IN SEARCH OF STUPIDITY
Over 20 Years of High-Tech Marketing Disasters
SECOND EDITION

IN SEARCH OF STUPIDITY

Over 20 Years of High-Tech Marketing Disasters
SECOND EDITION

Merrill R. Chapman

Apress®

In Search of Stupidity: Over 20 Years of High-Tech Marketing Disasters, Second Edition

Copyright © 2006 by Merrill R. Chapman

ISBN-13: 978-1-59059-721-7

Lead Editor: Jim Sumser
Editorial Board: Steve Anglin, Ewan Buckingham, Gary Cornell, Jason Gilmore,
    Jonathan Gennick, Jonathan Hassell, James Huddleston, Chris Mills,
    Matthew Moodie, Dominic Shakeshaft, Jim Sumser, Keir Thomas, Matt Wade
Project Manager: Elizabeth Seymour
Copy Edit Manager: Nicole LeClerc
Copy Editor: Kim Wimpsett
Assistant Production Director: Kari Brooks-Copony
Production Editor: Katie Stence
Compositor: Dina Quan
Proofreader: Elizabeth Berry
Cartoon Artists: Marc F. Richard (http://www.lartiste.com), Wolfgang Niesielksi
Cover Designer: Kurt Krames
Manufacturing Director: Tom Debolski

Library of Congress Cataloging-in-Publication Data

Chapman, Merrill R., 1953-
  In search of stupidity : over 20 years of high-tech marketing disasters / Merrill R. Chapman.
-- 2nd ed.
     p. cm.
  Includes bibliographical references and index.
  ISBN 1-59059-721-4
  1. Computer software industry--Management--Case studies. 2. Computer industry--
Management--Case studies. 3. Business failures--Case studies. I. Title.

  HD9696.63.A2C53 2006
  338.4'7004--dc22

                        2006029296

Printed and bound in the United States of America 9 8 7 6 5 4 3 2 1

Trademarked names may appear in this book. Rather than use a trademark symbol with
every occurrence of a trademarked name, we use the names only in an editorial fashion and
to the benefit of the trademark owner, with no intention of infringement of the trademark.

Distributed to the book trade worldwide by Springer-Verlag New York, Inc., 233 Spring
Street, 6th Floor, New York, NY 10013. Phone 1-800-SPRINGER, fax 201-348-4505,
e-mail orders-ny@springer-sbm.com, or visit http://www.springeronline.com.

For information on translations, please contact Apress directly at 2560 Ninth Street, Suite
219, Berkeley, CA 94710. Phone 510-549-5930, fax 510-549-5939, e-mail info@apress.com,
or visit http://www.apress.com.

To Ruth, Lili, Alfie, Winston, and, of course,
Charlie in heaven.

CONTENTS

FOREWORD TO THE SECOND EDITION

I LOVE THIS BOOK. When telling stories about some of the finest fiascos in our industry, the author offers unique insight and humor. The result is a book that is both readable and worth reading. That's a powerful combination that I find increasingly uncommon. I was a fan of the first edition of *In Search of Stupidity*, and I am honored to be writing this foreword for the second edition.

I am particularly fond of the title of this book. Taken completely out of context, it suggests that if you want to find stupidity in our industry, you have to search for it. I envision a typical person who wanders accidentally into the Software and Computers section of his local bookstore. He sees this book on the shelf and believes that stupidity in high tech is difficult to find.

Aw, never mind that. People are not so easily fooled. Anybody who reads the newspaper can easily look at our industry and see that stupidity is like beer at an NFL game: Half the people have got plenty of it, and they keep spilling it on the other half.

As of August 2006, here is what the average person knows about the world of high-tech products:

- The FBI just spent $170 million on a software project that completely failed and delivered nothing useful. Most of us would have been willing to deliver them nothing useful for a mere $85 million or so.

- We each get 50 e-mails a week from eBay, none of which actually came from eBay. So we find somebody who knows about computers and ask why, and he starts spewing stuff that sounds like *Star Trek* technobabble.

- The movie industry wants us to buy all our DVDs again so we can see them in "high definition," but it can't decide which new format it wants to support. Either way, this comes in the nick of time, because as we all know, the central problem with DVD technology is the atrocious picture quality.

- The time between the initial release of Windows XP and Windows Vista is roughly the life span of a dog, and apparently the main new feature is that it will be harder to use digital music and video content. Oh yeah, and it looks prettier.

The world of high tech is fouled up beyond *all* recognition, and everybody knows it.

But everybody loves reading about it. When it comes to failed software projects or dumb marketing mistakes, the mainstream news media is eager to print anything they can get their hands on. Nobody writes stories about software projects or marketing efforts that succeed.

The funny part is that most of the stupidity never makes it into print. Those of us in the industry know that things are actually even stupider than the perspective in the press. For example, most people know that whenever Microsoft announces a new product, it gives it a really boring name that nobody can remember. But those of us in the industry know that the boring name was immediately preceded by a "code name" that was memorable or even clever. It's almost like Microsoft has a department whose mission is to make sure their public image always looks lame and pedestrian compared to Apple.

And let's not forget that stupidity can show up in success as well as failure. Do you know the inside story of the Motorola RAZR? In the original plan, the powers-that-be at Motorola were convinced that the RAZR would be a "boutique phone," a niche product that would appeal to only a small segment of the market. It ordered enough components to make 50,000 of them. In the first quarter of production, the wireless companies placed orders for more than a million units. Motorola had the most popular cell phone on the market, and it was completely unprepared for it. It took them a year to get production capacity up to meet the demand. Today, Motorola is shipping RAZR phones at a pace that is equivalent to selling 50,000 of them every day before lunch.

In the news media, on the message boards, and here in this book, stories about product disasters in our industry are a lot of fun to read.

That's why the first edition of this book was great, and this one is even better. I applaud the author for the changes he has made in the second revision, giving more specific attention to the matter of learning from the marketing mistakes made by others. I imagine lots of people will enjoy that kind of thing.

But truth be told, not all of us aspire to such a high and noble station.

If you are like me, you probably lied to yourself about why you wanted to read this book. You told yourself how great it would be to learn from the mistakes of others. In reality, we don't want to learn—we want to gloat. We like to watch things crash and burn. This book is the marketing equivalent of the car chase scene from *Terminator 3*.

Wielders of clichés would say that misery loves company. Call it what you will, but let's just admit it together: We like to read about products and marketing efforts that exploded in balls of flame. It helps us feel better about our own stupidity.

And in my opinion, that's OK. In the vast constellation of unhealthy vices and guilty pleasures, this book isn't really all that harmful.

Eric Sink
Source Gear
http://software.ericsink.com/

FOREWORD TO THE
FIRST EDITION

IN EVERY HIGH-TECH COMPANY I've known, there's a war going on between the geeks and the suits. Before you start reading a book full of propaganda from software marketing wizard and über-suit Rick Chapman, let me take a moment to tell you what the geeks think.

Play along with me for a minute, will you? Please imagine the most stereotypically pale, Jolt-drinking, Chinese-food-eating, video-game-playing, Slashdot-reading, Linux-command-line-dwelling dork. Because this is just a stereotype, you should be free to imagine either a runt or a kind of chubby fellow, but in either case this isn't the kind of person who plays football with his high-school pals when he visits mom for Thanksgiving. Also, because he's a stereotype, I shouldn't have to make complicated excuses for making him a him.

This is what our stereotypical programmer thinks: "Microsoft makes inferior products, but it has superior marketing, so everybody buys its stuff."

Ask him what he thinks about the marketing people in his own company. "They're really stupid. Yesterday I got into a big argument with this stupid sales drone in the break room, and after 10 minutes it was totally clear that she had no clue what the difference between 802.11a and 802.11b is. Duh!"

What do marketing people do, young geek? "I don't know. They play golf with customers or something, when they're not making me correct their idiot spec sheets. If it was up to me I'd fire 'em all."

A nice fellow named Jeffrey Tarter used to publish an annual list, called the Soft*letter 100, of the 100 largest personal computer software publishers. Table 1 shows what the top ten looked like in 1984.

Table 1. *Top Software Publishers in 1984*

Rank	Company	Annual Revenue
1	MicroPro International	$60,000,000
2	Microsoft Corp.	$55,000,000
3	Lotus	$53,000,000
4	Digital Research	$45,000,000
5	VisiCorp	$43,000,000
6	Ashton-Tate	$35,000,000
7	Peachtree	$21,700,000
8	MicroFocus	$15,000,000
9	Software Publishing	$14,000,000
10	Broderbund	$13,000,000

OK, Microsoft is number 2, but it's one of a handful of companies with roughly similar annual revenues. Now let's look at the same list for 2001 (see Table 2).

Table 2. *Top Software Publishers in 2001*

Rank	Company	Annual Revenue
1	Microsoft Corp.	$23,845,000,000
2	Adobe	$1,266,378,000
3	Novell	$1,103,592,000
4	Intuit	$1,076,000,000
5	Autodesk	$926,324,000
6	Symantec	$790,153,000
7	Network Associates	$745,692,000
8	Citrix	$479,446,000
9	Macromedia	$295,997,000
10	Great Plains	$250,231,000

Whoa. Notice, if you will, that every single company except Microsoft has disappeared from the top ten. Also notice, please, that Microsoft is so much larger than the next largest player that it's not even funny. Adobe would double its revenue if it could just get Microsoft's soda pop budget.

The personal computer software market is Microsoft. Microsoft's revenue, it turns out, makes up 69 percent of the total revenue of the top 100 companies combined. This is what we're talking about here.

Is this just superior marketing, as our imaginary geek claims? Or is it the result of an illegal monopoly? (Which begs the question, How did Microsoft get that monopoly? You can't have it both ways.)

According to Rick Chapman (he's formally known as Merrill, but everyone calls him Rick), the answer is simpler: Microsoft was the only company on the list that never made a fatal stupid mistake. Whether this was by dint of superior brainpower or just dumb luck, in my opinion the biggest mistake Microsoft made was the talking paperclip. And how bad was that, really? We ridiculed the company, shut off the feature, and went back to using Microsoft Word, Excel, Outlook, and Internet Explorer every minute of every day.

But for every other software company that once had market leadership and saw it go down the drain, you can point to one or two giant blunders that steered the boat into an iceberg. MicroPro fiddled around rewriting printer architecture instead of upgrading its flagship product, WordStar. Lotus wasted a year and a half shoehorning 1-2-3 to run on 640KB machines, and by the time it was done, Excel was shipping and 640KB machines were a dim memory. Digital Research wildly overcharged for CP/M-86 and lost a chance to be the de facto standard for PC operating systems. VisiCorp sued itself out of existence. Ashton-Tate never missed an opportunity to piss off dBASE developers, poisoning the fragile ecology that's so vital to a platform vendor's success.

I'm a programmer, of course, so I tend to blame the marketing people for these stupid mistakes. Almost all of them revolve around a failure of nontechnical business people to understand basic technology facts. When Pepsi-pusher John Sculley was developing the Apple Newton, he didn't know something that every computer science major in the country knows: Handwriting recognition isn't possible. This was at the same time that Bill Gates was hauling programmers into meetings, begging them to create a single rich-text edit control that could be reused in all their products. Put Jim Manzi (the suit who let the MBAs take over Lotus) in that meeting, and he would be staring blankly and thinking, "What's a rich-text edit control?" It never would have occurred to him to take technological leadership because he didn't grok the technology. In fact, the very use of the word "grok" in that sentence would probably throw him off.

If you ask me, and I'm biased, no software company can succeed unless there's a programmer at the helm. So far the evidence backs me up. But many of these boneheaded mistakes come from the programmers themselves. Netscape's monumental decision to rewrite its browser instead of improving the old code base cost the company several years of Internet time, during which its market share went from around 90 percent to about 4 percent, and this was the programmers' idea. Of course, the nontechnical and inexperienced management of that company had no idea why this was a bad idea. There are still scads of programmers who defend Netscape's ground-up rewrite: "The old code really sucked, Joel!" Yeah, uh-huh. Such programmers should be admired for their love of clean code, but they shouldn't be allowed within 100 feet of any business decisions, because it's obvious that clean code is more important to them than shipping, uh, software.

So I'll concede to Rick a bit and say that if you want to be successful in the software business, you have to have a management team that thoroughly understands and loves programming, but they have to understand and love business, too. Finding a leader with strong aptitude in both dimensions is difficult, but it's the only way to avoid making one of those fatal mistakes that Rick catalogs lovingly in this book. So read the book, chuckle a bit, and if there's a stupid head running your company, get your resume in shape, and start looking for a house in Redmond.

Joel Spolsky
http://www.joelonsoftware.com
http://www.fogcreek.com

ABOUT THE AUTHOR

 MERRILL R. (RICK) CHAPMAN has worked in the high-technology and software industries since 1978 as a programmer, salesman, field sales engineer, and marketer. He is currently the managing editor of Softletter, a twice-monthly publication that focuses on the business issues of running a software company. He is also the author of *The Product Marketing Handbook for Software* and coauthor of *The US Software and Distribution Guide* and enjoys writing, lecturing, and consulting about various aspects of high-technology marketing. The companies he has worked or consulted for include MicroPro, Ashton-Tate, IBM, Inso, Microsoft, Novell, DataEase, Stromberg, Sun Microsystems, Terradata, Ziff-Davis, and many others. He currently resides in Killingworth, Connecticut, with his wife, Ruth; his daughter, Lili; a nine-pound feline, Alfie, who showed up at his house in the winter of 2003 as an orphan of the storm and graciously agreed to stay on as a permanent boarder; and a true miniature schnauzer, Winston. His previous dog, Charlie, a standard schnauzer who was misrepresented at the time of purchase as a miniature version of the breed, passed away in the summer of 2004 to his family's great sorrow after living a long and happy life. Based on his experiences, Mr. Chapman now recommends the standard schnauzer to anyone seeking to own a great dog.

For more information about this book and Mr. Chapman's other books and publications, please visit the following Web sites:

http://www.insearchofstupidity.com

http://www.aegis-resources.com

http://www.softwaremarketsolution.com

http://www.softletter.com

ABOUT THE ARTISTS

MARC F. RICHARD was born in France, where he studied at the school of Art Decoratifs in Paris for 4 years. He was commissioned by several companies, including Lufthansa and Monsieur Meuble, to develop artistic design material for advertising and promotion.

Mr. Richard moved to the United States in 1983 and started his own company as a freelance artist specializing in commercial art and cartooning. He has owned and operated his own studio in the Bay Area since 1989, offering clients various forms of artwork, including illustrations, logos, portraits, and caricatures. Some of his clients include Kemper Insurance, Hewlett-Packard, G.T. Global, Novell, Smith Barney, Sun Microsystems, Psychology Today, Goldman Sachs, Kaldair, Compaq, Lehman Brothers, Merrill Lynch, and Viacom. Mr. Richard's cartoons have been published in newspapers and books. He has designed numerous posters for retail companies, including Weatherford BMW and the Stinking Rose, "a garlic restaurant."

WOLFGANG NIESIELSKI was born in Germany, where he received his education. After his move to the US he owned and operated a design and garment printing company, called Wolf-Rose Screen Printing and Design, supplying design work and printed garments for companies like IBM, Apple, Sun Microsystems, Hewlett-Packard, and many others. He also specialized in caricatures and cartooning, providing his work to many companies as well. He has published a collection of his cartoons "A Parallel Universe."

He is also a writer, having published a suspenseful novel in the science fiction/horror genre, called "Touched by Choi" and is a columnist. His humor columns appear weekly in the Contra Costa Times, as well as other newspapers.

ACKNOWLEDGMENTS

JOHN F. KENNEDY once said, "Victory has a thousand fathers, but defeat is an orphan." Writing this book has certainly borne this maxim out: Not only did most of the people I spoke to during its development not want to be credited, but a few threatened me with dire bodily harm if I did.

Nonetheless, a brave few souls have agreed to allow their contributions to this effort to be recognized, and I'd like to take this opportunity to acknowledge their help and assistance. Those listed in my escutcheon of honor include Ted Finch, Adam Green, Randy Hujar, Maria Johnston, Steve Manes, Mary Marsden, Pete Peterson, Paul Somerson, Joel Spolsky, Jeffrey Tarter, and Alan Zenreich. Those who chose not to be listed also have my deepest thanks and appreciation.

Guy walks into a doctor's office, raises his arm, points to his shoulder, and says, "Doc, it hurts when I do that."

Doctor looks at him and says, "Then don't do that."

—Old vaudeville joke

Hegel remarks somewhere that all great, world-historical facts and personages occur, as it were, twice. He has forgotten to add: the first time as tragedy, the second as farce.

—Karl Marx

PREFACE

IN THE FIRST EDITION of *In Search of Stupidity: Over 20 Years of High-Tech Marketing Disasters*, I made a deliberate decision to avoid giving specific advice about how companies could avoid being stupid. At the time, I thought the process was fairly obvious; study the mistakes of the past, apply self-observation to your current behavior, and if you see yourself repeating a previous example of idiocy, stop and do something else. As I point out in Chapter 1, the claim that high-tech companies are constantly running into "new" and "unique" situations that they cannot possibly be expected to anticipate and intelligently resolve is demonstrably false (particularly if you read *In Search of Stupidity*). The truth is that technology companies are constantly repeating the same mistakes with wearying consistency (as this second edition makes even clearer), and many of the stupid things these companies do are completely avoidable.

But despite my fond expectations, many who read the first edition claimed they needed more guidance on avoiding stupid behavior and more detailed instructions on how to pump up the frontal lobes of the collective corporate brain. Thus, I've added helpful analyses and, where appropriate, checklists on specific actions you can take to both avoid acting stupidly and transform yourself into a marketing Einstein after suffering a brain hiccup similar to the one that afflicted Eric Schmidt in 2005 when he decided to go to war with the press after a member of the fourth estate demonstrated Google's potential to invade your privacy by googling "Eric Schmidt" (discussed in greater detail in Chapter 5). Although sometimes created in the spirit of tongue in cheek, the analyses and fundamental items in the lists **will** assist you in your quest to raise your marketing and sales IQ. Follow their sage advice, and you will find they offer you both redemption (good) and foresight (much, much better).

Another critique leveled at the first edition of *In Search of Stupidity* was its love of hindsight (also sometimes known as "history"). In the opinion of a fairly vocal minority, applying hindsight to the situations I wrote about was unfair; they believe I was picking on a band of dewy-eyed naifs wandering about a primordial high-tech Garden of Eden where original sin was unknown until introduced into paradise by Lucifer. (Prime candidates for the role of "Father of Lies" include Steve Jobs, Bill Gates, Larry Ellison, and a bevy of other industry movers and shakers from the period covered. The winner of the part depends on historical context and your personal opinion.)

For an overview of this viewpoint, I urge you to go to Amazon.com and read the *In Search of Stupidity* reviews, both good and bad, to see how people expressed themselves on the topic of hindsight. In my humble opinion, the words of Robert Hangsterfer "bob_hangsterfer" from Glendale, Wisconsin (two stars, "Rehashed stories, no guidance," May 10, 2005), best sum up the disdain of some for learning from the mistakes of the past: "The author berates the 'losers' of the PC software wars and laughs at their 'stupid decisions.' Yet, how were the executives supposed to know what decisions would lead to success or failure?" Bob calls plaintively from the virtual pages of Amazon.

Now, in all honesty, I don't regard this criticism as trenchant but rather somewhat tautological: "Nothing do I know; therefore I know nothing. So how can you expect me to act like I know?" But, the question deserves an answer. So, let's take Chapter 8 of *In Search of Stupidity*, which deals with Intel's $500 million+ meltdown over the Pentium's inability to properly handle floating-point math past four digits. How could Intel possibly have known the consequences of its actions? How could Intel have possibly predicted what would happen when a major brand is besmirched by a major (or at least a perceived major) flaw in a high-profile product? What clues existed that would have possibly informed poor, confused, lost little Intel that its course of attempting to cover up a flaw in its flagship microprocessor, refusing to acknowledge the impact of the problem, and not offering to make customers whole to the extent possible was a stupid path to take?

Well, Intel **could** have studied the 1982 example of Johnson & Johnson, when some cockroach slipped cyanide into capsules of Extra Strength Tylenol and murdered seven people. The poisoning immediately destroyed sales of the leading brand of acetaminophen, and most observers predicted that Tylenol was doomed. In the first days of the disaster, advertising guru Jerry Della Femina, author of the classic *From Those Wonderful Folks Who Gave You Pearl Harbor* (Simon & Schuster, 1970) and other tomes about the world of ads and admen, was quoted by the *New York Times* as saying that "I don't think they can ever sell another product under that name. There may be an advertising person who thinks he can solve this, and if they find him, I want to hire him, because then I want him to turn our water cooler into a wine cooler."

I assume that Jerry has drunk a lot of vino in the intervening 24 years because his prediction was dead wrong. Instead of shriveling away, Johnson & Johnson launched a PR campaign that by 1994, the year in which the Intel debacle occurred, had **already** become a model of what to do when circumstances damage a company's reputation or brand. The campaign included the following elements:

- An immediate press campaign by Johnson & Johnson informing the public about the poisoned capsules and warning them not to use any Tylenol product. Company executives were instructed to not obfuscate or deny the scope of the problem but instead cooperate with the media in getting the story out so as to ensure everyone heard about the poisoning.

- An immediate recall of all Tylenol capsule products on store shelves (at a cost of more than $100 million to Johnson & Johnson).

- An offer to immediately swap out all Tylenol capsules with Tylenol tablets.

- A series of forthright statements by Tylenol upper management expressing their shock and pain over the deaths.

- After the completion of the recall, an extensive PR announcement of the introduction of new Tylenol products in tamper-proof packaging, coupled with an extensive series of promotional programs offering the new products at reduced prices via price discounts, coupons, and so on.

When you read Chapter 8 of this book, contrast these actions with the ones Intel actually took.

The result of Johnson & Johnson's classic (and much studied) campaign rescued the product from the marketing grave. During the crisis Tylenol had seen its share of the market drop from 37 percent to 0 percent.

A few months after the poisonings, Tylenol was back up to 24 percent market share and today still reigns as the leading brand of this popular painkiller.

So, there's your answer, Bob. That's how Intel could have known what to do. With a little study, a little history (hindsight), and a healthy dollop of common sense, we know how Intel could have saved itself a world of embarrassment and derision as well as a cool $500 million+.

(Oh, how do we **know** this? Because, Bob, amazingly enough, the second generation of Pentiums also suffered from math problems! But, Intel had learned its $500 million lesson. The company promptly offered to recall the "defective" processors and make dissatisfied customers whole. Since most customers didn't really know what a floating-point unit [FPU] chip was and even more probably no longer knew how to do long division, the public—offered the security of Intel's "guarantee blankie"—decided not to bother fixing a problem that wasn't bothering them, and no one paid any attention to the whole imbroglio except for a small cadre of picky math people and hardware-obsessed geeks who took their new chips home and went away happy.)

Now, in all fairness, it's not just high tech that suffers from a reluctance to learn from the mistakes of the past. For just a moment, let's step outside high technology and take a look at what is perhaps America's most seminal business, the automotive industry. As I've noted in Chapter 1, by the 1970s the U.S. car industry had raised the practice of building shoddy buggies to an art form. I particularly remember toward the end of the decade an abomination produced by Chrysler called the Cordoba, which was, we were assured by pitchman Ricardo Montalban, clad in "fine Corinthian leather." It is a virtual certainty that all that survives of these cars are the leather seats; the bodies long ago turned to rust. Chryslers of this era were matched in this respect only by the Chevy Vega, a car that began to disappear in a cloud of iron oxide particles from the moment it was driven out of the showroom. If that wasn't exciting enough, for more thrills one could always buy the "Immolator," the Ford Pinto with that amazing, mounted-above-the-rear-axle-so-it-was-guaranteed-to-explode-when-smacked-hard gas tank.

But by the second half of the 1980s, a turnaround seemed to have taken place. Ford, General Motors, and Chrysler all appeared to turn important quality corners. Although no American cars have ever reached the benchmark standards set by Japanese carmakers, the situation definitely improved. Instead of dissolving in a heap of nano particles by 60,000 miles, the fate suffered by the hapless Cordoba, American cars started to be put together so well that people began to expect their homegrown tin to hit the 100,000-mile mark. U.S. carmakers latched on to the Japanese discovery that people like to "live" in their cars, and soon American cars had caught up with their overseas rivals in respect to the number of cubbies and cup holders festooning their buggies; Chrysler in particular was so diligent in this regard that some people began referring to their minivans and sedans as Slurpeemobiles. Even more telling, while K cars such as the Dodge Aries and Plymouth Reliant were never state-of-the-art automotives, 20 years after their introduction versions of each could be seen still limping up the frozen, rust-inducing streets of New York, New England, and eastern Canada (where they were sometimes known as Toronto Taxis).

The cult of quality continued to spread across the American auto landscape during these years; at Ford, quality was "job one"; the sort of legendary Lee Iacocca, when he wasn't driving the development of such abortions as the revived Chrysler Imperial, a 1970s K car with a 1960s design that appealed to people in their 80s, proclaimed that "if you could find a better built car, buy it." Not to be outdone, General Motors started a new division, Saturn, designed to prove that if you stuck a group of Americans in a remote location in the backwoods of Tennessee with nothing better to do, they'd build a small, underpowered, but pretty reliable car just as good as the Japanese were doing in the 1980s.

The result of all this attention to quality and reliability paid off; during the late 1980s and through much of the 1990s, American cars held their own against the Japanese and seriously dented the Europeans. But by the mid-to-late 1990s, American car companies had begun to backslide. Today, Toyota Camrys and Honda Accords routinely reach 150,000 and even 200,000 miles of reliable, trouble-free use while sporting ever more sophisticated designs, increased fuel economy, and more powerful engines. Doors and body panels on Japanese cars align with geometric precision; by contrast, the body panels of Chevys and Pontiacs often look like they've been attached to the car by assemblers suffering from problems with both depth perception and basic geometry. On European cars, interior plastic trim usually has a plush feel and pleasing patinas; on American cars, the plastic frequently appears as if it were made from recycled polyester double-knit leisure suits stored over from the 1970s. I've owned both a Pontiac Grand Am and a Bonneville over the past 10 years; both suffered from serious electrical problems before they hit 65,000 miles. (To add insult to injury, my 1999 Pontiac Bonneville in the course of 2 weeks underwent a transformation from transportation to tin at 69,000 miles when in quick succession the car's AC system ceased working and the engine's plastic(!) intake manifold cracked, drowning the buggy's innards in antifreeze.) By contrast, every electrical and mechanical component in my dispose-a-car **Hyundai Elantra** wagon still worked properly before I gave the thing away at 130,000 miles.

A Honda Accord's high-beam stick flicks over with a satisfying "snick"; by contrast, the action on a Pontiac Bonneville's light control stalk is equivalent to yanking on a stale stick of licorice. The Ford Focus, Lincoln LS, Pontiac Aztek, Chrysler 300m, and so on, and so on, have all been plagued with extensive quality complaints upon their initial introduction. *Consumer Reports*, the gold standard for objective auto ratings (yes, the magazine is not much fun to read, and it has that annoying left-wing, tree-hugger-life-was-better-in-the-19th-and-early-20th-centuries-when-choo-choo-trains-belched-smoke-into-the-air attitude, but it does **buy** its test vehicles and thus has no need to suck up to Detroit or Tokyo in the manner of publications such as *Car and Driver* and *Road and Track*) consistently accords Japanese cars with seas of little red bull's-eyes (top ranked) while American cars are awash in black dots (bottom of the barrel). This after 30 years of multiple opportunities to catch up and adjust to the new reality the Japanese had introduced to the market, namely, that well-engineered and highly reliable cars will be favored by buyers over cars that aren't.

Quality, reliability, and design issues had become such a problem in the U.S. auto industry that by 2006 General Motors and Ford bonds had been reduced to junk status; both companies were shedding plants, employees, and market share by the bucket load, and Ford scion William Ford had been reduced to making remarkably-just-like-the-ones-made-20-years-ago ads featuring smiling (presumably because they'd not been fired for making astoundingly unreliable first-year Ford Focuses) workers promising that Ford was (again) going to make reliable and well-built cars.

In defense of the indefensible, several auto-industry observers offered the feeble excuse that the reason for the reoccurrence of poor quality in

American cars was that Detroit had decided to focus on building big SUVs in its quest for profits and market domination. The problem with this theory is that while the Americans were pouring out tons of GMC Jimmies with front ends that wobbled like tops at about 60,000 miles and Eddie Bauer–version Ford Expeditions with body parts that tended to fly off the car's exterior at moderate velocities, the Japanese were turning out giant, global-warming-contributing and ice-cap-melting monstrosities that were also highly reliable and well made (as adjudged by *Consumer Reports*).

What possible justification can American cars (and I blame both the bosses and the workers for their failure to get it) offer to excuse their failure to at least match the Japanese in quality and reliability? Answer: there is no excuse. What we're dealing with is sheer idiocy and a failure to study the mistakes of the past (hindsight) so as to avoid doing the same stupid thing all over again.

I'm not quite sure why hindsight in general has developed a bad reputation amongst the high-tech cognoscenti, but I have several theories. One revolves around culture, specifically the culture of Silicon Valley, high technology's principal engine and driver since the late 1970s. Silicon Valley is located in California, a land of self-actualization and narcissism and home to some of the silliest cults to ever plague mankind. Take est, for example. Developed by former used-car salesman (of course!) "Werner Erhardt" (not his actual name, but who cares), est was built around the platitude of "What is, is." This was translated into a very profitable seminar program of how to arrive at "is" by getting "it."[1] The series was highlighted by a series of exercises that took the attendees on a trip through a tomato, allowed est trainers to yell rude things at the attendees, encouraged acolytes to ignore most social niceties, and didn't allow them to go to the bathroom (very often) during the est seminars. The core of the est belief system revolved around a mantra that "your beliefs, feelings, and experiences were the only things that were truly valid."[2]

---

[1] For a ribald but also highly informative look at est, I suggest you rent a copy of the 1977 film *Semi-Tough*. Possibly the best movie ever made by Burt Reynolds, its depiction of est (only thinly disguised in the movie) is both accurate and very funny.

[2] *Outrageous Betrayal* by Steven Pressman (St. Martin's Press, 1993)

est had its competitors, as you'd expect. At MicroPro, for example, many in upper management's inner circle were "graduates" of something called "The Laughing Men." This was an offshoot of est that taught, according to what I was told at the time, pretty much the same thing. (I assumed the reason the men were laughing was that they were allowed to go to the bathroom.) At Ashton-Tate, Scientology was very popular, with the company's founder, George Tate, being a practitioner.

est and its imitators were quite the thing in the 1970s and early 1980s and created large cadres of sociopaths[3] who felt they were immune from such interpersonal obligations as saying they were sorry when they misbehaved and totally focused on gratifying their every last whim and desire (which, come to think of it, characterizes much of upper management at many high-tech companies today). Some est graduates finally snapped out of it (often after receiving the divorce papers or a punch in the nose), and one day Werner Erhardt bailed out of the business and moved to Europe. But an examination of the current zeitgeist indicates est's solipsistic message of relying only on your experiences to "create your own reality" has taken hold in much of high tech (as well as in other industries), and there's probably not much of a market for teaching something everyone already believes in. And while you're busy tending to your own reality, you tend to not have much time for worrying about others' realities, particularly unsuccessful ones, since your reality will obviously not include their failures.

Another theory focuses on the underlying nature of engineers and programmers, many of whom continue to create new and innovative companies that they often then destroy by repeating past stupidity. The best programmers and engineers are usually "world creators," people who like to "live" in their work and are happiest when they have complete control over every aspect of the tools, techniques, and technologies they use to create products. The frequently written about "not invented here" (NIH) syndrome is a direct result of this ethos, and the damage it can wreak on a company is illustrated in Chapter 4, which discusses how a key programming group at MicroPro finally destroyed the company over the issue of product control. A corollary to NIH is

---

[3] I speak about this from personal experience, having had close acquaintances who went through the training and who remained unbearable for years.

DTMNBICTCAYD, or "Don't tell me nothing, because I created this company and you didn't," an affliction that also frequently leads to history repeating itself.

Again, it's not just high tech that suffers from these syndromes. In 1908, Henry Ford created the Model T, the car that allowed Ford to transform the face of America and become for more than 20 years the largest automotive company in the world. By the standards of the day, the T was high tech, well built, easy to maintain, reliable, and cheap. But car technology was rapidly changing, and in 1912, while Ford was away on a trip, several of his engineers built a prototype of a new Model T, an "upgrade" that incorporated improvements such as a smoother ride and more stable wheelbase. Ford's response to this attempt to improve "his" car without his exercising direct control over the process was to smash and vandalize the prototype while the shocked engineers watched.[4]

Now, in all fairness, some businesses insist on using hindsight to study past failures: the airline industry is a good example of this. After a crash or major flight faux pas, NTSB investigations do **not** normally follow these lines:

> *NTSB investigator*: "Uh, captain, I note you've just flown your airplane straight into that mountain and killed all your passengers."
>
> *Airplane captain*: By Jove, with the benefit of 20/20 hindsight, we can all see you're right! But, you know, I just had to experience catastrophic aerial failure for myself to truly comprehend it. Having lived through the disaster, I've absorbed on a deeply personal level just how bad crashing my plane and killing all my passengers can be and will in the future understand intuitively why it's an experience to be avoided in the first place!

Instead, after a crash or serious operating mistake by a flight crew, the circumstances are analyzed, broken into their constituent parts, and then programmed into a flight simulator, which can be thought of as an electronic box stuffed full of hindsight. After this, flight crews from all over the world are periodically summoned to attend simulator classes so they can directly learn from all this hindsight until their instructors are satisfied they are unlikely to repeat another's mistake.

---

[4] *The Reckoning* by David Halberstam (William Morrow, 1986)

But, enough preaching. If you're one of those sturdy types who march to their own drummer, who seeks to squeeze the juice of life from sources pure of the carping calls of second guessing, and who desires to personally experience every emotion directly so as to live a life unadulterated by the pallid personas of those cowards who shrink from the whip of disaster and scourge of financial failure, let me salute you and bid you good luck and Godspeed!

Just do me one favor. At some point, send me your e-mail address and a description of what you're up to. I'll need some good material for the third edition of *In Search of Stupidity*.

one

INTRODUCTION

IN 1982, HARPER & ROW published *In Search of Excellence: Lessons from America's Best-Run Companies* by Thomas J. Peters and Robert H. Waterman, Jr. *In Search of Excellence* quickly became a seminal work in the category of business management books and made its authors millionaires. Although it's no longer the literary obsession of freshly minted MBAs that it was in the 1980s, the book's distribution and influence have proved long lasting and pervasive. After its introduction, the book stayed on best-seller lists for almost 4 years and sold more than 3 million copies. A survey by WorldCat, an electronic catalog of materials from libraries in the United States and other countries, ranks *In Search of Excellence* as being on more library shelves than any other book in the world. With 3,971 libraries listing it as being in their collections, the book tops the list of 100 books held by libraries. It has held the number-one position since 1989.

In Search of Excellence, when it first came out, applied soothing balm to the raw nerves of the American psyche, and this helps account for its tremendous success. The 1970s had been a gloomy time for U.S. businesses. The Japanese had run American companies out of consumer electronics; Japanese cars lasted 100,000 miles, while American cars started breaking down at 20,000; and as the 1980s began, Japanese companies had just started making memory chips more cheaply than their American counterparts. The Japanese even announced they were starting a "Fifth Generation" project to build software that would make computers very, very smart indeed, leaving the poor old United States with software systems that would be the technological equivalent of Studebakers. (The project was a complete bust, like all the others emanating from the artificial intelligence hype machine of the 1980s, and it never developed much more than software capable of storing some nice recipes for sushi.) Yes, the United States was doing OK in this new market for little machines called "microcomputers," but the pundits universally agreed that eventually the Japanese were going to move into that industry as well and that would be it for the Americans.[1] Maybe

---

[1] In fact, the Japanese did introduce a plethora of CP/M and MS-DOS "clones." Like many other companies, the Japanese firms failed to understand the impact of the IBM standard on the industry, and none of the machines made a significant impact on the market. In Japan, NEC and Fujitsu attempted to establish independent hardware standards, but their efforts were eventually overwhelmed by IBM's PC standard. The most important long-term impact the Japanese had on computing technology was Sony's successful introduction of a standard for 3-inch floppies.

IBM would survive; after all, it did business like the Japanese anyway. For the ambitious young MBA, a start-up position in agribusiness, such as sheepherding, began to look like the fast track to the top.

In Search of Excellence helped buck everyone up. All the companies it profiled were **American** firms competing successfully in world markets. It seemed obvious that if you studied the organizations closely, learned the fundamental practices and techniques they used to achieve excellence, and then applied those practices and techniques to your business, it would become excellent too!

The basic thesis of *In Search of Excellence* isn't complex and can be summed up succinctly: Excellent companies create corporate cultures in which success flourishes. (Yes, this is something of a tautology, but it's a nice one and people always like reading it.) An excellent corporate culture is one that loves the customer, loves its employees, loves the company's products, and loves loving the company. Once enough love is flowing through the corporate veins, a company will organically become excellent and in turn create excellent products and services. This will lead to more customer, employee, product, and corporate love, lifting all concerned to even greater heights of selling and purchasing ecstasy. The cycle becomes self-sustaining, and a universe of almost sybaritic business success awaits those who master the Zen of Excellence.

Most of *In Search of Excellence* thus functions as the corporate equivalent of the Kama Sutra, profiling different companies as they bend and twist themselves into different postures and techniques designed to build customer desire for the company, increase customer love for the company's products, and provide lasting satisfaction with the company's service. The positions and techniques discussed vary widely and include being reliable, shooting for 100 percent, communicating intensely, being creative, talking about it, talking about it a lot, listening a lot, getting on with it, and so on. High-tech firms are particularly well represented in the book, with IBM, Xerox, DEC, and many others serving as exemplars of how to seize the business world by the tail via the practice of excellence.

For the next several years, copies of *In Search of Excellence* flew off bookstore shelves. Thousands of companies, including most in the high-tech sectors, took its maxims to heart. People walked, talked, and communicated with incredible intensity. Peters became a widely sought-after speaker and business consultant (Waterman dropped out of public sight). He wrote more books, including *A Passion for Excellence* and *The Pursuit of WOW!*, all of which continued the earlier book's quest for that ineffable corporate phlogiston that when ignited leads inexorably to success. America's affair with excellence appeared to be endless.

Unfortunately, while U.S. businesses were vigorously applying excellence to every nook and cranny of their corporate bodies, a few people began to note that many of the firms listed in Peters and Waterman's tome seemed to be, well, less than excellent. As early as 1984, *Business Week* published a cover story entitled "Oops!" that debunked some of the book's claims. Most people dismissed these early criticisms as journalistic carping, but over time it became more difficult to ignore that something was very wrong with the book's concept of business excellence.

Take, for example, its examination of Lanier, a major competitor in what is now a vanished world—that of dedicated word processors. The market for these single-purpose computers had been built and defined by Wang. As the market grew, companies such as Lanier, Xerox, IBM, and almost a hundred others competed fiercely for the privilege of selling $20,000.00 boxes that did what a $99.95 piece of software does today (actually, the software does much more). These dedicated devices were often the only experience many people had with computers throughout much of the 1970s, and to many people word-processing stations epitomized "high tech."

In Search of Excellence thought Lanier was **really** excellent, a company that "lives, sleeps, eats, and breathes customers." The book described how the company's top executives went on sales calls once a month, how the president of the company personally handled service calls (and if you believed **that**, you probably also went out and bought a famous bridge in New York City), how its service was even better than IBM's, and so forth, and so on.

And Lanier was a sharp marketing bunch, too! The company knew that the term "word processor" put everybody "off." That's why Lanier called its word processors "No Problem Typewriters." Sheer advertising genius.

The only problem with all of this was that Lanier wasn't an excellent company; it was a dead company, a shot-through-the-head dinosaur whose sluggish nervous system hadn't yet gotten round to telling the rest of its body to lie down and die. In 1981, an Apple II+ running AppleWriter or ScreenWriter[2] did everything a Lanier word processor

---

[2] An early attempt at a true What You See Is What You Get (WYSIWYG) word processor. The product displayed your text on a bitmapped screen and could show italicized and underlined text. On a 1MHz Apple II it also ran veery slooowly.

did, never mind an IBM PC with WordStar. By 1985, the market for dedicated word processing was as extinct as the Tyrannosaurus Rex, but Peters and Waterman seemed not to have noticed they were profiling a walking corpse.

Now, you can argue that market shifts can catch companies unaware and that Lanier was a victim of the unexpected. This, however, can't be true. *In Search of Excellence* was written in 1981 and published in 1982. By 1981, thousands of Apples, RadioShack TRS-80s,[3] Commodore PETs, and a wide variety of CP/M systems were selling monthly. The IBM PC was also launched that year. WordStar, AppleWriter, and Scripsit (popular on the RadioShack systems) had been available for years. Hundreds of ComputerLand stores, one of the first national franchises dedicated to selling desktop computer systems, were doing business nationwide, and dozens more were opening on a monthly basis. Yet somehow Lanier, the company that apparently did everything but have sexual relations with its customers, never found out from a single one of them that they were interested in buying an IBM PC or an Apple with a good word-processing program that did everything a Lanier word processor did at a fraction of the cost and did other things as well, such as run a nifty type of new program called a "spreadsheet." You would think an excellent company would have caught on much sooner.

It only became worse as time passed and people kept track of the book's list of "excellent performers," particularly the high-tech ones. For instance, Data General: gone into oblivion.[4] Wang: moribund by 1987. DEC: PC roadkill. NCR: a mediocre performer bought up by AT&T that passed into extinction without leaving a trace. Texas Instruments: the

---

[3] The first computer I ever owned was a used RadioShack TRS-80 Model I, semi-affectionately known by its owners as "Trash One." The reliability of early models was less than stellar, and the paint tended to rub off their keyboards, leading older systems to develop a rather decrepit appearance.

[4] Data General made its own contribution to stupidity with the introduction of the Data General–One in 1985. This was the first "clamshell" portable and, in terms of weight and functionality, a breakthrough. A fully loaded system cost about $3,000.00, weighed about 12 pounds, supported up to 512KB of RAM, could hold two 3.5-inch double-sided 700KB floppies, and featured an LCD screen capable of displaying a full 80×25 lines of text, an unusual feature for a portable in that era. It also had enough battery life to allow you to get some work done from your airplane seat. Unfortunately, the LCD screen also sported a surface so shiny and reflective you could literally comb your hair in it, making it almost impossible to view the screen for everyday computing chores. No one could ever quite figure out what had possessed Data General to release a system that basically functioned as a $3,000.00 personal grooming system. I still own one of these systems and once tried to sell it at a garage sale for $25.00. I am happy to discover they're currently worth about $500.00 in the collectibles market.

company that coinvented the microprocessor saw its TI99/4A tossed out of the computer market by 1984. IBM: In 10 years it went from an American icon to an American tragedy.

Xerox, on the ropes by the late 1990s, was on the book's list of hero companies. By the mid-1980s, industry mavens were already puzzling over how a company could develop the graphical user interface (GUI), mouse, object-oriented programming, and Ethernet and fail to make a single successful product from **any** of these groundbreaking innovations. Instead, Xerox made its inaugural debut into the PC market with an obsolete-before-its-release clunker of an 8-bit CP/M machine with the appetizing name of "Worm" that sold just about as well as you would expect.

Atari, for God's sake, even made it to the book's Hall of Excellence. In 1983, the year after *In Search of Excellence*'s publication, the company was close to death after releasing the worst computer game of all time, E.T. (based on the movie). Before its product hit the store shelves, an "excellent" company would have used the plastic cartridges that contained this all-time turkey to club to death the parties responsible for producing the game that ruined the Christmas of 1982 for thousands of fresh-faced video game junkies.[5]

It wasn't simply the companies profiled in *In Search of Excellence* that proved to be disappointments. During the 1980s, it was impossible, especially in high tech, to escape the training seminars, book extracts, and corporate programs that sprang up dedicated to ensuring everyone was excellent all the time and every day. Yet, despite all the talking, walking, and communicating, high-tech firms kept doing stupid things. Again and again and again. And every time they did they paid a price. Again and again and again.

One key to the problem may be that in 2002, Peters announced the data used to "objectively" measure the performance of the companies profiled in the book was faked. Oops. Well, remember, excellence means never having to say you're sorry.

---

[5] It has been my privilege to meet the person who holds the world record for getting the highest score ever achieved on this game, a young man who worked for me in the late 1990s. (The E.T. game and original Atari 2600 game system are somewhat collectible and still used by those interested in retro gaming. If you want to experience the horror that was E.T., you can download the game and a 2600 emulator for your PC from various Internet sites.) I won't reveal the name of this stalwart gamer because my revelation might permanently damage his career. When I knew him, he suffered from insomnia, and after playing many hours of E.T., I can understand why.

But despite this little faux pas, a more important answer lies in the types of companies analyzed in *In Search of Excellence*. With only a few exceptions, they were large firms with dominant positions in markets that were senescent or static. IBM ruled the world of mainframe computers. DEC and Data General had carved out comfortable fiefdoms in minicomputers. Xerox reigned over copiers. Wang and Lanier both possessed principalities in dedicated word processing.

In these types of business environments, affairs proceed at a measured pace and plenty of time is available for navel gazing. Their vision clouded by all that lint, companies such as IBM and DEC decided it was their natural goodness that made them successful, and therefore they were successful because they were naturally good. By the time Peters and Waterman got around to interviewing them, most of these firms were ossifying, their internal cultures attempting to cement employee mindsets and processes in place in a futile attempt to freeze the past so as to guarantee the future. These firms weren't excellent; they were arthritic.

For high-tech companies, navel gazing is a particularly inappropriate strategy because markets tend not to stay stable very long. In 1981, for example, distinct markets for spreadsheets, word processors, databases, and business presentation products existed in the software industry. By the late 1980s, word processing alone was a $1 billion category. By 1995, all of these categories had been subsumed by the office suite (particularly Microsoft's).

What, therefore, accounted for the success of companies such as Microsoft, Oracle, and Symantec and the failure of other firms such as Novell, MicroPro, and Ashton-Tate? Was it Microsoft's "respect for the individual," something *In Search of Excellence* told us IBM had in abundance? Well, Bill Gates once stood up at the start of a presentation being given by a new product manager, fixed the unfortunate fellow with a cold stare, and asked, "Where the fuck did we hire you from?" before leaving the room.

Hmm. Perhaps not.

Perhaps it was a "seemingly unjustifiable overcommitment to some form of quality, reliability, or service"? IBM had that in abundance also. Well, Dell is currently the reigning king of PC hardware, not IBM. Although Dell's service is OK, the company isn't "unjustifiable" about it. Oh, Dell pays lip service to the concept of great customer service, and within the constraints of its business model, it does the best it can. If you don't like your PC, Dell will probably take it back if you're within the warranty period and you scream loudly enough and pay for the shipping and maybe fork over a restocking fee if you're a small business. If your PC breaks, the company will do its best to get **you** to fix the thing. But Michael Dell, unlike the excellent CEO of Lanier, won't be calling your house to handle affairs personally.

That's because Dell has figured out that what people really care about these days in a computer is high performance at a low price. Dell has learned over the years to build such machines. IBM didn't and ended up exiting the PC business in 2005 muttering about "commodization" and "focusing on core competencies" while Dell grew its revenues that same year to almost $50 billion on sales of servers, notebooks, desktop systems, printers, and related items. Computers are very reliable and on a statistical basis don't break down often. If the ones made by your company do, it **is** possible to sell a great many of them if you price them cheaply enough, as in the case of Packard Bell, a company that briefly became a powerhouse in PC retailing. Alas, the machines were of poor quality, they broke often, and few people ever bought a second Packard Bell computer.

On the other hand, Dell computers rarely break (though they have been known to erupt in flames).[6] You, the customer, know that. You're willing to buy a Dell PC because you've made a bet in your mind that the risk that the computer you buy won't work isn't worth the extra money it would cost to have your fanny kissed in the event of a breakdown. People who buy desktop PCs aren't a high-roller audience, and it makes no sense to treat them like one.

Let's move on.

---

[6] In June 2006 at a seminar in Osaka, Japan, a Dell laptop was photographed burning up because of a defective cell in its lithium ion battery. The pictures were quickly distributed worldwide throughout the Internet. The story was particularly embarrassing because Dell had over the past year cut back its not-very-world-class support to levels that invoked the ghost of Packard Bell, proving once again that today's high-tech hero is only one stupid decision away from becoming tomorrow's computing clown. To its credit, Dell immediately announced it was spending $100 million extra in customer support, presumably so it would no longer have to hire so many Indian workers who announce in impenetrable accents that their name is "Ralph" instead of "Ramesh" and ask you to do things like "please to remove the solid drive to check to the connection orifice for proper adherence" (an actual quote I transcribed during a Dell tech support call). At least Dell customers hoped so.

Or perhaps it was "autonomy and entrepreneurship"? Motorola, a company with a history of allowing different autonomous groups within its phone division to tear at each other's throats while firms like Nokia tore away its market share, surely has **that** in abundance. In the entrepreneurial spirit of "up and at 'em," these groups managed to build what was perhaps the coolest-looking cell phone of its time, the StarTAC. The only problem with the StarTAC was that when it was first introduced it was a very cool analog system when everyone wanted digital phones.

And it was certainly entrepreneurship that led Motorola to launch its Iridium project. Motorola spent $5 billion plus to put 66 low-earth satellites into orbit so that anyone could phone anytime from anywhere with a Motorola phone. Unfortunately, the satellites spend 70 percent of their time over our planet's oceans and aren't usable for much of their life (unless perhaps you're adrift in the middle of the Atlantic); the phones, though they may have worked from the top of Mount Everest, didn't work indoors, in the shadows of buildings, or under trees (early demos of the system enjoined purchasers to "make sure the phone is pointed at the satellite"[7]); the service's monthly cost was high; the phones were huge; and every major metropolitan area already had cheap and reliable cellular systems. In other words, Iridium had no market. After the last satellite was launched, the system quickly went bankrupt.[8] Despondent Motorola stockholders, watching the value of their shares plummet as Iridium crashed and burned, suggested sending up the project's marketing and engineering teams in rockets without space suits to join their orbiting financial debacle, but current law forbids this. You would think an excellent company with entrepreneurial instincts would notice that 70 percent of Earth's surface is water.

Uh huh. Maybe that isn't it.

In fact, if you examine high-tech companies, only one factor seems to constantly distinguish the failures from the successes. This factor is stupidity. More successful companies are less stupid than the opposition more of the time. As Forrest Gump astutely noted, "Stupid is as stupid does."

---

[7] I was present at such a demo. I interrupted the demonstrator to inquire "Which one?"

[8] The system was sold to a group of investors for the fire-sale price of $25 million.

One of stupidity's most endearing traits is its egalitarian nature. Its eternal dull lamp beckons endlessly to those dim bulbs who seek to rip open the hulls of successful companies and ideas on the sharp rocks of bad judgment and ignorance. With stupidity, your reach never exceeds your grasp; any company, no matter how large or small, can aspire to commit acts of skull-numbing idiocy and have a hope of success.

Take, for example, the creation of the worst piece of high-tech marketing collateral ever developed, the brainchild of the founder of a small company, Street Technologies. The front page of Street Technologies' expensive, four-color, 8½ × 11 corporate opus posed the following challenge:

"How to eliminate half your work force."

The inside of the brochure provided the means to rise to the task:

"Get the other half to use your software!"

When it was pointed out to the president of Street Technologies that a marketing campaign designed to create mass unemployment and spark a brutal Darwinian struggle for personal survival in its target audience might not be the most effective of all possible approaches, he airily dismissed the issue with the observation that "the piece was not aimed at the employees but their bosses." He'd apparently not considered the issue of who was going to be opening the mail.

Creating silly collaterals isn't a task reserved only for high tech's small fry. The second worst piece of marketing collateral ever created was a noble effort by software giant Computer Associates. This was a brochure designed to be included in a direct marketing campaign for a bundle of OS/2 business software. The piece trumpeted the presence of a free goodie that buyers of the bundle would receive upon purchase—a package of canned sounds you could use to liven up your OS/2 desktop. Sounds highlighted in this amazing bit of literature included "farting," "pissing," and "orgasm." One can only mourn that the package didn't include the noise made when a marketing manager is summarily decapitated for committing an act of boneheaded silliness, such as developing and printing thousands of patently tasteless and offensive four-color brochures.

The reason for the absence of stupidity can vary. In some cases, firms avoid stupidity because the company's culture creates more intelligent behavior. In other cases, it's because a company's personnel is smarter than the competition's and thus avoids making stupid mistakes. In yet others, it's because a business's leadership is smarter than the competition's and thus tends not to behave stupidly. Usually, it's a varying mix of all three. In a sense, the reason for not acting stupidly doesn't matter—the avoidance of it does. By reducing the number of stupid actions you take vis-à-vis your competition, you're more likely to out-compete them over time.

Some may object that stupidity isn't quantifiable, but in fact, the opposite is true. Stupid behavior is both quantifiable and identifiable. For example, it's stupid to create two products with the same name, price point, functionality, and target audience and attempt to sell them at the same time. This may seem stunningly obvious, but somehow one of the world's largest software companies, MicroPro, publisher of WordStar, a product that once ruled the word-processing market, did precisely that. A few years later, Borland repeated very much the same mistake with very much the same results. Then Novell. After you read Chapter 3 and learn precisely why this is a stupid thing to do and what the likely outcome is, you'll be less likely to make this mistake in your own marketing and sales efforts. That puts you one up on your competition who, unless they've also read this book, are far more likely to repeat MicroPro's fatal blunder.

Nitpickers like to claim that context often changes the nature of what is stupid behavior, but this principle is vastly overstated. For instance, if you spend many millions of dollars successfully creating a consumer brand, and then, when your most important product is revealed to be defective, stupidly attempt to blow off the public (as I describe Intel attempting to do in Chapter 5), you'll suffer. It really doesn't matter what industry you're in or what product you're selling. Expect to be immolated.

Or take the example of Syncronys, publisher of the immortal, never-to-be-forgotten SoftRAM "memory doubling" utility for Windows. Introduced in May 1995 with a list price of $29.95, SoftRAM was designed to "compress" your computer's memory using your computer's memory to give you, effectively, twice the memory you had physically installed (the problem with this concept should be apparent once you think about it). SoftRAM was quite the best-seller upon its release, with the Windows 3.x version selling more than 100,000 copies and the

Windows 95 version selling more than 600,000. The company's president, Rainer Poertner, was dubbed Entrepreneur of the Year by the Software Council of Southern California. Syncronys stock jumped from $.03 per share in March 1995 to a high of $32.00 per share in August 1995.

SoftRAM was a handsome-looking piece of software that after installation presented buyers with a snazzy dashboard that supposedly let them increase their PC's RAM with the touch of a button. Unfortunately for both purchasers of SoftRAM and Syncronys, the software didn't actually *do* that. Actually, it didn't really do *anything* except change a configuration setting in Windows that increased the amount of memory that could be swapped to disk, an operation a Windows user could perform manually in less than a minute for free.

It turned out that SoftRAM was an example of what Syncronys coyly called "placeboware," the software equivalent of a deed to the Brooklyn Bridge. The concept annoyed the spoilsports at the Federal Trade Commission (FTC) greatly, who forced the company to stop selling the package and promise to give everyone their money back. (Interestingly enough, no one was prosecuted for fraud in the case, the FTC apparently having bought the argument that the difference between computer sales reps and car salespeople is that car salespeople know when they're lying.) It would seem obvious to anyone with even half an uncompressed brain that no one would ever buy a product from Syncronys again, but in an act of supreme idiocy the *company actually tried to sell other software packages*[9] after the SoftRAM debacle. Sheer imbecility, because Syncronys promptly went out of business.

However, more than just a few trenchant examples of stupidity are needed to support a substantive examination of the subject, which brings me to the point of this book. *In Search of Stupidity* was written to provide you with a more comprehensive look at the topic. Within these pages are documented many of high tech's worst marketing and development programs and strategies, as brought to you by some of its most clueless executives. In my quest to bring you the best of the worst, I selected from a wide range of companies, from arrogant smaller hotshots on the path to meltdown to sluggish giants too muscle bound to get out of their own way.

---

[9] For instance, it tried to sell a utility called "Big Disk."

In the interest of fairness, I haven't included hard-luck stories. No natural disasters, plane crashes, or tragic deaths played a part in any of the disasters discussed. All of the blunders, snafus, and screwups described in this book's pages were avoidable by the individuals and companies that made them and are avoidable by you and your company. After reading this book, you'll know what they are and you'll be in a position to act less unintelligently. For you, history won't repeat itself.

Of course, it *is* possible you'll make other stupid mistakes, ones not chronicled in these pages, but not to worry. If your competition is making the mistakes I describe in these pages, as well as all the others, you'll still probably prevail. Remember, the race goes not to the strong, the swift, or the more intelligent, but to the less stupid.

Besides, I'm planning a sequel.

Best of luck!

two

FIRST MOVERS, FIRST MISTAKES:
IBM, Digital Research,
Apple, and Microsoft

THE BIRTH OF WHAT we now think of as high tech began in 1975 with the introduction of the Altair, the world's first affordable and practical microcomputer, from Micro Instrumentation and Telemetry Systems (MITS) of New Mexico. Units such as the French Micral and the American Scelbi were introduced prior to the Altair, but you couldn't do much with them. The brainchild of former U.S. Air Force Engineer Ed Roberts, the Altair was sold in kit form for $397.00, a price that put the unit within reach of a mass audience. Built around a powerful (for its day) 8-bit Intel 8080 processor, an assembled Altair was capable of doing real work, once you added a keyboard, a monitor, memory, storage peripherals (such as a paper-tape reader), and software, none of which were in great supply when the unit was first introduced. However, a generation raised on Isaac Asimov, Robert A. Heinlein, Robby the Robot, and *Star Trek* (particularly *Star Trek*!) wasn't going to let a parts shortage stop them from getting cracking on building the new world. Bliss was it in that dawn to be alive, but to be a young geek was very heaven! (With apologies to Wordsworth.)

~

The Big Bang: The Altair

The Altair exploded upon a universe ready to accept it, but as with the big bang, its time as a force in microcomputing was brief. MITS was mismanaged and destroyed by its own rapid growth, a pattern that would repeat itself many times in the industry. But as the Altair's bright fire burned down and faded away, it left behind a busy new world inhabited by Commodore PETs, Apples, TRS-80s, Cromencos, Osbornes, and a score of other systems now long extinct.

But high tech is a place of fast change, sharp elbows, and ruthless competition. Soon, great powers began to stir, roused by the hum of commerce and the rustle of dollars being exchanged in this virgin world of microcomputing. Covetous eyes gazed upon an unconquered landscape and began to plot to make it their own.

A Fistful of Chips

Of all the entities converging on the world of microcomputing during its early formation, none was more dominant than IBM. To many, IBM wasn't simply a high-tech company; IBM *was* high tech, other companies being simply minor stars in an IBM firmament. By 1981, admiration, reverence, and fear of IBM had reached neocult status. IBM was "Big Blue," and its chief competitors in the mainframe business were referred to as "The Seven Dwarfs."

Nonetheless, IBM, almost against its will, was increasingly drawn to examine the unknown force that was driving people to go buy hundreds of millions of dollars worth of "toy" computers. By the early 1980s, IBM had come to the realization it needed to understand this force, participate in its growth, and control it. The IBM PC was IBM's first bid to achieve these ends.

A great deal of mythology surrounds the introduction of this now legendary system. The prevailing belief among many is that microcomputing before IBM's arrival was a rough-and-tumble frontier, full of ornery software and colorful hombres tough enough to buy and tame herds of uncooperative boxes of lowing, obstreperous silicon. But as has so often been the case with historical events, truth and legend are often at odds.

The truth is that the microcomputer industry just before IBM's appearance resembled not so much a rude cow town but rather a spanking-new steam train, trimmed in polished brass and covered in fresh paint. Most of the passengers boarded the train at Start-up Junction and are looking forward to the ride to Prosperity, the town just up the line. On board and seated in a fancy Pullman car is a diverse set of well-to-do-looking characters, all gussied up in fancy store-bought clothes they've purchased from the proceeds of successful IPOs and healthy sales. These are the hardware dudes, who include Apple, Commodore, and RadioShack, as well as a score of manufacturers of 8-bit computers running the widely used CP/M operating system. They're a happy-looking lot—they're shipping units to businesses as fast as they can manufacture them.

The home market is equally energetic, though not nearly as profitable, with every general store in town packed at Christmas and every other holiday with parents and their eager-eyed offspring snapping up every VIC-20, Commodore 64, Atari 800, Texas Instruments 94, and Timex Sinclair they can grab. (In 1982, Macy's,[1] at the time a power in consumer electronics, ran out of *every* home-oriented microcomputer at its flagship Herald Square store in New York City a week before Christmas.)

Riding in the car just in front of the hardware merchants are the software peddlers, and they look almost as content. They're selling copies of VisiCalc, WordStar, and PFS File as fast as they can stuff them into cardboard boxes. In many cases cardboard isn't required; demand is so high that customers are willing to take their software home in plastic baggies. Boom times indeed!

Fabulous Fruit

Of all the characters waiting expectantly for the train to pull out of the station, Apple was probably the best positioned of the early denizens of Microcomputerville to become the town's mayor. Apple's mainstay system, the Apple II, and its immediate successor, the Apple II+, were triumphs of industrial design and utility. Sleek and low slung, the units provided an attractive contrast to the stark industrial designs common to business machines. The Apple was reasonably priced (a fully configured system with a whopping 64KB of RAM, color monitor, and dual floppies cost only about $4,000.00). Its integrated color graphics gave it crossover appeal to the home market, and the system was supported by

---

[1] At the time I was working at Macy's as a salesman in a fully staffed and stocked high-end retail computer store that was built within the company's flagship Herald Square location on 34th Street. This store was authorized to sell "high-end" systems such as the IBM PC and the Apple II and III, but until it was completed I was put to work in the consumer electronics section of Macy's, which sold "low-end" systems such as the VIC-20 and the Atari 400s and 800s. Several days before Christmas, the only units available for sale to disappointed moms and dads were a few forlorn Sinclairs that were finally scarfed up by desperate shoppers. For a while in 1982, this store became something of a focal point for celebrities and the PC elite because it was one of the few places in the New York area where you could purchase an IBM system without an inordinate wait. Tony Gold, founder of *PC Magazine*, showed up one day at the store to buy systems for himself and several staffers at the magazine. Famous science-fiction writer Isaac Asimov showed up one day to learn about microcomputers. I escorted Asimov to a station where he sat down at an Apple II, typed in a bit of BASIC code, and was promptly stuck because he had no idea how to interrupt the loop he had just initiated.

a wide selection of business and entertainment software. A small company called Corvus had even developed a system for networking Apples together. All in all, it was a compelling, up-to-date package, and buyers loved their Apples.

Yes, the system did have its idiosyncrasies. You had to buy a hardware upgrade to type in lowercase. Connecting your floppy drive to your Apple incorrectly caused the hapless disk unit to seemingly explode as an internal capacitor[2] blew with a loud pop and a rush of blue smoke out the drive door, but people were willing to overlook these little peccadilloes.

Just as important as its hardware design was that Apple was the first system to run the first spreadsheet, VisiCalc, microcomputing's first killer application. A *killer application* is defined as a product so compelling you'll buy the necessary hardware just to run that particular piece of software. VisiCalc qualified for this rare and honored appellation—once an accountant or CFO saw rows of numbers rippling across a spreadsheet grid as she automatically updated, that person was hooked for life: She *had* to have the product. Management information systems (MIS, later to be called "information technology," or "IT") departments may not have cared for the loss of centralized control that these little boxes represented, but it's a well-known axiom of corporate life that "you don't say no to the CFO." And once the CFO's secretary (now called an "administrative assistant") tried a word-processing program, that was it. Apples, along with any other computer that ran VisiCalc, or some of its early competitors, quickly proliferated across a business frontier that was grateful to get them.

Also contributing to Apple II's success was its relatively flexible and extensible hardware and software architecture. Unlike most of its competitors, Apple's system was "open." Popping off the cover of an Apple II revealed *slots*, connectors into which it was possible to plug in a host of different accessories and upgrades, including memory extenders, accelerator cards, copy boards (hardware devices you used to help make bitmapped images of software for, er, "archival" purposes), extended graphics cards, CP/M boards that allowed you to run CP/M

---

[2] I observed this happen at a training course for Apple repair certification. I'm an authorized Level I Apple repairman (circa 1982) and an Apple Consumer-Oriented Retailing Education (CORE) graduate. How would you like that Apple III sent to your office?

software on your Apple II, and so on. An extensive industry focused on providing third-party accessories and upgrades quickly coalesced around the Apple II, helping drive sales even further.

In fact, from Apple's point of view, the system was entirely *too* open. By 1980, a burgeoning clone and "gray" market was developing around Apple's flagship as units with names like the Pineapple[3] and the Orange started being shipped into the United States in growing quantities from Taiwan and other points east. Domestically, Apple even had its own Compaq, a New Jersey company called Franklin Computers, which offered a well-made Apple clone that even let you type in lowercase letters right out of the box.

Apple's reaction to this turn of events foreshadowed its future behavior with respect to the Macintosh market. It summoned an army of attorneys who were given the mission of shutting down the clone market. The lawyers accomplished this by convincing the courts that it was illegal for companies to simply copy the Apple basic input/output system (BIOS), the built-in set of software instructions that enabled the system to communicate with its internal peripherals. Once this principle was established, the clone market quickly withered because the machines were built by simply replicating the Apple's hardware chassis and equipping it with ROM chips that contained the now "pirated" BIOS code. (Most people obtained the Apple operating system, Apple DOS, by simply copying the floppy on which it came, though Franklin had gone to the trouble of creating its own version of the Apple operating system.) The Taiwanese all sailed back to their island to concentrate on building IBM clones, and the last time Franklin Computer made any noise was at the industry's 1983 COMDEX trade show in Las Vegas. It hired the Beach Boys to regale attendees at a party that turned out to be a musical swan song to the company's imminent wipeout.

At the time, CP/M (short for "Control Program/Monitor" or "Control Program for Microcomputers") was considered by many to be Apple's great rival (though both Commodore and Tandy systems had their devoted acolytes). Developed in 1974 by Gary Kildall, founder of the whimsically named Intergalactic Digital Research (later just Digital Research), CP/M was designed to run on Intel's widely used 8-bit microprocessor, the 8080, and its several clones, most notably Zilog's Z80

---

[3] I briefly owned Pineapple and Franklin Apple II clones.

chip. Unlike Apple DOS and its other competitors, CP/M was less closely coupled to a particular microcomputer's underlying hardware. Digital Research capitalized on this trait to build a profitable and growing business licensing CP/M to several dozen companies, such as NCR, Televideo, Sol Processor, RadioShack (its variant was known as "Pickles and Trout" for some forgotten reason), and one of the industry's earliest and most spectacular flameouts, Osborne Computing, creator of the first "portable" (at 25 pounds) computer.

CP/M suffered from one tremendous drawback, however. Although it could be easily adopted to run on a wide variety of computers, no de facto hardware standard for CP/M machines existed. Printer ports, monitors, and in particular floppy drives all differed from machine to machine. As a result, a person who purchased MicroPro's WordStar word processor for his Vector system had no assurance the floppy on which the software was stored could be read by a Cromenco computer, despite that both used the CP/M operating system. For a while, resellers such as Lifeboat Systems in New York City did a nice business simply supplying CP/Mers with the software of their choice on floppies their computers could read.

Exploding disk drives and noncompatible floppy formats aside, our train has built up a head of steam and begins to chug forward. But as the engine begins to pull out of the station, a lone rider appears suddenly in the distance, his horse galloping madly in pursuit. Reaching the last car before the train has come up to speed, the outlaw grabs hold of a railing and quickly swings himself up onto the rear platform. As he does, we can see the pursuer is a lean bandito wearing a tattered poncho, his features obscured by a tattered hat pulled low over his face. He enters the train and strides through it toward the special Pullman where our hardware merchants sit unsuspecting. When he reaches their car they turn to face the intruder, trepidation writ large on their faces. There's a long moment of silence. Then the stranger lifts his hat to uncover ice-blue eyes that show no pity and throws back his poncho, revealing a three-piece suit matched with a white shirt and sensible tie. Strapped around the stranger's waist are a pair of 8088s, deadly six-guns with the phrase "16-bit" inscribed on their chromed barrels. Pulling out these engines of destruction by their off-white pearl handles, the stranger mercilessly guns down the hardware dudes one by one. Only a handful escapes the initial carnage.

The IBM PC has arrived on the scene.

Building the Perfect Beast

The history of the development and design of the original IBM PC has been told so many times in so many different venues that I need simply to cover the basics before examining the system's long-term impact on the industry. Realizing the microcomputer industry was approaching hypergrowth and worried that IBM might be cut out of the action, a small group of IBM executives decided to act before it was too late. At a meeting of IBM's top management committee in 1980, this group of pre-scient individuals pitched then–IBM President Frank Cary on the necessity of the company building its own PC and doing it quickly. The IBM PC, by the way, was not IBM's first stab at building a microcomputer: An earlier effort in 1975 had produced a management-by-committee machine that was clunky, overengineered, and overpriced. No one wanted it, and no one bought it.

To avoid making the same mistake again, IBM agreed to allow an "off-campus" skunk works to be established to build a new IBM micro-computer, out of the reach of the behemoth's bureaucracy. Heading up the effort were Bill Lowe, Jack Rogers, Jack Sams, Don Estridge, and several others. Estridge, put in charge of the project's day-to-day opera-tions, would one day be known as the "father" of the IBM PC. The location they picked for the project: Bill Lowe's Boca Raton, Florida, lab. Code name for the project: Chess. Code name for the new com-puter: Acorn. Time to project completion: 1 year.

To meet its self-imposed deadline, the IBM team decided on a radical departure from standard IBM practice. Rather than attempt to build and manufacture the new computer internally, the PC would be built mainly from parts bought from third parties. IBM would assemble, ship, and support the machines, which would possess the IBM brand identity, but the contractors would supply most of the critical components, including the unit's microprocessor.

Having made this decision, IBM now had to decide on its new machine's fundamental architecture. Would it be a closed box design or open and accessible like the Apple II series? Apple's success in rapidly building third-party support for its system impressed the PC impresarios of Boca Raton, who regarded Apple as their biggest competitor. After some hesitation and internal debate, the group chose the Apple model. The IBM PC would have slots and an architecture open to third parties.

The chip chosen to be the brains of the PC was Intel's 8088, a less buff version of Intel's new full-fledged 16-bit chip, the 8086. The 8088 was a design compromise, a hybrid chunk of silicon with 16-bit internals and an 8-bit data path for peripherals. IBM liked the 8088's price and 8-bit bus; it brought the cost of the computer down and made it easier for hardware manufacturers to build new accessories to fill the PC's slot.

On the software side of things, IBM purchased the industry's most popular language, BASIC, from Microsoft, the publisher of the industry's most popular variant of that language. For the PC's operating system, IBM, in a contretemps of which the details are still controversial, didn't pick what many regarded as the industry standard, CP/M. The one IBM did pick, MS-DOS, again from Microsoft, very much "resembled" CP/M and, like Digital Research's offering, was highly transportable to other Intel-based computers.

From a cost standpoint, IBM's use of third-party parts meant a fully loaded IBM PC would cost you only about $4,000.00 to $5,000.00, give or take an accessory or two. This was more than an Apple II but not a huge financial barrier for the small businesses IBM anticipated would be the system's primary customers. To soften any perception that PCs were expensive, IBM even produced a stripped loss-leader model for only $1,265.00 (with 16KB of memory, no monitor, and no floppies). These units turned out to be much prized, because enterprising buyers often bought them,[4] added cheaper, non-IBM parts to make them functional, and in some cases even resold them at a profit to a gray market hungry to get its hands on any unit it could.

In fact, IBM, having made the commitment to an open system, took Apple's original open hardware gambit and surpassed it in several key areas. Unlike Apple, which had used control over its BIOS to shut the cloners down, IBM published its BIOS specifications.[5] It didn't allow you to directly copy the BIOS code, but once everyone understood how

---

[4] Including yours truly. I purchased two of these models while at Macy's and sold one at a nice markup to a friend of mine who worked at a computer store in New York's Greenwich Village. I used my profits to help outfit the other unit.

[5] IBM actually thought this was a clever tactic to prevent cloning, because by publishing its BIOS it thought it would be hard for companies to find programmers to reverse engineer it who could prove they had never read its widely published specifications. But, apparently, IBM was wrong, because several companies successfully built BIOS "clones" within 12 months of the PC's release. It seemed plenty of people had never seen those BIOS specs. At least they said so, and IBM's legal department realized it's very, very hard to prove someone has read something.

it integrated with the PC, it was a relatively easy process for smart programmers to reverse engineer its functionality and produce an equivalent BIOS that did everything IBM's did. And IBM also made the PC's hardware interface specifications widely and cheaply available and made no attempt to enforce patents it held on several aspects of the PC design.

Its path firmly set, IBM moved rapidly and built the IBM PC in a year. Its release in August 1981 was greeted with almost universal huzzahs and overwhelming consumer acclaim. Some of the gearheads of the time argued interminably about whether the computer was really a 16-bit machine, but most sensible people ignored them. The IBM PC was (relatively) inexpensive, was powerful enough for any future anyone could foresee (fully loaded, it supported 640KB of memory, and who would ever need more memory than that?), had a great keyboard, supported color graphics, looked fairly sleek for its day, and came in any color you wanted as long as it was off-white. And, of course, the fact that it was IBM selling it sealed the deal. The PC was an instant sales success.

And then, IBM, having introduced a well-designed, highly functional computer with a sterling brand name and an open architecture, did the last, most significant thing it would ever do in the microcomputer hardware business. It did nothing. And it did it for 6 crucial years.

With this "action," IBM unleashed the industry's first and to date only "hardware virus." Once introduced into the environment and left to fend for itself, the initially microbial PC hardware standard began to mutate into an enormous Silicon Beast that over the years grew ever larger. Eventually, by dint of its size and influence, the PC standard created a hardware ecosystem around itself that allowed it to continue to grow and flourish without IBM's help or influence. But by the time IBM awoke to the consequences of its historic inaction, it was too late. The Silicon Beast had ambled clear of the ability of any one company to control or manipulate it to its exclusive benefit. A flourishing and open hardware universe had come into being, one that dominates the technology industry to this day.

During this critical period, IBM did introduce new computers, the most notable being its IBM AT in 1984, a system that surpassed the original PC in market acceptance and sales. But the underlying PC platform and architecture remained open and comparatively royalty free. Anyone could, and many did, jump into the market to make clones of the PC and AT, including firms such as Compaq (maker of the first "luggable" PC), Dell Computer, and for a period of time, literally hundreds of others, most of whom have vanished unremembered into PC history.

To get a sense of how unique this state of affairs is, consider that today, more than 20 years after the release of the original PC, anyone can, if the mood strikes her, assemble a state-of-the-art computer from standardized parts available from hundreds of vendors. Try doing that with a Macintosh or a Sun Microsystems SPARC (or for that matter, your TV, VCR, DVD, or even your toaster). Apple finally took a stab at allowing a clone market to develop around the Macintosh and the Mac operating system (OS) in 1994, but after his reascension to the Apple throne, Steve Jobs promptly squashed the Mac clones. In the late 1980s and early 1990s, Sun Microsystems made great noises about how it was going to unleash its SPARC chip and architecture on the industry and create an open, alternate hardware platform. But despite all of Sun Microsystems CEO Scott McNealy's noise and posturing on the issue, the company, via restrictive licensing terms and subtle tweaks to its hardware platform, kept all potential competitors on a tight leash and prevented a free-for-all clone market from ever coalescing around the SPARC.

In 1987, IBM attempted to take it all back and stuff the PC standard back into its cage with the introduction of its PS/2 line. PS/2s sported a new hardware architecture and, in contrast to the PC, IBM closely guarded their hardware specifications in the name of "quality control" and demanded comparatively stiff royalties for its use in competing systems. Fierce, drooling patent attorneys with sharp fangs were called out of their legal kennels to stand guard over every chip, connector, and clump of BIOS over which IBM laid exclusive claim. To show it wasn't kidding about its intent to replace the PC with PS/2, IBM announced soon after the introduction of the new machines that it would discontinue selling PC-type computers.

The PS/2 effort was a complete failure. Yes, the new bus was better and faster than the earlier PC standard. But the PC bus was more than good enough for the hardware of the time and remained good enough for several years after the PS/2 introduction. A group of IBM's competitors, led by upstart Compaq, quickly banded together and proclaimed the existence of the royalty-free Extended (no longer IBM) Industry

Standard Architecture (EISA) for those who *really* needed more performance. To IBM's chagrin, almost no one came calling with hat in hand to build PS/2 clones, and IBM was forced to retreat from its "only PS/2 for you" stance and continue making good old PCs while the PS/2 began a long and miserable slide into irrelevance. Most manufacturers ignored both new hardware architectures and simply continued pumping out cheaper and cheaper PC clones to a public eager and ready to buy them. Instead of leading the pack, IBM now found itself yoked by the nose to its own creation, forced to drudge along abjectly behind the growing behemoth with the rest of the hoi polloi.

In the meantime, the Silicon Beast slowly and steadily moved into new pastures, wreaking devastation wherever it browsed. First to be driven to extinction were the CP/M machines, comparatively fragile creatures, none of which individually had enough market share to allow it to survive for long. Then the Beast chewed through the Apple II's grazing range, driving it from the business market and into the home and education niches, where it eventually withered and died. The commodity nature of the PC standard made it possible to build ever-cheaper PCs, and the Silicon Beast ambled into the home market where it slowly suffocated prosaic creatures such as the Commodore 64 and even more exotic species such as the Amiga and the Atari ST. All disappeared beneath the Beast's massive bulk, their dying cries scarcely catching the market's attention.

For a brief period, Apple's success with the Macintosh offered the company a chance at battling the Beast by creating one of its own, but as with the II and II+, Apple chose a different path. It created the Macintosh reservation, today a delicate biosphere maintained by Mac fanatics and the print and graphics market. Roped off from the rest of the computing world by fancy industrial designs, yuppie-pleasing cutting-edge colors, and the forbearance of Bill Gates, who has found Apple's continued existence useful as a means of fending off the Feds, the Macintosh lives a rarefied, hothouse existence. In 2006, Apple possessed a 3 percent to 4 percent market share in hardware and had become the world's largest irrelevant $14 billion computer company (though the company has found a second life in MP3 music players with the iPod).

Unfortunately for IBM, the Silicon Beast proved to be no respecter of parentage. Almost by accident, the Beast devoured the Peanut, the IBM

PC's smaller cousin, in the mid-1980s (an event you'll examine in the next chapter). Next on the menu, as already noted, was the PS/2. The Beast then moved on to cut IBM's mainframe computers off from new pasturage. This market, once the heart of IBM's business model, became first a static and then a slowly shrinking environment. Ditto for the once flourishing Silverlake (the code name for IBM's highly successful AS400 minicomputer line).

Still not sated, the Beast turned its eyes in the 1990s to lucrative UNIX markets and ambled off in search of fresh grazing grounds. Niche UNIX vendors such as SGI found themselves starving for profits as their markets were flooded with high-end PCs stuffed with inexpensive memory and increasingly fast processors. And now even mighty Sun Microsystems sees the possibility of an eclipse as the Beast grows larger, its bulk swollen by huge influxes of cheap PCs running Linux, a free UNIX clone that has begun to compete with Solaris, Sun Microsystems's version of UNIX, in power, performance, and reliability.

The long-term consequences of the choices IBM made in building the PC impacted more than just computer manufacturing. The PC's creation led to the decoupling of software from a reliance on proprietary silicon. Prior to the appearance of the IBM PC standard, firms had rarely purchased computers per se; rather, they bought packaged solutions that combined a company's hardware, software, and services. In this tightly bound environment, IBM had clawed its way to overwhelming dominance by dint of ruthless marketing and good products.

But in IBM's brave new (and unexpected) world, the competitive environment had been recast. For example, prior to the existence of the PC, little attention was paid to the microprocessor, the actual computer that resided at the heart of any system. But as it became obvious to everyone that PCs were simply collections of standardized parts that anyone could assemble, interest grew in the actual distinguishing characteristics of one computer from another. Intel would recognize this opportunity and take advantage of it in the coming years to become the closest thing the industry has to an arbiter of hardware standards, though the company's ability to dictate terms and conditions to the market has never approached IBM's imperial authority.

Even more significant was that the creation and spread of the PC standard meant that software, not hardware, now formed computing's nexus of power. With computers reduced to a growing aggregation of almost identical silicon clones, control over operating systems, data formats, application programming interfaces (APIs), and Web standards would determine market supremacy and company profitability. As IBM slipped from the apex of power, another company would rise to supplant it, a tiny upstart that better understood this new world's new rules and what it would take to master them. Big Blue was fated to be eclipsed by Great Green.

~

Great Green Rising: Digital Research and Microsoft

In its 2001 rankings of the 100 largest independent PC software companies in the United States, Jeffrey Tarter's *Softletter* publication reported that Microsoft represented 69 percent of total revenues. In the categories of operating systems, business applications, development tools, Internet browsers, database management systems, and server software of different types, Microsoft had a monopoly, dominant, or substantial market share. As the 21st century dawned, Microsoft had replaced IBM as the company most people were likely to admire and revere or distrust and hate. And today, no one "ever gets fired for buying Microsoft."

Reluctant Ahab

As with the IBM PC, many myths surround the rise of Microsoft to high tech's position of paramount leader. The seminal myth hearkens back to the company's anointment as the supplier of the OS for the PC, the single greatest coup in the history of business. The popular story (backed up by such sources as *The Pirates of Silicon Valley*, an interesting and well-acted film that does a complete disservice to the cause of truth) is that IBM intended to use Digital Research's buff new 16-bit operating system, CP/M-86, for its new PC.

Kildall, through a series of misunderstandings and miscommunications that to this day are the stuff of legend, refused to talk to IBM's representatives. IBM then turned to Microsoft for its OS. Despite that Microsoft had no such product, the company bamboozled IBM into agreeing to buy a nonexistent product and then turned around and scarfed up Quick and Dirty Operating System (QDOS) from a small computer company, Seattle Computer Products. QDOS was written by Tim Paterson to support an 8086[6] prototyping board that the company was selling to software developers.

The reality is a bit different. In 1981, the industry's biggest fish first swam up to Microsoft, not Digital Research, in search of both computer languages and an OS for the PC. At the initial meetings, Gates candidly informed IBM that Microsoft had no OS to sell. At the time, Microsoft made most of its money from the sale of languages, particularly BASIC. Microsoft was overjoyed at the chance to sell its products to IBM, but it suggested that for an OS, IBM representatives should contact Kildall and Digital Research to talk about CP/M-86. Dutifully, the Big Blue Whale traveled south to California to meet with Kildall, who didn't think the initial conference important enough to attend and allowed his wife, a vice president at the firm, to conduct the opening ceremonies. There was an argument about signing a confidentiality letter, neither group found much to like about the other, and IBM left Digital Research without even a preliminary agreement to talk about CP/M-86.

The IBM contingent then asked Gates to talk to Kildall and persuade him to be more receptive to their overtures, but even this led nowhere. IBM was "the establishment," and many programmers brought up in the 1960s and 1970s regarded the company with a certain disdain. IBM was big, bureaucratic, and its machines, although beloved by big businesses everywhere, weren't accessible to hackers and hobbyists. Kildall, in tune with the spirit of the Altair and doing a nice business with CP/M, wasn't overly impressed by IBM and saw no need to kowtow. It was only after these initial rebuffs that Microsoft stepped into the OS situation and agreed to provide one for an IBM becoming increasingly nervous about meeting its ship dates for the IBM PC. After all, if IBM couldn't ship its PC, it wouldn't need Microsoft's BASIC. Fortunately for everyone concerned, except Kildall, the serendipitous existence of QDOS made it possible for Microsoft to deliver on its promise.

---

[6] Ads for this board appeared in *BYTE* magazine.

Over the years, rivers of ink have been spilled bemoaning Kildall's rotten luck and the cruelty of an unfair world, but most of the hand-wringing seems misplaced. Kildall had been placed in the unique position of having had the largest of large blue whales swim up to his door, beach itself in his office, roll over on its belly, and point to the spot where the harpoon should be placed, and he had refused the shot. A fair person can hardly blame Gates for stepping up to the prow for his own throw at the great beast, and unlike Kildall, Gates's aim was true. The contract he negotiated with IBM turned out to be Microsoft's first step on the road to industry supremacy.

Yet, even this happy turn of events for Microsoft was not all it seemed. It would take further blundering on the part of Digital Research before the company was truly and finally fish food.

When the PC first shipped, PC DOS was indeed the operating system of record. But this didn't mean as much as it seems. DOS wasn't pre-loaded on the IBM PC. The unit had no hard disk, and DOS wasn't stuffed on a chip in your PC. You booted your OS from a floppy every time you turned on the machine.[7] Nor was DOS bundled into a purchase of a PC. It came in a separate box and you paid for it separately. During the initial rollout, IBM had put no extensive marketing push behind DOS; all of its emphasis was on the PC. But as the system's sales momentum built, IBM did, however, make much of the fact that no less than three OSs were available for the PC: PC DOS; the UCSD p-System, which was really a development system for programmers interested in developing "write once, run anywhere" software (no, Java wasn't the first time someone had that bright idea); and . . . CP/M-86.

CP/M-86? How did that get in there? Hadn't Kildall blown it in those legendary meetings and phone calls?

Well, not completely. As the enormity of what he had done began to sink in, Kildall took a close look at a copy of the forthcoming IBM OS and noticed that, by golly, it sure looked a lot like CP/M. And that didn't seem fair at all. There quickly ensued some legal harpoon rattling, a

---

[7] As a salesman at Macy's "professional" computer store, I attempted many times to sell prospective customers CP/M-86 instead of IBM DOS. Having worked with CP/M in its 8-bit incarnation, I knew it was a superior choice, but the product's pricing made it almost impossible to sell.

quick visit to Boca Raton, and voilà! CP/M-86 was now an officially supported IBM OS that shipped in an IBM box and was available directly from IBM.

CP/M-86 was late to market, but despite this, shortage of software support would be no problem for the still feisty DOS competitor. The press and most technical gurus regarded CP/M-86 as superior to DOS, and publishers of older CP/M software hadn't found it hard to port their applications to the new OS. For example, MicroPro, at the time the world's largest microcomputer software company, had ported WordStar, the industry's leading word processor, as well as most of its other business packages, to CP/M-86. Ashton-Tate, publisher of the best-selling dBASE II, had a CP/M-86 version of the program. Other companies produced spreadsheets, games, utilities, and other products in anticipation that CP/M-86 would quickly sweep DOS from the market.

Nothing of the sort happened. Compounding his initial errors, Kildall had made a fundamental pricing mistake with CP/M-86. Upon the introduction of the IBM PC, the cost of PC DOS had been set at $40.00 (when anyone actually paid for it; the product was heavily pirated). This decision by IBM had reset market expectations as to what an OS for a microcomputer should cost (a reality the company would find out 6 years later applied to itself during the introduction of OS/2). CP/M-86 upon its release cost $240.00, a price close to that paid by purchasers of the 8-bit CP/M. The huge disparity in price made it almost impossible to sell CP/M-86 to retail purchasers, and the OS began to wither almost immediately.

Years later Kildall would claim that IBM had decided on the price difference between the two operating systems. There is good reason to question this statement. At CP/M East[8] in the autumn of 1983, the last

---

[8] This show was the first I attended as a MicroPro employee. I spent most of my time demoing InfoStar for CP/M-86 and was one of the people who tracked Gary Kildall down to discuss the pricing issue destroying CP/M-86. This event became legendary among MicroPro employees for what became known inside the company as the "Schmuck 'n' Shark" riot. MicroPro rented out the New England Aquarium for an evening and handed out about 700 tickets for a surf-and-turf dinner with an open bar. Approximately 3,000 people crashed the event, and a few drunken revelers had to be forcibly restrained from doffing their clothes and diving into the shark tank for a swim. A radical contingent from MicroPro was in favor of allowing the partygoers to jump in with the sharks and watching what happened, but the more conservative faction prevailed.

major trade show ever held dedicated to promoting Kildall's brainchild, a group of people[9] from various companies publishing CP/M-86 software cornered Kildall on the busy show floor to discuss pricing and the OS's future. In the impromptu discussion that followed, Kildall was repeatedly implored to adjust CP/M-86's price so that it could compete with PC DOS and warned that failure to do so would kill the product. Kildall was polite, pleasant, and adamant that CP/M-86 was "priced just right." "The market understands the difference between a toy OS and a professional product," he proclaimed before disappearing into the show crowd.

CP/M-86 was effectively defunct by the end of 1984.

A despondent Digital Research would try to make a comeback with GEM, a Macintosh look-alike shell for DOS that enjoyed a brief measure of success before it was crushed by a litigious Apple. In 1987, Digital Research obtained a more solid measure of revenge when it released DR DOS, a "clone" of MS-DOS (though who was the actual clone is a legitimate matter of dispute). Though no major PC vendor ever picked up the product, for a couple of years Digital Research did a brisk business selling DR DOS to second- and third-tier manufacturers while simultaneously giving Microsoft and Gates minor fits.

The fun came to an end when Microsoft struck back by placing messages in beta versions of Windows 3.1 that warned users of possible "problems" that might occur if you used DR DOS with Windows.[10] This was all nonsense; DR DOS worked fine with Windows 3.1 and public pressure eventually forced Microsoft to back away from this unsavory tactic, but in the interim a great deal of marketing damage had been done.

More significant were the changes Microsoft made in its licensing agreements that made it difficult to buy MS-DOS without also purchasing Windows and tied discounts to exclusive purchases of Microsoft products. These were tough tactics, and they would come back to haunt Microsoft during its defense against the U.S. government's charges of predatory and monopolistic business practices. But even if Microsoft had been a kinder, gentler opponent, unless a major player such as IBM

---

[9] I was one of those individuals.

[10] Wendy Goldman Rohm, *The Microsoft File: The Secret Case Against Bill Gates* (New York: Times Business Books, 1998). I was a DR DOS user and personally experienced this situation.

had intervened, DR DOS could never have amounted to more than a minor presence in a market moving inexorably to a GUI model of computing à la the Macintosh.

Attack of the Clones

The second great myth surrounding Microsoft's rise to power is that the original DOS contract with IBM immediately provided the company with a massive and unfair advantage over its competition. Again, the truth is somewhat different. Over time, Microsoft's DOS contract *did* prove to be a cash cow of legendary proportions, but it took idiocy of monumental proportions on the part of IBM, Apple, and other industry players to transform Microsoft's good deal for its quick-and-dirty DOS into the industry's shiniest gold mine.

From a financial standpoint, the original DOS deal put a nice bit of up-front cash in Microsoft's pocket and provided the company with a lucrative revenue stream from royalties on sales of PC DOS. But far more significant was that the contract gave Microsoft the right to resell DOS to other companies, something the company promptly began to do under the rubric of MS-DOS.

This, however, didn't turn out to be as lucrative a business as Microsoft had initially thought. Many of the first "clones" of the IBM PC weren't true clones; rather, they tried to improve on the PC's design. These machines, from companies such as DEC, Otrona,[11] RadioShack, Victor, Texas Instruments, Hyperion, and many others that have vanished into obscurity, were collectively known as "MS-DOS clones." Some offered better hard disk support, sported different keyboard layouts, and provided better graphics capabilities, an area in which the original PC was considered weak.

It was the issue of graphics support and compatibility that proved lethal to the MS-DOS machines. Developers for the IBM PC had discovered something about MS-/PC DOS early on: It displayed graphics slowly. To solve the problem, software developers quickly learned to bypass the OS and directly access IBM's graphics hardware to improve screen performance.

---

[11] I had use of an Otrona, a "light" portable (around 20 pounds) for about a year in the early 1980s. The unit was retrofitted with a compatibility board that let it run most IBM PC software.

The appearance of the MS-DOS clones presented software developers with a dilemma. Should they build customized versions of their software to support these new computers, most of which didn't possess substantial market share? Or should they hedge their bets and use MS-DOS to handle screen updating? Most hedged, and buyers of MS-DOS clones soon got used to watching their software work veeery slooowly on their systems while IBM PC users enjoyed word processors and spreadsheets that seemed to snap to attention. Interest in the MS-DOS clones, which had been high, was soon replaced by skepticism, and then derision. No one wanted an MS-DOS clone; everyone wanted an IBM PC or a true PC compatible, one able to run IBM PC software out of the box. The MS-DOS clone market quickly collapsed, and Microsoft's advantage seemed less significant than it had been.

But fortunately for Gates and company, IBM had unleashed the Silicon Beast. As quickly as the MS-DOS clones withered from the market, they were replaced by hordes of IBM compatibles able to work with PC displays and graphics without any need for machine-specific customization. All the new generation of clones required to go to market was an MS-DOS license. Microsoft's IBM deal started to turn golden indeed.

Microsoft's good fortune was compounded by a decade of fumbling stupidity on the part of IBM as it sought a replacement for MS-DOS. First to flop was TopView, a clunky, multitasking, character-based pseudo-OS released in 1985 just as Apple's Macintosh was educating the market on the benefits of a GUI. Next to fail was something called CP-DOS (one of its many names), an abortive attempt to create an OS that took full advantage of the IBM AT's 80286 chip. Along the way, IBM continued to break Kildall's heart with flirtations over different versions of CP/M-86 that never lead to consummation. OS/2 has earned its own inglorious chapter in this book. In the mid-1990s, after its storied divorce from Microsoft, IBM even attempted to sell its own version of DOS in the retail and original equipment manufacturer (OEM) markets and did as well with it as it had with OS/2.

But IBM would never succeed in developing a successor to DOS. Apple would never follow its own early example with the Apple II and liberate the Macintosh OS from its sterile preserve to grow and flourish in an open environment. Digital Research would eventually fade away, unable to ever recover from its early missteps.

Over the next 20 years, Microsoft would make the most of its competitors' mistakes and stupidity as it slowly leveraged its advantage in desktop OSs into absolute control over what would prove to be high tech's most strategic terrain. Using the generically named Windows as its base, it would slowly branch out to take control of the business applications market and then move from there to a position of preeminence in web technologies such as browsers. Like its competitors, Microsoft wouldn't always be completely ethical or nice in the way it did business. But unlike them, Microsoft would consistently avoid making stupid mistakes again and again and triumph from this ability.

three

A RATHER NUTTY TALE:
IBM and the PC Junior

TO FULLY APPRECIATE the tale you're about to read, we must take a trip back through time. We begin our journey in search of ancient high-tech stupidity by boarding a time machine of the imagination. Step into the conveyance, sit down, hold tight, and let's begin our journey to modern high technology's Paleolithic era. Even the word "microcomputing" gives us a sense of antiquity and great age; these days, we say "desktop computer" or "workstation." Relax as we travel through eons of high-tech time—in fact, all the way back to the early 1980s! Enjoy the ride.

As we arrive safely at our destination and fly over the Lost World of Technology, we see it's a strange and archaic place inhabited by the even stranger dinosaurs of computing. Let's land, leave our time machine, and explore a bit. It should be fairly safe on the ground—for the most part, the creatures we see are friendly, if a bit hard to use, and won't "byte."

As you step out of the time machine, look over to your left. There you'll see the vanished Elysian Fields of CP/M. Note the wide variety of species. For example, there's a common blue-case Osborne and its rarer brethren, the earlier brown-hide variant. It's a placid beast unless you try to pick it up; then it's liable to dislocate your shoulder. That's because it weighs about 30 pounds. Ouch. Nonetheless, it's the first portable computer! The Osborne came in a sewing machine–style case that included a 5-inch CRT, dual floppies, and an incredible software bundle consisting of CP/M, WordStar, SuperCalc, BASIC, and later even a database. And all for only $1,795.00! It went extinct when it grew too fast and tried to give birth to a new IBM-compatible offspring before it was ready. You can read more about this fabulous creature in John Dvorak's classic tome, *Hypergrowth: The Rise and Fall of the Osborne Computer Corporation* (Avon, 1984). Sad.

To the right of those Osbornes, note the Sol Processor unit. It's a handsome beast, with its polished walnut flanks. Lumbering about behind it you can see varieties of Northstars, Morrows, Kaypros, Cromencos, and similar ungainly-looking creatures. We suggest you not get too close—if one of those beasts falls over on your foot, you're liable to break a toe.

Directly ahead you'll see verdant green meadows inhabited by various species of Apple IIs. No shortage of them! Much harder to spot is the rather fragile and delicate Apple III. When it was first introduced, the new system seemed not to work well unless you read an Apple service bulletin advising you to pick the unit up and drop it from a height of several inches to help reseat its memory chips. We believe this species went extinct from sheer embarrassment.

In those woods to your right you'll see many colorful and interesting specimens of the home computer family, including Commodore VIC-20s and 64s, TI99/4As, Atari 800s and 400s, and a bevy of Sinclairs. These species tended to be short-lived, with the exception of the Commodore 64, which was prolific. If you look closely, you'll see a truly fascinating hybrid, a Coleco Adam. This odd beast was the offspring of Coleco's fabulously successful Cabbage Patch Kids line of amazingly ugly dolls. The company used the profits from the Kids to go high tech, and the Adam was the result. The unit was aimed at the home market but ran the CP/M operating system, which loaded from an integrated tape drive. Historians believe these units were actually designed and built *by* the Cabbage Patch Kids; this would account for the fact that about one-third of the Adams that shipped were DOA and that putting the cassette with your OS on top of an Adam's built-in printer tended to erase it.

If you look directly behind you, you'll notice a giant off-white herd thundering our way. These are IBM PCs, but if you look carefully at the hides of these magnificent beasts, you can see they're undergoing an interesting transformation. The "IBM" is slowly fading from their bodies, and soon the only strong identifying mark on these creatures will be the "PC" mottling. We'll need to move out of the way when the herd gets closer because these voracious beasts devour any other computer in their path.

Now, look closely at the edges of the herd. See those little creatures scuttling out of the way and peering at us from under those rocks? They're rather small and ungainly-looking things: "peanut" sized, in fact. They're IBM PC Juniors, and they have an interesting tale to tell.

~

The Gods Themselves, Coming to Your Home Soon

After the IBM PC's release, the Gods of IBM at Boca Raton were feeling, well, pretty godlike. The PC was selling like gangbusters. IBM's initial projections of 221,000 units over 4 years had been laughably wrong: The company actually shipped 200,000 PCs in its first year on the market and by 1982 couldn't keep up with the demand. The PC's big brother, the PC XT, basically a PC with more memory and a hard drive, proved to be an even stronger seller. IBM's "Little Tramp" advertising campaign, based on the famous character created by silent-screen star Charlie Chaplin, was regarded as a triumph of successful product branding. An IBM authorization to sell the PC was a license to become a millionaire. The units were in such demand that gray market purchases of PCs were used as money-laundering vehicles for various enterprises of dubious origin.

The question now arose: What next? IBM had a new rock-'em, sock-'em box in development, the AT, but it would be a couple of years before it was ready. The Gods of IBM at Boca Raton cast their Olympian gaze about the land, and it came to fall on the home computer market. It seemed a place ripe for exploitation and conquest.

This is because in 1982 a fairly sharp dividing line separated the world of business and home microcomputing systems. The business market was dominated by the IBM PC, RadioShack, and a bevy of CP/M systems, all of whom were losing market share to the PC on an almost hourly basis. Apple's III system, intended to replace the Apple II as the company's mainstream business machine, had proved to be an embarrassing flop. The Apple II was still a player in the business market, but it was increasingly seen as a pricey and premium home system.

The market for "computers for the home" was controlled by Apple and a supporting cast of interesting players, including Atari, Commodore, RadioShack, and Texas Instruments. Aside from Apple, none of these was particularly healthy. Atari, with its 800 computer, should have been in fine shape. This system, the direct ancestor of the even more fabulous Amiga, was almost a decade ahead of its competitors with graphics and sound coprocessors and even a primitive version of today's USB bus. Unfortunately for the company's computer aspirations, by 1982 Atari's core market, gaming consoles, was undergoing a storied meltdown.

The inferno had been lit by the release of the worst game in computing history, an E.T. title based on the movie of the same name. Unleashed on an unsuspecting American public just in time for the 1982 Christmas season, E.T.'s idiotic story line, ugly graphics, and tedious and illogical game play transformed what was supposed to be a treasured holiday gift into a lump of coal left under the tree. The game was sold in the hundreds of thousands during the holiday season[1] and carted back to stores in almost equal numbers after the season was over, the deluge of returns driven by the screams and wails of America's disappointed tykes. Almost single-handedly, E.T. the game destroyed the American video game industry of the 1980s and transformed Atari's 2600 cash cow game console into cow flop in the living room. The market wouldn't recover from the E.T. debacle until Japanese manufacturer Nintendo revived it by ensuring that only games that adhered to basic standards of quality control reached America's TV screens.

Commodore's VIC-20 and C64 units were shipping like crazy and appeared to present a more formidable challenge. Commodore was headed by the semilegendary Jack Tramiel, a Holocaust survivor who had started in the business as a typewriter repairman in the Bronx. Tramiel, who liked to periodically proclaim that "business is war" followed a "computers for the masses, not the classes" strategy of relentless price-cutting. As a result, finances always seemed dicey at Commodore, and although the company shipped lots of units, profits were slim. Quality control was also an issue: When the C64 first shipped, at least 25 percent of the units were DOA.[2] If business was war, no one doubted that IBM would blow Tramiel out of his trenches with a Big Blue cannon.

---

[1] As already noted, I briefly worked in Macy's consumer electronics department. E.T. was rolled out in time for the 1982 Christmas season, and I personally sold many copies of this gaming abomination to parents eager to satisfy the consumer longings of their offspring. I must confess I told some people the game was "OK," an act for which, if there is an afterlife, I will undoubtedly pay a suitable penance.

[2] Despite this discouraging start, the unit did go on to have a fairly long and successful run, particularly as a gaming machine. Software emulators exist that allow you to experience the joys of early 1980s 8-bit computing with the Commodore 64 on your PC today.

RadioShack was too busy trying to figure out how keep its business systems alive in the face of the IBM juggernaut to spend much time worrying about its color computer, though the unit would find a second life overseas in Britain. And speaking of the mother country, British inventor Clive Sinclair's namesake, the black-and-white Sinclair ZX80, was cheap and the computing curious bought quite a few of them, but it was difficult to find someone who actually used the system for much. Industry analysts proclaimed it the first closet computer. You bought it, played with it a bit, and then tossed it in your closet and bought a "real" computer.

Finally, another major contender in the home market, Texas Instruments' TI99/4A, would soon disappear from the market. The TI99/4A was perhaps home computing's most luckless system, the ongoing victim of an incredibly stupid marketing campaign that included

- shipping the unit with no way for software publishers to write software for it,
- threatening third-party publishers who did figure out how to write software for it,
- hiding the existence of a software language shipped with the machine that made it easier to write software for it,
- providing no storage system for the computer until months after it shipped (not even a cassette player),
- shipping the unit with a power supply that tended to explode,
- shipping the unit without any type of fuse in the power system, leading to the possibility that Texas Instruments could electrocute its customers,
- and, finally, initiating a price war with Commodore, the discounting kings of computing, that led to Texas Instruments losing up to $50.00 on every unit shipped.

Texas Instruments would withdraw from the home market in 1984 after losing about $500 million on the TI99/4A. This may not have been the last time the industry heard from this system; some observers postulate that the TI99/4A returned from the grave in 1998 and possessed the souls of thousands of Internet marketers. Others believe the problem lay in Texas Instrument's charming practice of firing older and more experienced workers while at the same time bringing in cheap hires out of college. This, coupled with a shameless policy of laying off people who had almost reached their 20-year retirement and pension, earned the company the internal nickname of the "Training Institute."

~

The Market Goes Nuts

Thus, with the home front in varying degrees of chaos, confusion, and despair, the time seemed right for IBM to bring its brand of peace and order to the market. A new IBM PC for mom, pop, and the kids code-named "Peanut" was decreed and announced to a market agog to know more. To heighten industry interest, IBM blanketed the project in tight secrecy, and few accurate details about the machine leaked out before its 1983 release. Only a handful of resellers were allowed to see the machine while it was in development, and loose lips were sealed by IBM's threat to relieve blabbermouths of their valuable license-to-print-money IBM authorizations. (IBM wasn't kidding about the Peanut's security—an indiscreet electronics buyer at Macy's who leaked some accurate details about the Peanut to the press lost his job.)

The Peanut's announcement immediately threw the industry into an orgy of feverish speculation. In the months leading up to the system's rollout, an entire mini-industry sprung up dedicated to making pronouncements and prognostications about the Peanut's feature set, its impact on the market, and its effect on the competition. As the Peanut's release date neared, the buzz reached a higher and more frantic pitch. Guesses about the system's configuration and capabilities included statements such as the following:

- The Peanut would have an 8086 processor (the big brother of the PC's 8088).
- The Peanut would have an 80286 processor (the chip that would be the brains of the IBM AT).
- The Peanut would have an 80386 processor (an Intel chip that wasn't built yet).
- The Peanut would have a huge amount of memory, maybe even a whopping 1MB of the stuff (most IBM PCs maxed out at 640KB).

- The Peanut would have a hard drive like the XT, only bigger.
- The Peanut would have multiple coprocessors à la the Ataris and Commodores.
- The Peanut would be a supercomputer in a box.
- The Peanut would be a supercomputer in a box and be incredibly inexpensive.
- The Peanut would be a supercomputer in a box and be incredibly inexpensive and look incredibly futuristic and cool.
- The Peanut would help solve world hunger and war. (No, I'm not kidding. You know, because everyone would have a supercomputer on his desktop, he'd be able to communicate with others and thus reach across national/ethnic/religious/political boundaries to create a new world of greater understanding and harmony, etc., etc., kumbayah, kumbayah.)
- The Peanut would have great graphics.
- The Peanut would have *really* great graphics with fabulous symphonic sound.
- The Peanut would have a matter transporter unit that would dematerialize you à la *Star Trek* and then rematerialize you inside the computer so you could play games in the first person! (OK, yes, I *am* kidding, but speculation peaked just a bit under these levels.)

But the most interesting bit of prognostication offered about IBM's newest offspring was that the Peanut would be so wonderful, so powerful, and so cheap that everyone would want one instead of an IBM PC. Industry watchers spent much ink and time speculating about how IBM would deal with this new wonder box that would immediately cannibalize the market of its incredibly profitable and fast-growing PC franchise. Pity was expressed on behalf of this amazing colossus that didn't even know its own strength.

But whatever the unit did or didn't have, everyone was sure that when it shipped it would be a huge smash. The IBM PC and XT had already proved that IBM could do no wrong. Retailers fought for early allocations of the precious few units that would be available upon the system's official unveiling. Buyers feverishly flooded into stores and laid down their money in advance so they could be the first on their block to have a precious Peanut. The press drooled. The pundits prayed. The clock slowly ticked. The minutes dragged by. People's hearts felt as if they would seize in their chests. And then . . . in November 1983 . . . the unit . . . shipped.

And the world . . . shrieked.

~

The Nut Grinder

Not in approval, mind you. With the shell of secrecy surrounding the Peanut finally cracked, it was immediately apparent to observers that something had gone terribly wrong. For starters, the unit was ugly, an ungainly white lump of a system that just seemed to lie there. No swoopy futuristic curves or neat little design fillips. If the PC Junior represented computer designs of the future, the future looked like Mr. Spock's box of Kleenex. And it was an expensive box: A base PC Junior with a monitor cost about $1,000.00. Not that different from a PC.

The PC Junior was also not richly appointed with accessories by any means. It had one measly 5-inch 360KB floppy drive and no room for another inside the system. And even in 1983, one floppy drive wasn't enough storage to get much done. Worse, disk access to the floppy was glacial, IBM having opted to not include a specialized chip found in the PC that speeded things up. There was no hard drive, and it wasn't easy to add one. There *were* two cartridge slots, which developers had learned to avoid like the plague because shipping software in large bulky plastic chunks drove the cost of goods of your product up by several thousand percent.

There were no slots, either. Instead, you added expansion capabilities to the PC Junior via what were called *slices,* ungainly small white lumps you stuck onto to your ungainly large white lump to make a computer that was even lumpier. And they were expensive as well. In fact, all the PC Junior's accessories were expensive.

A look into the PC Junior's innards was even more disappointing. Not only were there no exotic graphics and display coprocessors, but you also had to buy extra memory to look at an 80-character display instead of the unit's default 40 characters. OK, the unit had 16 colors, and the PC had only 4, but still. You couldn't even add the crummy math coprocessor, used to speed up spreadsheet operations, that you could on the IBM PC. And there was no 8086, 80286, 80386, or any other superchip on Junior's motherboard—just the same stolid 8088 used in the IBM PC running at an unexciting 4.7 MHz.

Adding the final insult to injury was the pièce de résistance of the whole ugly, expensive ensemble: the infamous "chiclet" keyboard. This abomination consisted of a plastic slab festooned with small, flat, stiff, rectangular rubbery keys that looked like pieces of chewing gum and provided little feedback when struck. Because these keyboards could be built cheaply, Atari, Texas Instruments, and Commodore had used variants of this design in some of their systems, but users loathed them. Trying to touch-type on the PC Junior's unyielding slab was a wearying and frustrating experience; one commentator who received the PC Junior as a Christmas gift described the feeling like that of "having one of Santa's elves continuously whack on your fingertips with his little hammer."

Adding fuel to the fire was that the original IBM PC's keyboard was a storied design loved by many. Many people swore by their IBM boards, which sported a "clicky" and pleasant tactile touch, and vowed they would give them up only when they were pried from their cold, dead fingers. IBM clearly knew how to build something a typist could live with. But this wasn't it.

In short, the PC Junior was obviously a chopped and crippled version of the IBM PC, and after some initial head scratching by the market, people decided they didn't want a second-class computer. Not even promotions like a free replacement keyboard and other goodies could save the PC Junior. Over the next 2 years the system died an ugly and painful death, as did IBM's reputation for marketing invincibility.

What had gone wrong? Well, obviously the Gods of IBM at Boca Raton (now reduced in rank to midlevel deities) had been listening very carefully to the words of those who had wondered about the Peanut cannibalizing sales of the PC and had taken very explicit measures to ensure this would never happen. But to achieve its goal, IBM had committed two great marketing sins.

The first, perhaps most forgivable sin was failing to understand the power of the Silicon Beast the company had unleashed on the industry. As early as 1982, the IBM PC's architecture was regarded as the industry standard. Even IBM needed to tread carefully if contemplating changes to it, as the reaction to the PC Junior's slices illustrated.

An alternate strategy did exist to IBM's chop-and-change approach: "embrace and extend." Although IBM found the market would fiercely resist arbitrary changes to the existing PC hardware standard, the company was, in 1982, still in a position to improve it with proprietary extensions. For example, IBM could have introduced a new graphics coprocessor system (and charged royalties to use it). Or it might have added a new high-speed extension to the PC's underlying bus architecture, perhaps something similar to today's USB technology (and charged royalties to use it). A smarter company than IBM, Microsoft, would learn from these mistakes and years later use the embrace-and-extend strategy to meet the challenges of "open" standards by converting them to proprietary technologies Microsoft could control and sell.

~

The Nuttiness of Subtractive Marketing

IBM's second, more serious sin was committing the unholy practice of subtractive marketing. *Subtractive marketing* works by taking a successful product and subtracting key capabilities and features until the product is clearly different from, and inferior to, the original. The subtractive marketer then attempts to pawn off her second-class creation by advertising it as a "value" or a "money saver." It never seems to work. People will, if they have the choice, always refuse to buy something that brands them as not being able to afford anything better. Even people who are thrifty like to go in style; they just don't like paying for it.

Examples of subtractive marketing abound both inside and outside the high-technology market. In the auto industry, a classic example is the Ford Falcon. The brainchild of "whiz kid" Robert McNamara, the Falcon was designed from the get-go as a "people's car." In other words, it couldn't go very fast, it got good gas mileage, and it was economical to run. Extolling these virtues was the car's deliberately plug-ugly design, one that proclaimed the vehicle was in the service of the lumpen proletariat, those who only drive and serve. The lumpen proletariat didn't appreciate the sentiments the Falcon reflected, and although people who couldn't afford anything more bought the Falcon, they drove the car without joy and bought few of the optional accessories that made selling the car profitable.

On the other hand, the Ford Mustang when it was released in 1964 was a phenomenon, and Ford couldn't make enough of them to meet demand. Mustangs were fun, sexy, and desirable. Mustang owners were intelligent and cool people with a great sense of value, the type of folks you wished would invite you to a barbecue at their place. Of course, the Mustang also wouldn't go very fast (though it looked like it could), got good gas mileage, and was very economical to run. This is because it was, underneath its alluring sheet metal, nothing more than a reskinned Ford Falcon. But by dint of good design and the addition of key features that proclaimed the car wasn't for old farts (such as a snazzy steering wheel and bucket seats) and sporty options (such as high-profit, high-performance engines), the Mustang became a car you could aspire to whereas the Falcon was just a cheap set of wheels.

The Ford Mustang illustrates the other path IBM could have taken in the design of the PC Junior. Prototypes of other PC Juniors were built and examined before the disastrous "chopped" version was decided on—models that had faster microprocessors than the PC (one promising design incorporated the 80186,[3] a hot little chip for its day), much improved graphics, a hard drive, the PC's bus, and so forth. In fact, several of these proposed designs were indeed more powerful and advanced than the IBM PC. Could any of them have been introduced without cannibalizing PC sales?

Easily, by executing a "building toward" marketing strategy. The PC Junior was intended to be a computer for the home, and games and entertainment are an integral part of that environment. To keep the PC Junior out of business, all IBM had to do was

- integrate a joystick directly into the PC Junior's keyboard,
- superglue several ROM chips containing the most addictive game titles IBM could find to the PC Junior's motherboard,
- make the addictive games immediately available to the user at the push of a key (a dedicated "Game" button on a normal keyboard would have been a nice fillip), and
- provide a "one-touch" screen blanker capability.

---

[3] In fact, Tandy Corporation later introduced a PC based on the 80186, the 2000.

These features not only would have ensured Junior would not be bought by businesses, but you also would probably have been fired for bringing one into the office. No company would have touched a machine that permitted its employees to play games at their desktop at the touch of a button. Yet no one could have criticized IBM for building a computer that did exactly what it promised to do. And providing the PC Junior with advanced capabilities would have justified its premium pricing.

Subtractive marketing has also proved to be a particular peril for software developers because code bases are so malleable. Again and again companies have taken a popular software product, yanked out some key features (Whoops! There goes the spelling corrector!), slapped a quick coat of marketing "paint" on the skeletal remains, and voilà! A "lite" product is born. Over the years, publishers have created myriad "executive" word processors, "student" spreadsheets, "simple" data-bases, and so forth, all based on existing and popular products. None has ever been particularly successful.

And, in fact, several software publishers followed the PC Junior down the subtractive path, creating chopped versions of their flagship products. MicroPro, for instance, created a "Junior" version of its market-leading WordStar program.[4] Tens of thousands of copies of the product ended up in the remainder sections of major retailers and in the back pages of *Computer Shopper*. Not having learned its lesson from WordStar Junior, MicroPro made the same mistake with a later "lite" product, Easy.

Amazingly enough, IBM's experience with the PC Junior seemed to teach the company little. With the exception of the IBM AT in 1984, which would be its last unqualified success in the desktop market, IBM continued to release a steady stream of computing clunkers, including the IBM Convertible and the IBM Portable, that missed the mark. IBM's funniest flop was a little-remembered debacle called the XT/286. This was an attempt to shoehorn an AT into an XT case. The XT/286 sported a cacheless microprocessor setup (*cache* is memory dedicated to storing programming instructions for the chip and speeds up operations), thus ensuring the system ran dog slow, and a case design that prevented

---

[4] I spent a tedious 3 days in 1984 at a trade show in Boston demoing WordStar for the PC Junior to an audience already cognizant that the system was doomed.

buyers from inserting most AT accessory cards into the computer. The XT/286 quickly went to a well-deserved repose in the same landfills holding stacks of unsold PC Juniors and discarded chiclet keyboards.

It all culminated in the disastrous launch of the IBM PS/2 line in 1987, a marketing fiasco that demonstrated to the world that the PC standard now existed independently of IBM's control. Throughout the 1990s, IBM steadily lost ground in a market it had once owned. In 2004, almost a quarter century after the release of the first PC, IBM announced it was exiting the PC desktop market, selling out to Chinese company Lenovo, unable to compete with a company launched by a college kid in his dorm room (Michael Dell), an upstart cloner (Compaq), and a guy who talked to a cow (Gateway).

four

POSITIONING PUZZLERS:
MicroPro and Microsoft

In the 1970s, fortunes were once again to be found on the West Coast of the United States, though instead of gold, the new wealth was hacked out of silicon and on computer terminals. As had occurred in the 1840s, hordes of young people from the East Coast headed west seeking fame and fortune (the 20th century threw in the added benefit of an IPO). One of these hardy pioneers was a fellow by the name of Seymour Rubinstein, a New York transplant who upon his arrival out west soon found work with one of the industry's pioneers, IMSAI, a company building clones of the seminal Altair system. Rubinstein served as the company's marketing director but soon decided the real gold lay in selling software and left to found his own company, MicroPro.

~

Death by Doppelganger: MicroPro

Rubinstein's initial goal in founding MicroPro was to develop and publish a high-end database management system (DBMS) designed to compete with Ashton-Tate's dBASE and similar products, but during his stint at IMSAI, he learned the CP/M market needed a good programmer's text editor. Because developing one would take less time than a full-blown DBMS system and provide the company with a revenue stream until the database product was ready, Rubinstein hired Rob Barnaby, a top-notch assembly language programmer, to build the product. Barnaby, in an inspired burst of creativity, wrote 137,000 lines of code in 4 months and produced both the editor and a high-speed sorting program intended to be the first component in the forthcoming database program, Supersort.

A Star Is Born

Barnaby's text editor was christened WordMaster and upon its release in 1976 sold so well that Rubinstein decided to take the next step and release a full-featured word-processing program based on WordMaster. The new product, named WordStar, hit the market in 1978 and quickly became the dominant product in the CP/M market. The product was so highly regarded that it even became popular on the Apple II, as people bought CP/M computers on a board and slipped them into their Apples so they could use WordStar.

There were several reasons for WordStar's early success. The first was power: For its day, the product was feature packed. The second was what came to be known as WordStar's *Control-key interface*. Rubinstein had deliberately designed WordStar to meet the needs of touch typists. To enter commands in the program, you held down the Control key (most CP/M systems of the time had one) and pressed a key. WordStar's layout was not mnemonic; instead, in the interest of fast typing, Rubinstein designed the interface so that all cursor movements were performed with the left hand while less common operations fell to the right hand. WordStar users came to swear by this system, and today diehards still retrofit Microsoft Word and other products with add-ins and utilities that resurrect the WordStar keyboard system.

The third and most important factor was that WordStar was the first What You See Is What You Get (WYSIWYG) word processor. Prior to WordStar, formatting text with a software product meant sprinkling formatting commands amongst blocks of text, printing the document to see the results, and then sprinkling in more commands and reprinting until you were satisfied with the results (a process very similar to working with raw HTML and an editor today). WYSIWYG, a term coined by Rubinstein, meant something far different in 1978 than it means today. WordStar, like all early CP/M and IBM software, ran on character-driven screens that couldn't display different fonts or combine graphics with text à la the Mac or a Windows machine. Nonetheless, the software accurately displayed line lengths and paragraph breaks (assuming you were willing to concede everything you would print was set in 10 pitch) and allowed you to set margins and tab stops onscreen. Soon most word processors were emulating this new approach to editing.

By 1983, WordStar's success had made MicroPro International the largest microcomputer software company in the world, with sales peaking that year at close to $70 million. During this period, MicroPro attempted to diversify into other markets, publishing InfoStar, Rubinstein's long-dreamed-of database product; ChartStar, a business graphics product; and even an unfortunate spreadsheet called CalcStar. (It was unfortunate because the product was infamous for its bugs. Until the product went to its well-deserved and unheralded demise, an entire row of the CalcStar workspace was nonfunctional, and internally the product was known by such nicknames as "WoofCalc" and "DogSheet.") MicroPro even briefly attempted to manufacture its own CP/M computer, the PBM[1] (supposed to remind you of IBM) until someone came to his senses and shut the project down. However, none of these other software products sold particularly well, and WordStar remained the pillar on which the company's fortunes rested.

Version 3.3 of WordStar for both IBM and CP/M computers was released in 1983 and sold briskly, and all seemed right with MicroPro's world. Unfortunately, the situation soon changed. Rubinstein had gotten into a contretemps with his WordStar development team, and they, depending on who is telling the story, either a) quit or b) were fired. (The departing programmers promptly set up shop in an office not far from MicroPro headquarters and proceeded to found a new company called NewStar, which published a WordStar clone called NewWord. Their fate and MicroPro's would become closely intertwined.)

In any event, at just about the exact moment MicroPro needed to ship an update to WordStar, it had lost the ability to do so.[2] No update to WordStar would appear in 1984 or even in 1985. A 12- to 18-month upgrade cycle had become the norm in the software industry, and competitors were busy building new products that matched, then began to surpass, WordStar's capabilities. Things looked bleak until an unexpected savior appeared on the scene.

This white knight was brought to MicroPro courtesy of AT&T. The phone company was about to begin a disastrous foray into microcomputing by introducing a line of new desktop-based UNIX computers that

---

[1] These computers were assembled in San Rafael, California, on the checkout counters of a former A&P supermarket. They sported dual Z-80 processors, a 5MB hard drive, a quad-density single-sided 5-inch floppy, and Televideo terminals, and they were preloaded with MicroPro software. Only about 100 were ever built, and they were sold to the company's employees. The units were originally supposed to be called "SyStars" (for Seymour Rubinstein). Rumor had it that the reason MicroPro went briefly into the hardware business was that Seymour was jealous that his friend Adam Osborne had a computer named after him.

[2] One of the difficulties in upgrading WordStar lay in the practice, common at the time, of implementing bug fixes by directly modifying the binary executable rather than updating the source code and reassembling the program (reassembling was a lengthy process). When the development teams working on WordStar examined the original 8080 source code, they found it didn't match the WordStar.exe files being shipped in the latest product. The lack of documentation on what fixes had been implemented made working with the WordStar code base very difficult.

would fail to sell in any significant quantities. AT&T decreed that some choice software fodder needed to be produced for its forthcoming line of white elephants, and the company proposed that MicroPro port WordStar to its UNIX operating system and the C language in return for some cold, hard cash.

MicroPro actually lacked the capability to do this, but a seeming bit of serendipity intervened. Rubinstein got wind of a new software product developed by a programmer outside the company that was written in C, ran under UNIX, and cloned WordStar's functionality and design. Seymour took a look at the embryonic word processor, bought it, hired the programmer who had written it, and told him to hire a small team of coders and port WordStar to UNIX.

Operating outside MicroPro's normal corporate structure, the team worked busily for several months at their task. When they were done, the results of their work weren't what Seymour had originally envisioned. The new "WordStar port" used a mnemonic set of Control key–based commands, possessed some features that WordStar lacked, lacked some features that WordStar had, and sported a new file format completely incompatible with the original product. It was written in C, and it did run on PCs and the AT&T UNIX boxes. And it was clearly not WordStar.

But by this time MicroPro was desperate. It was now more than a year and a half since the release of WordStar 3.3, and the program was growing very long in the tooth indeed. MicroPro decided to make the new product the focus of its future sales and marketing efforts. The new product was named WordStar 2000 (the idea for the "2000" was lifted from the logo of a local furniture store). WordStar 2000 was priced at $495.00, then the median price for a high-end word processor, and rolled out in 1985. The original WordStar remained on the shelves (it was still selling strongly, though sales were slowly declining) at its suggested retail price (SRP) of $495.00.

All hell promptly broke loose. With its release of WordStar 2000, MicroPro had just committed a fundamental positioning mistake. The company would pay dearly for this mistake, ultimately with its very existence.

The Doctrine of Positioning

Positioning as a marketing concept became all the rage in the 1970s and 1980s, and a great deal of time and ink has been dedicated to the topic. The Orthodox Creed of Product Positioning, as decreed by one of the great cardinals of high-technology consulting, Regis McKenna, is that positioning is a

> . . . *psychological location in the consumer's mind, pertaining to the relative qualities a company, product, or service may have with respect to its competition.*

The "relative" qualities a company, product, or service may aspire to in the buyer's mental geography include the following:

- Low price
- Best quality
- Fastest
- Most popular

And so forth.

The virtual locations most desirable for your product or service depend on its particular characteristics, your market, and your competition. For example, in the case of Joe Whitebox's local computer company, it can't credibly claim that it's the leading manufacturer of desktop computers; Dell, Compaq, Hewlett-Packard, or another company owns that "location" in the market's mind. But Joe Whitebox might seize the "service" terrain because he runs a local business and has a shot at making that claim stick.

The Orthodox Creed has, however, often proved inadequate to the needs of software companies. This is because software, by its nature, is an abstraction. The Reformed Creed of Product Positioning for software states that positioning begins with describing a product in such a way that the purchaser can tie it to a real-world process or object. On the face of it, this seems like an easy, straightforward thing to do, and sometimes it is. For example, when word-processing software for desktop computers was first introduced, most people quickly grasped the idea that these products put "a typewriter in your computer." The benefits of fast revisions, spelling correction, and flexible formatting of documents were immediately apparent.

But for other categories of software, positioning has proved to be far more difficult. One of the most famous examples is Lotus Notes. If you're in the software industry, you've certainly heard of Notes and you may even use it. But when the product was first introduced in 1989, Lotus seemed unable or unwilling to explain what the heck the product did. The Lotus Notes 4.0 documentation, rather pathetically, highlights the problem best:

What Is Notes Anyway?

People have been asking that question since the beginning of time (or at least since Notes first came onto the market). It has been hard for people to define Notes because you can use it to do so many things.

—FROM THE *Notes 4.0 Beginner's Guide*, PUBLISHED IN 1996

Actually, this documentation never **does** tell you exactly what Notes "is." As you can imagine, the Lotus sales force had a great deal of trouble explaining why someone should buy Notes when the company that published it couldn't explain what it was.

(Oh, what does Notes do? Well, its most popular function is as an e-mail management program, a post-office system for your computer network. The most obvious feature that differentiated the product from its competition was that the electronic letters you sent back and forth could be annotated with notes and comments. Other people could see your comments and add their own "under" yours. It's not that hard to explain and tie to the real world, but Lotus somehow could never bring itself to do so.)

Positioning Wars

MicroPro's positioning mistake was of a different nature than Lotus's and far more difficult to manage. The release of WordStar 2000 created an irreconcilable positioning conflict that pitted MicroPro against itself. After the product's release, the WordStar user base took one look at WordStar 2000 and decided no thanks, opting instead to sit on its hands until MicroPro released an upgrade to its favorite product. As a result, MicroPro now found itself selling two high-end word processors called WordStar for $495.00 to people using IBM PCs. Precious marketing resources had to be expended in creating collaterals, ads, and promotions for the two products while attempting to provide a convincing rationale for the existence of both.

It was an impossible task. A day selling WordStar 2000 to the market went something like this:

MicroPro: Hi there! We're here to tell you about WordStar 2000, our new word processor!

The Market: Great to see you! But, we have to tell you that although WordStar is a wonderful product, it's hardly new. You must mean this is the new upgrade. Great! I'm so excited! Let's take a look!

MicroPro: No, no, this is WordStar **2000**! It's really totally new!

The Market: Oh. *(Long pause.)* When are you releasing the upgrade to WordStar? In 2000?

MicroPro: No, no, the upgrade to WordStar will be released real soon now!

The Market: Oh. *(Longer pause.)* Well, why will you release a new product in 2000 when you haven't released the upgrade to WordStar?

MicroPro: No, no, WordStar 2000 is available right now! We just call it "2000" because it's new and powerful and easy to use! But you don't have to wait until 2000 to enjoy all those benefits!

The Market: Oh. *(Dead silence.)* In other words, WordStar, which won't be upgraded until 2000, is old and not powerful and hard to use?

MicroPro: No, no, no. WordStar is a classic and is powerful and has a wonderful interface for touch typists!

The Market: Oh. Does that mean you can't touch-type with WordStar 2000?

MicroPro: Don't be silly! Of course you can! It's easy to type with WordStar 2000's new mnemonic commands!

The Market: Then is it hard to type with WordStar's regular commands? And don't call me "silly."

MicroPro: Sorry about that! No, you can type quickly with WordStar!

The Market: Then you have to type slowly with WordStar 2000?

MicroPro: Uh, no. You can type really well with both of them!

The Market: Oh. *(Long, long pause, dead silence.)* Now, what's the difference between WordStar and WordStar 2000 again? And why do I have to wait until 2000 for an upgrade to WordStar?

And so it went. Endlessly. Instead of answering why prospective users should buy WordStar, the MicroPro sales force for years tied itself in knots attempting to explain the difference between two products named WordStar.

The confusion within MicroPro was just as pernicious, as the company began to split internally along WordStar/WordStar 2000 fault lines. Within MicroPro there were WordStar aficionados and WordStar 2000 mavens, and each side wondered what the other saw in its choice of a word processor. At one point, the head of the WordStar product development team forbade team members from talking with WordStar 2000 programmers. (A neat trick, because both programming teams worked in the same building.) By 1987, as MicroPro wrestled itself to the mat, it had ceded its leadership of the word-processing market to Microsoft Word and Corel WordPerfect.

Yet when things were darkest, MicroPro seemed to come to its senses. A new president, Leon Williams, and new product management, including myself, were brought in to try to sort out the mess. Two things needed to be done immediately. An upgrade for WordStar had to be released ASAP, and something had to be done about the conflict between WordStar and WordStar 2000. I was given the task of figuring out the positioning strategy.

The first thing Williams did was trot down the street to NewStar software, buy the company, and use its NewWord product as the foundation for an upgrade for the long-suffering WordStar user base. The upgrade, called WordStar version 4.0, sold well into the WordStar installed base, though its feature set wasn't truly competitive with other products of the time. MicroPro even released a new CP/M[3] version, which did surprisingly good business and garnered the company much favorable PR. The gloom surrounding MicroPro started to lift.

Repositioning WordStar 2000 was a more difficult task. The logical thing to do would have been to simply shoot the product. Unfortunately, this wasn't practical. Since WordStar 2000's introduction, a fair number of people had bought the program, and its sales represented an important revenue stream. Despite MicroPro's fervent wishes, WordStar 2000 was going to stick around for a while.

My short-term answer to the positioning conflict was an approach I came to call "façade." This strategy consists of taking a look at two products in conflict, deciding what key features differentiate them, and repositioning one product "away" from the other. In *The Product Marketing Handbook for Software* I describe the goal of a façade program as an attempt to

> *. . . Buy time . . . to maneuver yourself out of having to explain the differences between the two products so that you can talk about what the products are and why the buyer wants them.*

By its nature, a façade approach to a positioning conflict is a transitional strategy. When done correctly and with finesse, it can provide a company with the opportunity to decide whether it's possible to kill one of the conflicting products, either via a migration strategy or via a merger, or perhaps relaunch it into a completely different market.

After a quick analysis of the options, WordStar 2000 was rechristened a "word publisher" (the actual phrase was coined by one of MicroPro's top salesman, Jim Welch, who, along with the rest of the MicroPro sales force, was slowly going insane attempting to explain the differences between the two products). And what, you may ask, is a "word publisher"? Well, a word publisher is a word processor with exceptional laser-printing capabilities, a particular strength of WordStar 2000 at that juncture. Of course, this claim couldn't withstand market scrutiny over time; in reality, there was no such thing as a word publisher. The claim to differentiation was credible only as long as WordStar 2000 was

---

[3] WordStar 4.0 for CP/M was the last major commercial release of software for this OS. I have a copy on 8-inch disks.

superior to its competition in this particular aspect of the product. But in the short term, the campaign worked as intended and bought MicroPro some time and maneuvering room. Sales and market share of both MicroPro word processors increased, and the price of MicroPro stock rose.

Stupid Printing Tricks

As a "reward" for my efforts, I was "promoted" to group product manager and given responsibility for the product management of the resurgent WordStar. A new version, WordStar 5.0, designed to build upon the momentum built by the successful 4.0 release, was being hurried along to market. If MicroPro could launch it in a timely fashion with a competitive feature set, there was a chance the company could regain its lost market leadership, or at the very least generate enough revenue to branch out to new and more lucrative opportunities in other software categories. The product was slated for release in early 1988.

The first thing a product manager does when he or she is assigned responsibility for a new product is take a look at it, and I was soon handed a fistful of disks that contained the latest version of WordStar. Like any upgrade, it had a raft of new features and capabilities, but to my annoyance you couldn't print with it. A quick look at the files that made up the program revealed why: The newest version of WordStar lacked a printer database.

Now this was odd, because if there was one thing MicroPro had learned to do over the years it was to support printers. In the pre-Windows era it was the responsibility of software developers to obtain, test, and debug printers and their drivers to ensure they worked with their particular products. As of 1987, MicroPro had built a quality database of more than 300 printer drivers. The information in this database represented years of careful debugging, testing, and implementing capabilities specific to each printer. When you installed a printer in WordStar and told the program to print, you could be fairly confident your text wouldn't appear upside down or in a character set that resembled Sanskrit.

What made the omission of the database even more puzzling was that in 1985 a decision had been made at MicroPro to base all future printing code for other products on the WordStar 2000 printer database.

It was tested and debugged, and it was extensive. MicroPro had introduced a low-end word processor, Easy, that utilized the 2000 database. Why wasn't it in WordStar 5.0?

Several inquiries made by me to the development group elicited vague responses about "new support" issues and "implementation questions." A sense of dread began to haunt my soul. A heavy weight seemed to descend upon my shoulders. More inquiries elicited even vaguer answers. The weight pressing down on me grew heavier. It was time to find out what was going on.

As a product manager I had developed the habit of periodically stopping by the MicroPro development center to schmooze with the programmers about product features and problems while providing them with feedback on what our customers liked and disliked about our programs. One fateful day I headed to the center and floated by the section occupied by the WordStar programming team. While skulking about, I saw a group of agitated programmers pointing at a screen and arguing heatedly.

Sidling closer, I listened to their conversation with growing horror, and then I heard a word that confirmed the bad news I'd been overhearing. The impact of this word on me was stunningly physical. On hearing it, a bright light burst upon my eyes and filled them with a dazzling clarity, one that let me see the future. Simultaneously, the great weight was lifted from my shoulders. This wasn't because I was feeling better; rather, it was because I no longer **had** any shoulders as I underwent a miraculous transformation from product manager to small gray rat desperate to abandon a ship I knew would soon be sinking.

That word was "pointer."

As in a hierarchical pointer. As in a hierarchical database pointer. As in the development group had decided to discard the WordStar 2000 database and replace it with a new one based on hierarchical database technology. It was an incredibly foolish thing to do, and it sealed MicroPro's fate.

To understand why this was a disastrous course, you need to have an understanding of database technology, something that I, having once worked as a DBMS programmer, possessed (and something the previous product manager had not). WordStar 2000's printer database was basically a flat relational table. When you installed, say, an HP LaserJet printer, the WordStar install program looked up the driver information for this unit from a row in the printer database. Specific printer functions, such as boldfacing and italicizing letters, were stored in columns within this row.

The new hierarchical database being built for WordStar discarded this paradigm. Printer information was stored in something that resembled a tree. Pointers were used to locate specific information about printer functions within the tree.

In all fairness, there were some minor technical advantages to this new printer structure. For instance, it would be smaller than the 2000 database. MicroPro might save the cost of a floppy in the WordStar cost of goods. But I also knew that hierarchical systems had fallen into disfavor after the introduction of relational technology. No commercially available programming tools or utilities were available on our desktop development platforms to convert the current flat table structure to a hierarchical one. Porting the printer database to the new model would first require building a series of custom programs to accomplish the task. This would take months. Then the tools themselves would have to be tested for proper operations, which would take more time. Of course, once the database had been ported to the new structure, all printer operations would have to be retested to ensure the accuracy of the process, which would take even more months. There was no way WordStar 5.0 was going to meet its projected ship date or even come close to it.

Once I confirmed what was going on,[4] I went squeaking to my boss, the vice president of sales and marketing, and warned him of our impending shipwreck. VP to VP, the head of MicroPro's development assured the head of sales and marketing I was exaggerating the situation. Officially, WordStar 5.0 was still on track in development and would ship on time.

As the weeks went by and WordStar still refused to print, I prepared to move myself and my skinny pink tail to what I hoped would be a more favorable clime (I was wrong, by the way) I accepted a senior

---

[4] Final confirmation, from my point of view, came during an impromptu basketball game near MicroPro's headquarters. Steve Evangelou, a talented programmer at the company, and I had gotten into the habit of driving to a nearby court to shoot some hoops and discuss company gossip. During a lull in our game he informed me that the WordStar 5.0 project faced some "issues." Before he went further, I interrupted him and said, "Let me guess. You guys have decided to discard the WordStar 2000 database in favor of some hierarchical system, and you have no idea of how to port the data. And we're not meeting our ship dates." He looked at me and said, "I guess you've got a handle on this after all."

product management position at Ashton-Tate (the company had a lousy word processor, but I was pretty sure it would print) and handed in my resignation with a final warning to all that financial projections based upon WordStar 5.0 revenues needed to be revamped. On my last day at MicroPro, as I left corporate headquarters and walked through the parking lot to my car, the company's director of direct promotions bustled over to say good-bye. Before I pulled out of the lot for the last time, he informed me that that morning the vice president of development had finally confessed that WordStar 5.0 wasn't going to meet its ship date. Nor could he provide a firm estimate of when it **would** ship. He quoted my boss as saying, "Rick Chapman told me this was going to happen."

The WordStar development group's decision to discard the company's existing printer technology delayed the critical 5.0 release for more than half a year. When the release did ship in late 1988, the new version was widely criticized for having a printer database about one-third the size of that of previous WordStar products. Upgrade sales, as well as sales to first-time buyers, were disappointing. Time spent re-creating the printer database was also time not spent on adding new features to the product that would have made it more competitive. The cumulative effects of three blown financial quarters and disappointing sales led to MicroPro's upper management, including Leon Williams and my former boss, being marched out and treated to a summary executive execution. MicroPro had lost its last chance to regain its footing in the market, though the company staggered on in zombie-like fashion for several more years, living off its steadily decreasing installed base of WordStar users. WordStar finally faded away in the early 1990s, subsumed in a merger with a flock of similarly unsuccessful and second-rate software companies. It was an ignominious end to the career of a great piece of software.

The question that remains, of course, is, why? What had possessed the development group to embark down such a destructive path? What were their motivations? The technical case for their actions was never strong. That this was the wrong thing to do from a business standpoint was even clearer.

The answer lay in the positioning conflict unleashed within the company. While MicroPro worked hard to placate a confused market, within the company the WordStar versus WordStar 2000 struggle raged on. The WordStar programming team hated WordStar 2000 with a passion and wanted nothing from that product to pollute "its" WordStar.

Its decision to rip out the existing printer technology was based on emotion, not a rational cost-benefit analysis of the consequences of such a course.

Positioning problems constantly plague high-technology companies, particularly software ones, because of the industry's rapid pace of change, the malleable nature of software, and acquisitions. In 1991, Borland International split itself along Paradox versus dBASE lines via its purchase of Ashton-Tate. Novell, like MicroPro, would shoot itself in the foot by creating two competing product lines with its purchase of UNIX from AT&T. Today, Sun wrestles with the issue of Solaris vs. Linux. And in 1993, Microsoft demonstrated with the release of Windows NT that previous success doesn't necessarily provide protection against future stupidity.

~

Two Software Nags: Windows 95 vs. Windows NT

The buildup to NT began after the incredibly successful launch of Windows 3.0 in 1990. For the next 3 years, Microsoft spent considerable time proclaiming that this new version of the product, once known as OS/2 3.0, would be the 32-bit successor to the 16-bit Windows 3.x product line. But as NT neared completion, complaints began to surface that the product was too big and resource hungry to fit the existing desktop profile. Microsoft had heard these complaints before with other products, but Moore's law that, roughly paraphrased, states computing capacity doubles every 18 months, had always bailed out the company in the past. In a rare case of Microsoft losing its nerve, NT was quickly hustled offstage and repositioned as a local area network (LAN) alternative to Novell's NetWare where, with Novell's unwitting assistance, it enjoyed tremendous success.

Microsoft then cobbled together a DOS-based 32-bit hybrid that would eventually be known as Windows 95 and switched promotional gears, telling everyone that **this** product was in fact the desktop upgrade Microsoft had been promising. Windows 3.x's huge installed base,

IBM's ineptitude in marketing the competing OS/2, and a massive promotional campaign all contributed to Windows 95's tremendous sales success. But over time, the positioning problem grew in the critical desktop arena. Windows NT, then 2000 (the more things change . . .), had always been available in a "workstation" version that directly competed with the Windows 9x family. After all, both product lines were called Windows. They were both 32-bit operating systems. The desktop versions were comparably priced. They even looked alike. So, which to buy?

Microsoft tried to help customers make the decision via a classically bad 1996 ad campaign many referred to as "Two Nags Racing." A two-page spread, it featured a picture of two horses running neck-and-neck with the caption "You See a Horse Race. We See Two Thoroughbreds." Apparently no one at Microsoft had realized that, well, yes, but the horses **are** racing. And as we all know, only one horse can win. So, which customer is going to ride the losing steed? Faced with such a choice, corporate America paused (and the ad was quickly yanked). Two years after the release of Windows 95, more than 60 percent of the U.S. corporate market was still using Windows 3.x. This didn't seem to particularly bother Microsoft; after all, businesses would have to upgrade sooner or later, and they had only one choice. A Microsoft choice. Right? Right.

~

Some New Nags

And then Java appeared. With its siren call of "write once, run anywhere," corporate America, frozen in place by indecision, decided to give the newcomer a close look. Perhaps this was a safer choice than attempting to pick the right pony in the Microsoft OS competition. Microsoft, taken by surprise, was forced to "embrace" Java via a humiliating agreement to license it from archrival Sun Microsystems. That done, Microsoft spent enormous amounts of time, effort, and money trying to convert the supposedly platform-independent Java into a proprietary extension of Windows (whichever Windows) **and** introducing a new programming language, C#, to compete with it.

To complicate matters further, Linux, an open-source OS based on UNIX that came with its source code, began making a considerable splash in the market. Bundled with a freeware Apache Web server by such firms as Red Hat, Linux eventually relieved Microsoft's NT, Sun Microsystems's Solaris, and Novell's NetWare of significant market share.

Java's future and Linux's ultimate success in loosening Microsoft's iron grip on the OS market is unclear. Microsoft finally learned its lesson and announced that in the future there would be only one Windows product line, XP, with different versions aimed at different users and platforms. But it's also unclear how long and how successful Microsoft's plans to migrate users from all the other Windows variants will be. As of this writing, Windows 98, really no more than an upgrade of Windows 95, is still in use by approximately 20 percent of Windows users, though in July of 2006 Microsoft discontinued support for this version of the venerable OS. What's clear is that Microsoft's situation would have been very different if the market had been focused on how to upgrade from Windows 3.*x* and not on what to upgrade to. Also, more than ten years after the Netscape IPO of 1995, the combination of software as a service (SaaS, the successor to the earlier ASP fiasco) and new technologies such as mashups and Ajax threaten to make the mid-1990s dream of using the Internet as a platform to bypass the desktop operating system a reality.

Making matters even more interesting (and demonstrating that companies need to learn the same lesson again and again) is that Microsoft has announced that Vista, its long-delayed upgrade to Windows XP, will come in no less than **six** versions. (Not to mention the "N" products, versions of Windows absent the media player and instant messaging utilities the company has been forced to develop in Europe and Korea because of the fallout from its antitrust case loss.) Microsoft probably hopes that Windows customers will be so busy trying to figure out which Windows to buy they'll be too exhausted to give any alternative a try. But as we've seen, when you give customers a reason to shop, you can be sure they will. The ghosts of WordStar and WordStar 2000, still locked in eternal combat, gibber from high tech's graveyard, a warning to all of the grim fate that awaits those who dare to repeat MicroPro's positioning sin.

five

WE HATE YOU, WE REALLY HATE YOU:

Ed Esber, Ashton-Tate, and Siebel Systems

IN 1987, WHILE WORKING at MicroPro as a WordStar product manager, I was assigned to participate in one of high tech's hoariest rituals: a press tour. A press tour consists of arranging for members of your senior management team to meet with key members of the fourth estate and analysts who write about and cover your market. The hope is that once you've established a backslapping, hail-fellow-well-met relationship with an editor from *PC Magazine* or a guru from Gartner they'll be more inclined to write nice things about your company and its products. Sometimes it works out that way. The quid pro quo driving the tour is that in return for putting up with you disturbing their day, you'll provide fresh news for the press and buy research from the analysts. Sometimes it works out that way as well.

Tour personnel usually consist of at least one member of upper management, one member of middle management capable of giving a comprehensive product demonstration (informally, this person is referred to as "the demo dolly"), and a PR person. For this tour, upper management was represented by Leon Williams, then president of MicroPro; I appeared in the role of the demo dolly; and rounding out the group was a sad little PR type who confessed at the end of our trip that she really didn't like working with members of the press. Once you've been on one or two press tours, most people regard them with the same affection as root canals. Most tours consist of a trip to New York, Boston, and San Francisco, the three major hubs for high-tech media and analysis.

Our itinerary included a side trip to Austin, Texas, to meet Jim Seymour, long-time editor and columnist for the Ziff Davis publishing empire. On the day of our appointed meeting, we trekked out to Seymour's house in the Austin hills, where I dutifully demonstrated the latest, greatest version of WordStar 5.0, the one that couldn't print. Luckily for me, Seymour, engrossed by the Macintosh (as were most members of the press at the time), paid only cursory attention to the demo and instead insisted on demoing his latest Mac toys for us. Once everyone was done showing off, we settled down for the obligatory period of chitchat before heading off to the airport and our next stop in the never-ending tour.

~

Heart of Darkness

For no particular reason that I can remember, the topic turned to Ashton-Tate, publisher of the widely popular dBASE database program. Seymour started talking about a meeting he'd attended with other members of the press where Ed Esber, CEO of the database giant, addressed the group. As he began talking about Esber, his face suddenly developed an expression of contempt. He told us how during the speech Esber had stated at one point that he wasn't necessarily the smartest guy in software. Seymour paused, then looked at our group, and said, "We were all thinking, boy, you've got that right, Ed." The venom in his voice was surprising.

I didn't pay much attention to the exchange at the time, but after leaving MicroPro to become a product manager at Ashton-Tate, I later realized I'd had my first glimpse into the dark heart of one of software's biggest and most unexpected meltdowns. As events progressed in the industry, it became clear that as far as the PC press was concerned, it was "Ed Esber. He's dead." They wanted his head on a stake.

Ashton-Tate at its height in the 1980s was one of software's "Big Three," the other members of the triumvirate being Microsoft and Lotus. Microsoft had DOS, Lotus ruled spreadsheets, and Ashton-Tate was the database king. The lucrative word-processing franchise was being fought over by MicroPro, WordPerfect, MultiMate, Microsoft with its Word product, and a host of smaller players.

dBASE was originally designed to help place winning bets in football pools and was the creation of Wayne Ratliff, a contract programmer at the U.S. Jet Propulsion Laboratory. Although Ratliff didn't get rich on sports betting, he did decide his new software program had commercial potential. Named "Vulcan" in honor of the home planet of *Star Trek*'s Mr. Spock, Ratliff placed his first ad for the product in the October 1979 issue of *BYTE* magazine. At its release, Vulcan was priced at $50.00, and though there was flurry of initial interest,[1] the stress of trying to

---

[1] I was one of the initial purchasers. After purchasing my copy of Vulcan, I taught myself how to program in it and began developing applications that ran on CP/M and MP/M, the multiuser version of CP/M. My specialty was in building inventory tracking and control programs for beer and soda distributors in New York City.

ship, support, and manage a one-man company was overwhelming. Ratliff was on the verge of ceasing operations when software reseller George Tate contacted him.

Tate and his partner, Hal Lashlee, took a look at Vulcan, quickly realized its potential, and bought exclusive distribution rights. At the time of the deal they were running a not-very-successful mail-order software company called Software Plus. Believing that Vulcan would turn things around for their company, they renamed the company Ashton-Tate to give it a more "upscale" image. (A great deal of speculation has centered over where Tate came up with "Ashton"—no one who worked at the company had that name. The general belief is it was picked because Ashton sounded "British." It should be noted, however, that Tate had a pet parrot named Ashton.)

After a quick trademark search uncovered potential problems with the name Vulcan, the product was rechristened dBASE II. There was no dBASE I, but even in the early 1980s people were reluctant to buy 1.0 releases of software products. The company upped the cost of dBASE II to $695.00, a very competitive price for a product in its class and with its capabilities, and placed full-page magazine ads featuring a picture of a sump pump and the proclamation that while the pump might suck, dBASE didn't (or words to that effect). Sales took off, and by 1985 Ashton-Tate's revenues were more than $100 million a year and climbing, mostly from sales of dBASE II and its successors, dBASE III and III+. The company also enjoyed modest sales success with its Framework, an integrated product. *Integrated* products attempted to combine word processing, database management, a spreadsheet, and graphics all within a single program. Framework was considered the best of breed in this market segment, but the integrateds, which included software such as Lotus Symphony and Ability,[2] never sold in the numbers projected, and the category largely disappeared in the early 1990s.

---

[2] The success of Lotus 1-2-3 convinced the industry that if adding rudimentary graphics and some simple sorting capabilities to a spreadsheet was good, then adding the kitchen sink had to be better. Integrated products usually added word processing, more graphics, better database capabilities, and communications to the mix. Some of the integrateds simply extended an existing product further; Lotus Symphony, for instance, allowed you to create documents in one big cell in a spreadsheet. Ashton-Tate's Framework operated on an outline paradigm. Integrated products tended to be big and cumbersome wads of code that lacked robust capabilities, the worst of both worlds.

In addition to ads featuring plumbing, another reason for dBASE's quick rise to prominence was that the company made much of the fact that dBASE was a *relational database management system* (RDBMS). The relational model was first introduced in a paper published in 1969 by an English computer scientist, Dr. E. F. Codd, who worked for IBM. More flexible and expandable than competing technologies, relational products over time were adopted by most DBMS developers and users.

In addition to a table-oriented paradigm, Codd's definition of an RDBMS also incorporated several key capabilities and functions a product needed to possess before it could be called a "truly" relational system. None of the early RDMBS systems for the PC incorporated all of Codd's requirements, and religious arguments raged constantly over which product was "more" or "less" relational than another. dBASE II was probably "less" relational than some of its competitors, but that also meant it could run on systems with less memory and reach a broader audience. Despite the pooh-poohing of purists, for several years dBASE became almost synonymous with the relational concept.

In 1985, Tate died unexpectedly of a heart attack at the age of 40, and Esber, his second in command, took over the leadership of Ashton-Tate. Esber was a Harvard-trained MBA and a former product manager at VisiCorp, the company that had seen its VisiCalc spreadsheet eclipsed by Lotus 1-2-3. Esber announced he was going to bring a more professional management style to Ashton-Tate, replacing Tate's more hands-on and emotional approach. Despite having a bachelor's degree in computer engineering, Esber didn't have a reputation of being technically astute.

Esber did fancy himself something of a business guru, and one of his favorite quotes was "A computer will not make a good manager out of a bad manager. It makes a good manager better faster and a bad manager worse faster." He had something there. It had taken Tate about 5 years to build Ashton-Tate to software giant status; it would take Ed Esber only 2½ years to put the company on the road to ruin. And Esber had a PC on his desk the entire time.

The key to Ashton-Tate's downfall lay in Esber's idiotic mishandling of the dBASE development community and the impact his actions had on the public's perception of the company. Developers were key to dBASE's early success. This was because in addition to its relational status, dBASE II was one of desktop software's first major "shelfware" products. Despite the inevitable claims that dBASE II was "easy to use," thousands of people who bought it and tried to use it quickly put the product away on a shelf or gave it to a programmer friend. The next database they bought was usually a dirt-simple "Rolodex-in-a-box" bit of software such as PFS File or even Ashton-Tate's own Friday product.

The reason for this was simple and remains true to this day: Powerful database programs are intrinsically hard to learn and use. Properly organizing and structuring data for a task of any size and complexity requires a great deal of thought, planning, and design. As a result, DBMS products are primarily bought by people who write programs for other people.

With dBASE's head start in the market, relational capabilities, and reasonable pricing, a massive aftermarket quickly sprang up around Ratliff's creation. There were programming utilities that extended the product and made up for its deficiencies, books that taught you how to program in dBASE, training programs that provided hands-on instruction in the product, and thousands of programmers and consultants dedicated to building products and services around dBASE. This third-party market was an invaluable asset to Ashton-Tate because it served as an unpaid sales force of influencers and recommenders that helped push dBASE into new accounts and markets.

Over time, however, Esber came to resent this third-party market, and relationships began to sour between the company and the developers. One area of friction lay in the delicate balance the company had to maintain between publishers of third-party utilities for dBASE and Ashton-Tate's natural desire to enhance its product. Ashton-Tate began to develop a reputation among the development community for spotting a profitable opportunity in the dBASE utilities market and then prematurely announcing it was going to release an addition to dBASE that would incorporate the third-party product's functionality in the soon-to-be-released update. The inevitable result of these announcements was that sales of the third-party product would immediately come to a screeching halt as the market waited for the real thing to be released from Ashton-Tate. Unfortunately for several of these companies, many of Ashton-Tate's announcements proved to be hype and vaporware. These antics succeeded in destroying several third-party firms, most notably Fox & Geller, pioneers in providing add-ons for dBASE II and III. The development community began to bubble with resentment toward what it perceived as Ashton-Tate's highhanded and misleading tactics.

An even greater area of friction lay in the nature of dBASE itself. At heart, the product was simply a language and not much more. Products such as dBASE III and III+ provided a simple code-generating shell that allowed neophytes to build very basic programs, but experienced developers used the language and a variety of third-party tools to build more advanced applications. Once an application was complete, it would be distributed with a "runtime" module, a piece of the dBASE code that could run programs but didn't allow you to modify them. Ashton-Tate charged hefty fees for its runtime product. To avoid these fees, developers started building *compilers*, programs that would take dBASE instructions and transform them into *machine code*, .exe files that ran completely independent of any Ashton-Tate product. Sales of the dBASE runtime quickly disappeared, a development Esber didn't appreciate. Worse, he realized that the logical next step was the development of third-party products that combined the dBASE language and a compiler. These programs would compete directly with the company's flagship.

In an attempt to forestall the competition, Esber began to rattle legal sabers, threatening lawsuits against people who he thought were poaching the dBASE franchise. At the beginning, Esber was a bit vague about exactly what the dBASE franchise consisted of, but nonetheless his threats went over very poorly with the dBASE community, who felt it "owned" a piece of the product as well. After all, it was the community's utilities, evangelizing, and development efforts that had helped make Esber a rich man and Ashton-Tate a market leader. Just who was Esber, a man who had probably never written a line of dBASE code in his miserable MBA existence, to threaten them?

While preparing to unleash the legal dogs of war, Esber simultaneously embarked on an ill-thought-out plan of diversification. In 1985, Ashton-Tate purchased MultiMate, then a leader in the word-processing market, and in 1986, Ashton-Tate bought Decision Resources, publisher of a leading line of business graphics. Although on the face of it the acquisitions made sense, both proved to be big mistakes.

Hartford, Connecticut–based MultiMate got its start in the early 1980s when an insurance firm hired a small group of contract programmers to write a clone of the Wang word-processing system to run on their PCs. Once the project was complete, the group founded a software company to market their new Wang work-alike. For a few years the MultiMate word processor enjoyed brisk sales, particularly in corporations that already had Wang systems installed.

By the mid-1980s, however, MultiMate was already running out of steam. The company wasn't particularly well managed, and some of its marketing and advertising programs were amateurish and misfired. One of the company's funniest blunders was its "All He Could Do" ad series. Seeking to capitalize on the fact that the company sold only word-processing products, MultiMate ran a full-page four-color ad that featured Babe Ruth with the caption "All He Could Do Was Hit." Apparently no one at MultiMate realized that when the Bambino was traded from the Boston Red Sox in 1918 he was an all-star pitcher **and** outfielder. (Ruth's lifetime record as a pitcher: 94 wins, 46 losses, .671 pct., 2.28 ERA. After his trade to New York, he pitched infrequently.)

Of more concern was that MultiMate was a nasty and recalcitrant piece of code. From a performance standpoint, the product emulated a 1970s-era Wang word processor all too well; for example, it allowed you to see only one page of a document onscreen at a time, a holdover from an era when memory requirements imposed that limitation. The product's underlying architecture consisted of a poorly documented mass of assembly language spaghetti that over time proved increasingly difficult to extend and improve.

By 1987, MultiMate was consistently placing near the bottom in press reviews and competitive rankings, and sales began to run out of steam. After the best programming minds at Ashton-Tate spent months reviewing the situation,[3] the decision was made that the only way to solve the problem was to rewrite MultiMate from the ground up (or buy a new product and call it MultiMate). Of course, the company was planning to release a new OS/2-specific word processor, and that would probably be the final answer to all the problems. In the meantime, Ashton-Tate began resorting to "stuffing the channel" to keep sales of MultiMate moving.

Channel stuffing is a time-honored tactic used by high-tech firms to mask slowing sales. It works by inducing distributors and resellers to accept large amounts of inventory in their warehouses, shipments the

---

[3] I attended some of the meetings in order to provide marketing input into the deliberations. I spent a great deal of time saying "You really, really need to ship an update to the product soon" but was ignored for the most part.

company then books as revenue. Incentives include crazy low prices, generous payment terms, and most important of all, agreeing to take all the inventory back if it can't be moved. At one point, inventory representing about 2 years of sales of MultiMate lay moldering in warehouses all around the country.

Decision Resources proved to be a similar headache. The ChartMaster family of products was a poorly architected mass of BASIC language spaghetti that over time proved increasingly difficult to extend and improve. By 1987, the ChartMaster product line, like MultiMate, was consistently placing near the bottom in press reviews and competitive rankings. The company did have an "ace in the hole," a minicomputer graphics program that had been ported to the PC that Decision Resources extolled during its negotiations with Ashton-Tate as "state of the art." After the purchase, a closer examination of this graphics gobbler, later released in a fit of desperation as "Draw Applause," revealed a program with an interface so obtuse and illogical that an internal marketing team evaluating the product was reduced to giggling hysterics[4] as they attempted to use it.

As with MultiMate, sales began to rapidly run out of steam. After the best programming minds at Ashton-Tate spent months reviewing the situation, they decided the only way to solve the problem was to rewrite ChartMaster from the ground up (or buy a new product and call it ChartMaster). Of course, the company was planning to release a new OS/2-specific business graphics product, and that would probably be the final answer to all the problems. In the meantime, Ashton-Tate began resorting to stuffing the channel to keep sales of the product moving. Soon, inventory representing about 1 year of sales of ChartMaster lay moldering in warehouses all about the country.

The Decision Resources purchase also proved to be an open morale sore within Ashton-Tate. Many of the employees of what was now the company's new East Coast graphics and word-processing division soon realized that Ashton-Tate had bought their companies based strictly on an analysis of their cash flow contribution. It became clear to them that Ashton-Tate had little interest in investing in the MultiMate and ChartMaster products, and resentment in the company's "orphan" division flared. One expression of the bad feelings was the release of

---

[4] I was a member of the evaluation team.

Ashton-Tate's very own underground comic entitled *Graphic Violence*.[5] Different strips included depictions of company employees shooting down upper management, Ashton-Tate's development group as a bunch of stoned druggies, and Draw Applause as an overweight superhero munching on memory. New releases of *Graphic Violence* became much prized within Ashton-Tate.

~

Making Ed's Day

The year 1987 also proved to be a time of decision in another way, as Esber formally declared war on major segments of the dBASE community. An independent committee of third parties that had started an effort to create a "standard dBASE" specification was threatened with a lawsuit if it continued its work.[6] The committee promptly stopped work on the dBASE standard and began work on efforts to create what was now a "standard **xBase**" specification.

Fresh from this triumph, Esber struck harder and deeper. The company announced that the dBASE language was "proprietary"[7] and couldn't be used without permission[8] from Ashton-Tate. He was quoted in the press as calling the third-party companies "parasites." Ashton-Tate mailed out legal cease-and-desist letters to consultants such as Adam Green, one of the industry's most noted dBASE gurus, to stop using the name "dBASE" on many of his training and teaching materials. At a Software Publishing Association conference, Esber got up before a crowd of developers and bellowed "Make my day!"[9] while threatening to sue anybody who dared build a dBASE-compatible product.

---

[5] I still have a complete set of the series.

[6] *PC World* magazine, April 1989.

[7] The company made the announcement by way of a lawsuit filed in federal court against the Santa Cruz Corporation and Fox Software in 1989.

[8] See http://www.lgu.com/publications/softcopy/14.shtml.

[9] Several members of Ashton-Tate's management were in the audience when Esber made his threat, including Product Manager Randy Hujar, who remembers cringing as Esber spoke.

Nor did Esber restrict use of his honeyed tongue to people outside Ashton-Tate. Once at a company party he took the occasion to tell Ratliff, a figure much revered in and out of Ashton-Tate, that he was just as valuable to the company as its janitors.[10] Observers believe Esber was probably just trying to advance the theory that everyone at Ashton-Tate was a cog in one big happy marketing machine, but Ratliff apparently missed this subtle point and soon after left the company.

One of the potential targets of Ashton-Tate's legal jihad included a company called Fox Software, publisher of a dBASE "clone" that was increasingly well thought of by the dBASE community. Interestingly enough, Ashton-Tate attempted to buy the product with the idea of using it as the next major upgrade to dBASE III+, but the negotiations fell through. Soon after the release of dBASE IV, Ashton-Tate did indeed sue Fox.

As the development community became steadily more roiled and resentful, word began to circulate that Esber was "ashamed" of dBASE because he thought it wasn't "relational" enough. Because most people felt that Esber wasn't technically astute enough to distinguish between a relational database and a close relation, this observation simply exasperated everyone further. Esber then made a puzzling deal with Microsoft to jointly market a SQL server product from Sybase. SQL applications are designed to store actual application data on remote computers called *servers* while a desktop PC (the client) processes the code that deals with screen displays and data entry and then transmits records to and from the servers.

The new partnership had many in the industry scratching their heads. It was no secret that Microsoft was looking longingly at the database market and seeking entry. Ashton-Tate was still the unchallenged PC database leader and possessed the resources and clout to buy or partner with a major SQL provider on its own. To many the deal seemed a public confirmation that Esber lacked confidence in dBASE and its capability to adapt to the future, a viewpoint not appreciated by a development community that depended on dBASE for its livelihood. (Ashton-Tate eventually did purchase its own SQL software, but by that time the company was so badly damaged it was unable to do much with the product.)

---

[10] This story was mentioned in an article on Ashton-Tate that appeared in the *Wall Street Journal* after Esber's departure from the company.

The legal push finally culminated in Ashton-Tate filing papers in court attempting to declare the dBASE language the property of the company.[11] The move was seen by many as an attempt by Ashton-Tate to lock them out of the market and take the bread off their table. By this time Esber was thoroughly loathed by the dBASE community with a passion never before seen in the software industry.

Esber apparently didn't realize that as he was making himself public enemy number one with every dBASE developer and programmer on Earth, he was also making himself radioactive from the press's viewpoint. In high tech, as in many other industries, writers and editors rely on a stable of gurus and notables to provide them with quotes and background information on the companies they cover. Beginning in 1987, when members of the press called up their favorite dBASE experts to ask them their opinions about the latest developments and news from Ashton-Tate, they were often treated to observations such as "Ed Esber is a diseased amoeboid life form with the intelligence of a sick protozoa" (an actual quote[12]).

This type of thing takes its toll, and as 1988 rolled by and the industry waited for the release of Ashton-Tate's next big product, dBASE IV, Esber fell about even in popularity with Satan in the eyes of the developer and press communities. Not helping things was the fact that as dBASE IV kept slipping its release date, promised features whose announcements had helped kill and wound several third-party products and companies began to drop out of the final version. Third-party market resentment swelled to a crescendo.

Also not helping the situation was that Ashton-Tate's dBASE IV development effort was seriously broken, but no one seemed to know it. An important reason for this was because, lulled by Ashton-Tate's mid-1980s success, Esber had hired a new company president, Luther Nussbaum, to run the company's day-to-day operations. Esber remained in overall charge as CEO and spent his days thinking deep strategic thoughts while simultaneously pursuing his campaign of becoming the most hated man in software.

Nussbaum's hiring was a mistake. Less technically astute than even Esber (he had previously worked at a company that built diesel engines),

---

[11] *PC World* magazine, April 1989.

[12] As relayed to me by an enraged dBASE developer while I was working in product management for Ashton-Tate.

he quickly developed a reputation within Ashton-Tate for preferring to rule by bullying and intimidation. Management by fear can be an effective tactic (at least in the short term), but it doesn't work well if you're not sure what you're threatening people about. In his new role of supreme corporate-strategy guru, Esber had stopped coming to critical meetings that tracked the development and release date of dBASE IV, and he was out of touch with the technical difficulties surrounding the development effort. The result was that upper management was unaware of the true nature of the product they finally released in October 1988.

~

The Horror, the Horror

The dBASE IV launch was a disaster. The product had serious memory management issues, contained plenty of bugs, and lacked promised capabilities such as an integrated compiler. In the words of dBASE maven Adam Green, it "didn't work." The reviews were devastating, and the development community howled loudly in disdain at a product one developer publicly stated was "an abortion in a box."[13]

Now, there's no question that dBASE IV had serious deficiencies, and Ashton-Tate should have expected to take its well-deserved lumps. Nonetheless, the reaction to dBASE IV was out of line with normal industry scenarios. Database products are some of the most complex pieces of software to develop, and the industry is rife with examples of full-point releases (i.e., 3.0 to 4.0) that "don't work" (just ask any longtime Oracle user). When faced with this situation, an astute company positions the new upgrade as an "opportunity to learn" about the release, "test" its features, and build "prototypes." In the meantime, the publisher works frantically to fix bugs and push out the "4.1" and the "4.2" releases, the ones that actually *do* work. If the company is in good odor with the press and its developers, this approach can often help finesse a new release flop. The press will spank the publisher, but

---

[13] I was present in 1990 at a New York special interest group (SIG) meeting devoted to dBASE when a developer stood up and made this comment, but I can no longer remember his name.

developers and third parties will tend to rally round the product because their self-interest is involved. They'll begin developing programming workarounds, exchange tips on dealing with problems, and assure the press that once the bugs are all worked out the new release is eventually going to be mondo boffo.

This dynamic was absent at Ashton-Tate. Sensing blood in the water, the dBASE community had no intention of letting up until it had Ed Esber's testicles in hand. It had all become personal. When the press called up a dBASE developer the first time for quotes and comments, they received an earful about the horrors of dBASE IV and the awfulness of Ed Esber. The ensuing bad reviews and karma upset all the other developers, who saw their investment in dBASE training and development threatened, thus ensuring that the *next* time the press called they received an even louder earful about the incredible evil that was dBASE IV and the intergalactic menace to humanity represented by Ed Esber.

None of this was helped by the fact that Ashton-Tate, instead of quickly acknowledging dBASE IV's problems and embarking on a crash course to fix them, spent 6 months denying the problems existed and then told everyone it was planning an OS/2 version of dBASE that would make everything better. At this juncture, the press began hearing from the development community that dBASE IV was a genocidal plot against all sentient life in the universe and that Ed Esber wasn't simply as bad as Satan but was Satan himself. This unvirtuous marketing cycle unleashed a mob mentality whose goal was Esber's destruction. The corresponding devastation of Ashton-Tate was simply collateral damage.

Revenue growth at the company came to a screeching halt in 1989 as sales of dBASE IV stopped. Spooked by the turmoil surrounding the company, the distributors and resellers decided this might also be a good time to return all those copies of MultiMate and ChartMaster gathering dust in their warehouses. Ashton-Tate, whose size had peaked at about $350 million, lost more than $60 million over the next several quarters. In 1990, its legal case against Fox Software was tossed out of court when it was ruled that because Ashton-Tate had failed to disclose that dBASE was based on the JPLDIS language, the company had no proprietary rights to the dBASE "dialect." Shortly thereafter the board of directors tossed out Esber and brought in an innocuous fellow by the name of Bill Lyons to head the now barely twitching company. Lyons astounded everyone by convincing Philippe Kahn of Borland in 1991 to pay $440 million (in stock) for Ashton-Tate. There was speculation that Philippe, a French immigrant, thought he was counting in francs instead of dollars.

~

100 Percent Loyal

During the late 1990s customer relationship management (CRM) software was one of software's hottest new categories. CRM products are bulked-up versions of sales contact managers such as ACT! and GoldMine that became popular in the late 1980s and early 1990s. CRM packages are designed to move beyond managing sales prospects and, in theory, offer companies the ability to manage every aspect of their customer relationships, from buying through returns.

In the late 1990s, CRM's 800-pound gorilla was Siebel Systems. Founded by Tom Siebel in 1993, the company by 2000 was worth approximately $1.25 billion and was the dominant player in various segments of the CRM market. As Siebel grew, both the company and its founder and CEO developed a reputation as being arrogant, inaccessible to the press, and difficult to deal with (much like a certain large database company of the 1980s). Like enterprise resource planning (ERP) products, a successful CRM deployment requires a company to make a profound commitment to reengineering its internal business computing platforms, practices, and policies to ensure eventual success. Tremendous amounts of time and resources have to be dedicated to customizing the software, testing, and deploying it as well as retraining company personnel to use the new system. The process is never smooth and can often be snarled by internal politics, software deficiencies, and implementation costs that can quickly spiral past initial optimistic estimates.

Making things worse is that despite the claims of the industry and the availability of CRM "suites" that supposedly integrate disparate customer databases across the entire enterprise, the truth is this integration is often more real in the minds of CRM software vendors than on their customer's computer systems. As an August 26, 2003, report by *DM Direct* magazine pointed out, "Few CRM suite suppliers package integration between their own campaign management offerings and their own contact centre, e-commerce, or customer self-service applications!" As a result of these issues, the entire CRM category came into some disrepute as "shelfware," a category of software that companies bought, attempted to deploy, gave up on, and then relegated to an inglorious position tucked away on some IT worker's shelf.

As the dot.com bubble burst, Siebel, along with many other firms, suffered as shrinking IT budgets and a tighter focus on measurable ROI from technology washed over the software industry. Siebel did not escape the tide. By 2002 the company's growth had slowed sharply, and the CRM publisher experienced an 18 percent drop in third-quarter revenue and a loss of $92 million, in contrast with a profit of $35 million during the same period in 2001.

Siebel's PR chickens came home to roost when in June of 2002 a small, obscure research firm, Nucleus Research, thrust itself into the limelight when it decided to survey 66 customers Siebel had posted on its site as marquis reference accounts. Of these 66, 23 responded to the Nucleus questionnaire and, to Nucleus's (stated) surprise, the survey found that 61 percent of these accounts did not believe they had achieved any measurable ROI on their investment in Siebel software after two years. (The average sale to this group was approximately $6.6 million over a 3-year period.)

The Nucleus survey also stated the following:

- 65 percent of Siebel's customers had problems customizing and performance tuning their software.

- 78 percent said the product suffered from a "lack of user-friendliness."

- 57 percent said deployment took longer than planned.

- 55 percent said their system rollouts went over budget.

- Several respondents also said they thought Siebel was an arrogant and unresponsive bunch.

The press, no great fan of Siebel, gleefully jumped all over the Nucleus report, giving it widespread coverage in every major print publication and Internet site devoted to software and IT issues. The report also appeared and was discussed on several business-oriented TV shows.

Siebel's response was an almost textbook example of ham-handed spin control. The company first proclaimed the survey was "random" in nature. This argument was unconvincing since the customers surveyed at "random" were presumably Siebel's best accounts. The point made by Rebecca Wettemann, VP of Research at Nucleus, who said, "If their success stories are having a difficult experience, what does that tell you about the broader population of Siebel customers?" was never convincingly refuted by Siebel.

The company then hired a research firm, Satemetrix, to conduct its own study of the Siebel customer base. Not surprisingly, Satemetrix announced the following:

- Siebel had 90+ percent customer satisfaction.
- Siebel had nearly 100 percent customer loyalty.
- Siebel's customers did not regard Siebel as an arrogant and unresponsive company.

Unfortunately for Siebel, skeptics and Nucleus immediately pointed out that Siebel was a minority owner of Satemetrix, the study had not allowed respondents to answer survey questions anonymously (unlike the Nucleus study), the loyalty question was designed to force a "loyal" response, and the satisfaction and loyalty percentages cited for Siebel were suspiciously close to the numbers Saddam Hussein polled before the war in Iraq.

CEO Tom Siebel compounded matters further by giving a clumsy interview with *Computerworld* in which he stated that "a number of these customers who were quoted in there are pretty upset that the comments were misrepresented." Siebel was not, however, willing to say which of its marquis customers were "upset." He then credited Nucleus with a nice bit of "guerilla marketing." Since Nucleus, unlike Satemetrix, was an independent company, it was unclear to everyone precisely who the guerillas were. Overhanging the entire mess was the rich irony that a company selling customer relationship software designed to help you understand your customers didn't seem to have good relationships with its customers or understand them.

Siebel's competitors wasted no time in attempting to capitalize on the controversy. PeopleSoft quickly announced that it had filched a half dozen unhappy customers away from Siebel. SalesForce.com, a software-as-a-service (SaaS) rival and the particular bête noire of Siebel in the sales automation segment of the CRM market, launched a well-publicized special promotion designed to entice Siebel customers to jump ship.

Many years ago an interesting ad campaign ran on TV that depicted a weary CEO looking at his assembled management team and announcing that a major customer had just "fired" the company on the grounds that its customers no longer "knew" who they (the company) were. In the ad, instead of hiring a research firm to prove that the customer didn't know what he was talking about, the CEO handed out plane tickets to his staff with orders to go on the road and reconnect with their clients.

This ad exemplified the approach Siebel Systems should have taken to the Nucleus report. Siebel should have done the following:

- Thank Nucleus for bringing these problems to their attention.

- Announce the company was putting together a task force to remedy the problems the Nucleus report had uncovered.

- Visit every reference account to ensure the task force's objectives were completely understood and explained (and make no attempt to isolate the "unhappy 23"). The truth is that Siebel's sales force probably knew almost precisely who was unhappy with its software.

- Develop a proactive campaign of managing post-sales accounts so as to ensure ongoing customer satisfaction.

- Develop a timeline of steps the company was taking and goals that would be achieved and then make sure the timeline was widely distributed among the press and the analysts. Had Siebel followed this course, it would still have been inevitably embarrassed by the Nucleus revelations, but the focus of the story would have quickly shifted.

Instead of the press enjoying the sight of Siebel engaging in a fruitless argument with Nucleus and, by extension, its own customers, the story would have turned, over time, into an ongoing examination about how Siebel was learning from its mistakes and ensuring its customer's satisfaction. The use of the timeline would have enabled the company to shape the story to match the normal journalist desire to cover events that encompass a conflict, hero, climax, and happy ending.

Siebel did none of this, and problems at the CRM giant continued to fester in the wake of the Nucleus disaster. In the spring of 2004, with Siebel sales still sharply down from their earlier highs and its revenue flat, company founder Tom Siebel announced he was stepping aside and hired a new CEO, IBM veteran Mike Lawrie, to take Siebel to "chapter two" in its corporate evolution. Chapter two came to an abrupt end when Siebel announced Lawrie was retiring in the wake of more financial bad news. The Siebel Systems saga came to an end when in September of 2005 the CRM pioneer disappeared down the maw of Oracle. To many observers, it was a corporate match made in heaven, because Oracle had a reputation for irritating customers every bit as much as Siebel in its prime, and a nice new CRM would be just the thing to help smooth out the rough edges.

six

THE IDIOT PIPER:
OS/2 and IBM

Almost from the moment IBM signed its first contract to use MS-DOS with the original IBM PC, the company began planning to replace the Microsoft OS with something else. Even by the standards of the time, DOS was regarded by many as a "toy" OS. It was a given that IBM would replace it with a more serious system as the PC market grew and developed. The question everyone was asking was, with what?

After several fits and starts, it turned out that "what" was something eventually christened "OS/2," the real OS that Big Blue intended to follow in the footsteps of other classic IBM OSs such as VM and MVS. Once IBM had made up its mind about what it wanted to do, no one doubted that OS/2 was destined to be the next chapter in IBM's unmatched record of sales triumphs. Sure, the company made occasional missteps such as its Stretch computer of the 1950s and more recently its bungled development of the PC Junior, but to many these were mere sideshows. IBM had designated its next-generation OS for its PCs as "strategic," and when IBM made a proclamation like that, the die was cast. OS/2 was destined for greatness.

It didn't turn out that way. Instead of being a new chapter in "success," OS/2 turned out to be a tragicomedy that played out for more than a decade and ended in disaster for IBM. Before OS/2, IBM was a company apart from all others that people viewed with a sense of awe that bordered on reverence. The company was famous for its no-layoff policy, feared for its power, and worshipped for its profitability. To be an IBM employee meant one was automatically a member of America's working elite. IBM CEOs were always promoted from within, their ascension to the Big Blue throne treated by the American business press as minicoronations.

After OS/2's collapse, IBM's iconic status in the eyes of America was lost. Upstarts such as Compaq, Dell, and Gateway decimated IBM's PC business. Microsoft and a handful of others carted away the desktop software riches IBM had assumed it would one day inherit. As its mainframe and minicomputer businesses shrank, IBM lost billions in the 1990s—almost $5 billion alone in 1992, which proved to be a mere warm-up for 1993's $8 billion shortfall.[1] The no-layoff policy was scrapped, and 200,000 people eventually lost their jobs. IBM CEO John Akers was summarily tossed off the Big Blue throne, and cigarette salesman Lou Gerstner was installed in his place. And while Gerstner

---

[1] Gary Rivlin, *The Plot to Get Bill Gates* (New York: Times Books/Random House, 1999).

stopped the flow of red ink and made the company mildly profitable again, IBM's growth during the 1990s was lackluster: a 3 percent compound annual rate—not very impressive when compared with the company's 10.6 percent annual rate in the 1980s. To the world at large, IBM had become just another company: still big and powerful but also often sluggish and stupid.

The fallout from OS/2's failure also had a serious and, in some cases, fatal impact on many of the companies that had followed IBM's lead. Before OS/2, IBM had played the role of pied piper to the industry's software publishers. Whenever Big Blue's dulcet tones sounded, companies dutifully lined up to follow. After OS/2, IBM's flute was broken. In the words of the founder of a small utilities company that bet big on OS/2 and lost, "OS/2 took a lot of us over the cliff. The product was IBM's Idiot Piper."

But in 1985, the piper's tones were still clear and seductive. That year, as a member of MicroPro International's far-flung sales force (I had been flung to Secaucus, New Jersey, microwave antenna capital of the United States, in the role of support engineer attached to the local office), I was summoned to Marin County, California, to attend the company's national sales meeting. This event consisted of 3 days of sales briefings, gossip, and some serious wining and dining, and it was normally the highlight of the company's year. I, however, showed up in a cranky mood, and nothing about the next few days of frivolity changed it.

I maintained my despondent demeanor throughout the meeting's gala finale, a dinner at which special achievement awards were handed out. By the end of the meal my bad humor should have disappeared. I had won an award for field sales engineer of the year and had been told informally by the powers that were that I had a shot at moving into product management, something I badly wanted.

Unfortunately for my peace of mind, a couple of weeks before the national sales meeting, I had attended a regional IBM trade show in New York City,[2] where I had spent an excruciating day demonstrating MicroPro's latest word processor, Easy. Easy was the brainchild of

---

[2] The ostensible highlight of this show was supposed to be the IBM Convertible, yet another hardware gobbler that continued the process begun with the PC Junior of puncturing IBM's image of marketing acumen and invincibility. The unit lacked serial and parallel ports, meaning you couldn't use a modem or print with the computer unless you bought a pricey option.

then–MicroPro President Glen Haney, a nice but fairly clueless fellow. For some reason, Haney had gotten it into his head that the most important thing MicroPro could do was compete with PFS Write from Software Publishing Corporation (SPC). Founded by Fred Gibbons, SPC had made its mark in the industry with PFS File, an easy-to-use database program for the Apple II, and then the PC. The company had subsequently spun off several new PFS-brand products, including Write, and had done fairly well with them. Haney was sure MicroPro was losing future market share to Gibbons and was determined to do something about it. Hence Easy.

When it was introduced, Easy had two main claims to fame. One was that it was, er, easy to use, at least by the standards of the time. As with all such products, much of this ease of use was achieved by stripping out a good portion of WordStar's feature set. The product thus had no appeal to WordStar or WordStar 2000 users, who were used to paying more for a WordStar upgrade than the full retail price of Easy. Like all the other "lite" word processors, Easy never amounted to much and eventually faded away.[3]

~

A Dog's View

Easy's other mark of distinction was its much-heralded TopView compatibility. TopView was IBM's first attempt to steer an independent course from Microsoft, and its introduction in 1985 had given Bill Gates a severe case of heartburn. TopView was a "shell" that added rudimentary cut-and-paste capabilities between programs as well as multitasking to DOS. Multitasking would allow a user to, for instance, call up WordStar while recalculating a spreadsheet in Lotus 1-2-3. Unfortunately,

---

[3] MicroPro attempted to use Easy as the foundation of a new version of WordStar, and several members of the press were invited to view the work in progress. Invitees included Paul Somerson and Steve Manes, journalists for *PC Magazine*, coauthors of *Underground WordStar,* and publishers of StarFixer, a WordStar "tune-up" utility. After sitting through a demo of the prospective new WordStar, they and several other members of the contingent warned members of the MicroPro staff that if MicroPro released the new WordStar in the form they had just seen it, the company would undoubtedly be very unhappy with the press reaction. The Easy-to-WordStar project was quickly discontinued.

this capability was somewhat theoretical. TopView sucked up most of the resources of any PC it ran on, making multitasking any but the smallest applications difficult, if not impossible. TopView was also character based, unlike the Mac OS and Windows. It was therefore unable to integrate graphics and text within a document or display different fonts and type sizes.

For products written specifically to the TopView API, the integration between products became more robust, and memory management became somewhat more effective. MicroPro had spent a considerable amount of time and internal development resources learning how to integrate TopView into its software. The company expected this investment would pay off in big dividends in increased functionality in future MicroPro products and stronger sales.

Despite these expectations, TopView compatibility hadn't gone over well at the conference. For one thing, a bunch of Macophiles from the press had for some reason shown up and taken a great deal of pleasure in torturing me during demos of Easy. "Show us again how you cut and paste text," they'd say. "You call **that** easy?! Bwwwaaaaahhhhhaaaahhhhhaaaa!" they brayed as I banged on a keyboard instead of brandishing a mouse. "Now, how do you display a font onscreen? You **can't**?! Wow! We can see why TopView is so fabulous!" they howled as they held their sides and laughed hysterically.

By the end of the show I hated Mac users and Macs.

On the other hand, PC types had hardly been more complimentary. At one point, John Dvorak, the long-time columnist at *InfoWorld* who was now working at *PC Magazine*, strolled by.

"Hi, John!" I called out brightly. "Care to see a demonstration of Easy, the TopView-compatible word processor, in action?"

He stared at me with distaste. "I have no desire to see, hear, or do anything that has anything to do with TopDog," he stated with emphasis. "When is the next update of WordStar shipping?"

"Uh, real soon now! In the meantime, would you care to see a demonstration of WordStar 2000?"

He walked away without saying a word. Great.

A few minutes later, up walked a pleasant-looking gentleman whose show badge indicated he worked for the IT department of a major New York bank.

"Hi! Care to see a demonstration of Easy, the TopView-compatible word processor from MicroPro, publisher of WordStar?" I chirped.

He looked sad. "I don't think so. We're a major IBM customer, but when we brought in some copies of TopView and showed them to our PCs, they began to whine and howl and tried to crawl off their desks and hide under the chairs. By the way, could you let me know when the next version of WordStar is shipping?" He gave me his card and walked away.

Another fellow stepped up briskly to my demo station, stopped abruptly, and peered intently at the monitor. His greasy hair and slight but redolent tang of BO told me before I glanced at his badge that he was a programmer.

"Hello!" I caroled. "Care to see a demonstration of Easy, the TopView-com—"

"TopView? **TopView**?!" he interrupted hoarsely. "I want to know when the next version of WordStar is shipping!" Gobbling sounds began to issue from the back of his throat. He made the sign of the cross at me and hurried away.

It was a long, long day.

The memory of my humiliation fresh in mind, I decided to do something about it. After all, I was the field sales engineer of the year, damn it. I stalked over to the table where MicroPro's vice president of development was peaceably minding his own business, sat down, and announced in what I hoped were my richest, most persuasive tones that "We need to forget about TopView and support Windows."

He blinked at me. "Rick, we're talking about IBM. TopView is endorsed by IBM. Bill Lowe has personally told me that TopView is the future of IBM operating systems on the PC. And IBM is the company that sets the standards."

"No," I countered. "The wisdom of the field says that TopView is doomed. Customers don't like it. They've seen the Mac; that's what they want on their PCs. The press hates TopView; they think the Mac is where it's at. Developers hate TopView; they want to make cool Mac-like things for PCs. Everyone hates TopView! On the PC side of things, the only viable thing close to the Mac is Windows. If we write for Windows, we can do a cool Mac-like word processor for the PC and be the only one! By default, we'll lead the PC market in our ability to do things like display graphics and text within a document."

"Besides," I said, my enthusiasm reaching a fevered pitch, "Why spend so much time supporting IBM? They're notorious for working with companies and then stealing their good ideas and driving them out of business. We need to work with Microsoft! They're much smaller and will be far easier to deal with!"

Rarely is one privileged to be so right for so wrong a reason.

As I had predicted, the market, enthralled by the Mac and discouraged by TopView's sluggish performance, rejected IBM's first attempt at breaking free from Microsoft's yoke. TopView was out of sight by the end of 1985; the company literally could not give the thing away.

Chastened by its failure, IBM paused to consider its options. It had two basic tracks down which it could go. It could simply cut the cord with Microsoft at some point and develop its own desktop OSs. Or it could decide to remain in partnership with Microsoft and ship new versions of DOS on its PC and eventually Windows, the GUI extension to DOS that Gates had been pushing since 1983 and had finally shipped in 1985.

After pondering the situation a bit, IBM decided to do both. It would stay in partnership with Gates but make the little geek jump through hoops building a new OS that did all the things IBM thought it needed to do, up to and including supporting old TopView applications, all two or three of them, despite that no one cared about this. Oh, and IBM programmers would develop significant parts of the new OS. Oh, and the new OS would come in two versions, one that Microsoft could license to third parties à la DOS and another higher-end version that would have additional capabilities and run only on IBM PCs (in theory—this turned out not to be true). And oh, by the way, everyone agreed that Windows could stick around for a while. The first edition had gotten bad reviews, and the product was clearly harmless.[4]

Gates, in a display of manly fortitude (well, perhaps not that manly. Gates would have supported **Commodore DOS** if that's what it took to keep IBM's business) that paid off handsomely, agreed to everything IBM wanted. Work on the next generation of PC OSs commenced.

---

[4] Windows was formally introduced to the world at large at the 1983 Las Vegas COMDEX trade show, which I attended with MicroPro. It was impossible to walk around the show floor and not see demo screens of an evergreen viewed through a window (get it?). Windows wouldn't actually ship until late in 1985, and when it did, it was viewed with contempt by GUI gurus enamored of Apple's far more polished system.

~

An OS Is Born

While IBM and Microsoft were involved in their negotiations, rumors of the new PC OS began to float throughout the industry. For a while it was called CP/DOS, or DOS 286, or DOS 5.0, and then finally Presentation Manager. It would have multitasking and multi-threading (whatever that was) and semaphores and all manner of good stuff, but most important, it would have a GUI, just like the Mac! This interface would be based on Windows, only much better, obviously, and Windows and the new interface would be so similar that anyone who developed a Windows product could port it to Presentation Manager when it was ready to ship with a snap of the fingers and a twinkle of a compiler. Write two products for the price of one. And boy, that sounded really good to all the developers!

And though no one would actually confirm the date on which the new wonder OS would ship, everyone assumed it would be sometime in 1986 or at the very least 1987. And that sounded good, too, because by 1986, Atari ST [5] owners had a pretty sophisticated GUI for their machines, for God's sake, whereas PC types still had to clunk along in character-based DOS. And PC owners were sure getting tired of all those Mac snobs laughing at them and twirling those damned mice under their noses and getting all the girls because Macs were so cool. In fact, a fair number of them started buying up Macs so they could twirl mice and be cool, too. But most were still content to wait for IBM to ship a cool Mac-like OS so that they could twirl their mice while avoiding paying Apple those 50 percent profit margins it got on its systems. But they were sure eager to get their hands on that new OS and those mice.

Then IBM threw SAA into the mix, and everything changed.

---

[5] The Atari ST OS TOS (Tramiel Operating System) was based on Digital Research's GEM. The ST was the brainchild of Jack Tramiel of Commodore fame. After losing control of Commodore, Tramiel and his sons took control over Atari's nearly defunct computer business and had some short-term success in reviving it. The ST series launched Atari's rebirth under its new management, and for a while the system enjoyed some success in the market, particularly as an inexpensive music synthesizer (the ST included a MIDI port). I purchased an Atari 520 ST running TOS in 1985 (and I still have the unit). Tramiel, as always, relied on a low-price strategy, but over time Atari was driven out of the market by the inevitable depredations of the Silicon Beast.

SAA, which stood for Systems Application Architecture, was an attempt by IBM to develop a cross-platform OS (or something close to it) that would run on all IBM mainframes, minicomputers, and PCs. (An inadvertently hilarious book about this heroic effort was written many years ago. It was referred to by industry wags as "The Soul of a Giant Three-Ring Binder.") This initiative had been sparked by IBM's annoyance at having to listen to its archrival in the lucrative minicomputer market, DEC, trumpet that it, DEC, "had it now."

What DEC[6] had "now" was a unified OS and application environment for its entire product line. In theory, no matter what size computer you bought from DEC, they all used the same OS and ran the same software. (This wasn't entirely true in practice, but DEC certainly was way ahead of IBM in this regard.) By contrast, IBM supported more than a dozen incompatible hardware and OS platforms. Moving an accounting package from, for example, an IBM minicomputer system to a mainframe required an extensive rewrite of the software.

SAA was designed to close this perceived competitive gap, but IBM was targeting a chimera. True, in the late 1980s, DEC's profits and revenue presented the picture of a company in the pink, but this was an illusion. In reality, DEC's appearance was more akin to the hectic flush a consumptive develops before death. DEC's business model consisted of selling minicomputers and small mainframes to companies at the departmental and divisional level. This was precisely what the market companies such as Novell and 3Com were targeting with their networking OSs. Herds of Silicon Beasts yoked together with NetWare were a fraction of the cost of DEC's expensive and overengineered hardware products and required less support. LAN systems were also

---

[6] DEC had taken a stab at the market for small systems in the early 1980s with the simultaneous introduction of no less than three incompatible microcomputers. The most widely publicized and purchased system was the Rainbow, an MS-DOS–compatible machine that also sported a Z-80 processor for running 8-bit software. The machine quickly met the fate of all the other MS-DOS clones. The computer is best remembered for DEC's obnoxious practice of shipping the machine without a format program for its unusual nonstandard floppy drives, ostensibly forcing users to purchase amazingly expensive preformatted floppies directly from DEC. (Enterprising programmers soon developed several freeware formatting programs for the Rainbow, and the ploy failed.) DEC also developed a hilarious series of ads that depicted style-conscious yuppies drooling over the Rainbow's sleek keyboard and monitor, with the big bulky computer itself absent from the picture. Urban professionals nationwide were treated to a nasty surprise when they bit on the ads, bought a Rainbow, and developed hernias lugging their I-got-far-more-than-I-expected PC out of the store.

starting to offer a broader and cheaper selection of software to compete with the minicomputer market's offerings.

Some ominous reports from the field began to filter into DEC head-quarters over defections in the company's customer base, but these were ignored until it was far too late. Over time, the concept of much cheaper and more choices beat "has it now" hands-down, and DEC, along with most of the minicomputer market, disappeared in the late 1990s. For good measure, SAA proved to be a massive waste of IBM's time and money and eventually sank without a trace as well.

Nonetheless, what IBM said still went, and work on integrating SAA technology into Presentation Manager moved forward. Much of this work involved building support for a whole host of IBM mainframe ter-minals into the new OS. This all took much time and effort, and it was soon apparent there would be no wonder OS in 1986. In fact, the new OS with the cool graphical interface would not be ready until 1988. Oh, and you know all that stuff about a simple recompile being all you needed to do to port your Windows product to Presentation Manager? Forget it. You were going to have to do a major code rewrite to get your product to run under the new OS after all, which, by the way, was going to be called OS/2. A nice fit, IBM thought, with its new PS/2 line of microcomputers.

Then, in an act of supreme stupidity that would characterize IBM's marketing of OS/2 for the rest of the product's ill-starred existence, the company announced it would indeed ship the first version of OS/2 in 1987. Only it wouldn't have a cool Mac-like GUI—just the same DOS-like character interface everyone was heartily sick of. Few cared that underneath the hood of the new OS was a quantum-leap improvement over DOS in functionality. With this single stroke, IBM had created TopView II.

IBM's motive for this act wasn't hard to discern. OS/2 had become a draftee in the company's war on the hardware cloners, and it had been assigned to ride shotgun alongside its new computers into battle. By 1987, the company had woken up to the consequences of unleashing the Silicon Beast on the market and was looking to take it all back. The PS/2 line would ship with a new bus, the Micro Channel, that had more patents stuck to it than bugs on a fly strip hanging from the ceiling of a Texas gas station. The new BIOS chip, called Advanced BIOS (ABIOS), reared up and bit you on the finger if you tried to reverse engineer it. The units shipped in April 1987 with plain old DOS, and IBM badly wanted something that could better showcase their new darlings. OS/2 1.0 was it.

Although this was all well and good for IBM, software publishers were less than thrilled. Companies were being asked to throw a considerable amount of time and money into supporting an OS version whose sales prospects were dubious. Making everyone feel worse was IBM's pricing of OS/2 1.0: $340.00 for a retail copy, a price that generated sticker shock. IBM had established a low price point for desktop OSs with the introduction in 1981 of DOS 1.0 for $40.00, and no one thought the OS/2 pricing strategy was a smart move. Once a market's pricing structure is established, it takes time and effort (and perhaps a helpful monopoly) to change it, if you ever do. Yes, many people would eventually obtain the product via bundling, but strong retail sales would help kick start acceptance of OS/2 and generate sales of OS/2-specific products. And that was unlikely to happen with a $340.00 desktop OS that lacked a GUI.

And speaking of pricing, IBM and Microsoft had placed a $3,000.00 price tag on the OS/2 software development kit (SDK). That was no problem for larger software companies, but smaller firms complained bitterly. Microsoft practically gave away its Windows development tools. Even Apple set more reasonable prices for its SDKs.

IBM also seemed oblivious to the need to provide marketing assistance to independent software vendors (ISVs) building OS/2 applications. The company had no direct mail programs a third party could access that would help promote new OS/2 products. IBM had no expertise or influence in software distribution channels and seemed uninterested in developing any. IBM made no attempt to garner critical "shelf space" in major resellers. There were no co-op advertising programs. There were only a few scattered attempts to build a supporting infrastructure of books, publications, shows, and events that would stimulate interest in buying OS/2 and OS/2-related products. IBM's attitude was that what had worked for the company since the Great Depression would work today. And, to an extent, it did. Several major publishers, including Ashton-Tate, Lotus, SPC, and MicroPro, as well as a few daring start-ups, committed themselves heart and soul to OS/2.

Exacerbating all the aforementioned issues was an event beyond IBM's control: a rapid spike in memory prices during the OS/2 introduction. This was a big problem because OS/2 required a "whopping" 4MB of memory to be useful, 8MB to step along smartly, and 16MB to really hum. A 1MB memory stick that was projected to sell for about $100.00 shot up to almost $400.00 before the bubble burst.

What wasn't beyond IBM's control was that the company was one of the largest producers of memory in the world at the time and in a position to take advantage of a rare opportunity to use hardware to drive software sales. As a glum product manager from DeScribe, a start-up that was introducing an OS/2-specific word processor, pointed out, "OS/2 without memory was a $1,000.00 upgrade. Bundled with a handsomely discounted 4MB memory stick, it was a million-copy seller." But IBM was unresponsive to that idea.

The name "OS/2" also proved to be a problem. Many people assumed the new OS ran only on IBM's PS/2 computers, a misperception IBM did little to dispel. And the existence of two versions of the product, the "standard" and "extended" editions, didn't help matters.

All these factors combined to ensure the introduction of OS/2 1.0 was an unmitigated flop. No one bought the package, and no one made any money developing software for it. The desktop market as a whole was becoming restive and showed signs of slipping from IBM's control. Its PS/2 line met stiff resistance from competitors such as Compaq, which spearheaded an effort to develop an independent hardware platform, EISA. After examining IBM's stiff licensing and royalty demands, most potential OEMs decided to stay with the existing PC architecture and refused to build PS/2 clones.

Still, this was IBM after all. It set the standards. The software industry turned its impatient eyes toward OS/2 1.1, the "real" OS/2, the one that would finally ship with that cool Mac-like interface. After due deliberation, IBM announced it would ship OS/2 1.1 in October 1988. Considering that by then Mac users would have been using a modern GUI for 4 years while PC users labored in computing's version of the Stone Age, this seemed rather tardy, but OK. Most people were still ready to wait, though sales of Macs continued to grow briskly.

And while you were biding your time, there was this increasingly interesting Windows alternative. Windows 2.0 had shipped in April 1987, and though the critics still mocked it, 2.0 was clearly an improvement over the last version. There was even a special version, Windows 386, that took advantage of some of that chip's special features. You could do some real work with Windows, especially the 386 version, and now there were even some good software packages for it: desktop publisher PageMaker, for one, and Microsoft's new spreadsheet, Excel, which had received glowing reviews upon release. When you bought the package, which came in well under $100.00, it said it had Presentation Manager. In other words, you were sort of getting a sneak preview of IBM's new wonder OS. That was a nice little bonus, when you stopped to think about it.

Microsoft had also done something really quite clever. It had released a runtime version of Windows[7] to developers, ensuring that if you didn't have Windows, you could still buy a Windows application you could run on your system. If you were a PC user with a 386 and Windows, you might not be ready to twirl that mouse, but you were certainly entitled to swing it a bit. Windows 2.0 sales started to become quite robust, hitting about 10,000 units a month through the retail channels. But no one got carried away. OS/2 1.1 was on the way.

IBM kept its promise. OS/2 1.1 with the Presentation Manager GUI was officially released in October 1988, on Halloween. It had a cool Mac-like GUI, though by now GUIs weren't really that cool anymore, just necessary if you wanted to be competitive. The market sighed in relief. There was a flurry of initial purchases. OS/2 appeared ready to take off!

And then everyone found out you . . . couldn't . . . print . . . with OS/2 1.1.

This was because in addition to providing no support for third-party software developers, IBM had also made no attempt to garner support for manufacturers of non-IBM hardware.[8] And although IBM made some very nice printers, most people hadn't bought them. They had

---

[7] The runtime version of Windows was discontinued with the introduction of version 3.0 despite the dismayed screams of many software publishers.

[8] IBM did take some stabs at addressing the situation. For example, at a seminar held for the press extolling the virtues of OS/2, several attendees pointed out that the difficulty of obtaining drivers for printers and other types of hardware was hurting OS/2 in the market. An IBM employee held up a disk he claimed had several hundred drivers and announced IBM was prepared to sell the collection to all comers for $300.00. Many members of the press were utterly dazzled by this display of silliness on the part of IBM and promptly went out and bought Windows.

bought a wide variety of different printers from different manufacturers, most notably HP LaserJets, and OS/2 1.1 had no idea of what to do with them.

And, unfortunately for IBM, memory prices had remained high as well. Because OS/2 1.1 needed even more memory than OS/2 1.0, upgrade costs were around $2,000.00 per PC. And no, IBM hadn't changed its mind about a hardware/software bundle of memory and OS/2.

The company then proceeded to make the day of OS/2 developers everywhere by announcing it had licensed the NeXTStep interface from Steve Jobs's NeXT Software. Rumors immediately began to spread that NeXTStep would become a part of OS/2.

NeXTStep ran on the NeXT computer, Steve Jobs's incredibly cool black-cube desktop PC that cost $10,000.00 per unit. At that price, no one actually intended to **buy** a NeXT box, but everyone hoped someone would buy one for them so they could put it on their desk and look as cool as Steve Jobs. The NeXTStep interface was certainly state-of-the-art, with chiseled icons and slick graphics—no one had ever doubted Steve Jobs's ability to create great-looking icons. But if it were true that it was going to eventually replace Presentation Manager, why write applications for OS/2 now? Everything would have to be extensively rewritten once NeXTStep was integrated into OS/2. Better to wait. On the other hand, everyone was just sick to death of character-based interfaces. (IBM never did anything with NeXTStep.)

The market lowed and shifted about restlessly. More people went out and bought Macs. Had Apple not been in its way every bit as stupid as IBM, the company was in a position to become the Microsoft of OSs. But we all know how that turned out.

Sales of Windows 2.0 hit 50,000 units per month.

OS/2 1.2 shipped a few months later. Most people still couldn't print with it. IBM announced it was now talking to a company called Metaphor about **its** really cool OS and interface. (IBM never did anything with Metaphor.)

The lows and the bleatings became louder. The tension rose higher. It was now 1990.

Microsoft announced Windows 3.0. It looked pretty good. It was inexpensive. It supported 16MB of memory but ran OK in 4MB. The memory bubble had burst. Windows really needed a mouse. Several good programs were available for it, including spreadsheets and word processors, the most popular applications. You could print with it. It was 6 damn years after the Mac had first shipped.

The market bellowed loudly and stampeded toward Windows 3.0.

IBM shipped OS/2 1.3. It could—usually—print. It was highly functional. IBM's Desktop Software division even had a lineup of nice OS/2-specific applications available for it. When did it ship? It doesn't matter. No one cared.

Before the herd broke, IBM had one last chance to stop the stampede. In 1988, the company had formed its Desktop Software division in Milford, Connecticut. The group was deliberately staffed with young honchos from outside the company who were supposed to show IBM how to succeed in the rough-and-tumble world of PC software. In short order, Desktop Software built a fairly polished stable of OS/2 applications, including word processing, business presentation, and desktop publishing products. All the programs were scheduled to be available in Windows versions, though these were going to ship well after their OS/2 counterparts were out the door.

Alarmed at the growing presence of Windows and aware that OS/2 needed more time to build momentum in the marketplace, the Desktop Software group petitioned to meet with no less an august personage than IBM President John Akers himself to explain the situation. They had taken a close look at Windows and, despite Microsoft's soothing words, realized it presented a serious competitive challenge to OS/2. They were also aware that the development market was on the cusp; if events broke the wrong way, software publishers might be forced to abandon OS/2 if they thought Windows would allow them to meet the pent-up demand for GUI-type products on the PC. After submitting their request, they were duly granted an audience before the Big Blue throne.

At this point, IBM still had the ability to checkmate Microsoft's plans for Windows. One way was to buy a new OS from a company called GeoWorks. The company had developed a highly optimized product with a slick GUI that could run in a small hardware footprint; GeoWorks ran with amazing alacrity even on the original IBM PC. This was the path favored by the Desktop Software division.

Another option, one widely discussed within IBM and Microsoft, was to release a version of DOS with the Presentation Manager interface. And, as it had been since 1981, Digital Research was still sniffing about forlornly while proffering GEM and DR DOS. If all else failed, IBM's final option was to simply threaten Microsoft with termination of the joint development agreement between the two companies and strike out on its own. At this point, IBM still held the upper hand in the relationship and in the marketplace, and Microsoft would have had to back down.

The day of the meeting arrived, and the Desktop Software contingent, led by Product Marketing Manager for IBM Corporation Randy Hujar,[9] was escorted before IBM's reigning monarch and given the chance to make their case. Akers received a detailed briefing on the situation, as well as a series of recommendations. When the team was done, he called them "a group of good kids" and proceeded to explain the facts of life to the naïfs before him. IBM, he told them, controlled these markets and set the standards, and it always would. Bill Gates "was a nice boy," and IBM fully understood how to position OS/2 vis-à-vis Windows. It was all well taken care of. They could go back to their cubicles and not worry their precious little heads about the problem.

The Desktop Software group was then escorted out of the august presence and reoccupied their cubicles. IBM proceeded to develop a ludicrous agreement with Microsoft that said that Windows was just great for "low-end machines" (i.e., the ones that most people had) and that OS/2 was great for "high-end machines" (i.e., the ones they would one day own). Windows 3.0 shipped as planned.

IBM shut down its Desktop Software group in 1992, just in time to ensure that the division's applications wouldn't be available to support the rollout of OS/2 2.0. That same year, Akers was kicked out of the CEO position at IBM. Microsoft was estimated to have shipped approximately 30 million Windows 3.0 and 3.1 licenses by that time.

---

[9] I first met Randy when we were both product managers at Ashton-Tate.

Who Killed OS/2?

Yet, despite IBM's record of stunning marketing and sales incompetence, OS/2 refused to die. Work continued on the product despite the Microsoft tsunami, and in 1992 IBM released OS/2 2.0. This version of the product was years ahead of Windows in terms of raw functionality, and only until the release of Windows 2000 did a comparable product exist. Unlike the 16-bit Windows and OS/2 1.*x*, 2.0 was a 32-bit OS that could take full advantage of the 386, 486, and Pentium processors. It sported a powerful new "object-oriented" interface that, though initially confusing to many, made older approaches to GUIs seem toy-like in comparison. It even had decent hardware support and could print, most of the time.

IBM had also made a few improvements in its attempts to sell OS/2. It had consolidated all marketing and development efforts in its Austin, Texas, facilities; this helped provide some focus to the OS/2 effort. The new Austin unit founded the IBM Independent Vendor League (IVL), a business group chartered to help encourage the development of OS/2 books, courseware, certification exams, and similar aftermarket materials. IVL also helped launch two magazines dedicated to OS/2: *OS/2 Professional* and *OS/2 World*. In addition, several prominent online forums were founded to extol the virtues of OS/2 and encourage its use, foremost among them being Will Zachman's Canopus forum on CompuServe.

Helping the situation along was the fact that the industry was learning that Microsoft could be every bit as tough and brutal a competitor as IBM in its heyday. As the company tightened its grip on the desktop OS environment, it used its cash and intelligent marketing to drive toward dominance of the lucrative desktop applications markets. IBM's competitors were increasingly in a panic. OS/2 offered, perhaps, an opportunity to regroup and regain lost market share and revenue on a more level playing field.

Unfortunately for these hopes, although IBM had learned a few lessons, it hadn't learned enough. The aforementioned shutdown of IBM's Desktop Software group robbed OS/2 of critical application support when it needed it most. In addition, IBM had entered into yet

another OS deal, this one with Apple. This was Taligent, a joint development effort between IBM and Apple that burned up about half a billion dollars before collapsing of its own weight.

Taligent started out as an attempt to build yet another next-generation OS, which then morphed into a half-witted effort to build an OS that would run other OSs. When this proved unfeasible, Taligent decided to waste more time and money creating a series of middleware tools that no one understood or bought before someone woke up and pulled the plug on the entire fiasco. But in the meantime, the industry was abuzz with rumors that OS/2 was simply an intermediate step on the way to this newest wonder OS. Then rumors began to spread that IBM and Apple would merge and that OS/2 would soon adopt the **Macintosh** interface. OS/2 developers had heard all this before, and fortunately for IBM, many chose to ignore the idiot mutterings from Big Blue and focus on trying to sell their software.

This wasn't easy, because another lesson IBM still hadn't learned, despite the success of IVL, was the need to help software companies sell their products in order to ensure OS/2's success. The company still had no direct marketing and distribution channel programs in place to help get OS/2 applications seen and bought. Several attempts were made to convince the powers that were to create software promotional bundles with OS/2, or at the very least include trialware versions of applications in retail units of the product. All such attempts foundered.

The problem of developer support was compounded by yet another IBM mistake: the decision to incorporate Windows 3.0 and 3.1 into different versions of OS/2 2.0 and 2.1, respectively. IBM positioned OS/2 2.0 as a one-size-fits-all OS capable of running DOS, OS/2, and Windows applications. In fact, IBM regularly claimed in its marketing literature that OS/2 ran Windows better than, well, Windows. This immediately raised the question of why anyone should buy an OS/2-specific application if Windows solutions ran so much better in OS/2. It also raised a credibility issue, because it seemed unlikely to many that IBM would be able or inclined to provide increased functionality and support for what was now OS/2's bitter rival. And the existence of Windows within OS/2 allowed developers who were under pressure to develop OS/2 applications to fudge the issue by claiming that "Yes, indeed, our applications run under OS/2 (Windows) just fine."

In adopting this strategy, IBM was ignoring the lessons of history. Other attempts had been made in the past to create one-size-fits-all computers and OSs. In the early 1980s there was the Dimension computer,[10] a system that ran Apple DOS, TRS-DOS (for the RadioShack line), and CP/M via plug-in boards. What all the makers of these products soon found out was most people didn't want a one-size-fits-all product; they wanted a single product that did what they wanted and did it quickly and well. Mastering the complexities of multiple OSs within a single desktop environment was something that was of interest only to a small group of hobbyists and IT experimenters.

And even though IBM's other marketing processes had improved, the company's marketing groups still managed to provide some inadvertently hilarious lessons in how not to execute the basics. For example, IBM printed an infamous OS/2 brochure whose front piece showed a yuppie type flinging open a window to explore the wonderful new world of OS/2. Behind the window was a viscous green mass in which the yuppie had immersed his face. It looked a lot like what happens when the Blob ingests its victims.

Then there was IBM's sponsorship of college football's Fiesta Bowl (soon known internally as "The Fiasco Bowl"). To many observers, it was unclear what benefit IBM derived from slapping the name "OS/2" on a second-tier sporting event. No demographic information seemed to exist that indicated that people who watched the Fiesta Bowl were also highly interested in 32-bit OSs, and there wasn't much proof that watching a college football game would make people more inclined to rush home and demand computer resellers stock up on OS/2.

Regardless, after buying the sponsorship, the Fiesta Bowl was duly renamed the "IBM OS/2 Fiesta Bowl," and the organizers of the event asked IBM for their lineup of sponsors. "Uh, what sponsors?" the IBMers replied. At this point, IBM learned that along with the right to advertise its own products during the football game, it had also bought a series of time slots it was supposed to allot to the third-party vendors of its choice. IBM's Austin group had no experience with this sort of

---

[10] I first saw this system in action at the first PC Expo, held in 1983 in New York City's now defunct Coliseum. For years PC Expo was considered the industry's second most important trade show after COMDEX.

activity, and the news sparked a series of frantic phone calls out to local Austin businesses[11]—barbecue restaurants, transmission shops, auto dealerships, and so forth—asking if they'd like to advertise their wares during the IBM OS/2 Fiesta Bowl. (Eventually a professional was brought in to manage the process.)

But despite IBM's best efforts, OS/2 proved to be a survivor and soldiered on. The technical excellence of the product was hard to ignore. Windows, still a 16-bit application with firm DOS roots, was looking increasingly antique and out-of-date in contrast with OS/2 and its sleek, object-oriented interface. The release of Windows NT, the 32-bit OS originally intended to be the successor to Windows 3.*x*, and the announcement by Microsoft that it was developing yet another 32-bit OS for the "home" and the "desktop," a product that would eventually be known as Windows 95, were generating intense confusion in the market. And developer antagonism toward Microsoft was rising steadily. But IBM was up to the challenge. With the introduction of OS/2 3.0, the company finally managed to put a stake through OS/2's tough little heart.

The 3.0 release of OS/2 in early 1995 was accompanied by a name change. Henceforth, OS/2 was to be called OS/2 "Warp." The genesis of this truly unfortunate moniker began with IBM's habit of using code names lifted from the popular and seemingly eternal TV and movie series, *Star Trek*. Previous beta versions of OS/2 were named "Borg," "Ferengi," and "Klingon" (all alien races on the show), and the 3.0 beta version was called Warp (as in "warp speed," as in really, really fast). But as Warp neared its release date, IBM puzzled over what to call the released product, until Chairman Lou Gerstner decreed that the product should be known as . . . Warp.

It seemed an excellent idea! Earlier versions of OS/2 had been criticized by some as being slow, though this was more a function of memory requirements and setup than a technical deficiency. *Star Trek* was cool, futuristic, and familiar, a seemingly perfect match of product image to functionality. IBM moved ahead and designed a marketing campaign around a *Star Trek* theme. They rented a hall in New York City and invited hundreds to see Patrick Stewart, the then-current captain of the

---

[11] I was consulting for IBM's PSP group at this time. This organization had responsibility for all OS/2 marketing and promotion programs, and I learned about IBM's Fiesta Bowl woes firsthand from the people responsible for these programs.

starship Enterprise to help roll out the product in a gala event. (Stewart was a no-show.)

The only problem was that no one at IBM had bothered to check with Paramount, owner and guardian of the *Star Trek* franchise and all related trademarks and marketing rights, about what it thought of this idea. Now, Paramount had no right to trademark the name "Warp"— science-fiction writers had been using the word since the 1930s. But IBM's public use of "Klingon" and "Ferengi" had annoyed Paramount, and the company wasn't about to let IBM appropriate *Star Trek* for its own marketing purposes. Sharp letters were sent to IBM, and threats were voiced. As a result, IBM decided to drop any *Star Trek* marketing concepts for Warp.

This was a problem. Without a cool futuristic concept tied to the word and the product, IBM had to rely on the traditional meanings of the word. Like "Bent." "Twisted." "Warped." "Out of shape." And other, less conventional meanings. For instance, if you were alive during the 1960s (if you **remember** the 1960s), "warped" was something you became after ingesting certain substances that time and experience have shown to be bad for memory recall and possibly your genetic heritage.

The result was that IBM ended up creating a very odd advertising and marketing campaign redolent of hash brownies and magic mushrooms. Twisty "Age of Aquarius" type was splashed across ad posters all over the land, proclaiming that people were "warping" their computers. Edwin Black, publisher of *OS/2 Professional* magazine, described in an editorial of nearly having an apoplectic fit[12] as he gazed upon one such IBM ad plastered up on the walls of Chicago's O'Hare Airport. It featured Phil Jackson, former coach of the mighty Michael Jordan–led Chicago Bulls and the flower child of NBA basketball with the New York Knicks in the 1970s, smiling through his bushy mustache at the prospect of "warping" **his** computer. Everyone, of course, was thrilled at the prospect of running a psychedelic, warping OS that smoked dope and had flashbacks when you asked it to retrieve a file.

---

[12] Edwin had many such moments in his dealings with IBM's marketing and sales system. He later wrote a scathing article in *OS/2 Professional* about IBM's marketing and sales mishandling of an excellent search utility for OS/2, SearchManager, called "DOA." This was an editorial act of some courage, as IBM accounted for a large percentage of *OS/2 Professional*'s advertising budget. Edwin took over the product, renamed it "Bloodhound," and had some sales success with it before OS/2 died.

But despite even this, OS/2 continued to squirm and twist toward survival. Microsoft's increasingly public woes with the U.S. Department of Justice seemed about to slow the Windows juggernaut down a bit. The slow trickle of OS/2-specific applications coming to market began to swell. Sales of OS/2 through the retail channel became brisk. At IBM's 1994 Technical Interchange trade show, many vendors offering OS/2 applications had sold out by the event's end.[13] Although OS/2 was far from reaching parity with Windows, it was close to achieving the status of a strong second-place contender with significant market share.

Then IBM rolled out the big guns: IBM PR and Lou Gerstner himself.

~

Coup de Grace

In the pre-PC era, IBM's PR strategy was a conventional but effective "big company" approach that garnered IBM a great deal of public respect. The company invested in public charities, sponsorships of select TV and theater programs, advertising, and the usual editorial placements in a wide variety of publications to build and maintain its public image. Its approach was held up as a model of effective PR and marketing communications.

However, as was true of most IBM marketing programs, its PR program was highly centralized, not designed to communicate with its product marketing groups, and technically ignorant. This didn't work well in the new era of press reviews and analysis that sprang up in the 1980s. Powerful columnists and influencers such as John Dvorak (an OS/2 fan) and Jerry Pournelle had little interest in IBM's sponsorship of Hallmark's annual showing of *A Christmas Carol* or its contributions to the United Way. But they were very interested in discussing the newest and hottest technology, playing with the latest technical toys, and having their egos stroked by people who were knowledgeable about the industry.

Over time, IBM developed an involuntary two-track approach to PC press relations. The first track consisted of IBM's conventional PR

---

[13] I was present at this event and gave a series of presentations to OS/2 software publishers on effective high-tech marketing practices.

program, which clanked along, oblivious to its increasing irrelevance in the new world.

The second track was an unruly back channel of former and current IBM employees who talked to the press on an ad-hoc basis, churning out gossip and fueling speculation. A mini-industry of "IBM watchers" sprang up, who were dedicated to deciphering the various statements and pronouncements of the different officers, divisions, and spokespeople.

Even worse was that IBM had no formalized approach to managing its products' review cycles, a problem that has plagued IBM since the release of the IBM PC and that continues to this day. Once an IBM software product is released, the product is on its own. Not surprisingly, very few IBM software products ever receive stellar reviews.

The first body blow to the long-suffering OS/2 occurred when, in a major speech to business analysts, IBM CEO Lou Gerstner was quoted in August 1995 by the *New York Times* as saying that worrying about OSs was fighting the "last war."[14] Later in the speech, he added that it was too late for IBM to "go after the desktop." Several newspapers immediately reported this speech as an admission by IBM that OS/2 was a failure. The *New York Times* article was headlined "IBM Chief Concedes OS/2 Has Lost Desktop War."

The fallout was immediate and wide-ranging. OS/2 software vendors began to publicly question whether it made any sense to further invest in the OS. Many large corporate accounts that had committed to installing OS/2 on an enterprise level announced they were reconsidering their positions. Key advocates and columnists such as Will Zachman began to publicly question their support of OS/2.[15]

The next, and even more devastating, blow came from a completely unexpected source. In his August 6, 1995 piece in the *New York Times* "Technology Column," Peter Lewis ran a story called "OS/2 No Longer at Home at Home." It was full of juicy quotes from an IBM spokesman. Among them: "OS/2 is a great operating system" but "Sony's Betamax was a better system than VHS . . ." and "I'm going to put Windows 95 on the machines in my house."

What made these quotes truly memorable was that the source was David Barnes, IBM's Mr. OS/2 himself. Highly photogenic and comfortable in front of a crowd, Barnes had traveled thousands of miles over the

---

[14] "IBM Chief Concedes OS/2 Has Lost Desktop War." *New York Times*, August 1, 1995.

[15] On Zachman's OS/2 advocacy forum, Canopus.

previous 3 years conducting competitive demonstrations of OS/2 and Windows, had been a keynote speaker at trade shows, and had appeared on radio and TV extolling OS/2's virtues. It was as if Bill Gates had been quoted as saying that Windows was really an inferior product to OS/2 and he wouldn't be caught dead using the thing himself.

Reaction in the OS/2 community made the Gerstner faux pas seem insignificant. Online OS/2-friendly forums exploded. Tens of thousands of messages were posted electronically over the next several weeks, most asking for an explanation of Barnes's remarks. Famous long-time OS/2 aficionado James Fallows, columnist for the *Atlantic Monthly*, former editor of *U.S. News & World Report*, and a noted writer, posted several public messages[16] asking what on Earth IBM was doing.

After the Barnes story broke, IBM did nothing for several weeks. Corrections weren't published; Barnes didn't write a letter of clarification to the editor of the *New York Times*; no IBM spokesperson appeared on any online services, Usenet forums, or SIGs to correct or explain Barnes's statements.

Finally, after more OS/2 customers announced their defection from the product, IBM reacted. Barnes published a statement claiming that Lewis had taken his statements out of context. IBM assured everyone it was still committed to OS/2. Various IBM spokespeople made comforting noises. No one read any of these statements, and before Microsoft had even released Windows 95, its desktop OS, OS/2 was truly dead.

Cynics have pointed out that perhaps IBM was attempting to signal to the marketplace that it was discontinuing its support for OS/2. If this is true, it's hard to imagine a more self-defeating strategy. At the very least, IBM could have waited until after Windows 95 had shipped to judge market response. But after the Gerstner/Barnes remarks, Microsoft could have waited another year to release Windows 95. It wouldn't have mattered.

As already noted, OS/2's failure not only had a profound impact on IBM, but it also altered the fate of many companies in the industry. Perhaps the saddest case was that of SPC, the firm that through no fault of its own had years ago inadvertently yoked me to TopView for that one miserable day. SPC had divested itself of its PFS line by the late

---

[16] Including on Zachman's Canopus forum.

1980s and, via its purchase of Harvard Graphics, was for a brief period the leader in the PC presentation graphics market. SPC made a "bet-the-company" wager on IBM and OS/2 and developed InfoAlliance, a high-end OS/2 database product. Such was SPC's confidence in OS/2's future that it literally ordered its sales force to cease selling its market-leading Harvard Graphics package and concentrate on InfoAlliance. Whoops. When it became clear this bet wasn't going to pay off, SPC turned around and spent 2 years rewriting the package for Windows, but by the time the project was done, the company was out of cash and market share.

Even those companies that avoided being sucked into OS/2 development efforts ended up paying the price. Many mistook the market's failure to adopt OS/2 as a repudiation of GUIs. They had several clues this wasn't true—the enthusiastic reaction to Microsoft Excel and Word for Windows being but two examples. Apple's Macintosh success, despite that the company was held in distaste by much of corporate IT,[17] was another. But such was IBM's hold on the market's perception that many believed DOS would remain supreme on PCs for several more years.

Had companies such as Borland, Lotus, and WordPerfect committed to Windows development efforts in 1988 or 1989, they would have been in a position to compete with Microsoft on a fairly level playing field when Windows 3.0 took the market by storm in 1990 and 1991. The opportunity was certainly there; during this time period Microsoft was desperate to garner third-party support and went to great lengths to court potential developers.[18]

---

[17] Especially after Apple's "Lemmings" ad, which ran during the Super Bowl the year after its famous "1984" ad. The "Lemmings" ad featured a group of IBM-crazed corporate IT types marching to their demise over the edge of cliff while maniacally chanting "Hi ho, hi ho, it's off to work we go." IT managers worldwide developed an instant dislike of Apple, and the ad was being thrown back in the company's face years after its first and only airing. IBM would later fulfill Apple's apocalyptic vision with OS/2 and the software publishing community.

[18] From 1983 through 1989, Microsoft sent "evangelists" out to other software publishers at every opportunity, especially during trade shows. Prior to the widespread adoption of e-mail and the Internet, these events were considered prime opportunities to beg and cajole other companies to support Windows. During this time frame, the company was ready and eager to share technical specifications for Windows, do joint marketing, and make wide-ranging concessions in return for developer support. Most companies, with the exception of a handful such as Micrografix, a Texas-based publisher of graphics and drawing programs, rejected Microsoft in favor of IBM's strategic OS for the desktop, OS/2.

Much ink would be spilled in the mid-1990s over Microsoft's creation of "secret" API calls that supposedly gave it an unfair advantage over its rivals. Most of this was nonsense. What hurt these companies was not code but time—the time they had to take to play catch-up with Microsoft, which was ready to release what the market wanted: robust, GUI-based Windows products.

Even more ink has been spilled in bemoaning Microsoft's supposed perfidy in taking advantage of poor old trusting IBM in their joint venture to bring OS/2 to market. Such sympathy is wasted. IBM bears almost complete and direct responsibility for the failure of OS/2. From advertising and pricing through to positioning and naming, it's difficult to find a marketing mistake IBM **didn't** make. The truth is that by 1990, the PC market was ready to accept almost any GUI-based system that worked, and Microsoft simply provided what everyone wanted. Bill Gates is undoubtedly a very smart guy, but someone with half his brains could have whipped IBM.

What ailed IBM then and what ails it today is that the company is simply too big. Although no one has ever been able to identify exactly when a company becomes so huge that it can no longer effectively compete, by the early 1990s IBM had clearly reached that point. With 400,000+ employees and products that competed in every segment of the market in almost every country of any note, IBM of necessity had to manage and assign priorities to a welter of competing interests and initiatives. It was a task of dizzying complexity, and perhaps a business genius could have managed it. Large organizations, however, tend not to promote geniuses to top managerial positions. Geniuses tend to be monomaniacal in their focus, less than solicitous of other people's feelings, and often make those around them uneasy (a description that reminds many of Bill Gates). Smart politicians are the types who usually climb to the pinnacle of corporate success in large companies, but a company of IBM's size needs more than an affable organization man to kick it in a desired direction. Though during his tenure at IBM Lou Gerstner was lauded by the press for the company's modest turnaround, his financial accomplishments came more from cost cutting and retrenchment than renewed business growth. And shortly after Gerstner's departure, his successor announced that, yes, things were still rather slow at IBM and more layoffs would be coming.

The answer to IBM's problem, ironically, was discovered by the U.S. government in the 1970s when it attempted to break IBM up. IBM fought the government tooth and nail and eventually prevailed, allowing the company to remain an increasingly unresponsive muscle-bound giant unable to get out of its own way. By the early 1990s, John Akers decided the government had been right after all and developed a plan to split the company into several autonomous divisions. Akers was shown the door before he could put his plan in motion and IBM remained intact, but these were Pyrrhic victories. As the years progressed, IBM was forced in effect to do just as Akers recommended as it shed businesses, such as printers and PCs, in which it could no longer compete. But IBM remains big, bloated, and no longer at the center of high technology. 'Tis always better to reign in bureaucracy than serve in competition (with apologies to Milton).

seven

FRENCHMAN EATS FROG, CHOKES TO DEATH:
Borland and Philippe Kahn

From its inception, Borland International was the *Animal House* of high tech, a group of self-proclaimed software barbarians who broke all the rules and had all the fun. Led by its wide-girthed founder, Philippe Kahn, a Frenchman who started the company with no green card and very little cash, Borland seemed to lead a charmed life for the first few years of its existence. But the trouble with barbarians is their appetites. They tend to like to sit down at the table, rip off a big slab of meat from a half-cooked haunch, and eat rapidly without properly chewing their food. Combine this unfortunate habit with Kahn's Gallic background, and the stage was set for tragedy. Confronted with software's biggest frog, the Frenchman's savage nature got the best of him, and he choked to death attempting to swallow what any civilized person would have realized was a very unpalatable amphibian indeed.

Borland made its debut in the industry in a big way with the release of Turbo Pascal in November 1983. Turbo Pascal was a port to DOS and CP/M of Anders Hejlsberg's COMPAS Pascal, and it was rereleased by Borland at a price that seemed amazing at the time: $49.95, about one-tenth the price of comparable products. With a single stroke, Kahn had upset the price structure of a market category, a tactic he would employ again and again in the future. Even better for buyers was the product's capabilities: Turbo Pascal[1] integrated an editor, debugger, and compiler in what would later become known as an *integrated development environment* (IDE). The product was a runaway smash, and to this day Borland dominates the market in Pascal-based development tools.

Turbo Pascal was a breakthrough in another way. It was the first product of its type to bypass the software distribution channel and be sold directly to customers. Readers of *BYTE* magazine who bit on Borland's full-page ads for Turbo Pascal sent their 50 bucks straight to the company. Borland's marketing coup heralded the beginning of a struggle that high tech wrestles with each day: the desire of companies to bypass the intermediary and sell directly to their customers versus the power of distribution systems to "break bulk" and reach a wide audience of potential buyers quickly.

---

[1] Those interested in exploring a piece of software history can download Turbo Pascal 1.0 for free from the Borland web site (http://www.borland.com).

As befits its *Animal House* antecedents, Borland pulled off a frat house–style prank to get its advertising placed that has entered the annals of industry legend. As Turbo Pascal neared completion, the company found itself long on chutzpah but short of the cash needed to place its ad in *BYTE*. Borland dealt with the problem by inviting a *BYTE* ad salesperson to visit Borland and meet Kahn to discuss ad placement. While this individual waited outside Kahn's office, the *BYTE* ad salesperson managed to "overhear" a conversation between the company president and a company employee masquerading as a salesperson from a rival magazine discussing Borland's advertising plans with that publication. Ad salespeople having the morals of, well, software barbarians, the *BYTE* representative agreed to cut a deal that allowed Borland to place its ad in *BYTE*[2] without an up-front payment if Borland would agree to change its placement strategy and "emphasis." Borland was glad to agree, and history was made.

After Turbo Pascal's introduction, the company continued to release a steady stream of successful utilities and programs, including a keyboard macro product, a low-end database, more languages, and most famously Sidekick, the first of a short-lived class of *terminate and stay resident* (TSR) products. TSRs took advantage of an oddity in DOS that allowed them to stick around in memory after they'd been shut down. A keystroke combination recalled the product, which popped up in a window over your current application. Sidekick integrated an editor, a calculator, a phone dialer, and some other goodies in a neat little package that gave buyers an early taste of the joys of a multitasking software environment.[3]

Borland was aided in its growth by Kahn's astute handling of the media. In addition to his ability to sweet-talk the publishing side of the PC press, Kahn was also a favorite of editors and writers. Kahn played saxophone, was a karate black belt, gave good quote, and always seemed to be involved in some newsworthy antic, such as Borland's wild

---

[2] *BYTE* magazine, perhaps the microcomputer industry's most respected publication for much of the 1970s and 1980s, ceased print publication in 1998, though an online version of the magazine still exists (http://www.byte.com).

[3] The age of the TSR would prove to be short. This class of software had sharp little virtual elbows, and different programs didn't play together well. Loading more than one TSR into your system frequently led to system lockups and crashes.

toga party[4] at the 1984 COMDEX trade show. He also possessed a talent for getting under Bill Gates's skin, and the press always appreciates a good gladiatorial contest.

An example of Kahn's persuasiveness was demonstrated when he convinced *PC Magazine* to give Borland's minor-league TSR spelling and thesaurus utility, Turbo Lightning (for a while practically every product in Borland was "turboized"), front-cover status. The accompanying article was a breathless piece that discussed how Turbo Lightning was going to revolutionize . . . uh . . . spelling. (The author of the article, pundit Paul Somerson, was still living that one down years later.)

Kahn was also quick to promise end users that they too would share in the booty when Borland's conquest of the software universe was complete. He became famous in the mid-1980s for decrying the high price of software, proclaiming that it should be priced like a "book," and pointing to the pricing of Turbo Pascal as the wave of the future. The crowds, as could be expected, roared their approval, and for a while Philippe Kahn was the most popular man in software.

~

Barbarian Conquests

Borland made its first play for big-league status with its 1987 purchase of Ansa and its Paradox database. Now buried in the Corel Office suite, Paradox, first released in 1985, has never received the credit it deserves for its innovative design and breakthrough performance. The product's initial claim to fame was its introduction of *query by example* (QBE) capabilities to PC relational databases. Instead of typing in long lines of obscure queries, a Paradox user could quickly recall records by simply checking boxes from an onscreen image of the database and then save these visual queries for future use. This capability, combined with powerful form creation and scripting features, made the product a viable competitor to Ashton-Tate's dBASE and the various Xbase clones. The product often, if not always, came in first in reviews and competitive

---

[4] This is **not** the storied 1983 toga party held by Borland in San Francisco but a more impromptu affair that was the talk of that year's COMDEX.

analyses, and by the 3.0 release Paradox was widely considered to be the "best of breed" in the DBMS desktop market.

Even better from Borland's standpoint was that the product couldn't be easily cloned. The Paradox scripting language manipulated "objects" such as queries, reports, and forms within the Paradox environment and resisted compilation technology. On the other hand, Paradox was accessible enough to allow third parties to develop utilities for and extensions to the product. The combination of power, price, and third-party push helped Paradox begin to make major inroads into a market formerly dominated by Ashton-Tate and the Xbase alternatives. By the time of Borland's takeover of Ashton-Tate in 1991, Paradox owned about one-third of the market for PC desktop databases. Interestingly enough, Borland kept the price of Paradox at $695.00, then the median price for high-end database products. It seemed the software barbarian was willing to ape the ways of civilization when they suited his purposes.

After Ansa and Paradox, Borland purchased the Surpass spreadsheet from Seymour Rubinstein of WordStar fame,[5] renamed it "Quattro," and entered the spreadsheet market with barbarian zest. As part of his slash-and-burn tactics, Kahn launched what became known as a *competitive upgrade* promotion against Lotus, which had lagged in releasing its new 3.0 version of 1-2-3. The competitive upgrade works by offering the user of another product your product at a reduced price in return for the user ostensibly "turning in" her current product—a desirable marketing "twofer" because the upgrade increases your installed base while simultaneously decreasing your competition's. Quattro's pricing was initially less than the $495.00 median for spreadsheets, but as with Paradox, by 1990 it was repriced to match industry standards. The competitive upgrade was kept sharp and at hand in Borland's promotional arsenal, and periodically the company launched one when it spotted an opportunity. Wielded in the hands of barbarians, cutthroat pricing and competitive upgrades were fearsome weapons, but they were ones that more civilized warriors could also employ, as Borland would one day discover.

---

[5] Seymour Rubinstein decided to sell Surpass after determining he didn't have the resources to compete with Lotus and its market-leading 1-2-3 spreadsheet. As you would expect, Rubinstein first offered the product to MicroPro. Leon Williams, the then president of the company, asked my opinion about the purchase. I advised against it, because I thought MicroPro was having enough trouble selling word processors and was in no position to compete with Lotus. Another case of being right for the wrong reason.

In 1991, Borland reached more than $200 million in annual revenue, mainly on the strength of growing Paradox sales. Kahn was now at the height of his ambitions and looking for new conquests. Casting his fierce gaze about, it came to rest on Ashton-Tate, a wounded company that seemed ripe for the picking. Negotiations commenced between the barbarian and his intended prey. Alas, a group of smooth-talking and decadent civilized men seem to have seen the savage coming and talked him into forking over the princely sum of $440 million in Borland stock for the privilege of raising the Borland tribal standard over once mighty Ashton-Tate.

Ashton-Tate upon its purchase proved to be a pretty warty property and by no means worth what Kahn shelled out. (A sum in the neighborhood of $200 million would have been more realistic. Maybe.) The company's "crown jewel," dBASE IV, was an ugly frog that showed no inclination to turn into a prince anytime soon, and the rest of Ashton-Tate's software portfolio was pretty toad-like as well. Its MultiMate word processor was obsolete, and sales were dying. Ditto for its ChartMaster family of products. There was also an unsellable desktop-publishing program, Byline. Framework was a fine little bit of code, but the brief day of the integrateds was almost over. Ashton-Tate's Mac products weren't bad, but by 1991 it was becoming clear that Windows was going to reduce Macintosh software to a niche market, and Kahn wasn't interested in investing in it. Reduced to its essence, what Borland had bought for its $440 million was a mailing list of dBASE customers and an installed base that was quickly rotting away as developers fled dBASE into the arms of the Xbase alternatives or Borland's own Paradox.

Making matters even more problematic was Microsoft's purchase of Fox Software and its FoxPro product line for $173 million. FoxPro was considered to be the best of the Xbase clones, and many people thought that if Kahn wanted to compete in the dBASE market, this was the product he should have bought. Fox's programs were fast, stable, and state-of-the-art and could have been bought for much less than what Borland paid for Ashton-Tate. Large portions of the dBASE market had already defected to FoxPro, and Borland would need to provide a compelling reason for the migration to stop.

From an employee morale and company-building perspective, the purchase was a fairly savage affair. On the day of the Borland takeover of Ashton-Tate, Kahn, with that unique blend of tact and subtle under-standing of the sensibilities of others for which the French are so famous, flew down to Ashton-Tate's Torrance, California, headquarters so he could watch the company logo taken from the building and dumped in the office parking lot the minute the deal was official.[6] Borland's internal company briefings on the reorganization made it clear that the Ashton-Tate employees were second-class citizens in the Borland empire. Barbarians, after all, don't pussyfoot around when they swagger into conquered territory.

The conquered population demonstrated their appreciation for the barbarian point of view by performing numerous acts of petty van-dalism, destroying customer databases, and leaving the merged firm as rapidly as they could find jobs elsewhere. On the way out, many took time to call key dBASE gurus and influencers to commiserate on how it had all turned out. The whole process ended up rubbing raw nerves even rawer within what was a rapidly shrinking dBASE community.

The purchase of dBASE also unleashed a positioning conflict within Borland similar to the one that had bedeviled MicroPro years ago with its WordStar versus WordStar 2000 battle. There was no natural tech-nical synergy between the two products; they approached the task of creating applications so differently that there was no hope of ever "merging" them into one product. The Paradox development commu-nity thus paid no attention to dBASE and continued to focus on its side of things. From an emotional standpoint, Borland personnel had been taught to regard dBASE as the database product from hell. The company had even once started to build a dBASE clone (yes, Turbo Base) but had canceled it because, in the words of Kahn, "dBASE is a dirty language."[7]

From the Ashton-Tate side of things, many of the surviving employees had little incentive to care about dirty old dBASE and were uncertain about the product's future. A new version, 1.1, released before the takeover, had fixed some of 1.0's many bugs, but dBASE was no longer competitive with the clones and didn't include the long-promised

---

[6] In the interest of fairness, Kahn contacted me after the first edition of *In Search of Stupidity* was published to claim he was not present when the Ashton-Tate sign came down and in fact never visited the company's headquarters. However, other people present at the time claim he did. I leave it to readers of this book to make up their own minds about the facts of the matter.

[7] *BYTE* magazine, October 1987.

compiler. It seemed clear to many that if you wanted to survive and prosper as an employee at Borland, Paradox marketing and development was the place to be. Complicating matters was the fact that customer and developer interest was turning increasingly toward the release of Windows-based databases.

Borland only made the situation worse with the positioning strategy it finally did hammer out. In this scheme, dBASE was to be the "high-end" product, whereas Paradox was repositioned to be the "end-user" database. Borland, however, didn't reprice Paradox to reflect its new end-user status, and the Paradox development community[8] never considered throwing away the time it had invested in mastering the product in order to learn a language it had already decided it didn't like. Instead, the community just politely asked Borland when the next version of Paradox would ship, mailed in its wish lists, and continued about its business.

The dBASE community appreciated Borland's nice sentiments but was more interested in action. If Borland was going to hold onto the dBASE market, it would have to initiate a crash program of releasing high-quality, competitive products as quickly as possible. This didn't and wouldn't ever happen during Borland's stewardship of dBASE. Despite public pronouncements to the contrary, it soon became clear that Paradox remained Borland's fair-haired darling. Paradox was assigned the bulk of Borland's advertising and marketing budget for its database products. New releases of Paradox were consistently released earlier and with greater fanfare than new dBASE versions. dBASE would always be treated by Borland as the company's ugly stepchild.

By 1992, the dBASE development community, fearful that the product on which it relied for its livelihood was doomed to become a dead end, was in an irascible mood. Borland found out just how irascible at its 1992 annual developer's conference, when the dBASE attendees began shouting at the dBASE IV 1.5 product manager during a product demo. The 1.5 version would have been a smash hit in 1988,

---

[8] Some of the main social events of the Paradox community were the yearly parties held at the New Jersey home of Paradox guru Alan Zenreich, author of *Paradox Programmer's Guide* (Scott Foresman Trade, 1990) and a personal friend of mine. These parties were 2-day affairs attended by leading Paradox developers from across the nation and were much anticipated by all attendees. I attended several of these gatherings, and even after the Borland purchase of Ashton-Tate, dBASE was never discussed during the festivities.

but by 1992 it was another me-too product and there was **still** no compiler. Previous experiences with Ed Esber had taught the developers that the best way to get a company's attention was to throw a miniriot, and though Borland was a much nicer company than Ashton-Tate, people tend to revert to type under stress. Bullhorns had to be brought in to quiet the crowd, and everyone from the dBASE side of things went home in a cranky mood. Upgrade sales of dBASE IV 1.5 were very disappointing, and the migration to Microsoft's FoxPro and the other Xbase products accelerated.

~

The Object of It All

In the meantime, Philippe Kahn underwent an experience common to barbarians and pagans throughout the centuries: He had, like Constantine, a religious epiphany. In his case, revealed truth came in the guise of object-oriented programming (OOP). Having been struck down by the light, Kahn arose a changed soul determined to bring his new truth to all of Borland's products. In the future, all of them would have big heaping dollops of objects integrated into their very beings.

The result of Kahn's conversion was a promotional strategy in 1992 and 1993 that centered around telling Borland's resellers and customers about the wonders of objects and the amazing benefits their presence in your software brought to humanity. Bemused resellers nationwide packed into crowded seminar rooms throughout the United States[9] to learn about the hottest new features in the latest releases of Paradox and Quattro were instead first treated to exciting lessons on encapsulation, polymorphism, and inheritance, key elements of object-oriented code. The launch was a less-than-stellar success, as the loud sounds made by stultified attendees slipping to the floor in a deep state of unconsciousness tended to be a distraction to those who successfully remained awake.

---

[9] I attended one such seminar and still have my free copies of Paradox for Windows and DOS that were handed out at the end of the session.

And speaking of OOP, what exactly is it? This excerpt from "What is Object-Oriented Software?" by Terry Montlick of Software Design Consultants (http://www.softwaredesign.com) should explain it all to you:

> *An object is a "black box" which receives and sends messages. A black box actually contains code (sequences of computer instructions) and data (information which the instruction operates on). Traditionally, code and data have been kept apart. For example, in the C language, units of code are called functions, while units of data are called structures. Functions and structures are not formally connected in C. A C function can operate on more than one type of structure and more than one function can operate on the same structure.*

> *Not so for object-oriented software! In o-o (object-oriented) programming, code and data are merged into a single indivisible thing—an object. This has some big advantages, as you'll see in a moment. But first, here is why SDC developed the 'black box' metaphor for an object. A primary rule of object-oriented programming is this: as the user of an object, you should never need to peek inside the box!*

From this, many potential buyers of Borland software derived the idea that a) Borland software came in black boxes, and b) it was potentially dangerous to open those boxes.

All humor aside, building a promotional campaign for business software around a technology that was incomprehensible to anyone but programmers was obviously a ridiculous thing to do, but preaching religious moderation to the newly enlightened is often difficult. Kahn didn't stop with Borland's promotions, however. He began to closely supervise the development process of Borland's products, particularly that of the in-the-lab Windows version of Paradox, in order to ensure it adhered to prescribed orthodoxy. Kahn became personally involved in making sure the product had enough object-oriented capabilities, possessed the right "methods," and of course, as a newly civilized man, was garbed in an appropriate color scheme. The scheduled release date predictably slipped under these ministrations, and the introduction of Paradox for Windows scheduled for early 1992 drifted into 1993.

It's a common reaction for the newly converted to build a monument to mark the occasion of their exaltation into the faith, and Kahn decided to build his. This was a new $120 million Scotts Valley, California, office complex (observers noted the design looked suspiciously like the Microsoft campus in Redmond, Washington) that company humorists designated "Versailles." The need for this expenditure was questioned by many, because as sales of dBASE IV continued to deteriorate, the company wasn't exactly rolling in profits.

Music is also part of the ritual of worship, and Kahn, an enthusiastic amateur saxophonist and jazz aficionado, began releasing CDs featuring him and other jazz enthusiasts playing their little hearts out. The cost of producing these CDs was about $300,000.00 a pop, and they didn't turn out to be profit centers. The need for these expenditures was also questioned by many, as Borland stock slid from a high of $86.00 to about $5.00 per share. (Those who listened to the CDs proclaimed the music to be "pleasant.")

~

Gates at the Barbarian

While Philippe Kahn was being ravished by the object-oriented light, Microsoft released its Office suite in 1991 for a retail price of $495.00 and immediately began to do serious damage to its competitors in the business applications market. Microsoft Office was not so much a well-thought-out strategy as it was an attempt by Microsoft to punish Borland for all those competitive upgrade promotions the company was constantly launching at its software rivals. When the suite was first introduced, firms such as Borland, Lotus, and WordPerfect proclaimed their confidence in the best-of-breed theory of software purchasing. Customers, they said, would reject a cobbled-together bundle of inferior software in favor of buying the best product from the best company and rely on Windows and their own ingenuity to achieve whatever integration between applications they felt was needed.

The only problem with this theory was that the competition didn't have the best-of-breed products; Microsoft did. Though Quattro was always well rated by the press and usually beat Lotus 1-2-3 in head-to-head competitions, it almost invariably was an also-ran to the top-ranked product, Microsoft Excel. WordPerfect's botched release of its first Windows-based word processor had landed the one-time ruler of the category in third place. First and second places were usually fought over by Microsoft Word and Lotus's AmiPro. Microsoft PowerPoint and Lotus Freelance usually struggled for the business presentation graphics crown, but the spreadsheet and word-processing elements were the most important factors in a buyer's decision. Advantage: Microsoft.

Both Borland and WordPerfect attempted to fight back with competing office suites assembled from each other's respective products (with SPC's faded Harvard Graphics thrown into the mix), but they were unsuccessful. Not surprisingly, the new suites lacked the integration of Microsoft Office, but more important, they were bundles of second- and third-class programs competing against top-ranked contenders. Lotus SmartSuite faced a similar problem. Lotus 1-2-3 for Windows never placed higher than second in competitive face-offs and usually came in third place (a shocking comedown for the one-time category leader). AmiPro sometimes outplaced Microsoft Word, but Lotus was, after all, the **spreadsheet** company. Freelance usually placed second to PowerPoint in reviews, and the suite's database, Approach, although a decent product, wasn't well known and brought little extra credibility to the package.

~

The Fall of the Barbarian Empire

Faced with both pricing and feature disadvantages, sales of Quattro, as well as WordPerfect, 1-2-3, and others, began to sag. Shocked out of his civilized demeanor, Kahn fell back on barbarian tactics. Borland launched an inept series of promotions designed to stop erosion in Quattro sales. The company accomplished the exact opposite instead, destroying the product's credibility.

The first disaster was the Quattro "WinDOS" bundle. The promotion was Kahn's idea, and he insisted on its execution over the strenuous objections of his marketing staff, who feared the promotion would puzzle the market. WinDOS included both the DOS and Windows versions of Quattro in the same box. Once launched, it quickly became clear that Borland's Cassandras were correct: WinDOS wreaked total confusion amongst prospective buyers. Some people thought that the WinDOS "product" was a hybrid of Windows and DOS. Some thought it was a DOS product that looked like Windows. Some thought it was a special Windows version of Quattro that ran under DOS. Some figured out the box contained the complete versions of both products.

In addition to being confusing, the promotion proved to be a sales killer. It turned out that someone who wanted the Windows version of the product had little interest in the DOS version, and vice versa. Many people took advantage of Borland's generosity to help friends and neighbors handle their spreadsheet needs with a leftover Quattro for Windows or DOS. As one observer noted, "WinDOS worked like a competitive upgrade's evil twin." The promotion was hastily canceled, and Kahn, in the spirit of "Le Roi can do no wrong," fired a few of the marketing personnel who had advised against the whole fiasco.[10]

WinDOS was followed by a series of price-slashing campaigns that finished what the earlier promotion had started. Although some of the early price cuts temporarily boosted sales, this soon stopped as the market wised up and tried to calculate just how low Borland would go. The answer turned out to be $29.95 for a product that a few months earlier had an SRP of $495.00. The pricing strategy reached its nadir when Borland actually ran full-page color ads announcing "Quattro Pro—That's like being offered a Lexus for the price of a Hyundai."[11] (Apparently Borland didn't realize that the type of people who actually offer you a Lexus for the price of a Hyundai are often named "Vinnie" and have five Rolexes wrapped around their arms and a car trunk full of

---

[10] In all fairness, Kahn apparently did have some second thoughts about the promotion before its launch. At the rollout of the WinDOS promotion, which took place in England at a swanky London hotel and featured large, billowing clouds of dry ice–generated fog, a giant stage-mounted vinyl WinDOS box that inflated on cue, enough flashing lights to restore the age of disco, and similar items of bad taste, a crowd of about 1,000 people consisting of key customers and journalists was kept waiting for more than an hour while Kahn and several Borland vice presidents considered revamping or canceling the whole idea. They didn't and thus was born one of high tech's most boneheaded marketing campaigns.

[11] In my work as a marketing consultant I had used the Lexus/Hyundai comparison for years as an example of the value of credibility in positioning a product, and I was very excited to find out a major software company had actually been stupid enough to create an ad of this sort.

laptops they'll sell to you cheap.) Interest in buying Quattro turned to skepticism as people wondered why Borland had to sell it at a bargain-basement price or speculated that the company was looking to dump inventory before unloading the product.

Complicating things further was that as its woes with Quattro grew, Borland saw its clout with the U.S. channel sharply diminish. Quattro had often functioned as a loss leader for Borland, a lever it used to ensure distributors and resellers also carried generous quantities of the company's more profitable but lower-selling databases. As the spreadsheet's sales and profitability collapsed, distributors and resellers decided they needed to carry fewer Borland database products and wanted better terms on those they did stock, putting increasing pressure on Borland's bottom line.

In the meantime, Microsoft announced it was going to be shipping its long-awaited Windows database, Access, in November 1992, beating Borland's Paradox for Windows to market by 3 months. This was surprising, because Microsoft had pulled the plug on an earlier effort to develop a Windows-specific product and had started again from scratch. Borland, however, in the grip of its object-oriented fervor, had decided it wasn't going to ship Paradox for Windows until it was "right," and it wasn't right enough in 1992.

Microsoft also informed everyone that the new database would have a $99.95 introductory price and would be part of the Microsoft Office suite. Borland immediately cried foul, but it was hard to feel much sympathy for the company. After all, wasn't Paradox supposed to be an "end-user" product? That's how Microsoft was positioning Access, with the Fox line serving as its high-end "developer" product, and $695.00 for a starter DBMS seemed a bit dear.

People also remembered that before Borland purchased Ashton-Tate it had launched a competitive upgrade program against its former rival, offering dBASE users a "lite" version of Paradox for $149.95. It seemed only fair that if the software barbarians were willing to swing the price sword, they should be prepared to defend against it.

Access 1.0 met its November ship date and was greeted with generally decent reviews. The product lacked certain features prized by developers, but it was surprisingly stable for a first release, it intelligently copied many of the ease-of-use features of Paradox, and the price was certainly right. It also incorporated a specialized version of Microsoft's Visual

Basic, allowing developers to leverage their existing skills when developing applications with the new product.

The release of Access could have triggered a positioning war within Microsoft à la what was happening at Borland, but Microsoft was able to finesse the situation. The acquisition of FoxPro had been very friendly, and former Fox employees, flush with Microsoft stock options and cash, were treated well and, in the main, were happy to cooperate with their Microsoft colleagues and their new database. For example, they helped integrate Fox's heralded "Rushmore" technology, a system of binary indexing that speeded up data querying and data retrieval, into Access, a move that helped make the product more competitive with Paradox. And though over the years Access received the lion's share of Microsoft's marketing and PR attention, a situation that engendered some resentment amongst Fox acolytes, FoxPro **was** regularly updated and improved. This helped soothe wounded feelings and, just as important, kept the dBASE community (or at least Fox's portion of it) from looking for other alternatives to buy and recommend.

January 1993 saw the long-awaited arrival of Paradox for Windows 1.0 at an introductory price of $129.95, Borland's counter to Microsoft's pricing gambit. Unlike with Access, initial reactions were decidedly mixed. Paradox for Windows had serious memory management issues and many bugs (if you've read Chapter 5, this should sound familiar). Features that the developers had requested and hoped would be in the product, such as macros, referential integrity checking, and a data dictionary, were missing. Reviews of the product were polite (Philippe Kahn wasn't Ed Esber) but not enthusiastic, and many urged buyers to wait until the next release. Sales of the product were disappointing.

From the standpoint of Paradox developers, there was a bigger problem. Paradox for Windows was indeed very object oriented. In fact, it was **so** object oriented that it was a completely new system. Developing applications in it meant learning a new scripting language and starting from scratch. Existing applications couldn't be ported to the Windows version but had to be totally rewritten. Borland now had three mutually incompatible development platforms: dBASE, Paradox for DOS, and Paradox for Windows. Only Paradox for DOS had any claim to the title "best of breed," but the DOS market was rapidly shrinking.

Speaking of DOS, although it was shipping Paradox for Windows, Borland also released a new version of Paradox for DOS. It was a solid improvement over the previous product in many ways, but it still lacked many key features that had been long requested. It did have Turbo Vision, though, an object-oriented new interface that required you rewrite a great deal of your previous applications. And it had a new object-oriented version of the old script language. Then Borland had also along the way introduced ObjectVision, which was sort of a database but really wasn't. Some developers began to think that all this object stuff was getting out of hand.

Faced with this dilemma, the development community hesitated. If they were going to have to rewrite and relearn everything anyway, perhaps it made sense to take a closer look at Access and even FoxPro. Microsoft was certainly selling a great many units of both and, unlike Borland, seemed to be in good financial shape. This is an important consideration to developers, who don't want to see the companies that provide their development tools go out of business and leave them and their applications stranded. Many did take a look, and some decided that Microsoft was the place to be.

Later that year, Borland shipped a new release of Paradox for Windows that fixed the bugs, but the learning curve and rewrite issues remained. The financial news at Borland had only gotten worse in the meantime. More developers left the Borland fold.

In the meantime, Microsoft released its first version of FoxPro for Windows in January 1993 to excellent reviews. The migration from dBASE to FoxPro and other clones accelerated. In March 1993, Borland released dBASE IV 2.0. It didn't include the compiler, but you could buy it separately. It was a decent product, but DOS was becoming increasingly irrelevant. No one appreciated that little game with the compiler, either. And where was dBASE for Windows? More dBASE developers slipped away from Borland's embrace. They were joined by yet more Paradox developers who were convinced it was time to leave a sinking ship.

In 1994, Borland finally shipped its first version of dBASE for Windows. Demonstrating that the company could be every bit as obtuse as Ashton-Tate at its finest, the product lacked a compiler. It was also difficult to use and master. Sales of Paradox, dBASE, and Quattro continued to collapse. By this time, the trickle of dBASE and Paradox developers leaving Borland had become a hemorrhage.

Desperate to regain its footing, Borland bought a Windows dBASE clone from a small company called Arago and released it not long after as dBASE for Windows. Unlike its first dBASE for Windows, this was a solid, high-performance piece of code with all the features the developers wanted. Incredibly enough, it even included a compiler. At this point, Borland had two incompatible versions of dBASE for Windows, dBASE for DOS, Paradox for DOS, and Paradox for Windows to market and support. Those who weren't confused were indifferent, as fewer and fewer people were buying any Borland database. The company was on the brink of extinction, and few people wanted to invest in development tools from a firm in that condition.

By this time the Borland barbarians were restive, and in 1995 a tribal revolt (in part sparked by Phillipe Kahn awarding himself a handsome "performance" bonus of several million dollars of increasingly scarce Borland cash) led to Kahn being kicked out of the company he had founded and of which he remained chief stockholder. Borland exited the business applications market as quickly as it could, selling off Quattro[12] and Paradox to Novell. Corel then proceeded to buy WordPerfect and PresentationPerfect from Novell, combined them with its Borland acquisitions in its own office bundle, and then demonstrated how to lose millions of dollars by attempting to sell a suite of second-tier products directly against Microsoft.

Borland then decided to change its name to Inprise. Half the market thought the company was called Imprise, and when they found out they were wrong, people often looked quite comical as they attempted to reprogram their vocal cords to say the word correctly. After some time had passed, everyone got tired of a name that made you simulate a speech impediment and Inprise went back to being Borland.

The company also decided to return to its development and language roots. Despite being given up for dead, Borland successfully morphed hoary Turbo Pascal into a spiffy new development application called Delphi and crawled back from the edge of the abyss. In 2001, Borland's revenue rose 16 percent to $221 million, and profits climbed 11 percent over the prior year to $23 million. Borland ended 2001 with nearly $300 million in cash. But by 2006 the company was again in financial trouble

---

[12] Kahn drove the sale of Quattro to Novell.

and announced it was leaving the software development market for good, divesting itself of TurboPascal's various progeny. The Borland roller coaster has not yet stopped rolling.

Philippe the Barbarian was dead, but Philippe Kahn survived and went off to found Starfish Software, a company that combined the long-forgotten Sidekick program with wireless technology. Motorola purchased Starfish Software in 1998 for $400 million. Kahn then went off and founded a new start-up called LightSurf Technologies, which VeriSign bought for $270 million. He then founded FullPower Technologies. Reportedly, his table manners these days are impeccable.

eight

BRANDS FOR THE BURNING:
Intel, Motorola, and Google

THE CONCEPT OF BRANDING has always held a special allure for marketers in all industries, and high tech has by no means proved immune to its siren call. Throughout the 1990s, numerous articles, seminars, books, gurus, and websites all proclaimed the "magic of brands." An unending supply of Microsoft PowerPoint presentations placed before the High Priests of Investment Wealth, the venture capitalists (VCs), fervently declared their fealty to the brand in different ways, some promising to "establish brands," others to "drive brands to the market," and yet others to create "universal brands." The Internet frenzy led to the brand's ultimate apotheosis in the late 1990s as millions of innocent dollars were burnt on the altars of sock puppets, consumed in the name of just-in-time snacks for slackers too busy to shop for themselves, and sacrificed in uncounted numbers at America's supreme religious rite of marketing, the Super Bowl.

The benefits of brand worship are said to be many. Brands are supposed to be able to

- make sure everyone knows who's selling the stuff they're buying (brand *identity*),
- allow you to charge and sell more of your stuff (brand *premium*), and
- help you sell new stuff (brand *extension*).

But alas for the Brand Acolytes, as in many cases the Gods of Branding seemed not to hear the piteous cries for profits emanating from their frenzied followers. Millions of their dollars vanished down the maws of the gods with no measurable return on investment (ROI). The Pets.com Sock Puppet ended up being recycled as footwear for the homeless. The slackers and their attendant love handles were forced back to the brick-and-mortar stores, where they resumed laboring joylessly at the task of buying and bagging their own sustenance. Hundreds of thousands of eager-eyed dot-com twenty-somethings were detoured off the fast path of success to employment opportunities in food courts and retail service. The Gods of Branding had failed them all.

Much agony and disillusionment could have been avoided if the people had understood more about the nature of the deities they worshipped. For although brands can be powerful and mighty, they suffer from many weaknesses and limitations, and they often turn on those who fail to understand their fickle nature. The gods often turn out to have feet of clay.

~

The Nature of Brands

To ensure a sojourn at the branding altar free from sin, it's vital to understand what a brand is. First, it is not, nor can it ever be, a product or service. This is a concept difficult for many marketers to grasp. Yes, you can buy a company. And you can buy its brands. However, you can never sell these brands to the customer. All you can ever sell is products or services.

This basic fact was ignored time and again during the dot-com and application service provider (ASP) boom of the late 1990s. Branding exercises were substituted for sustainable business models. Billions of investment dollars were lost as companies poured money into expensive media and PR campaigns without first analyzing or testing whether anyone would actually buy their offerings.

The reason brands can never be sold is that they're symbols— intangible entities created and charged by dint of product excellence, unceasing PR, advertising, and good collaterals with **positive** equity. Brands live in a symbiotic relationship with products and services. If a product or service offers value and utility, a brand "rides along" with the purchase decision, whispering a soothing string of assurances into the buyer's soul that he has done the right thing. The ultimate goal of investing in a brand program is the ability to charge a premium for a product or service, to increase market share, or to do both.

Please note the emphasis on positive equity. It's quite possible for a brand's equity to change from positive to negative, and when this occurs, you no longer have a brand. Instead, you have a liability, or an *antibrand*, if you will. WordStar is a classic example of a product's brand equity changing from positive to negative. At the beginning of the 1980s, WordStar represented power and market dominance; by the 1990s, WordStar stood for hard-to-use and out-of-date.

A more recent example of this phenomenon is the gruesome fate of the aforementioned Pets.com Sock Puppet. The Sock Puppet is an example of creating a *brand component* to support a corporate branding program. The Sock Puppet followed in the footsteps of his ancestors, Speedy Alka-Seltzer and the Pillsbury Doughboy, and was a huge PR success. Everyone loved that stuffed bit of cloth with buttons attached, so much so that when Pets.com collapsed, the company announced it was selling the rights to the Sock Puppet and listed it as one of the company's assets.

This was, of course, ridiculous. Some pundits claim that brands and brand components don't die. They're wrong, and sometimes something even worse happens. The brand component upon death undergoes a horrible transmogrification and emerges from the grave in a decayed, decrepit state. This awful fate befell the Sock Puppet. He became a mortuary icon, a symbol of death and failure, an antibrand. His decayed remains showed up in a Super Bowl commercial. He appeared in numerous mocking cartoons, his pathetic body subjected to all manner of indignities (run over, squashed, dismembered, torn apart) to illustrate the foolishness of the Pets.com (and the entire "dot-bomb") strategy of pursuing brand recognition and bigness while ignoring business realities.

What was the marketing value of the Sock Puppet? Nothing—unless, perhaps, you're in the business of selling coffins. (He finally did get employment in a comparable industry: selling auto loans to people with bum credit.)

~

The Sins of Branding

But even those who have learned that a brand is a symbol often fall into error by failing to understand that a brand can arise from only two sources. The first is as a result of product success. Most brand identities spring from this source. For example, Proctor & Gamble transformed Crest from just another contender to America's leading toothpaste for decades after persuading the American Dental Association that Crest really did help prevent cavities. For a time, Crest was the only toothpaste able to make this claim, and the moms and dads of America flocked to buy a product that could objectively back up its claim to be "better." Building upon this success, Proctor & Gamble was able to build a brand around Crest, introducing over time an entire family of related Crest-brand products including mouthwash, dental accessories, and variants of the toothpaste.

In high tech, most brand identities have also been built upon product success. Apple's powerful brand image flows from its introduction of the Macintosh computer in 1984. From this point until the early 1990s, the Macintosh was clearly superior to other systems in ease of use and functionality,[1] and many argue this superiority continues. And though it has become common practice for many to denigrate Microsoft technology, during the 1980s and early 1990s most of the company's applications, particularly Microsoft Excel, Microsoft Word, and PowerPoint, received favorable press mentions and often beat (or at least equaled) their competition in head-to-head comparisons.

The second source of brand identity is a branding program. This type of program is a deliberate attempt to create brand identity and recognition via massive PR and marketing campaigns. Such efforts are expensive, and usually only large companies with established product lines can afford them. Remember, you can't sell a brand—you can sell only a product or service. That means every dollar spent on their creation comes out of your marketing and sales budget. It can be difficult, though not impossible, for even large companies to calculate how many incremental dollars a branding program is generating. But if you have the resources and money to execute one, over time a corporate branding campaign can build tremendous market awareness for your products and company while also acting as a formidable barrier to market entry for your competition.

A second great error many marketers fall into is failing to understand the limitations and requirements of brand creation. For example, just because your products have high name recognition doesn't mean people will automatically buy them. Once Windows-equipped PCs had caught up to the Mac (or had at least become good enough) in terms of ease of use and flexibility, Apple's market share rapidly dwindled. In place

---

[1] However, this wasn't true in terms of stability and reliability. By the mid-1990s, Windows NT was widely acknowledged to be superior to the aging Mac OS in this regard.

of technical superiority, Apple has substituted "coolness" and innovative design. But this carries you only so far in high tech. Apple's current worldwide 3 percent to 4 percent market share in sales of new computer hardware attests to this. Everyone knows about Apple; not everyone buys a Macintosh (though the public does love to buy iPods, which it then connects to their PCs for the purpose of, uh, "sampling" music via Internet-based peer-to-peer networks).

The PC market also taught IBM the limits of branding. The Silicon Beast the company unleashed in 1981 made many of IBM's brand intangibles—reputation, safety, and market leadership—less important. Over time, the ability of former college student Michael Dell, who started his business assembling PCs in his dorm room, to manufacture desktop computers more cost-effectively than IBM has proved to be a more powerful market incentive than IBM's lofty reputation. IBM had the point driven home by the collapse of its PS/2 effort.

Nor do brands allow you to simply raise prices at will. Many companies learned this lesson the hard way. Throughout the 1980s, Porsche and Mercedes raised the prices of their products seemingly in defiance of the laws of economics as consumers developed a thirst for German engineering. When they were done, by the early 1990s a fun little two-seater, such as the Porsche 944, that you could have bought for $14,000.00 in 1982 cost almost $50,000.00, and a small family sedan, the Mercedes Benz 190, that initially went for $15,000.00 cost $45,000.00. Then Mazda introduced the Miata for about $15,000.00, and Porsche's sales disappeared. Toyota and Nissan introduced full-sized luxury sedans for $30,000.00, and Mercedes gave up U.S. market share and profits by the bucketful. IBM also learned this lesson when it introduced OS/2 in 1987 with a price tag of $340.00, a sticker-shock contrast to the $60.00 price tag buyers had become accustomed to seeing for the current version of DOS.

Changing market tides can also threaten the effectiveness of a branding program. During the height of the Internet bubble, Sun launched an extensive branding campaign entitled "Critical Decision." The ad's look was a hybrid blend of *Mission Impossible* and *The Matrix* and featured young metrosexuals dressed in black raincoats careening around dark, rain-slicked streets in pursuit of one another while being cheered on by desirable women wearing slash-red lipstick. The rationale behind all this high-tech hoopla was the servers the lean-cheeked hero of the piece was going to buy for the corporate IT department. After the geek vision of what Tom Cruise would look like if he had a computer science degree decided that "we're going with Sun," the ad cut away to a scene of a glowing phosphorescent ball rising with a neck snapping "whoosh" through the center of a boardroom around which was seated upper management. The ad ended with a sonorous voice proclaiming that "Sun" was "the dot in dot-com." The purpose of the ad was to tie Sun in the minds of the ad's viewers with all things Internet and, after innumerable airings, was starting to succeed in doing just that.

Then the bubble burst and so did Sun's dot. All of a sudden, Sun was the "dot in dot-bomb." One blogger referred to the dot as a black hole down which Sun's profits were disappearing. A presenter at an industry conference called the ad "Critical Unemployment Decision." Sun defended its "dot" branding strategy bravely at first and then quietly shelved the ad and the campaign, having nothing to show for expenditures of millions of dollars except sarcasm and a negative impression of the company.

The ability to extend brands can also be sharply limited. On the software side of high tech, companies such as Lotus, WordPerfect, Borland, and most notably Microsoft have built brand strategies focused on superior products and then attempted to extend their success to other products and markets. This isn't to say that the process is always successful. If your product isn't judged by the market to be equal or superior to the competition, brand identity is no guarantor of success. For instance, do you think that because you've (Lotus) created the market's best-selling spreadsheet (1-2-3), you can sell a new word processor (Manuscript)? Or because you're selling word processors (WordPerfect) like there's no tomorrow, you can also sell a database (DataPerfect)?

Finally, brands must be defended. This sounds logical and easy, but high-tech companies are often too arrogant to want to bother. Don't people understand that all this technology is . . . well . . . complicated? Don't they realize America's geeks are smarter than they are and understand this stuff? Haven't they learned that they need to be guided by an elite corps of intellectuals who had difficulty getting dates in high school and danced with themselves at the senior prom? In 1994, Intel thought so.

By the early 1990s, the commoditization of the computer market, sparked by the unleashing of IBM's Silicon Beast, was almost complete. Prior to this, if you had started talking about "microprocessors" to computer buyers, you'd as often as not have gotten a blank stare. People bought an IBM or a Mac, not a "chip." But purchasers were increasingly focusing on the functionality of the computers they bought, not intangible brand attributes. If a computer was fast, cheap, and reliable enough, and the company selling it provided decent service, people would buy it. Who really cared what company made it?

~

The Great Pentium Bunny Roast: Intel Inside

In this environment, semiconductor giant Intel spotted an opportunity. Earlier in its history, the company had launched a marketing campaign aimed at IT types that was designed to convince them they should be concerned about whether their computers were built around Intel's 386 processor. The program had been fairly successful, and now Intel believed it was time to be more ambitious and make Intel a household name. Though people increasingly cared less about what company manufactured their PC, they still wanted to compare their purchases and brag about them. As a consequence, computer owners had begun to worry about the specifications and speed of their processors[2] in much the same way that car owners obsess over the horsepower and cylinder specs of their respective buggies.

Intel reasoned that if people were going to worry about their microprocessors, the company might as well make them worry about not

---

[2] This obsession led to the phenomenon of *overclocking*, the unauthorized (by the manufacturer) boosting of a microprocessor's speed by ratcheting up its designated clock speed. The first modern overclockers were purchasers of the original IBM AT, who discovered they could open their units and easily replace the 6 MHz crystal that governed the AT's 80286 chip with a 8 MHz unit. (In point of fact, the 80286 chip in the AT was an 8 MHz unit.) The author occasionally indulges in this nefarious practice and has a collection of fried chips and motherboards to prove it.

having one made by Intel. And while Intel was at it, the company should provide disincentives to computer manufacturers in the rapidly growing home market for PCs from using anything other than Intel microprocessors inside the boxes being purchased by Joe and Josephine America. These dual motivations gave birth to the "Intel Inside" program, the most massive consumer branding campaign high tech has ever seen. The Bunny People were released on an unsuspecting world.

Intel Inside consists of two key components. The first, and perhaps most significant on a long-term basis, is the marketing development funds (MDF) (or bribe, depending on your point of view[3]) aspect of the program. Largely hidden from public view, Intel's MDF systems work by kicking back to manufacturers an average of 6 percent of the total average selling price of the company's worldwide monthly microprocessor shipments. In return, computer makers agree to display the Intel Inside label on their computers and in their advertisements.

The accrued MDF funds don't go directly to the vendors. Instead, Intel deposits the money in an Intel-managed account the manufacturers must use to pay for print, Web, TV, or radio advertising for their Intel-based systems. If they don't use the funding within 12 months, they lose it.

All Intel Inside participants must submit every ad, regardless of medium, to Intel for approval. Ads are checked for compliance with Intel corporate identity standards for

- size,
- color,
- prominence of Intel's logo,
- verbiage in the accompanying taglines, and
- click-throughs to Intel websites for Web advertising.

Intel also "manages" the percentage of the funds that vendors must use for advertising in each medium. Helping Intel manage the process is a 100-page manual of regulations that even dictates how ad copy must be written. Failing to follow Intel's guidelines and committing even

---

[3] MDF plays a similar role in the software industry. In 1988, I spent a day in Buffalo, New York, handing out what are called *spifs* (cash payments) to telemarketers at computer distributor Ingram Micro every time they sold a package of WordStar 2000.

a minor infraction can lead to all MDF funds being frozen. Adding a product that uses a non-Intel chip to an existing line leads to forfeiture of all Intel MDF for that line. The vendor must establish a new product line to maintain access to its Intel Inside funds.

Intel Inside has proven very successful in locking Intel's competitors out of the top end of the market. Of the top-ten PC makers, only HP currently uses non-Intel chips in its business desktop lines, though nine of the ten top PC makers use non-Intel chips in brands targeted at the consumer and small office/home office (SOHO) markets. Computer giant Dell, despite nonstop flirtations with Intel's main rival Advanced Micro Devices (AMD) that were designed to keep Intel honest, remained an Intel-only shop until recently and has only grudgingly admitted a small number of AMD systems into its product lineup.

Invasion of the Bunny People

The second and far more visible aspect of Intel Inside is a massive media campaign consisting of a series of ads and commercials featuring all sorts of jiggly, jiving critters. The first generation of Intel media pitchmen were known as the "Bunny People": dancing "technicians" who leaped around in the "clean suits" worn by the people who work in semiconductor fabrication plants. Just like real rabbits, the Bunny People have been supplanted by numerous descendants, including the Blue Man Group and animated aliens who look like Bunny People whose genes have been subjected to nuclear radiation in a hidden lab. In addition to the Bunny People, Intel also created a jingle (the company calls it a "signature ID audio-visual logo") placement program—that ubiquitous 3-second tad-dah-tad-DAH song snippet millions of Americans have had pounded into their subconscious during a Dell or Gateway TV ad.

The main thrust of Intel's media campaign was to convince people that computers are more fun, exciting, and colorful if they have Intel inside, and after spending a great deal of money, Intel succeeded in doing just that. Millions of people knew about Intel (though many weren't precisely sure what they knew), bought computers that had Intel inside, and were confident that in doing so they had assured themselves of the very best computing experience they could have. That's because their computers had Intel inside, and that was a good thing because . . . Intel had spent a lot of money to hire dancing Bunny People to say so . . . and because it costs a lot of money to hire dancing Bunny People, lots of people must be buying Intel . . . so Intel has lots of money to spend on dancing Bunny People and that's . . . a good thing!

By 1994, the Intel Inside program had built up a full head of steam, and that was a good thing, too, because Intel was about to introduce its Pentium chip, a major product and marketing milestone for the company. Prior to the Pentium, Intel had identified chips via a series of numbers that also corresponded to the chip's ancestry. The 286 was the second generation of the 8086 line, the 386 the third generation, and so on. However, Intel had been told by a very unsympathetic trademark office that it wouldn't be granted a trademark on a series of numbers, and that anyone could call their chip a "486" if they felt like it. Intel promptly renamed its 586 the "Pentium," and the Bunny People were instructed to leap about with enthusiasm to celebrate the event.

People responded favorably to all of this frantic dancing, and new Pentium-based computers flew off the shelves. The computers all seemed to work very well, undoubtedly because of the Intel inside them, and America was a happy, happy place. And then a disturbing serpent appeared in Intel's sales paradise as a rumor spread through the Internet and the media about a flaw in Intel's latest microprocessor. It appeared the Pentium inside in your computer couldn't . . . well . . . count.

The Rabbits Fail Math

The problem was with the Pentium's *floating-point unit* (FPU). An FPU speeds up the operations of software that does extensive calculations involving decimal-point math. Unlike previous Intel microprocessors, all new 58 . . . er . . . Pentiums integrated an FPU directly into the chip itself. Prior to this, if you wanted to obtain the benefits of an FPU, you often had to purchase a separate chip, usually called a *math coprocessor*, and install it inside your PC. Most people didn't bother; only a handful of software packages made much use of FPU math operations.[4] But people

---

[4] Foremost among the applications supporting the Intel's FPU chips was 1-2-3 from Lotus. For the first several years of its existence, 1-2-3 almost exclusively drove sales of Intel math chips. Interestingly enough, Intel also had a text coprocessor it periodically marketed to word-processing companies, but none of them ever developed for it.

who were concerned about math operations did buy them or bought chips that had FPU capabilities, and being math types, they tended to be quite picky about the answers the chips provided.

One of these picky people was Thomas Nicely, a math professor at Virginia's Lynchburg College. In the summer of 1994, while checking the sum of the reciprocals of a large collection of prime numbers on his Pentium-based computer, Nicely noticed the answers differed significantly from the projected correct values. He tracked the error down to the Pentium by running his calculations on an older system that used a previous generation 486 chip. This unit spit out the right answers.

Confirmation in hand, Nicely promptly sent off some inquiries to Intel about his results. Intel, wrapped up in the care and feeding of its Bunny People, ignored him. Nicely thereupon posted a general notice on the Internet asking for others to confirm his findings. Intel, after realizing Nicely was not going away, talked of hiring the professor as a "consultant," and Nicely signed a nondisclosure agreement that basically said he wouldn't discuss further developments on the issue. The cat, however, was out of the bag—to Nicely's, and Intel's, great surprise.

What was actually happening inside the Pentium was fairly obscure (except to picky math people). The Pentium contains what are called *lookup tables*, rows of values embedded in the chip that speed up math calculations. When creating these tables, someone had put a zero in one of the columns. What should have looked something like this:

123456789

looked something like this instead:

123456089

The real-world results of that misplaced zero were that the Pentium would give incorrect answers on numbers that went past four decimals. What should have read

5505001/294911 = 18.666651973 *(486 with FPU)*

instead came out as

5505001/294911 = 18.66600093 *(Pentium)*

Making matters worse for Intel was that as the investigation into the Pentium's problems continued, other, even more obscure problems surfaced with the chip's math processing.

As Intel was quick to tell everyone, a bug in a microprocessor's embedded code or data isn't a new phenomenon. An *errata sheet,* a document listing known problems with a chip, accompanies practically every major CPU released by Intel, Motorola, AMD, and so forth. Engineers are used to dealing with these problems and devising workarounds. Usually, the chip's maker issues a software patch to deal with any programming or application issues, the fabrication plant makes an inline change to its manufacturing process, and that's that. After all, these things happen, and Intel had never promised you a rose garden.

Um, well, yes, it had. Somehow, as the Bunny People had leaped and cavorted on the screens of America's TVs, they had failed to mention errata sheets. Software patches. Workarounds. They hadn't mentioned those at all! Millions of computer buyers were confused and amazed.

Intel's actions subsequent to the disclosure of the Pentium's FPU faux pas epitomized techno-geek stupidity at its worst. As news about the problem spread, Intel announced that

. . . an error is only likely to occur [about] once in nine billion random floating point divides . . . an average spreadsheet user could encounter this subtle flaw once in every 27,000 years of use.

Critics responded by noting that although it might be unlikely you'd get a wrong answer, if your calculation met the right conditions you could be **sure** of getting a wrong answer. And worse, there was no way of knowing **whether** you had gotten a wrong answer. In the meantime, IBM halted shipment of Pentium-based computers (which wasn't that big a deal because they were still selling more of the older 486 units) and told everyone that "Common spreadsheet programs, recalculating for 15 minutes a day, could produce Pentium-related errors as often as once every 24 days." Wow! That sure sounded more often than 27,000 years!

Then it was disclosed that Intel had known that the Pentium flunked math before it shipped and hadn't bothered to tell the public. OK, it would have been odd to have the Bunny People dancing around with signs on their chests that proclaimed "1 + 1 = 3," but still! We the people expected our Intels inside to be able to count, for God's sake.

Not content to leave bad enough alone, Intel then compounded what was a rapidly growing PR nightmare by having Intel CEO Andrew Grove issue an apology over the Internet while the company was simultaneously telling everyone it wasn't planning a mass recall of the Pentium and intended to sell its existing inventory of math-challenged chips until it was exhausted. After this you could presumably buy a computer that counted correctly. At this point the Bunny People were leaping about to the point of cardiac infarct, but not many people were watching them anymore. People were starting to get really angry or were telling mean jokes about the Pentium. Jokes like this:

> **Question:** How many Pentium designers does it take to screw in a lightbulb?
>
> **Answer:** 1.99904274017, but that's close enough for nontechnical people.

> **Question:** Complete the following word analogy: Add is to Subtract as Multiply is to
>
> **a)** Divide
>
> **b)** Round
>
> **c)** Random
>
> **d)** On a Pentium, all of the above

Top Ten New Intel Slogans for the Pentium

9.9999973251 It's a FLAW, Dammit, not a Bug

8.9999163362 It's Close Enough, We Say So

7.9999414610 Nearly 300 Correct Opcodes

6.9999831538 You Don't Need to Know What's Inside

5.9999835137 Redefining the PC—and Mathematics As Well

4.9999999021 We Fixed It, Really

3.9998245917 Division Considered Harmful

2.9991523619 Why Do You Think They Call It *Floating* Point?

1.9999103517 We're Looking for a Few Good Flaws

0.9999999998 The Errata Inside

Intel didn't think these jokes were funny at all, but the company wasn't yet done exploring the depths of marketing stupidity. Shortly after Grove's unconvincing Internet mea culpa, Intel announced that yeah, OK, for all those whiners out there, yeah, the company will swap out your Pentium if you're prepared to explain why you need a computer chip that can count right. And buddy, the explanation had better be good.

By now the Bunny People were achieving leaps of absolutely stratospheric heights, but no one was watching, no one at all. A new joke about the Pentium began making the Internet rounds. It wasn't that funny, but to a great many people, it sounded highly accurate:

> **Question:** What's another name for the "Intel Inside" sticker they put on Pentiums?
>
> **Answer:** Warning label.

The Dark Bunny Dream of Andy Grove

At this juncture, rumors began to spread that members of Intel's PR and marketing groups, perhaps even Andy Grove himself, were suffering from a recurrent dream, a terrible nightmare that some began calling "The Dark Bunny Dream of Andy Grove." They described it like this:

> *In the dream I am always Andy Grove, and the dream always begins the same way. I am looking at a typical American town on a typical American day. The yellow sun shines brightly in a royal blue sky spread over a sea of prim tract houses of varying tasteful hues, each placed with geometrical precision in the center of a perfect green lawn. A neat, white picket fence surrounds every home, and each garage holds two cars, at least one being a sensible and reliable Japanese import. (Yes, we're all Americans here, but we need to make sure we get to work on time every day!)*
>
> *In each perfect house is a perfect PC, all of which have Intel inside. This is a good thing because . . . Intel had spent a lot of money to hire dancing Bunny People to say so . . . and because it costs a lot of money to hire . . . well, we already covered this. In any event, each perfect PC has become an integral part of each perfect family's productive and happy life. As the dream continues, I (Andy) realize I am floating above the home of Joe and Josephine America and their son, Joe America Jr. I have taken the*

form of a techno-ghost, an unseen spirit who can hear and see everything that is going on in the Americas' home. But today all is not well. I feel more than see the ominous dark cloud that appears on the horizon and rushes toward their snug little abode. Quickly, before the black billows can reach me, I sink through the roof of the home below me.

Once inside I see that, like everyone else on their block, the Americas have a PC with Intel inside. Dad comes home each night to use the PC to catch up on some office work and check sports scores across the nation. Mom uses the PC to store recipes and manage her family's busy social calendar. Junior uses the PC to help him in his schoolwork as he prepares to become the sensitive and caring yet assertive and forceful high-wage earner his parents know he can be.

As I drift through the Americas' home I pass by the kitchen and see a woman sitting at the table of a dinette set with her head in her hands, shoulders shaking from the silent sobs that rack her body. It is Josephine America. On a table beside her is a letter she has just opened. What news can it contain to cause her such grief?

At the same time, I hear the wheels of Joe America's Honda crunch on the gravel driveway, then the slam of the car door and the sound of Joe's footsteps proceeding to the front entrance. When Joe returns home from work he normally comes bounding into the house to greet Josephine with a hug and a kiss, but today he hesitates to enter, his hand frozen on the doorknob as some unseen force, some unknown instinct, warns him that something is wrong. Very wrong. Inside, Josephine has heard him. Gathering up the letter, she steels herself for the ordeal ahead. The next few minutes will be hard, terribly hard, but she must be strong. For him. (Outside the home the day darkens as thunderclouds build rapidly above the Americas' home.)

Gathering up his nerve, Joe turns the knob and enters his house to see a grave-looking Josephine facing him, holding the letter by her side. Neither says a word for several seconds. In the stillness, the distance between them seems to stretch like Turkish taffy. Finally, Joe breaks the silence.

Joe: (Quietly) Hello, Josephine. What is it?

Josephine: Hi, Joe. We need to talk.

Joe: (Again, quietly) I can see that. (Long pause.) What's the problem? What's wrong? I assume it has something to do with that letter?

Josephine: Yes, Joe, it does.

Joe: What does it say, Josephine? Are you ill? Has someone died?

Josephine: No, Joe. It's about Joe Junior.

Joe: Joe Junior? What's wrong, Josephine? Has *he* been hurt? Is he ill?

Josephine: No, Joe, he's OK. Physically, he's OK.

Joe: Then what is it, Josephine? For God's sake, tell me.

Josephine: (Hands Joe the letter.) Joe Junior can't count, Joe. This report from school says he has the mathematical abilities of algae. A potato can multiply better than Joe Junior. The only thing Joe Junior can subtract is food from our refrigerator. His teacher feels that to allow him to add his genes to the pool would be a crime against computation. (Thunder crashes outside the Americas' home as the storm begins.)

Joe: (Hoarsely) My God, Josephine! How could this have happened? Who is responsible?

Josephine: It's the computer, Joe. It can't count.

Joe: You mean, our state-of-the-art PC with Intel inside? The computer that Joe Junior uses to do his homework and spends all his spare time playing Alien Invasion on? That computer?

Josephine: Yes, Joe. It's the Pentium inside the computer. It can't count. It's in all the newspapers. On TV. Everyone's talking about it. It has made our boy dumber than DOS.

Joe: My God. My God. I can't . . . quite . . . comprehend this. Not yet. That boy had all the talent in the world. I always knew Joe Junior was destined for greater things, bigger things than I could ever aspire to. He was going to graduate from an Ivy League school. Get his graduate degree, maybe an MBA. I hear there's something big coming along, something called the Internet. All the guys at work are talking about it. They say it's huge, really huge. They say it's going to change everything, that one day we'll all be buying toys, groceries, furniture, even pet food on the Internet. I thought Joe Junior might be part of that—get rich, retire young, buy us a retirement home in Florida, make the old man proud.

But none of that is going to happen now. What can a boy who can't count aspire to? A life in middle management at Taco Bell overseeing the chalupa and chimichangas stations? A permanent spot in french fry preparation at McDonald's? A job as an apparel folding and hanger specialist at The Gap?

(Joe walks over to the living room couch, sinks down in despair, and buries his head in his hands, a broken man. Josephine sits next to him and puts her arm around his shoulders. They are silent for a minute. Suddenly Joe sits up, resolve stiffening his spine.)

Joe: Well, we're not going to sit here like the other sheep and take it, Josephine. Not the Americas! Those callous, cold-hearted corporate bastards, putting the almighty buck over our son's opportunity to be one of America's top one-percent wage earners! They're not going to get away with selling us a computer that can't count! They're not going to get away with destroying our son's future! I tell you, Josephine, we're going to get justice. We're going to fight for what's right! We're going to sue!

And I wake up screaming.

Joe and Josephine were as good as their word, and several class action lawsuits were filed against Intel. At this point, someone at the company finally yanked the IPU (idiot processing unit) out of the company's PR and marketing machine, and Intel capitulated. It agreed to replace its faulty Pentium unconditionally to anyone who asked and announced that the flawed chips[5] were heading to the landfill. By the time it was all over, the whole mess ended up costing Intel about $500 million.

The Bunnies Hop to It

It didn't have to happen this way. But Intel had embarked on a corporate branding program aimed at consumers without understanding the ramifications of its actions. The company had spent millions of dollars promising people that having an Intel inside their computers would make their machines, and by extension their lives, better. Once publicity and perception had compromised this promise, it was incumbent upon Intel to react immediately to redeem itself. Taking refuge in technical minutiae and engineering doublespeak wasn't an option. Instead, Intel had to chart a course of

- groveling;
- groveling mixed with effusive apologies;
- immediate promises to make it all better;
- the ritual execution of several middle managers, if necessary; and
- if absolutely necessary, the ritual execution of several selected members of upper management, up to and including the CEO (think Enron).

Intel could have saved itself tens, perhaps hundreds, of millions of dollars if the company had immediately offered to replace any "defective" chip, no questions asked. Far fewer people than the number who actually did ask for new chips would have bothered, but the hysteria whipped up by the whole mess roiled the market and raised awareness and concern over the issue.

---

[5] Well, most of them. For a while there was a lively gray market for cheap "defective" Pentiums.

Still, when it was all over, Intel seemed to recover rather nicely from the whole fiasco. In 1994, people were buying PCs like there was no tomorrow, and Intel had the millions available to learn its lesson. These days, the company's website brags that

> *Today, the Intel Inside Program is one of the world's largest co-operative marketing programs, supported by some 1,000 PC makers who are licensed to use the Intel Inside logos. Since the program's inception in 1991, well over $7 billion has been invested by Intel and computer manufacturers in advertising that carried the Intel Inside logos. This has created an estimated 500 billion impressions, while building Intel's worldwide name. Today the Intel brand is one of the top ten known-brands in the world, in a class with Coke, Disney and McDonalds, according to various rankings.*

It's hard to argue with success like that! And, after all, though bunnies know how to multiply, whoever said they could count?

~

Digital DNA: A Day in the Life of Alfred E. Motorola

It's a hard fact of life for the hardware guys and gals of high tech that it's usually the software geeks who get most of the glory. When software people code a software failure, they usually look like their reach exceeded their grasp; when hardware types build a flop, they look like dorks. With software, a timely patch can often erase the ugliest blemish; with hardware, mistakes are set in silicon, so to speak.

The Loneliness of Being Hardware

A fairly recent example of this principle in action occurred with the release of Palm Inc.'s m130 handheld computer. Before it released its latest personal digital assistant (PDA) in March 2002, Palm bragged that the device's 16-bit screen could display more than 64,000 different colors, but it turned out the m130 could actually show far fewer. Exactly **how** many fewer was a matter of some dispute. A spokesperson for the company was quoted as saying that by "blending techniques," such as combining nearby pixels, the m130 could display 58,000 "color combinations," which isn't quite the same thing as 64,000 colors. Palm profusely apologized for its mistake but made no offer to take its drabber-than-expected PDAs back despite the screams of some annoyed buyers. It **did** tell everyone it was busy thinking about some way to make it up to its disappointed customers. Industry wits immediately suggested that every m130 be shipped with a big box of Crayola crayons.

No, it's not fair, but that's the way it is.

Oh, there are a couple of exceptions. A few people know who Michael Dell is, though most people think he's that young guy who says "Dude!" in all those TV commercials. But Dell is really a boring company once you get to know it. Its main business is selling large numbers of square beige computers shipped in square white boxes. It's a great business, and Dell is a very, very successful company, but there's not much glamour there. Dell isn't cool, and it isn't glorious.

Then there's the guy (Ted Waite of Gateway) who talks to the cow, but cows aren't very cool (though the cow is kind of funny). And his company is losing a ton of money. That's not very glorious.

And maybe Scott McNealy of Sun Microsystems? Well, that's a tough one. He spends most of his time talking about Java and the Internet, though the company actually makes its money selling expensive computers running some incomprehensible OS called UNIX. Isn't Java software?

There **is** Steve Jobs of Apple. Jobs has a genius for hiring people who can design wonderfully colored and shaped computers that about 4 percent of the market wants to buy. He's the guy who brought us the movie *Finding Nemo* and Buzz Lightyear, and he also looks pretty sharp in Nehru shirts. Some guy from the television show *ER* even played him in that interesting but completely inaccurate movie *The Pirates of Silicon Valley*. Yeah, Steve Jobs is pretty cool. Too bad more people don't use his computers.

But after that it all becomes kind of fuzzy. Who's the Father (or Mother) of the PalmPilot? Who's the Disk Drive King? The God of Monitors? The Queen of Keyboards? The Prince of Uninterruptible Power Supplies? The Master of Removable Media?

No one knows. No one cares. It's tough to be in hardware.

On the software side, however, superstars abound. There's Bill Gates. Paul Allen. Steve Ballmer. Larry Ellison. Marc Andreessen. Steve Case. Peter Norton. Dan Bricklin. Ray Noorda. That Linux guy from Sweden—or is it Norway?—Linus Torvalds? Some incomprehensible Englishman named Tim Berners-Lee whom everyone calls "the Father of the Web." Heck, even Gary Kildall is famous just for failing big time. Michael Cowpland of Corel used to be pretty well known too (though most people remember him for that wedding-day picture of his trophy wife draped across a Lamborghini[6]).

There is, however, one hardware company that has some major media mojo attached to it. After years of dancing Bunny People, the Blue Man Group, and hyperactive space aliens, that company is Intel. Microprocessors are the hardware heart of the technology revolution, and Intel makes them. Most people aren't exactly sure how a microprocessor works, but they do know Intel produces a lot of them and many know they have an Intel in their computer. Intel is the semiconductor industry's ultimate glamour boy, hardware's Ken doll.

But as we all know, envy exists in this world. Our Ken has a jealous rival, someone who looks at our clean-cut builder of CPUs from the periphery of the admiring throng and grinds his teeth in frustration. "Why is everyone so crazy about him?" our hardware Iago wonders. "I make CPUs too. I'm a multibillion-dollar company. My technology helps drive commerce and industry worldwide. Why doesn't anyone care about me?"

Too frustrated to watch anymore, the observer turns away and strides by us. A quick glance at his countenance confirms his identity. Who else possesses that peculiar combination of dull stare, pockmarked skin, sandy hair, prominent dental gap, and eternally vacant expression?

Yes, that's him all right. Alfred E. Motorola.

Memories of a Crushing Blow

Motorola has envied Intel's marketing prowess since the companies first clashed in the early 1980s during the rollout of their respective 16-bit

---

[6] She looked marvelous.

microprocessors. Motorola had the better chip, but Intel had "Crush," a prototypical kill-the-competition campaign put together by William H. Davidow. Described in Davidow's book, *Marketing High Technology* (Free Press, 1986), Crush integrated PR, marketing communications, and advertising in a comprehensive effort to convince customers that Intel's ability to outdevelop, outsupport, and outsell the competition made an investment in Motorola's technology a bad bet regardless of technical merit. Motorola was caught flat-footed by Crush and could never develop a credible response. The company ended up ceding the bulk of the glamorous and profitable market for general-purpose microprocessors to Intel.

Motorola has never forgotten Crush, and the success of Intel Inside only rubbed salt in the wound over the years. In 1999, the company decided it couldn't stand it anymore and that it too needed to have a big corporate branding program. Thus was born Motorola's "Digital DNA" program, a waste of $65 million that demonstrated the company had learned little from the body slam Intel dealt it years before.

Bad, Bad Genes

The first problem with Digital DNA was that Motorola never deigned to pay anyone to stick the Digital DNA logo, a sticker that read "Digital DNA from Motorola," on their hardware. This alone was enough to doom the program. Motorola didn't want to pay out MDF because of the expense but was missing the point. Intel's MDF campaign allowed it to sell and charge more for its chips over rivals such as Motorola and AMD. The calculation was simple: For every dollar spent on MDF, Intel saw two dollars back via chip sales and profitability. The lack of an MDF component to the campaign also robbed Motorola of the ability to direct the marketing and advertising efforts of Digital DNA participants à la Intel Inside.

The second problem was the program's target audience—Motorola's customers, not the customers of their customers. Motorola's advertising for the program was thus aimed at phone makers, car manufacturers (big buyers of embedded computer systems), and electronics makers, not the buyers of phones, cars, and electronics. This strategy ensured no consumer demand for products with Digital DNA inside them would be generated. It also put Motorola in direct competition with those companies to whom it supplied chips, such as cellular phone manufacturers. Companies such as Nokia and QUALCOMM regarded the prospect of putting a Motorola logo on their phones with little enthusiasm. Again, Motorola had completely missed the point of the Intel approach, which was to make **consumers** demand computers with Intel inside, thus pressuring manufacturers to buy more Intel chips.

The third problem was schizoid execution. Having made the decision to target its customers, the company also diverted precious advertising budget dollars to running print-based consumer advertising as well. This wasn't money intelligently spent; an effective corporate branding effort requires a massive and extensive media blitz carried out over an extended period of time. A few million dollars spent in newspaper and magazine ads wasn't going to create any significant consumer interest in Digital DNA.

After a couple of years of wasted time and money, it became clear that Digital DNA was genetically defective. The program generated no end-user demand for Motorola products, no increased awareness of Motorola, and no increased demand other than that dictated by normal business necessity for Motorola products among its customers. Digital DNA was allowed to quietly wither away into obscurity.

The last time Ken passed Alfred on the beach, he kicked sand in his face.

~

The Eternal Darkness of the Clueless Mind: Google, Eric Schmidt, Sergey Brin, and the People Who Brought You Tiananmen Square

As usage of the Internet exploded in the mid-to-late 1990s, the problem of how to find stuff in an environment of tens of millions of web pages loomed large. The answer initially was America Online (AOL), the largest online service that had morphed fairly quickly into a launching point for more than 32 million subscribers in the United States, Europe, Latin America, and Japan. However, AOL was a paid service, and from 1996 to 2001 a plethora of new companies jumped into the fray, offering free search capabilities with the intent that advertising sales would subsidize the search functions of the site. The value of search engines to Net surfers was that a good engine could quickly help you locate useful information, and it didn't take long for businesses to figure out that it would be very useful and profitable to be the first bit of useful information found. Some of the early contenders for the crown of search engine king included such firms as AltaVista, AskJeeves, HotBot, Yahoo, and in 1998 a little known company called "Google" (the name is a play on the word "googol"—a one followed by a hundred zeros).

Google was developed by Stanford University graduate students Larry Page and Sergey Brin. Their system introduced a new concept to the search paradigm, link popularity. Google's search engine looks at the connecting links between web pages and, based on the number of links it finds germane to a search term, ranks pages in order of relevance. Google also developed a minimalist interface, one that presents the user with nothing more than a search box and a few text links that take the user to some further options and the engine's more advanced query capabilities. This was in sharp contrast to sites such as Yahoo and AOL, which positioned themselves as "portals," web locations where it was assumed you wanted to live your virtual life surrounded by calls to chat with friends and family, blandishments to buy stuff from advertisers, requests to read the news, online shows to see, and, of course, an unending stream of ads to view 24/7/365. Google also eschewed putting paid ratings into its search results, unlike the other search sites. The combination of this policy, its interface, and the quality of the results produced by Google searches quickly led to the upstart engine establishing itself as the premier search site on the Web. So good was Google in returning accurate results that portal sites such as Yahoo used Google to provide search for their visitors, a practice that stopped as Google became a competitive threat.

From serving an initial 10,000 queries per day, Google grew to the point that by 1999 it was handling more than 500,000 daily and on its way to surpassing its competitors. The company moved from, sigh, yes, a garage into a huge HQ in Mountain View, California, known as the

Googleplex. Early in 2000, Google introduced its AdWords system. Following Google's minimalist strategy, AdWords were simple text ads on the right hand side of the search results page. Google added the ingenious twist of allowing advertisers to bid on the search terms they would appear for and left the control of running the campaign to advertisers. You can select payouts of anywhere from five cents to a dollar per click, decide to run multiple ads, and run as many campaigns as you want. The first AdWords customer was a live lobster seller, and within six months of its introduction AdWords and related systems were pouring torrents of revenue into Google's coffers. Later in 2000, Google introduced the Google toolbar, a Microsoft Internet Explorer plug-in that made Google the browser's default search engine. Then, in 2001, Google announced it was hiring former Novell CEO Eric Schmidt (who had not covered himself with glory while in Utah trying to revive NetWare's star) to be its new chief executive on the theory that the latest young, entrepreneurial spawn of Silicon Valley needed adult supervision.

In 2004 Google announced it was going public, and the public frenzy surrounding the forthcoming IPO reminded people of the Internet bubble. But unlike the host of Internet companies who came to market with balance sheets dripping red ink, Google could boast 2003 revenues of $961.9 billion with profits of $106.5 million. With that flare for the unexpected Google had shown since its inception, the company announced that shares for the IPO would be available to the public via an auction process that allowed investors to obtain bidder IDs and submit a buy order that included how many shares they wanted and at what price. Google went public on August 19th, 2004, with its shares trading at an initial $100 and quickly climbing to more than $350. By 2005, Google accounted for more than 40 percent of all U.S. web searches and had a market capitalization of approximately $52 billion. The company followed up its successes by launching a popular web-based mapping application that caught the web user's fancy by allowing browsers to fly over a virtual Earth and, in some cases, zoom down almost to roof level over their own homes; a new free web-based e-mail system; a desktop suite of light applications; a shopping system (Froogle); a chat application; and more.

By 2006 Google had become one of high-tech's most powerful firms and was in a position to impact the profits of numerous companies across the globe. For example, every so often the Google search engine reshuffles its results, an event known informally as a "Google Dance." These search engine gavottes cause tens of thousands of business owners to clench their teeth (and other parts of their anatomy) until the rankings settle down again. In November 2003, perhaps the most significant Google Dance (nicknamed "Florida") in years occurred when the engine unleashed several new filtering algorithms on an unsuspecting Internet. Previously high-ranking sites lost their positions, and some seemed to disappear completely. Commercial sites seemed particularly hard hit, with many prominent sites being replaced in the rankings by odd choices that sometimes referred to a keyword but clearly were not the most relevant choice the engine could have provided (I confirmed this by inspecting many of the high-tech keywords I am most familiar with). Indignation ran high because losing a high Google ranking can be a devastating blow to many companies, and many people voiced the suspicion that Google was discriminating against commercial websites in the hope these firms would now buy Google's text ads. (A similar change rippled through Google in 2006, with similar complaints.) In February of 2006 yuppie panzerwagon maker BMW found its German website banned from the search engine's rankings when the company was caught "gaming" Google's ranking system. BMW, smarting in its lederhosen from its Google-administered spanking, promptly capitulated and removed the dubious material from its website, after which the chastened automaker was allowed back into the indexed database.

High tech was agog over the latest superduper young billionaires from Silicon Valley and very, very relieved that Google was making money. Media praise and fawning articles rained on the company thicker than hits on a website generated from owning the number-one keyword position on the noun "sex." In 2004, ABC News announced it had discovered that Silicon Valley's latest wonder boys had not been jaded by all that wealth and remained humble, "jes folks" like you and me:

Larry Page and Sergey Brin are not your typical billionaires. In fact, if you type "billionaire" into Google, the picture that emerges—fancy cars, private jets, mansions, jewels, supermodel girlfriends—isn't anything you'd find in the lifestyle of the Google guys. Page drives a Prius, which costs around $21,000. Brin gets around for the most part on inline skates, and he still lives in a rented apartment.[7]

Making it all even more wonderful was Google's idealistic corporate mantra of "Do no evil" that branded the company as something very different from the hordes of greedy Internet companies that a few years ago had depleted the bank accounts and stock funds of dewy-eyed investors worldwide. The rags-to-riches story of cofounder Sergey Brin also had strong appeal. Brin's Jewish parents had immigrated to the United States with the future billionaire when Brin was five and the Soviet Union was still the Evil Empire, a place where people whose religious, political, and economic views differed from communist doctrine were widely persecuted. It seemed Google could do no wrong.

And then a scribbler from the press decided to google (by this time, Google had achieved branding nirvana, and the company's name had become a verb)[8] the name "Eric Schmidt." And the Great God Hubris stirred, stretched out his august hand, and decided to teach the world's coolest company a lesson.

The 2004 film *The Eternal Sunshine of the Spotless Mind* describes a man who deliberately erases a portion of his past memories in a quest to experience a better future. To achieve this happy outcome, the hero of the film undergoes a physical process that inflicts, in the words of one of the characters, "brain damage." When evaluating Google's 2005 fiasco with CNET.com, a major high-tech site that reports on events, companies, and gadgets, one is forced to the conclusion that the executive staff of Google had all seen this movie and taken its central conceit to heart, forgetting that movies are generally fairy tales and their scenarios rarely apply to the real world. Most of us (at least most boys; girls are usually too intelligent to make this mistake) learn this at an

---

[7] http://abcnews.go.com/Entertainment/print?id=309165

[8] Google became an official English verb in July of 2006 when the venerable Merriam-Webster included the new transitive verb "to google" in its latest update.

early age after we see or read our first *Superman* comic book and leap off our beds in an attempt to fly, only to crash heavily to the floor in a tangle of pajamas, bed clothes, and sometimes a broken limb.

The Google contretemps began on July 14th, 2005, when CNET reporter Elinor Mills, as part of a larger article on privacy issues and concerns, decided to google CEO Eric Schmidt. The reason for this was that as Google's search engine reach and capabilities increased, some people and organizations started to become uneasy about the company's ability to invade your privacy. After all, Google stored every search query made through its system, and the information it stored included the IP address of the query's author, making it possible, in theory, for Google to tell other people the names of all those porn sites you never visited. (In 2006, the company disturbed people even further when it developed a desktop search utility that used Google's servers to index your hard drive's contents, making it possible, in theory, for Google to tell other people about all those pictures of Pamela Anderson you didn't download.)

Mills's search returned a wealth of "personal" details about the petulant CEO, courtesy of Google. Among the tidbits she uncovered (all from publicly accessible sites) were such details that Schmidt flies airplanes; gave money to the Gore campaign; lives in Atherton, California; is worth about $1.5 billion; and has attended the Burning Man art festival (a pretentious pseudo-religious jamboree held in the Nevada desert that allows the attendees to carry on the-way-they-dreamed-of-but-were-prevented-from-doing-so-by-alert-counselors when they were sent off to sleep-a-way and Boy Scout camps). It was not exactly the stuff of tabloid dreams but was an excellent example of the power of Google to intrude into the personal life of individuals to an extent not previously possible without the expenditure of considerably more time and effort than most people have been able or willing to commit. The article went on to make the point that Google also tracks a considerable amount of information about you and me that the company's search engine does not make available to the general public, and it speculated on the possible danger to privacy this concentration of information in the hands of one company poses.

Now, Google by this time was a large, very successful company (like Microsoft and Siebel Systems) and had to expect to undergo periodic scrutiny at the hands of the press; that's what the press does to large companies or to firms who occupy a "strategic" topic in the minds of readers and reporters. Google indeed has made search both widely accessible to the world in a way that its competitors haven't, and CNET's comments on Google's power to impact privacy are legitimate (and inevitable). It's the price a company pays for big-time success and a highly elevated stock price.

Google, however, had decided it was not yet ready to doff its jammies for the sober garb of corporate responsibility. When the CNET story was published, Google CEO Schmidt had a royal hissy snit and announced, with the type of haut grandeur guaranteed to make the press's collective teeth ache, that the company would not deign to speak to CNET for one year, presumed punishment for the news organization's act of lese majesty. The outcome of this silly behavior was completely predictable.

First, the blogs picked up the story and spread it far and wide, mocking Google while making fun of its paranoia. The UK division of CNET asked with mock plaintiveness whether Google's vow of silence applied to them. Then the major TV business shows ran with the story, with Eric Schmidt and Google receiving sardonic mentions and raised eyebrows on MSNBC, CNBC, Fox's Cavuto show, and so on. Finally, and inevitably, the august *New York Times* weighed in on the whole mess. On August 24th, writer and reporter Gary Rivlin wrote an article called "Relax, Bill Gates; It's Google's Turn as the Villain" that described how "venture capitalists, entrepreneurs, and technologists gather in Silicon Valley," to grouse "about Google, complaining about everything from a hoarding of top engineers to its treatment of partners and potential partners. The word arrogant is frequently used." It quoted a Mr. Levchin, who exclaimed, "I'm surprised at how fast the company's reputation is changing." It highlighted the observations of a Mr. Kraus who declared, "Microsoft is becoming I.B.M. and Google is becoming Microsoft." (This presumably was in regard to the mean, old, illegal monopolist Microsoft pre-DOJ spanking, not the newly chastened, good corporate citizen of recent vintage. Or maybe not.)

To drive the *New York Time*'s point home, a few days later, on August 28th, *New York Times* reporter Randall Stross wrote another article about Google and CNET entitled "Google Anything, so Long as It's Not Google." The article had more fun observations, such as "the company reacted in a way better suited to a 16th-century monarchy than a 21st-century democracy with an independent press" and "Mr. Schmidt and his staff have had six weeks to restore a working relationship with CNET (and to apologize)."

More articles and mean and nasty stories were issued from a thoroughly aroused fourth estate, and Google's corporate mojo began to drain away in a welter of sarcasm and derision. Finally, on September 26th, Google threw in the towel by way of a phone interview with not just CNET but with the offending Mills herself. But the damage had been done. In addition to its new and rapidly developing posture of the enemy of privacy, Google now faced another, longer-term problem. The press was mad at Google, and the press has a long institutional memory. The flow of laudatory stories abruptly stopped, to be replaced by far more skeptical and balanced coverage.

But the great god Hubris is not easily satisfied once aroused to action. In January, 2006, the U.S. Justice Department, its curiosity stimulated by the passage of the Child Online Privacy Protection Act (COPA) act, requested the records of millions of searches made on Google, Yahoo, AOL, MSN, and the other popular search engines in an attempt to find out just how many people weren't visiting porn sites with pictures of Pamela Anderson and other popular and well-endowed celebrities. The other search engines complied with Uncle Sam's request and turned over their search results sans information that would allow the feds to track down a particular IP address's specific visit.

Google, however, raising the banner of privacy and freedom from snooping, refused to hand over the requested data. For a couple of weeks Google was once again the darling of the media, basking in the glory of its role of Privacy Knight, a nice turnaround, it felt, from the CNET mess.

The knight was promptly unhorsed when it was reported that Google had bowed to the wishes of the Chinese government and began to censor its search engine so as to remove information unpalatable to the country's reigning dictatorship. All of sudden, if you were Chinese, terms such as "Tiananmen Square" (the place where thousands of Chinese protesters were slaughtered by the Chinese government), "falun gong" (a religious group whose members have been arrested and killed by the Chinese government), or "human rights in China" (something many Chinese and most Tibetans don't enjoy, courtesy of the Chinese government) were replaced by pictures of happy tourists visiting

Tiananmen Square and a message that Google wasn't showing them the complete results from their query.

Now, other search sites had cooperated with the Chinese dictatorship, most notably Yahoo, which had turned over information that helped lead to the arrest and incarceration of a journalist,[9] and Microsoft, which had shut down blogs distasteful to the unelected masters of Bejing. But money and profits had always been Microsoft's chief concern, and the Chinese market was very big with a huge profit potential. Yahoo was run by a fellow from the entertainment industry, a place where mothers are routinely sold in order to facilitate the closing of deals; in light of this, the site's willingness to hand over a mere newspaper guy was not surprising. Neither Microsoft nor Yahoo had ever publicly proclaimed that a moral principle underlay its business model.

In light of the contradiction between Google's words and actions, the brand was permanently besmirched. Not helping matters was the disclosure that humble Google founders Page and Brin had bought themselves a big 767 jet, were decorating it in early "Cave of Ali Baba," and had begun squabbling over which billionaire could have a king-sized bed in his respective onboard private cabin (with a wisdom worthy of Solomon, Google CEO Schmidt decreed that **both** Googlers could have any type of bed they wanted in their bedrooms.)[10]

Industry observers noted that perhaps Google's new motto should be changed to something like "Don't Do Evil But Don't Interfere With Those That Do" or perhaps "Only Evil When We're Talking a Market of One Billion+" or perhaps "As Evil As We Need to Be." Some people thought it odd that Google was willing to go to the mat for potential kiddie porn aficionados but was unwilling to stand up to a ruthless dictatorship. Many were struck by the irony that Sergey Brin, a person whose parents had fled a country where political and religious freedom was ruthlessly repressed, dissidents tortured and jailed, and journalists censored and thrown into prison was now censoring his search engine on behalf of a country where political and religious freedom was ruthlessly repressed, dissidents tortured and jailed, and journalists censored and thrown into prison.

---

[9] Reporters Without Borders, April 19th, 2006 (http://www.rsf.org/article.php3?id_article= 17180)

[10] Good Morning Silicon Valley, July 7th, 2006

nine

FROM GODZILLA TO GECKO:
The Long, Slow Decline of Novell

MOST PEOPLE HAVE ALWAYS had a sneaking love for those cheesy Japanese movies in which vast areas of Tokyo are always being subjected to large-scale urban renewal via the efforts of a huge, irradiated prehistoric creature with a bad attitude.

The undisputed king of the Japanese movie monsters was always Godzilla. Anyone who messed with this supercharged lizard that liked to spit radioactive phlegm was guaranteed a bad day. In various encounters he squashed Mothra the Giant Bug, blew away the Smog Monster, pulled the wings off Rodan the Giant Pterosaur (or whatever), and kicked King Kong's giant chimp butt. (Yeah, yeah, in the version shown in America the monkey wins, but in the **real** version shown in Japan, Kong gets a face full of nuclear halitosis and goes down for the count.) He never even paid attention to the plastic tanks and model airplanes the Japanese army threw against him.

Novell was once like that. The company started off its life in 1979 as Novell Data Systems, a Utah-based computer manufacturer and developer of proprietary disk operating systems. Its main offering, Sharenet, was a very expensive proprietary mix of hardware and software, and Novell had little success in selling it. By 1983, Novell was on the verge of collapse, but before the lights were turned off for the last time, the company brought in one of its investors, a gentleman by the name of Ray Noorda, to see whether anything could be salvaged from the mess. Noorda was not a technologist, but he was a shrewd businessman with an eye for value and an almost pathological focus on keeping costs down.

After poking around a bit, Noorda focused on the network operating system (NOS) that was Sharenet's software heart and decided Novell's redemption lay in this product. The NOS, soon to be christened "NetWare," was the pet project of the "Superset": a small group of contractors led by Drew Major and hired by Novell. It would serve as the foundation for what would become, for more than a decade, one of the industry's most powerful and influential companies.

NetWare's unique value was in how it allowed users to share files and resources on a network of connected PCs. Prior to NetWare's creation, competing NOSs for the PC market from companies such as 3Com simply partitioned a server (the remote computer on which the NOS ran) into virtual drives. You could store files remotely, but they were inaccessible to others. NetWare was far more sophisticated. The remote hard disk was treated as a common resource available to all users of the network. Individual users were granted rights to subdirectories on the server, and if the user had permission from the network administrator, he could easily transfer files across the network to others. In addition to its file-sharing capabilities, NetWare also made it easy for multiple users to share printers, an important issue in an era when a primitive dot-matrix unit cost about $600.00.

Another strength of NetWare was its independence of any particular vendor's hardware. NetWare could run over ARCnet, Ethernet, or Token Ring. Most of its competitors were tied to specific LAN types or LAN adapters. To communicate between the server and the desktop PC, the company relied on its proprietary Internetwork Packet Exchange (IPX) protocol. For a brief period in high-tech history, IPX became the de facto industry standard for network protocols. This would change as the Internet and TCP/IP gathered momentum in the 1990s.

Noorda initially offered his new NOS to some of the major players in the industry, most notably 3Com. Headed up by Robert Metcalfe, the coinventor of Ethernet, 3Com was the early leader in the NOS and networking environment. In a meeting at COMDEX in 1982, one that typifies the friendly, hail-fellow-well-met attitude so prevalent in high tech, Metcalfe threw Noorda out of the 3Com booth.[1] Metcalfe's reward for his intelligent behavior was to help ensure 3Com's eventual departure from the NOS market.

From this inauspicious beginning, Novell soon bulked up to become the Godzilla of PC networking. In a brilliant marketing move that could have been thought up by Bill Gates, Novell bought several network interface card (NIC) vendors and helped drive hardware prices down. Having ruined margins for several companies but having expanded the market for NetWare, Novell dumped most of its hardware business to focus on its OS.

By 1987, Novell was the baddest of the bad in the NOS arena. NetWare crushed Corvus, another early market leader in the industry.

---

[1] Noorda liked to tell this story in social situations, and I heard it from him first at the New York rollout of a fault-tolerant version of NetWare in 1985 and then in 1986 at a gathering in COMDEX.

Plucked Banyan's VINES. Body slammed 3Com. Kicked sand in the face of Microsoft's LAN Manager and IBM's LAN Server. From the early 1980s to the mid-1990s, Novell's dominance in LANs and NOSs was unchallenged.

Playing to its strengths, Novell also established itself as a major player in the "groupware" category with GroupWise. Noorda also drove the development of Novell's reseller education and certification programs and made a Certified Novell Engineer (CNE) certificate the most valuable networking designation in the industry from 1985 to 1995. Novell's CNE program was widely admired and copied in the industry. When Microsoft rolled out Windows NT, it made no secret that its Microsoft Certified Systems Engineer (MCSE) training regimen was based on Novell's program. Novell was big, powerful, and profitable. By 1994, yearly revenue exceeded $2 billion at "Big Red."

And then, just like in a Japanese movie, a nerd with glasses and a questionable haircut developed an incredible radioactive shrinking ray and turned it on the rampaging monster. When the ray had wreaked its incredible effect, the beast had been shrunk to gecko-like proportions.

To add insult to injury, the nerd didn't even bother to reach for a tank or a missile or a jet to apply the coup de grace to our miniaturized monster.

He used a cereal box.

~

Crunch Time for Novell

Novell's moment of truth came in the form of an aggressive direct marketing campaign Microsoft launched against the company in 2001. By then, Novell was a wounded lizard in the marketplace, losing market share to Microsoft almost on a daily basis while the press and the industry questioned the company's relevance in a server world dominated by Windows NT, Linux, and the Internet.

Desperate and clearly in over his head, Eric Schmidt, Novell's CEO, quickly arranged a shotgun marriage. The company merged with Boston-based Cambridge Technology Partners, a large but money-losing consulting and system integration firm. The company's corporate head-quarters was officially shifted from Provo, Utah, to Cambridge, Massachusetts. Jack Messman, CEO of Cambridge Technology Partners and former president of Novell from 1982 to 1983, became the head of the newly merged entity. It all felt very unnatural, as if Godzilla had married Mothra. Normally, Godzilla **eats** Mothra.

Microsoft, never reluctant to kick an opponent when it's down, wound up and tossed a "Microsoft Server Crunch" Novell's way. "Crunch" consisted of a clever bit of marketing collateral designed to look like a cereal box. The piece's copy made several statements about Novell and NetWare designed to tempt even the most devout of the company's many Mormons (a faith that discourages the use of coffee) to reach for a cup of java and some strong aspirin. These were the choicest nuggets in Crunch:

"What's the expiration date on that NetWare platform?"

"You're left with a server platform without the full support of its manufacturer, which means increasing costs as it rapidly becomes obsolete, forcing you to implement time-consuming retrofits."

"As a result of the recent Cambridge Technology Partners merger, Novell is shifting its focus from software development to consultancy services."

When I read about the Microsoft campaign I flashed back to the mid-1990s. Shortly after the merger of Novell and WordPerfect, I was invited to Provo, Utah, to train a combined group of Novell and former WordPerfect product managers on software marketing. During the training, the attendees ran up with an ad I now think of as "The Ship Slowly Sinking While the Band Plays On" piece.

The ad showed a picture of a person in a rowboat heading toward a sleek yacht in the distance. The rowboat was meant to symbolize WordPerfect; the yacht, Microsoft. The raison d'être for all this rowing was better service, as represented by the yacht. At its core, Microsoft was claiming it offered better customer service than Novell, a company that at the time was continuing WordPerfect's famous policy of offering 800 (that's toll-free) support to anyone who bought its products.

"This is outrageous," the trainees wailed. "What should we do?"

~

Famous Cheapskates

"Well," I said, "let's think this through. You could call Microsoft and complain that the ad is misleading and unfair and stuff like that, but, you know, while all that's going on you're not answering the charge that Microsoft is making. And I don't think they'll be very moved by your plight.

"Or, you could employ that famous marketing nostrum that proclaims replying to a negative ad gives it credibility and draws attention to the competition. Of course, that theory was propounded by someone who entered a sealed time capsule in the 1960s [when Godzilla was at his peak] and missed the development and refinement of the attack ad, which seems to work just fine, especially when you fail to answer the charges made by the other party.

"Or, you could consider answering the charges the ad makes in a strong and powerful way that makes Microsoft think twice about developing this type of ad in the future. What do you want to do?"

Everyone seemed to think the third choice was the best alternative, so we went to work.

"Well," I said, "how about this? I've been teaching you in the course that Microsoft has built a powerful brand element around the persona of Bill Gates. Gates is presented as a nonthreatening guide to computing for the masses. In public he usually dresses informally, he talks glowingly about the benefits of technology, and he never, ever, ever mentions money despite that he's one of the richest guys on the planet. Why? No one likes rich guys, usually. It's the 'Nobody Roots for Goliath' syndrome described by master marketer Wilt Chamberlain.

"So, let's create the following ad. We'll call it 'Famous Cheapskates.' We'll have a picture of King Midas, Scrooge, and that Getty guy, the one who put pay phones in his home to prevent guests from making toll calls at his expense. We'll put a caption under each cheapskate that tells his tale. And heading up the Hall of Cheapness will be a picture of Bill Gates. Next to Gates's picture we'll put a phone with a coin slot on the dial pad. Next to the phone will be a dime. The caption for the ad will read: 'Bill Gates has $30 billion [the approximate count at that time], but when his word processor doesn't work right, he wants you to spend **your** dime to get help.'

"What do you think? Microsoft isn't going to like this: It musses up the company's most important branding symbol. It's accurate. It's funny. And it accesses certain primeval emotions in the mind of the audience. Heck, show it to them before you run it. I bet they'll yank that boat ad if that's what you want."

There was a long silence in the room. I did notice one senior product manager from the WordPerfect side of the company giggling to himself and frantically taking notes. Finally, another senior product manager from the Novell side looked at me with a Utah-deer-caught-in-the-glare-of-the-headlights-of-an-18-wheel-semi-from-Seattle-bearing-down-on-it gaze and said, "Oh, Novell could never create an ad like this."

And so they did nothing, except finally sell WordPerfect to Corel at a loss of about $1.2 billion.

Now, to Novell's credit, new CEO Jack Messman went ballistic when the Crunch campaign appeared and called in the lawyers. Microsoft professed the proper amount of abashment, sent out a correction to the ad, said it was sorry, etc., etc., but all in all it was pretty weak tea. The ad had been sent, the accusations made. What was Novell's answer to these charges? And how would the company respond in front of the appropriate audience (the audience that wasn't found in a courtroom)?

The 1990s were full of similar crunch times for Novell, and the company rarely seemed able to rise to the challenge. No single problem led to Novell's loss of market leadership. Rather, a series of interlocking problems sapped the company's strength and drained the fire from its belly.

~

The Big Lizards

Novell from its inception was fundamentally a technology-driven company with a sales-oriented CEO. Like many such firms, Novell tended to regard its marketing operations almost as a problem to be managed, not a generator of opportunity. The problem was exacerbated by the position of the Superset within the company. This group consisted of a small group of elite programmers who had total control over the development of the NetWare kernel and the OS core, and it functioned almost independently of the rest of Novell. Over time, the Superset came to be regarded with almost religious reverence by the rest of the company, with Drew Major playing the role of chief pontiff to its small and self-governing techno-priesthood. You could suggest something to the Superset, but even Ray Noorda didn't give the group orders. For years the members of the Superset weren't even company employees.[2]

One result of the complete ascendance of technology over marketing at Novell was that the company's product management system was weak. Product managers had little ability to impact NetWare's product development cycle. For example, for years the Superset ignored the screams of users demanding a GUI for NetWare. At one juncture Drew Major proclaimed that there would never be a GUI for NetWare,[3] and for years, as Novell's product looked increasingly creaky and out-of-date in a GUI-driven world, he had his way. Another clue to marketing's weakness was its inability to provide compelling ROI arguments for purchases of NetWare and other Novell products. The company was good at developing long checklists of technical improvements to NetWare, but it made few attempts to tie these improvements to real-world benefits and savings.

Marketing's weakness carried over to other areas in Novell, particularly its GroupWise products. By the millennium, GroupWise, a powerful competitor to both Outlook and Notes with more than 35 million users (an interesting fact that Novell was excellent at keeping secret), had a mid-1990s interface badly in need of updating. Novell's product marketing group had known this for years but was unable to persuade the GroupWise development team to provide a modern look and feel for the product line.

---

[2] Robert X. Cringely, *Accidental Empires* (New York: Addison-Wesley, 1992), page 278.

[3] Major made this statement before a group of Novell resellers, including Pierre Chamberland of FaxTeam Software.

~

Island of Lost Souls

Another issue was culture. Until its merger with Cambridge Technology Partners, Novell, as noted, was headquartered in Provo, Utah. Utah is a land of decency, polygamy, and theocracy, all courtesy of the country's most successful homegrown religion, Mormonism. The state is an anomaly in the United States; it's a place of remarkable cultural, religious, and political uniformity. Mormons make up 63 percent of Utah's population and hold most statewide elective offices. Politically, white Republican males dominate the state legislature. Utah's entire U.S. congressional delegation is Mormon, as are both senators.

The result of this cultural and religious homogeneity proved a subtle problem for Novell as the company grew. Although Utah has fine universities that turn out decent numbers of programmers and sales and marketing types, Novell never held much appeal for people outside the Utah and Mormon milieu, and the company didn't make strong efforts to attract them. For instance, though Mormonism doesn't technically ban the use of caffeine, it doesn't look on its use with particular favor either. As a result, obtaining a cup of coffee at Novell headquarters wasn't an easy thing to do. This proved a minor problem in an industry that uses various java brews and caffeine-laced concoctions such as Mountain Dew and Jolt Cola to increase programmer productivity and happiness. After Novell's merger with Cambridge Technology Partners in 2001, new CEO Jack Messman made a point of handing out cigars (Mormons also don't believe in smoking) at a meeting of Novell resellers. Brigham Young may have been spinning in his grave, but Messman's point that the company was going to have to break out of its old mind-set wasn't lost on many.

The lack of acceptable sodas mirrored a more subtle intellectual issue that also dogged the company as it grew. Internally, Novell lacked the fizz and ferment of new ideas and concepts that the cross-pollination of employees coming and going generates in high-tech companies. As a result, Novell often seemed to regard itself as above the grimy realities of business. One clue to this attitude could be seen in Novell's intelligence-gathering operations. Industry observers have long noted that if you go to one of the various company-sponsored shows, such as a Microsoft's Exchange conference, you'll find IBM personnel (or their surrogates) in attendance, and vice versa for an IBM Domino/Notes show. However, you would rarely find a Novell GroupWise contingent sneaking about at a competitor's conference garnering information. It was just not the sort of thing Novell did.

Novell delivered a more subliminal message about its attitude toward the outside world with its infamous hotel, known informally in the industry as "Noorda's Nightmare."[4] For years, weary travelers who visited Novell at its corporate headquarters in decidedly unglamorous Provo were forced to sojourn at this "inn," because it was the only place for miles around where you could park your head in the evening. Novell's "resort" featured mediocre food, carpeting of a dubious color, threadbare towels, and much scratchy off-white linen drooped over tired mattresses. One corporate type who visited Novell to attend a high-level dog-and-pony show discussing the future of NetWare left Provo vowing to buy NT simply to repay Novell for the lethal case of heartburn he had developed eating the Nightmare's food.

And, of course, years of success also played a factor in Novell's insular attitude. When a company has done so well for so long, it's hard not to think it has got it all under control. But, as Bill Gates has always known, in a modern capitalistic society, they really **are** all out to get you. Properly channeled, paranoia is a useful management tool, but Novell for a long time seemed to lack any.

~

How to Miss Tokyo

The preceding two problems led to the development of a third: Novell's continuing inability to execute product-marketing fundamentals. Positioning and product naming seemed to be Novell's particular bêtes noires. In March 1993, with the introduction of NetWare 4.11, Novell decided to change the name of NetWare to "intraNetWare" in a

---

[4] I speak about the charms of the Nightmare from personal experience.

clumsy attempt to take advantage of all the Internet excitement. No good marketing group would have made such a mistake; the confusion this action generated was completely predictable. Everyone immediately assumed that Novell had discontinued NetWare and began to ask what had happened to the product. After all, there was still a huge market for conventional LANs, and it seemed Novell no longer stocked such an item. After a year or so of trying to explain to the market that, yes, Novell still sold LANs and that intraNetWare was also a LAN product but with intranet capability as well as all those terrific LAN capabilities traditionally associated with NetWare, Novell gave up and returned to the tried, true, trusted, and blessedly familiar "NetWare" (now with intranet capabilities) name.

More deadly have been Novell's ongoing positioning mistakes. In a reprise of MicroPro's fatal course, Novell created two competing group-ware product lines, GroupWise and Novell Internet Messaging System (NIMS, a development alliance with Netscape). Both products are close enough in functionality and audience to generate the dreaded "What's the difference?" question when prospective buyers are considering a purchase, instead of the desired "Why should I buy?" inquiry your sales force needs.

Of course, Novell would have survived all these problems handily but for a single pivotal event: the introduction of Windows NT in August 1993. Despite Novell's earlier success in stomping down Microsoft's LAN Manager, Windows NT was a tougher beast. Microsoft had studied Godzilla carefully and learned from its earlier mistakes. Its radioactive ray guns were primed and ready to take advantage of the beast's weaknesses.

~

Godzilla Meets NT, the Three-Headed Monster

Perhaps Godzilla's toughest opponent of all time was Ghidrah, the Three-Headed Monster. Launched by a team of bad Japanese special effects experts, Ghidrah was a tough dragon-like beast from outer space with, uh, three fire-spitting heads, perhaps worse breath than Godzilla, and, like his pseudo-prehistoric rival, the same desire to crush any plastic-and-balsa-wood Tokyo city models it could reach.

In the movie, Godzilla finally chases Ghidrah back to space with some help from Mothra the Giant Bug and Rodan the Monster Who Wanted to Be in *Jurassic Park* but Was Too Rubbery. Like Ghidrah, Microsoft's Windows NT attack on Novell was basically a three-headed affair. Unfortunately for Novell, no giant rubber allies were to be found in Utah at the time, and when the battle was over, Novell, from a sales and market share perspective, resembled Tokyo after Godzilla had completed one of his periodic sojourns through the city.

Ghidrah Does Demos

NT stood for "New Technology," and in contrast to NetWare, it looked like it. By 1993, 9 years after the introduction of the Macintosh and 3 years after the release of Windows 3.0, everyone was tired of command-line interfaces and X:\ prompts—everyone, that is, except technology-driven Novell and the Superset. In Provo, command-line interfaces remained just the thing, and Novell didn't intend to allow some ridiculous obsession with pretty pictures on a PC screen to mar their NOS's speed and stability.

The consequences of this decision were far reaching. The Windows NT interface made the product much easier to use and cheaper to deploy, and it reduced training and maintenance costs. This was an important point in an early 1990s world in which the principal purchases of LANs took place at the departmental level. As Microsoft gained control of the corporate departments, it positioned itself to attack the enterprise market, Novell's profit heart.

Sweet-Talking Lips

One of the least understood aspects of Microsoft's success over the years is its prowess in working with and communicating with the development community. Microsoft has always been good at making it easy and comparatively cheap to build Windows applications. It provides good-quality utilities, compilers, and frameworks on a timely basis. In line with its earlier efforts, it supported the rollout of Windows NT with several initiatives designed to encourage the development of new client/server applications for NT.

By contrast, developing products for NetWare in the critical 1993 time frame was difficult. Novell's tools were expensive and primitive. Developing an application for NetWare required a programmer to almost reprogram the OS itself. And despite numerous promises, Novell's widely heralded AppWare development framework never seemed to be available. Novell's attitude toward many NetWare developers was a mixture of equal parts distrust and disdain. The corporate zeitgeist at Novell was "If anyone is going to develop applications for our product, it should be us. We understand it and cherish it. If we allow just any hoi polloi to develop for our baby, they might change and deform it horribly." Sort of what happened to Godzilla when progressive aliens attempted to clone him as Mechagodzilla.

Novell helped drive this point home to developers with the shutdown of its Austin, Texas–based third-party development support center in 1994. This group consisted of more than 300 employees and was responsible for evangelizing software publishers to build NetWare-specific applications (called NetWare Loadable Modules, or NLMs). It has become a standard mantra to proclaim that NetWare was just a file-and-print server, but despite the obstacles the company threw in the way of programmers, a large and growing market of applications native to NetWare flourished up till the mid-1990s.

Novell was particularly well represented in the accounting and database markets, software that fits naturally into a network environment. Companies supporting NetWare included Great Plains, Macola, Peachtree, Oracle, Sybase, and Borland, to name a few. The Austin center supported Novell's ISVs with technical assistance and sold them development tools and utilities. Its marketing efforts encompassed helping companies reach customers via direct marketing campaigns, co-op advertising, and trade show appearances in partnership with Novell.

With the Austin center gone, most of Novell's third-party outreach programs went into limbo. Preoccupied with its purchase of WordPerfect, Novell didn't bother to fully reconstitute its Austin center in Utah for years. The development community, cast adrift, was thus primed to be receptive to Microsoft when it came calling with promises of NT development and marketing support.

Novell's contempt toward its development community also had serious long-term consequences as the Internet tide swept through high tech. Few new Internet applications were released for NetWare as the company spiraled toward irrelevancy. Novell's combination of high development costs, poor support, and shrinking customer base held little appeal to programmers and companies looking to enter new markets. Instead, Microsoft, with its history of providing inexpensive development tools and access to a huge market, and open source, with its even cheaper development costs and rapidly growing community of "anybody but Microsoft" acolytes, garnered the lion's share of new product investment. By the end of the 1990s, Novell had succeeded in converting the impression that NetWare was just a file-and-print server into a fact.

At the same time that Microsoft was stripping away Novell's development support, it was simultaneously wooing the top corporate executive community with a series of nationwide presentations. These presentations focused on highlighting the following:

- NT's spiffy new look (and that it was now actually possible to demo the product to upper management with the hope they would understand something of what they were seeing)
- NT's underlying functionality and stability (which was inferior to NetWare's when the product was first released, but it was a Microsoft representative doing the talking)
- NT's nice price (an NT departmental solution was far less expensive than its Novell counterpart)
- The fact that Microsoft had more money in the bank than many developing countries and was a safe and smart purchase

Bite and Hold On

Novell's response to Microsoft's relentless attack was initially to do . . . nothing. In this, it resembled those movie scenes in which one large Japanese monster is whaling on another downed Japanese monster that isn't fighting back, just sort of twitching in place like a pinned WWE wrestler. The company was sure the technical superiority of NetWare would speak for itself. The company **did** spend a lot of time telling IT types who reported to the CEOs and CFOs that Novell used far less hardware than Microsoft. Of course, as has happened only about 100 times in the past, Moore's law made this argument moot. As hardware prices plummeted, Novell's real and perceived pricing disadvantage only increased.

Godzilla Goes Ape

It took about 6 months for Novell to realize that, no, it looked like difficult-to-demonstrate technical superiority wasn't going to be enough to answer Microsoft's NT challenge. Something more was needed. Novell pondered the situation and then decided the answer was . . . UNIX. In December 1993, the company announced it was acquiring UNIX System Laboratories from AT&T, along with the UNIX trademark. Its strategic reason for the purchase: SuperNOS, a grand merger of NetWare with UNIX that was supposed to result in an NT killer. Due date: 1995.

The decision made no sense. As with MicroPro's WordStar and WordStar 2000, NetWare and UNIX on the server did basically the same things for the same people with the same hardware. Yes, AT&T's version of UNIX could also be used on the desktop, but Novell had neither the time nor the inclination to try to develop desktop UNIX for PCs. It couldn't sell the Windows applications it already had. "Combining" the best of the two OSs often meant no more than adding multiple ways of doing the same thing for an audience that had already decided on how things should be done.

And, as with MicroPro, Novell promptly broke into internal warring camps. Key members of the NetWare development group looked down on the UNIX side of the company and made no secret of their desire to see the end of UNIX. The UNIX side of the business resented being treated like second-class citizens and liked to rub UNIX's technical superiority in areas such as preemptive scheduling and virtual memory in the faces of the NetWare folks. To which the NetWare folks liked to retort with a ripping "Oh, yeah?" (a popular comeback among Mormons because they like to avoid swearing). Compounding it all, Novell released an interim version of UNIX it called "UnixWare," which wasn't SuperNOS and wasn't NetWare but sure sounded like it was some sort of mix of the two.

After about 2 years of this, Novell had enough. In 1995, it sold UnixWare and the rights to the UNIX operating system to SCO, and that was the end of that. Along the way, Novell made yet another attempt to provide developers with more useful development tools via an object-oriented programming effort called Serius, but that venture went down the same black hole as AppWare.

Then Novell completely lost its head and in 1994 purchased WordPerfect for $850 million.

To industry observers, the purchase by Novell of one-time word-processing leader WordPerfect Corporation never made any sense, and it was difficult at the time to find anyone even in Novell who would privately provide a convincing rationale for the deal. Publicly, the company stated it was buying WordPerfect to prevent it from "losing the desktop," but because Novell had never had a significant role to play in selling desktop and retail software, it was an unconvincing story. The most logical answer anyone could come up with was that because the two companies were located in Utah just a few miles from one another, it was a case of one Mormon-dominated company coming to the rescue of another.

WordPerfect had entered the 1990s in seemingly fine shape, but from 1991 to 1993 it had deteriorated rapidly. Since its inception as Satellite Software in 1979, the company had possessed one of the industry's oddest managerial systems. Ostensible CEO Pete Peterson[5] was actually one member of a governing triumvirate that included founders Bruce Bastian and Alan Ashton. Peterson acted in the role of tiebreaker in the event of a disagreement within the troika and played the role of stern daddy, keeping expenses under control and attempting to build a durable management structure for the fast-growing company. Under Peterson's regime, WordPerfect kept costs low and developed a fairly effective sales and marketing organization. The company was aided in its growth by the fact that then–market leader MicroPro was bleeding to death internally over its self-inflicted WordStar versus WordStar 2000 wounds.

Despite his CEO title, Peterson didn't have responsibility for development at WordPerfect; that was under the purview of Alan Ashton. In

---

[5] Peterson's brother Andre also worked for WordPerfect and was one of the company's best public speakers. He was legendary for his performances at SoftTeach, an industry-specific seminar series held by computer distributor Merisel. Andre's presentations began with a slide of his wife and multiple offspring and were enlivened by the wads of candy he threw into the audience.

1992, Bastian and Ashton, tired of Peterson's stern-daddy management style, decided they were ready to fly free on their own. Peterson was sent packing, and Ashton and Bastian promptly began to spend WordPerfect to death, raising employee head count from about 3,300 in 1992 to 5,500 by the end of 1993, a 40 percent increase. Simultaneously, WordPerfect's sales growth began to slow, though the company did see an increase in revenue from $570 million for 1991 to about $700 million for 1992. This increase wasn't enough to offset the tremendous rise in expenses engendered by WordPerfect's rapid expansion, and the company began to bleed cash. The problem became worse as sales growth continued to slow in 1993.

The main reason for the sales slowdown can be traced back to the first release of WordPerfect for Windows in late 1991. Despite the market's mad rush to Windows, WordPerfect had sent in the second team to develop its first Windows word processor. The company's best project managers and coders had preferred to stay with their tried-and-true DOS product, and Ashton, a "consensus" builder, had been unwilling to knock heads together in order to ensure the product's success. The result was that the first release of WordPerfect for Windows was slow, was buggy, lacked key competitive features, and received mediocre reviews. It was a critical mistake at a crucial juncture, and WordPerfect would never truly recover from it.

Compounding the problem was the release of Microsoft's Office suite. WordPerfect had lost its bragging rights to best-of-breed word processor, and the Office suite represented a tremendous value. WordPerfect had no Windows database or spreadsheet with which to build its own suite, and sales slowed even further. An attempt to cobble together a solution to Microsoft's challenge in concert with Borland, which did have a spreadsheet and database, received a poor reception from the market. The WordPerfect/Borland suite lacked Microsoft Office's integration, and its individual products weren't clearly perceived as market leaders in their respective categories.

Instead of a cash cow with promised sales of $880 million and an estimated $100 million in profits, WordPerfect proved to be a bum steer that showed up with rapidly declining sales and a tag on its ear that read "$100 million loss." Compounding its problems, Novell promptly fired most of the WordPerfect sales and marketing personnel. Novell, left with no expertise in the retail software business, was completely unprepared to fix the situation and ended up selling what was left of WordPerfect at the fire-sale price of $158 million to Corel in 1996 (the actual deal had very little cash up front attached to it).

In the meantime, Microsoft's deadly radioactive shrinking rays were steadily cutting Godzilla down to size.

Novell also missed an opportunity to exploit the positioning problem Microsoft had created for itself with the introduction of NT. At this point, Microsoft had created two 32-bit operating systems with the same name, similar pricing (at the desktop level), and almost identical interfaces. One was reliable and hard to use, and one was easy to use and hardly reliable at all. An astute marketing organization could have given Microsoft severe heartburn over this positioning conflict, but Novell didn't.

There were no moves to upgrade NetWare's look and feel with a modern GUI. No high-level seminars pointing out that Novell also had a lot of money in the bank, a huge installed base, and a better and more stable product. No pricing moves. No serious push to finally provide a competitive development framework for NetWare. Ultimately, Novell relied on the assumption that NetWare's superiority would speak for itself. And another assumption that people went out and bought a big expensive server with a pricey NOS installed and **then** thought about what to put on it—the exact opposite of real-life thinking.

Instead, for more than 3 years, Novell fought back by burning cash via pointless acquisitions while Microsoft kept demonstrating its up-to-date-looking product with its attractive price to decision makers. Several new CEOs were brought in to tidy things up, but Novell successfully resisted all change. Meanwhile, its sales shrank, and profitability went away. In 2001, Novell earned revenues of $1.04 billion, down from 2000's $1.16 billion, and lost $273 million.[6] Finally, the company decided the only way to deal with the situation was to sell out to Cambridge Technology Partners and move its headquarters to just out-side of Boston, a place where they drink lots of Sam Adams beer, smoke, and swear quite a bit. And quaff Jolt Cola.

---

[6] Novell press release titled "Novell Reports Fourth Quarter and Full Year Fiscal 2001 Results," November 29, 2001.

Now, to be fair, Novell finally woke up. Today, its pricing is competitive. It is making money selling Linux products, though the company's revenues and profitability have remained static as NetWare slowly dies (by the end of 2005, NetWare's worldwide server share stood at 6 percent and was projected to drop to 3 percent by 2007). It's now easier to develop NOS- and server-based applications for NetWare (though this no longer matters, because the company has said it will be phasing out NetWare in favor of its Linux products). The product now has a GUI (which also no longer matters). And many people who moved to Windows NT later regretted it. Although the Superset members weren't good marketers, they were wonderful programmers, and NT (now XP) has yet to match NetWare's stability and robustness.

But you have to wonder. The remake of Godzilla flopped at the box office in 2000. The movie was terrible. (Though this is perhaps not a fair criticism. All the Godzilla movies were terrible.) It just may be that Ghidrah has returned from outer space and triumphed at last. Certainly Novell thought so. On April 14th, 2003, Novell Chairman and CEO Jack Messman announced the next version of NetWare would be built on NetWare and Linux. Then, remaining true to Novell's history of ham-handed marketing, he called Linux "an immature operating system" and infuriated the open source community. He later apologized for calling Linux immature and, to show he meant it, bought Linux distributor SUSE. Then, in June of 2006, Messman was fired by a Novell board unhappy with the financial performance of the one-time networking giant.

Somewhere, Ghidrah is laughing.

ten

RIPPING PR YARNS:
Microsoft and Netscape

The high-tech industry has never grasped the dichotomy that exists between its vision of Microsoft and the public's. To industry insiders, Microsoft and Bill Gates are tough, ruthless, and predatory foes. To the public, they're something else entirely. This difference in perception is no accident. It's the result of almost 20 years of an unrelenting and masterly PR campaign. To comprehend and understand this campaign is to begin to grasp the Zen of Marketing.

Before you can proceed down the path of enlightenment, you must first undergo a purification ritual. Clear your mind of illusions and foolish cant. Sit down, assume the lotus position, and meditate. Allow your mind to become a limpid pool of clarity and reason.

~

The Zen of Marketing

As your gaze begins to pierce this world's veil of deception, you see three great myths lying about you. These myths take the form of great sayings. Approach one and its false words will ring in the air about you. Draw near the first myth and hear its cry:

Microsoft Products Are of Poor Quality and Have Succeeded Only Because of the Company's Market Monopolies

This is untrue. Since the early 1980s, Microsoft products have usually been well reviewed and received by both the press and the public. It's true that like every other major software publisher, Microsoft has preannounced products; practiced fear, uncertainty, and doubt (FUD) tactics whenever it could get away with them; and shipped products late.

However, Microsoft's products, when finally delivered, have usually been of decent quality and feature rich. The first version of Microsoft Word introduced style sheets to PC word processing, a concept since picked up by every desktop publishing product and most competing word processors. The DOS version of Word usually came in a close second to WordPerfect in product reviews and sometimes surpassed it. This state of affairs reversed itself after the release of the first version of Word for Windows in 1989. Word for Windows began to regularly beat DOS-based WordPerfect and all DOS products in the reviews; the advantages inherent in Word's GUI interface were just too compelling to ignore.

The Excel story is similar. When the 1.0 version shipped in 1987, *PC Magazine*, at the time the most influential PC-oriented publication in terms of the impact of its reviews, stated that "Microsoft Corp. has just unleashed a spreadsheet that makes 1-2-3 look like a rough draft." Most of the other reviews were just as laudatory, and all made much of the WYSIWYG functionality of the product.

PowerPoint at the time of its acquisition by Microsoft in the late 1980s was regarded as one of the top presentation products for the Macintosh. Once translated to Windows, the product received similar favorable reviews. Ironically, the purchase of PowerPoint was contro-versial within Microsoft, as the company had forked over the "incredi-ble" amount of $12 million for the software. A cornerstone of the Office suite, it would have been cheap at twice the price.

Microsoft Access when first introduced in 1992 competed primarily with Paradox for Windows. The first release of Paradox for Windows was eagerly awaited by the development community, but it shipped months late and was extremely buggy. By contrast, the first version of Access was regarded as competitive with Paradox for Windows in terms of its feature set and a bit more stable. It quickly established itself as a major contender in the DBMS arena, assisted by an aggressive upgrade promotional price of $99.95.

In the tools and language arenas, Microsoft's products have also been competitive. Since the 1980s, its C and other language compilers have usually received favorable reviews and have often won best-of-breed awards in their respective markets. Even those who dislike Microsoft concede that Visual Basic has been a powerful force in introducing object-oriented and visual programming to a wide audience. Despite Microsoft's public wrestling match with Sun Microsystems over Java, its first Java development system was universally acknowledged as one of the best tools available for the new wonder language. Microsoft has always been solicitous of the development community, providing it with tools, products, and information at attractive discounts. As a result, a huge ecosystem of third-party add-ons, training, and services has devel-oped around the company's panoply of software. Millions now rely on Microsoft for their daily income.

At the enterprise level, Windows NT was designed from the ground up in an effort led by technical god Dave Cutler of DEC fame. Although the product has always had its critics, it has also been widely praised for its overall stability, ease of use, and flexibility. Its SQL database, derived from relational DBMS pioneer Sybase, gives Larry Ellison of Oracle nightmares as it steadily improves in power and functionality. Its Internet offerings, though heavily criticized for security problems, are nonetheless flexible, relatively easy to configure, and powerful. And they're often free.

Microsoft has been widely criticized for not being an "innovative" publisher, but in this it differs little from its major competitors. Apple hijacked the GUI interface concept from hapless Xerox and made it a commercial success. Lotus became a major power via 1-2-3, a high-powered knockoff of the original VisiCalc. Borland made its initial splash in the industry with Turbo Pascal, a low-priced, high-performing language derived directly from .NET father Anders Hejlsberg's COMPAS Pascal. Borland grew rapidly during the 1980s on the strength of Turbo Pascal but then became a major player by buying the Paradox database and the Quattro spreadsheet. Satellite Software was by no means a pioneer in word processing and never succeeded in building a significant product other than WordPerfect. Ashton-Tate's dBASE was "derived" from the Jet Propulsion Laboratory's JPLDIS language. A third party developed its most innovative product, Framework. Linux is a UNIX derivative for Intel-based systems.

Microsoft has, of course, suffered its share of flops. Microsoft Access, a communications program (not the database of the same name introduced years later), was released in the early 1980s to scathing reviews. Microsoft quickly withdrew the program from the market, and now boxes of the product are considered minor collector's items. Microsoft Bob was another major faux pas, though analysts of the product have never criticized the product's feature set per se, and some believe it might have achieved some success if it had been marketed to children as a friendly front-end for Windows. And though everyone hated Clippy the talking paperclip, they kept buying Microsoft Office nonetheless.

Now draw near the second myth to hear its equally misleading claim:

Microsoft Has Always Been Feared and Hated by the Industry

Also untrue. Until the 1990 release of Windows 3.0, it was Apple, not Microsoft, that played the role of high tech's OS heavy. The success of the Mac OS, derived from Xerox's seminal Alto computer, gave Apple a tremendous competitive advantage for several years in the 1980s. Apple wasn't shy about using every legal tactic it could to defend its lead in GUIs, and for several years the company seemed to be on the hunt for every trash-can icon and drop-down menu it could sue.

Apple's first target was Digital Research's graphics environment manager (GEM). The GEM shell mimicked closely the look and feel of the Mac, though because it sat on top of DOS, it lacked much of the underlying functionality of the Mac OS. Regardless, Apple sued Digital Research shortly after the release of GEM in 1985 and forced the company to pull the product from the market for months. After the surgical removal of the GEM trash can from the desktop and minor changes to the menu system, GEM reappeared, but its enforced hiatus had cost the product precious time and momentum.[1] Everyone felt sorry for poor little Digital Research and very upset with big bully Apple.

Next up on Apple's legal agenda was Microsoft and by extension IBM. There had been labyrinthine look-and-feel negotiations between Apple and Microsoft over Windows 1.0 and the release of Windows 2.0 in 1987. This led to even more arguments about icons, graphics, and GUIs, and more legal threats. It was in this context that IBM and Microsoft invited a group of software publishers to come down to IBM's PC headquarters in Boca Raton, Florida, to preview the 1.1 release of OS/2, the one that would ship with the "Presentation Manager" interface. They were also asked to demonstrate their current OS/2 offerings to an internal conference of IBM employees. As the then product manager of WordStar 2000 for OS/2, I was sent to the event, where I spent a gloomy day showing off an OS/2-compatible character-based word processor and remembering TopView.

---

[1] GEM developed a fair amount of international support, particularly in Germany. However, the Windows wave eventually swept over Europe and GEM sank out of sight.

The day after the show, a series of presentations on the future of OS/2 were held for the ISVs. Attending from Microsoft were Scott Oki and Bill Gates himself. Gates gave an unremarkable speech on the coming glories of the new OS, and then Oki stood up to take the group on a tour of OS/2 1.1. Pointing to a spot on the Presentation Manager desktop where an Apple user would expect to find the trash can, Oki made a quip about how OS/2 would lack this most vital of features.

There was a long pause, and then the room exploded in laughter and appreciation for funny Scott and wonderful Bill and plucky-but-brave little Microsoft. How dare that big bully Apple push everybody around and build a litigation fence around a crummy trash can, for Pete's sake? Icons should be free.

You could feel the love. By 1991 the loving was over, but that's another matter.

Now it's time to approach the third myth. It proclaims the greatest falsehood of all, and once you study this great deception many things will become clear to you. Listen carefully as it proclaims:

People Don't Like Bill Gates

A great untruth. The software industry doesn't like Bill Gates. The public at large likes him just fine. It used to like him even more, but there **is** the matter of that U.S. Department of Justice (DOJ) deposition and 1997 lawsuit that Microsoft lost, an issue you'll learn more about as you proceed down the path to enlightenment.

~

Bill Gates vs. the DOJ: Sometimes We All Go a Little Bit Crazy

The public's affection for Bill Gates isn't an accident. It's the result of a long-term and brilliantly crafted PR effort that has paid off enormous dividends over the years. This effort was begun in the early 1980s by PR specialist Pam Edstrom, and since then Microsoft has spent years crafting Bill Gates's public image and using it as its chief branding symbol.

Building the Perfect Bill

Three major components have gone into the building of Bill Gates's public persona: dress, demeanor, and financial humility. In terms of his personal appearance, inordinate amounts of ink have been dedicated to Bill Gates's clothing and personal appearance. He wears glasses, not contacts. His sweaters are usually described as tattered and worn. His hair is often a "rat's nest" and usually untidy. It used to be widely reported he didn't bathe often enough (but his wife took care of that). He tends to fidget when his picture is taken. He wears lots of jeans and worn khakis. He almost never used to wear a suit and looks a bit uncomfortable when he does. (And you never saw in him those annoying master-of-the-universe, 1980s-style suspenders.) And that's a smart thing, because people always tend to distrust a man in an Armani suit with a yellow tie, red suspenders, helmet hair, and perfect nails.

Of course, as the years have passed, we've learned Gates has changed. Dandruff, wild hair, and greasy clothing have given way to more reasonable coiffures, better clothing, and even sometimes a suit if conditions demand it (like testifying in federal court during the penalty phase of an antitrust case). The ugly geekling has undergone a transformation into a mature elder-statesman-of-technology swan. It's a story with a nice arc. People respond to it.

Then there's Gates's demeanor. Over the course of his career, he's always avoided talking about or criticizing other companies and people (in public). There have been lapses, but not many. Gates has never indulged in such Sturm und Drang pronouncements as Larry Ellison's infamous "It's not enough we (Oracle) win, everyone else must lose."[2]

Gates is at his best when he's talking about the impact of computing on the future and its potential to enrich us all. He's not a good public speaker by conventional measures. His voice tends to be thin and reedy, though he is a disciplined presenter and always covers his main talking points. But Gates is a passionate speaker, one who believes in what he says, and this quality overcomes most of his technical deficiencies.

He wrote a book of deep thoughts about the future of technology, *The Road Ahead*. It's not a very good book, but people are OK with that. Richest man in the world, smart little geek, and talented writer might be a little too much to bear. And the book is just bad enough to

---

[2] Gary Rivlin, *The Plot to Get Bill Gates* (New York: Times Books/Random House, 1999).

convince people that Gates really tried to write it himself and didn't hire some slick ghostwriter to churn out more corporate propaganda. Gates wrote his **own** propaganda and he believes it. People like sincerity combined with the right dash of self-effacing ineptitude.

Finally, there's the matter of money. It's hard to ignore the fact that Bill Gates is the wealthiest man who has ever lived. But that doesn't mean you need to talk about it, and Bill Gates never does. Over the years Gates has acted like all this money just . . . happened. And Gates has done conventional humble millionaire things like taking coach flights instead of riding first class (and of course let everyone know it). He owns tons of Microsoft stock, but his executive compensation is moderate by current corporate standards. Americans like that. A dash of Uriah Heep and 'umbleness go a long way in creating a pleasing corporate persona.

Gates's personal rectitude has also helped reinforce his image. He didn't buy a yacht or sponsor one (always a bad PR move). Unlike Larry Ellison, who tried to buy a Russian Mig-29, he's made no attempt to buy any discarded military ordnance. He did buy a jet or two, but he doesn't talk about it. He does like fast cars, but what American boy doesn't? There have been no multiple succession of Mrs. Gateses—just the one with whom he's had three children. No discarded starlets and semifamous personalities dishing dirt to the tabloids. Before his mother's tragic early death from cancer, Gates called her every week.

He did spend a lot on his house ($50 million plus), but Microsoft PR spent a lot of time positioning Gates's Xanadu as both a giant geek toy and a multimedia laboratory. Those built-in electronic wall displays that can be programmed to project an endless variety of artistic images, you know. A bit of a stretch, but given Gates's past history they got away with it. And the man **does** have three kids. That's a big family in today's world, and you need a big house. Prodded by Mrs. Gates, he's caught on to the charity game and the noblesse oblige expected from the very rich. The Bill and Melinda Gates Foundation has subsequently given away hundreds of millions of well-publicized dollars. All the bases have been covered.

And Gates has also shared the wealth! No Enron-type scandals here; no poor bedraggled corporate drones deprived of their retirement funds and stock options earned from the exhausting task of depriving the state of California of power. Not only has Microsoft created more millionaires than any company in history (current estimates peg the number at about 12,000), but it has also created more **billionaires**: Gates, cofounder Paul Allen, Steve Ballmer, and Scott Oki. And Microsoft the company also gives away millions of dollars of stuff, mostly Microsoft software, valued at full retail price. (Normally, industry marketers call this "building an installed base," and no one pays full retail, but the stuff **is** free.)

There has also been a series of nice touches added over the years. In 1996, Microsoft initiated a program of private getaways (called "pajama parties") for journalists who get to spend personal time with the world's richest man and find out he's a regular guy after all. The theory behind this is that after you've met a fellow, shared a beer with him, and talked about the kids, it's a bit difficult to shove the journalistic knife in up to the hilt. You'll do your duty and nick him if that's what's called for, but you'll probably avoid homicide. The theory is, in the main, correct.

Combined, these components form the amalgam that is the foundation of Bill Gates's image. Once it was in place, the real selling of Gates could begin, and Microsoft pursued its mission with a vengeance. Despite all the talk about how Bill Gates dislikes taking time away from running (now technically guiding) Microsoft, he has somehow managed to spend a lot of time in front of various cameras during his career. Throughout the 1980s and 1990s it became difficult **not** to see pictures of Bill Gates holding a floppy disk, Bill Gates standing in a grove of redwoods, Bill Gates gazing into a monitor, Bill Gates talking about the information age (hastily revised to be the "Internet age" as events overtook the old buzzword), Bill Gates posing as A Handsome Guy on the cover of a women's magazine, etc., etc., all the while expounding on the future of the PC marketplace. The image Microsoft's PR effort finally succeeded in creating for Gates was of a friendly, nonthreatening technical wizard—a kind of high-tech elf. Completely harmless.

If you competed against Microsoft in the 1980s and were an astute observer of what was going on, you began to see Microsoft's PR effort beginning to pay off in the mid- to late-'80s. In 1987, *PC Week* published an article that claimed "Microsoft doesn't understand marketing, they just want to create great products."

Later that year, as Excel was being launched, Jerry Pournelle, influential columnist for *BYTE* magazine, commented that a Microsoft demo team was eager to show off the product because "they thought it was a neat hack." A "neat hack." Yes, the boys and girls of Microsoft weren't interested in all the money to be made in the market's second most lucrative segment (word processing being the first). They were just a group of friendly, naive hackers eager to show the world their latest trick.

To achieve this type of press is to master the Zen of Marketing.

Gates's public persona was, of course, completely at variance with his PC-insider reputation. A 1987 *Wall Street Journal* article detailing the 1985 negotiations between Apple and Microsoft over renewing Apple's license for Microsoft BASIC on its Apple II systems was one of the first to probe beneath the surface of Gates's carefully constructed public image. The article revealed a tough-as-nails negotiator and ultra-shrewd businessman who didn't hesitate to press an advantage over anyone he perceived as standing in his way. The deal's outcome led to Apple scrapping its innovative MacBASIC and many hard feelings between the two companies. But that was one article, and the press had people like Ed Esber to divert its attention. No one paid much attention to the *Journal*'s revelations.

The next several years saw Microsoft reap rich dividends from its PR effort as the company became the industry's 1,200-pound gorilla. The big dividends started in 1993. By then the high-tech industry was learning that Microsoft was every bit as brutal a competitor as IBM had ever been and much smarter. The OS wars, despite IBM's desperate attempts to make a comeback, seemed to be over. Microsoft Office, the company's marketing bet that combining a series of high-quality business applications into a semi-integrated suite would beat the best-of-breed approach still advocated by its competition, was paying off handsomely. WordPerfect, Lotus 1-2-3, Quattro, Paradox, dBASE, Harvard Graphics, and other competitors were all fast retreating into irrelevancy.

As you might imagine, everyone was screaming for the government to do something. (It's a truism that capitalists all believe in free markets until they have to live in one.) After all, Microsoft did have a monopoly in the desktop OS market. The company did engage in questionable business practices, such as forcing computer hardware manufacturers to buy licenses for DOS and Windows for every machine they made, thus effectively locking competitors such as Digital Research out of the market. Everyone in the industry had known for years that Microsoft was always ready to engage in a price war because it could use its DOS revenues to endure losses on any single product line for an indefinite period of time. A low-level probe of Microsoft's business practices had been launched in 1990 and was still burbling away out of sight of the general public's gaze. Important people were sure that the DOJ was going to pounce on Microsoft any moment and wrestle the gorilla to the ground.[3]

And, of course, Bill Gates was Satan. Everyone knew that!

Well, everyone didn't. In the United States the government reflects the will of the people, and the people were willing to leave Bill Gates alone. Sure, the lawyers wanted to sue him, but lawyers like to sue everybody, and they don't make people rich. Bill Gates had made a lot of people rich, and a lot of people knew it. And who was the government running to the rescue of? Big stupid IBM? No one felt sorry for that company. That French guy, Philippe Khan? Boy, we sure hate the French. Those Mormons from Utah? Don't they all have 6 wives and 30 kids? No wonder they need more money.

And Microsoft Office sure was a bargain! Imagine, where once you paid $279.00 (street price) for a word processor or a spreadsheet by itself, with Office you got Word, Excel, PowerPoint, and lots of other goodies for the same $279.00! Just how was John Q. Public being hurt by that?

And were any of the other companies any different from Microsoft? Jim Manzi of Lotus had spent years trying to hunt down Borland's Quattro spreadsheet with legal hit men. Apple had spent years suing anyone who put a picture of a trash can on a computer. Ed Esber of Ashton-Tate had sued people for using the dBASE language. In point of fact, everyone in the industry is constantly suing someone else over something: patents, false advertising, because it's Tuesday. Why should the U.S. taxpayers' time and money be wasted on trying to sort this all out? Let nature take its course and may the best geek win.

The Clinton White House, a poll-driven machine, took a look at Bill Gates's popularity ratings and reined in its legal hounds. In 1994, the U.S. government arrived at a fairly toothless settlement whose provisions wouldn't take effect until 1995. Microsoft agreed not to require hardware manufacturers to buy an OS license for every machine they made, regardless of whether the machine used Windows or DOS. This was a rather pointless restriction, as by the time the decree went into

---

[3] In April 1994, I had a lively discussion panel exchange with several IBMers at the OS/2 Technical Interchange in San Francisco during which I predicted the government wouldn't press its case against Microsoft.

effect there wasn't much else left to buy. Microsoft also agreed not to integrate new features and capabilities into its products if they were intended to "crush" the competition. Presumably, a gentle mauling would have to be sufficient.

Gates, however, in an action that signaled he had finally started to grow too big for his britches, made a mistake at this point. Having maneuvered a dream deal out of the DOJ's lawyers, Gates proceeded to hurt their feelings by swaggering about telling everyone that nothing had changed and that Microsoft would continue with business as usual. It was stupid behavior. Microsoft is big and has a lot of money, but the U.S. government is bigger and has **all** the money. Soft words and a humble attitude would have been the smart move. The political appointees at the DOJ didn't pay much heed to Gates's mouthing off, but in the eyes of the department's career attorneys, Bill Gates was a marked man.

Still, that was all in the future. In the meantime, a state of meaningless mutual satisfaction having been reached, everyone got back to watching Microsoft build its next monopoly in the applications market. The job was pretty much complete by 1995, just in time for the Internet and Netscape to show up.

Bill Strikes Back

It's no secret that the Internet caught Microsoft and Bill Gates flat-footed. Seemingly overnight, everyone was talking about new paradigms, the new economy, and new technologies. Microsoft, to its chagrin, wasn't perceived as a leader in any of them. Instead of Windows and Microsoft Office, proven and profitable monopolies, everyone was focusing on upstarts such as Netscape and recycled programming concepts such as Sun Microsystems's Java. Loud voices in the press announced that Microsoft was yesterday's news, old code, technology's new Edsel. Chained to the desktop, confined inside Windows, pushing "yesterday's" languages such as C and C++. Pundits proclaimed the company faced the imminent disappearance of its markets and a quick journey to irrelevancy.

Stimulated in part by fear and in part by the immensely big mouth of Netscape cofounder Marc Andreessen, Gates responded to the threat by focusing his complete attention and paranoia on all things Internet. In May 1995, he released a companywide memo instructing Microsoft employees to focus their energies on understanding the different opportunities and challenges presented by the Internet to Microsoft and Windows. On December 7 of the same year, he made a speech the industry nicknamed the "Pearl Harbor Day Manifesto" and announced that Microsoft was an Internet company. The software giant's legions of developers and marketers immediately began to change course and march inexorably toward a web-based future. Almost immediately, the press and the pundits changed their tune, and instead of obloquy they now heaped praise on Gates's ability to "turn Microsoft on a dime" and move the company in its new direction.

Time has shown that the praise, like the initial criticism, was overblown. Microsoft's counterattack was ham-handed, generated enormous public ill will, and led to a finding in favor of the U.S. government that the company had violated the nation's antitrust laws. Yes, Netscape was laid low in the end. But a marketing and development campaign that ends up with your company having the federal government playing the role of active partner in your business behavior for the foreseeable future isn't a triumph.

The company's development efforts can't be faulted; in this respect Microsoft performed superbly. Starting from nowhere, its Internet Explorer (IE) browser quickly caught, then surpassed, Netscape's Navigator and Communicator products in functionality and stability. By 1998, most reviews were giving the nod to Microsoft's product over Netscape's. Netscape, in a case of a company falling for its own propaganda, helped cut its own throat by going off on a half-baked quest to rewrite its market-leading browser in Java, a course that helped ensure the company would fall permanently behind Microsoft in the development race.

What did break down during the last half of the 1990s was Microsoft's PR machine. The decade began with Microsoft receiving, with very few exceptions, glowing media coverage and enjoying high public esteem. It ended with a slew of articles, books, and TV specials springing up dedicated to discovering the dark side of Bill Gates and Microsoft. A truly awful movie, *Antitrust*, was filmed with actor Tim Robbins playing an ersatz Gates, an evil billionaire who runs around killing lovable open-source programmers. (By the end of the film, most people are rooting for the evil billionaire.) As unflattering comparisons to earlier titans of industry such as Andrew Carnegie and John Rockefeller surfaced in the press, Gates began to undergo a public transformation from golden geek to gilded-age robber baron. And because Microsoft's PR machine had worked so assiduously to present Gates as Microsoft's official face, any blemish to his image reflected directly on his company.

This is all the more ironic when you realize that Bill Gates's initial reaction to the Internet was more prescient than people had realized. Microsoft has always been run as a real business that makes real profits, and in 1994 Gates immediately spotted the obvious: None of the Internet "business models" being bandied about described how anyone was going make any money on the Internet. The one place where profits could be found was in selling software that would allow **other people** to build websites where you could buy 30-pound bags of pet food at a loss. Microsoft promptly went out and did the intelligent thing and bought the leading web development package, FrontPage, from Vermeer Technologies. The acquisition led to Microsoft immediately becoming the leader in this new market category. But despite this initial display of good sense, Microsoft ended up buying into much of the Internet nonsense of the mid-1990s and allowed its behavior to spiral out of control.

Microsoft's first overreaction was to the development of Java. The new language was the brainchild of Sun Microsystems, a company that has released some interesting software technology over the years but has made little money doing it. Java was designed as a "Write Once, Run Anywhere" environment. It achieves this by allowing developers to write to a Java Virtual Machine (JVM), a software-based computer that's ported to different computer platforms. In theory, if your software meets the JVM specification, you can write a software program once and have it run on any machine with a JVM. Java wasn't specifically a part of the Internet's infrastructure, but the language's applicability to developing server-based software soon tied the two technologies together in the public's mind.

"Write Once, Run Anywhere" programming isn't a new idea. The concept had been tried before in the early 1980s, only then it was called the UCSD p-System.[4] You wrote p-System programs to the virtual p-System microprocessor and, in theory, your software would run on any computer with a virtual p-System machine. The problem with the

---

[4] The product was sold commercially by a company called Softech and later Pecan Software.

p-System and Java is that they require you to write to any particular piece of hardware's lowest common denominator, thus ensuring that a program's performance and interface are always far less than optimal. Developers could never resist tweaking their p-System programs just a bit to support a particular bit of silicon, but once they did, cross-platform compatibility disappeared. The primary difference between the two approaches was that a JVM could run in your browser, giving you access to a new universe of slow-performing web-based applications with standardized primitive interfaces running on all your computers. The p-System quickly faded as customers demanded applications optimized for their real, not virtual, machines. Java's "Write Once, Run Anywhere" claim proved just as chimerical as the p-System's, though the language is widely used to develop server-based applications.

Overwhelmed by the Internet roar, Microsoft made the mistake of licensing the Java language from Sun Microsystems, a move many saw as an acknowledgment that the company needed to play catch-up with its competition. Microsoft didn't need a license to provide "Java" compatibility and capabilities in its products; the Java language was highly cloneable. But use of the Java trademark **did** require that license.

Once the deal was struck, Microsoft promptly released a Java IDE that was widely praised for its performance and possessed, to no one's great surprise, "hooks" that, if used, optimized your Java programs for Windows (and made them incompatible with other platforms). Sun Microsystems and Microsoft promptly got into a noisy catfight about the purity of the Java language and cross-platform compatibility. Given that Java was proving to be about as cross-platform as the p-System, there didn't seem to be much point to the squabbling, but the episode damaged Microsoft's reputation in the press and with the public.

Microsoft's second, more important mistake was in allowing itself to be goaded into stupid behavior by Netscape's noisy declarations about browsers replacing Windows as an application portal. Netscape needed to make these grandiose claims for what was, and still is (though the advent of technologies such as Ajax and SaaS are finally changing this) primarily a viewing technology, because a browser is what Netscape had to sell. The idea that anyone was going to use Netscape or any other browser anytime soon to write documents, lay out publications, build budgets, store files, and design presentations was a fantasy. (The people who made these breathless predictions apparently never tried to actually perform any of these tasks in a browser.)

What has actually occurred is that desktop applications are slowly extending "out" across the Internet. For example, although it makes little sense for a word processor to be web based, it makes a great deal of sense for that word processor to be able to access a *web service* that allows multiple people to view a document, comment on it, and then distribute the revisions back to everyone on a distribution list. Prior to the Internet, proprietary products such as Lotus Notes provided this kind of functionality, but the Internet now allows these types of capabilities to be more broadly distributed. But building the software plumbing and infrastructure to support these capabilities is a development effort that's only now beginning and will take years to complete. Netscape had difficulties enough in building a competitive browser; its ability to construct a robust infrastructure of web services was nonexistent.

An Offer You Can't Refuse

Nonetheless, Microsoft, intent on its mission to destroy Netscape, rolled out across the industry with all the subtlety and attendant goodwill of Germany invading Poland. The first thing the company did after building IE was bundle it with the OEM version of Windows 95 and announce it was free. To be fair, this wasn't as aggressive a move as it appeared. Though the Netscape browsers (first Navigator and later Communicator) did have a theoretical SRP of $49.95, they were released on a trialware basis. You could download a fully functional copy of the browser and make full use of it without cost, though you were ostensibly supposed to pay up after an evaluation period. The products weren't crippled or time-locked in any significant way, and few individuals ever bought a copy, though Netscape did briefly make a nice living selling corporate licenses for its browsers.

But after this opening thrust, Microsoft ran rampant through the industry. The company threatened IBM and Compaq with the loss of their Windows licenses[5] if they offered Netscape instead of IE on their machines. It threatened Apple with the cancellation of a critical upgrade of the Mac version of Microsoft Office, the system's principal business

---

[5] Gary Norris of IBM testified during the Microsoft/DOJ trial that IBM, Compaq, and Hewlett-Packard feared loss of their Windows licenses if they considered offering OS/2 on their systems.

application suite, if it didn't yank the Netscape browser.[6] It offered "inducements" to companies such as KPMG to break volume purchase agreements they'd signed with Netscape.[7] It approached the major online services such as AOL, CompuServe, and MCI and cut deals with them to replace the Netscape browser with IE.[8] About the only thing Microsoft didn't do was kidnap the children of executives of companies using Netscape products and hold them hostage until their parents agreed to stop using Netscape's browser.

Microsoft employees also developed a bad habit of saying stupid things in public. In 1996, for instance, Microsoft Vice President Paul Maritz was quoted proclaiming that "We are going to cut off Netscape's air supply."[9] Although Maritz later denied saying it, the phrase nonetheless became particularly beloved at Microsoft and was repeated endlessly in internal e-mails, at company meetings, in conversations with the press, on online forums, etc. It all sounded tough and macho to the employees at Microsoft and rolled off the tongue in a satisfying fashion.[10] Netscape was going to suffer the same fate that befell Luca Brazzi and that treacherous little weasel of a brother-in-law in the movie *The Godfather*. But if Netscape was Luca Brazzi, what did that make Microsoft?

In Microsoft's defense, as with legal threats, tough talk in the industry is nothing new. Jim Manzi, after winning a look-and-feel judgment against Borland over its Quattro spreadsheet, had announced that he was going to perform a "cashectomy" on his foe.[11] (The judgment was overturned on appeal and Lotus never got a dime.) Ed Esber of Ashton-Tate had publicly bellowed "Make my day!" to companies daring to write dBASE language compilers. (Ashton-Tate never saw a dime either.) The difference is that when Jim Manzi and Ed Esber were shooting off

---

[6] Transcript of the videotaped deposition of Bill Gates, 1998, pp. 32–35.

[7] Rivlin, op. cit., pp. 198–199. This announcement was made in 1997 and involved KPMG pulling out 1,800 Navigator seats in favor of IE.

[8] Ibid, p. 198.

[9] Steve McGeady, a senior vice president at Intel, originally attributed this statement to Maritz at a 1995 meeting between the two companies.

[10] "US Takes on Microsoft." *The Boston Globe*, May 19, 1998.

[11] *Technology Update*, January/February 1994 (http://www.abanet.org/lpm2/magazine/tu941.html). This statement was perhaps the most famous of Manzi's entire career and was widely reported in every major PC and business magazine at the time of its utterance.

their mouths, they didn't have a bunch of resentful U.S. attorneys looking for an excuse to launch a federal antitrust action against their firms.

Viewed tactically, the Microsoft campaign was a success. By the end of 1998, Netscape and Microsoft were almost dead even in browser market share. Netscape was on the ropes and was saved from inevitable extinction only by being acquired by AOL.

Strategically, the campaign was a disaster. Microsoft had somehow convinced itself that its actions wouldn't bring down another DOJ lawsuit on its head, a calculation of almost incomprehensible idiocy. The feds came down with both feet on the company, and Microsoft found itself back in front of a federal judge explaining its behavior.

If Netscape represented the "Poland" phase of Microsoft's campaign, Gates's 1998 video deposition during the government's antitrust case was its "Stalingrad." The deposition was conducted in Microsoft headquarters over 3 days and featured a wan-looking Bill Gates nervously rocking back and forth and twitching while answering questions from David Boies, the government's lead attorney. His demeanor was a cross between that of Norman Bates in *Psycho* discussing "Mother" with Janet Leigh and Martin Short's Sweaty Nervous Guy of *Saturday Night Live* fame. (Sweaty Nervous Guy, a recurring character on the show, was a chain-smoking lawyer with an eternal caught-with-his-hand-in-the-cookie-jar expression who was constantly being interviewed by a Mike Wallace–type interlocutor about his various sleazy business deals.)

Gates demonstrated he had Sweaty Nervous Guy down to a "T" during the deposition. He never smiled during the sessions, and he never talked about the wonders of technology and all the good Microsoft was doing for humanity. He made few attempts to disagree with the premises of the questions, something you can do during a deposition. (He also seemed to feel sorry for himself, forgetting that no one feels sorry for billionaires.) Instead, he rocked back and forth, avoided making eye contact with his interrogators, and gave answers that were every bit as evasive, inane, and hilarious as Short at his best.

As Gates hit his stride, he had trial spectators and Judge Thomas Penfield Jackson guffawing in disbelief and amusement. One of the most widely reported gems was this:

David Boies: Do you recall speaking to anyone about the meeting referred to here between Dan Rosen and Jim Barksdale?

Bill Gates: No.

DB: The e-mail goes on to list six working goals, which are one, launch STT, our electronic payment protocol. Get STT presence on the Internet. Two, move Netscape out of the Win32 Internet client area. Three, avoid cold or hot war with Netscape. Keep them from sabotaging our platform evolution. Do you understand the reference to Win32 Internet client to be a reference to Windows 95?

BG: No.

DB: What do you understand it to be a reference to?

BG: Win32.

DB: And can you describe what that is.

BG: Thirty-two-bit Windows.

DB: Is Windows 95 a 32-bit Windows product?

BG: It's one of them.

Then there was this rib tickler:

David Boies: Does Microsoft have software that competes with QuickTime?

Bill Gates: Since QuickTime's a free runtime, you can answer that either yes or no. It's not a revenue source for Apple. But there is an Apple technology that has some common things with some Microsoft technologies.

DB: Do you believe that QuickTime software competes with any software distributed by Microsoft?

David Heiner (Microsoft attorney): Objection.

BG: Depends on what you mean by compete.

And this particular exchange practically brought down the house:

David Boies: Well, let me show you a document that has previously been marked as government exhibit 268. This is a document bearing Microsoft document production stamps ms 98 0110952 through 53. The first part of this purports to be a copy of an e-mail from Dan—Don Bradford to Ben Waldman, with a copy to you, Mr. Maritz and others, on the subject of, quote, Java on Macintosh/IE control. Did you receive a copy of this e-mail on or about February 13, 1998?

BG: I don't know.

DB: Do you have any reason to doubt that you received a copy of this e-mail?

BG: No.

DB: The first paragraph reads, quote, Apple wants to keep both Netscape and Microsoft developing browsers for Mac—believing if one drops out, the other will lose interest (and also not really wanting to pick up the development burden). Getting Apple to do anything that significantly materially disadvantages Netscape will be tough. Do you agree that Apple should be meeting—it reads, do you agree that Apple should be meeting the spirit of our cross-license agreement and that MacOffice is the perfect club to use on them. Do you have an understanding of what Mr. Bradford means when he refers to MacOffice as, quote, the perfect club to use on Apple, closed quote?

BG: No.

Judge Jackson paused from his enjoyment of this sidesplitting bit of theater just long enough to find Microsoft guilty of antitrust violations and recommend the company be broken up. Although Jackson was later removed from the case for injudicious conduct (i.e., telling anyone who would listen he thought Microsoft was guilty as hell), the finding was upheld on appeal and the guilty verdict sustained. All that remained to be determined was the punishment the company could look forward to.

The answer seemed to come when the government announced a settlement with Microsoft in which the company now agreed to

- allow people to yank things such as IE out of Windows (or hide it from view) if they so chose (Microsoft had previously announced this was "impossible," but apparently a guilty verdict in a federal antitrust trial can achieve miracles that would impress even Moses waiting to cross the Red Sea);

- play nice in the OEM market and not threaten trembling reeds such as HP and Dell with loss of their Windows licenses if they bundled products that competed with Microsoft on their PCs (and this time the government really really meant it);

- provide technical information on Windows APIs and protocols the company had previously kept proprietary;

- approve the payment of "billions of dollars" to the market in compensatory "damages," though much of said compensation seemed to consist of coupons that allowed people to buy Microsoft products at attractive discounts. Microsoft's sales and marketing group were said to be delighted with the concept;

- agree to allow the court to inspect Microsoft's business activities via a committee set up by the court for at least 5 years;

- and in general play nice in the future and act the part of good corporate citizen.

A group of spoilsport states and companies promptly announced they were unhappy with the agreement and spent a great deal of time trying to persuade U.S. District Court Judge Colleen Kollar-Kotelly, who had taken over upon Judge Jackson's abrupt departure from the case, to treat Microsoft far more harshly, but in November 2002 Judge Kollar-Kotelly issued a ruling that largely affirmed the initial settlement. The pundits promptly proclaimed Microsoft's total triumph in the case, and that seemed to be that.

Such proclamations were demonstrated to be premature a couple of months later when U.S. District Court Judge J. Frederick Motz decided in a separate lawsuit filed by Sun Microsoft that Microsoft had to bundle a spiffy, up-to-date version of Java in Windows instead of the obsolete hulk it had grudgingly agreed to stick into the OS in an out-of-the-way corner. Judge Motz was mightily impressed by the concept that Microsoft had been already found guilty of acting as an illegal monopolist and seemed inclined to kick sand in the face of the Redmond bully. When Microsoft objected and noted that Judge Kollar-Kotelly hadn't required this remedy in the government's case, Motz noted tartly that that was a different judge and a different case. He granted a preliminary injunction in Sun Microsystems's favor and ended up giving Microsoft 3 months to see the court's ruling implemented. At this point, Microsoft and others began to understand the long-term impact of losing an antitrust case to the U.S. courts: The company was now in many respects a 98-pound legal weakling who could be picked on by any judge having a "bad robe day." Over time, Microsoft could look forward to being nicked in courts again and again.

And it wasn't just Sun Microsystems looking for a pound of profits and revenge. Other companies, such as Be[12] and Burst, also had ongoing suits against Microsoft, and even a few diehard states, such as Massachusetts, announced they were going to continue worrying the software publisher's heels with sharp little legal teeth until they had extracted their own "justice" from the situation. And every time Microsoft lawyers walked into court, they could expect to hear an earful about how the company had been found "guilty" in the awful majestic eyes of the U.S. government of acting like a reincarnation of a 19th-century robber baron. (IBM, which managed to successfully fend off the U.S. government's similar charges, can give Microsoft some pointers on how this can affect a company's business environment over time.) The company had removed a thorn from its side in return for an anaconda around its neck.

Another casualty of Microsoft's Netscape blitzkrieg was Bill Gates's public persona. By the trial's end, Gates had become so closely associated with Microsoft's competitive knife work that he was in danger of becoming the high-tech version of Martha Stewart. It was judged necessary to ease him out of the company's CEO position by replacing him with second-in-command Steve Ballmer and settling him into the less visible role of company "chief technologist." Here, the scars and cracks Gates's behavior and comments during the deposition and trial had left on his carefully crafted and burnished corporate image could be slowly mended and repaired. In the meantime, Microsoft's PR machine went to work transforming Ballmer's attack-dog persona into something more warm and personable. Pictures of Ballmer's stout, bald-pated countenance sporting a beneficent expression soon began appearing on the front covers of business magazines everywhere. In the place of a high-tech elf, Microsoft now offered the world a high-tech teddy bear.

---

[12] Of all the companies baying after Microsoft, Be was perhaps the best example of a firm baking its own croissant but being unwilling to eat it. Be was the brainchild of Jean-Louis Gassée, who had spent much of the 1980s at Apple as vice president of engineering fighting any and all attempts to license the Mac OS to third parties. Gassée's efforts to keep the Mac OS proprietary were successful, ensuring Apple's descent from industry leader to niche player. After leaving Apple, Gassée founded Be, which briefly tried to replicate Apple's integrated hardware/software strategy before becoming a software-only firm. After failing to sell the Be OS back to proprietary Apple at the mind-boggling price of $300 million, Gassée underwent something of a conversion and attempted to position Be as an "open" OS. Not many people ever bought the company's products despite their considerable capabilities, and Be was eventually sold to Palm in 2001 for $11 million in stock, the high-tech equivalent of a handful of baguettes.

Microsoft could have traveled another path. Realizing the government was keeping a close eye on its every move, Microsoft could have moved forcefully but far more judiciously in its effort to compete. The company was on fairly safe ground in bundling IE with Windows and even offering it for free: Netscape was basically giving away its browser as well. The tie-in to Windows 95 in and of itself gave Microsoft a long-term advantage over Netscape that ensured it would pick up significant browser market share. And because it had bought and was successfully selling the market's leading web development package, FrontPage, Microsoft was in a position to leverage use of its browser on this front as well.

Where Microsoft needed to move carefully was in establishing its partnerships and picking the spots where it would apply maximum pressure. Blackmailing Apple was pointless; the company had all of 4 percent market share worldwide, and if every Mac user on Earth had sworn to commit ritual suicide on behalf of Netscape it didn't really matter. It wasn't necessary for Microsoft to chase Netscape off of every major online service; the AOL deal by itself was a major coup and ensured a huge pickup in user desktops. Threatening IBM and Compaq with loss of their Windows licenses if they didn't remove Netscape from their computers was an open invitation to an antitrust suit; simply ensuring that IE received equal billing on their PCs was more than enough to maintain the shift toward Microsoft.

It would also have been a smart move for everyone at Microsoft to have had an electronic collar fastened around their necks that gave off a severe shock anytime they said something mean about Netscape in public. Microsoft failed to understand that the public liked Netscape. It thought blonde, roly-poly founder Marc Andreessen was rather cute, kind of a high-tech panda bear. Netscape reminded them of another hot young technology company whose main spokesperson was also blonde, though he was now not so young and not so cute. And people hate it when other people are seen being mean to cute things. If you're going to club a baby seal to death, make sure you do it when the cameras aren't rolling.

Rather than sending out its unending series of blood-curdling announcements, Microsoft should have been lavish in its praise for cute young Netscape. It should have complimented the company on its cleverness and bright thinking while making sure everyone knew that IE was now being rated higher than Netscape's competing products. It should have praised the value of competition and welcomed Netscape as a "partner" in providing all Americans with access to the exciting new world of the Internet while simultaneously working to ensure IE's market share grew.

Microsoft should also have considered whether it was useful for Netscape to survive as a viable, but distant, number-two competitor. It's no secret that it's currently in Microsoft's best interest for Apple to stick around. While it does, Microsoft can make at least a semiserious claim that there's some competition in the OS market. Intel, another company that has from time to time felt the hot breath of the federal regulatory serpent, has also learned this lesson. The company has the power to crush long-time rival AMD in the microprocessor market if it chooses, but it has chosen not to do so. As with Microsoft and Apple, while AMD exists Intel can credibly claim that it faces real industry competition.

Still, it all could have turned out worse for Bill Gates and Microsoft. The change in administration in 2001 put a new, more business-friendly regime in power at the White House, and some of the pressure on Microsoft eased. Of course, having Judge Motz drop a new Java into Windows was the technical equivalent of having a big black fly expire in the middle of your fresh bowl of potato salad, but it seemed unlikely that the federal anaconda would squeeze the company into one or more parts. At least not right now. But it would stick around to keep an eye on its new friends, Bill Gates and Microsoft.

And Gates had clearly learned his lesson. The madness that had seized him during the 1998 deposition was nowhere in evidence when he testified on Microsoft's behalf in early 2002 at the remedy phase of the antitrust trial. He came to court dressed in an understated suit with a purple tie (a very spiritual color). His wife, Melinda, pregnant with their third child, accompanied him to court and held his hand.

During his testimony, in contrast with his Norman Bates/Sweaty Nervous Guy demeanor of 4 years ago, Gates was relaxed and under control, and he smiled genially and often. He even cracked a few jokes. He talked about how Microsoft had contributed to America's welfare with its technology. He portrayed the company as being at the center of a new industrial revolution. He reminded everyone that Microsoft played by the same rules as every other company it competed with.

Then, in 2004 and 2005, he and his wife went on several highly publicized trips on behalf of the Bill and Melinda Gates Foundation, proffering billions of dollars on behalf of the sick and diseased in Africa and India.

Bill Gates doesn't often make the same mistake twice.

~

Netscape and Marc Andreessen: Will You Please Just Shut Up?

If you like to go horror movies, you know the cast usually sports a character you've come to think of as The Idiot Who Deserves to Die. He's the knucklehead who runs screaming into the path of Godzilla just as the giant reptile is heading out to spend a relaxing afternoon destroying Tokyo, and gets squashed like a bug. The dimwit who sticks his noggin out of the deserted cabin in the woods and yells out "Mad slasher? What mad slasher?" just before the mad slasher decapitates him. The space-bound fumble-fingers who always manages to drop his blaster right when the Tentacle of Doom is zeroing in on him as lunch.

If Marc Andreessen, cofounder of one-time wonder company Netscape, ever gives up high tech for a career in horror movies, he'll play that character.

In 1993, Marc Andreessen, a computer science major at the University of Illinois at Urbana-Champaign, posted the first version of the Mosaic browser for download on several Internet sites. Mosaic was primarily the joint creation of Andreessen, who functioned as the product architect and idea guy, and Eric Bina, a programmer at the university who did most of the actual coding. Mosaic represented a radical step forward in browser design. It had, for the time, an easy-to-use graphical interface that a newcomer to the Internet could master in about an hour. It used HTML to display both text and pictures within the browser environment. Versions of it were available for UNIX, Windows, and the Mac. Mosaic, which would serve as the spiritual foundation of Netscape Corporation, swept through the Internet like a virus, only with a happier outcome. By the end of 1995, millions of copies of the product were in use, and to the general public the World Wide Web **was** the Internet.

In the interim, Andreessen, deprived of what he felt was his proper share of the glory for Mosaic's creation,[13] headed out west to make his fortune as a generation of high-tech expatriates had done before him. He quickly fell in with Jim Clark, one of the founders of Silicon Graphics, Inc. (SGI), and the two founded Netscape. The company promptly wrote a new browser that was eventually called Navigator to avoid legal problems with the University of Illinois, which owned the rights to Mosaic. Netscape's new baby was released over the Internet in December 1994.

Far more functional and feature packed than its competitors, including its Mosaic predecessor, Navigator quickly became the de facto market standard and by 1995 had approximately 80 percent of the browser market share. Netscape went public in the summer of 1995 (2 weeks before the rollout of Windows 95). The stock, pegged at a pre-IPO value of $28.00 per share, opened at $71.00 and closed at $58.25. Overnight, Netscape was a media sensation, and Andreessen, its vice president of technology, became one of the industry's latest on-paper multimillionaires. Even better, Andreessen also found himself at the tender age of 25 playing the role of spokesman and poster boy for the Internet company at a time when all anyone could talk about was the Internet.

It was a disaster.

The New Bill, Not the Same As the Old

On the face of it, it could have all worked out. Andreessen is a big, soft-looking fellow with stocky blonde good looks. Yes, he was young, but Bill Gates was still drinking Shirley Temples when he founded Microsoft and he was only 26 when he negotiated the famous IBM deal. Andreessen is fairly literate and very intelligent. He looks good in pictures and is comfortable on camera. People naturally warm to him, and he has a good speaking voice. On the face of it, a nice PR package. Unfortunately, what was missing from the package in the mid-1990s was even an ounce of common sense.

---

[13] Charles H. Ferguson, *High Stakes, No Prisoners* (New York: Times Books/Random House, 1999), p. 52.

Once he'd gotten a taste of the limelight, Andreessen, along with the rest of Netscape, promptly decided that the very smartest thing they could do was to bait and threaten Microsoft. Andreessen began his big push to guarantee his company's destruction at the hands of Microsoft by taking an early look at Java in 1995 and telling the world that this new language, in conjunction with Netscape's browsers, was the application platform of the future and would replace Windows. This immediately got Bill Gates's full attention. Windows is Microsoft's most valuable franchise and what threatens it threatens the company. Not one to let an opportunity slip by, Andreessen proceeded to ensure Gates would stay fully focused on him and Netscape for the foreseeable future by allowing himself to be quoted in the trade press predicting that Windows would be reduced to a "poorly debugged set of device drivers."

After his immortal "device drivers" bon mot, Andreessen was hardly through. Over the next few months he proved to be an endless source of witty and memorable observations, all of which were widely reported on in the press and collected by Microsoft, the owner of those poorly debugged device drivers. Some of his most pithy comments included the following:

"It was like a visit to Don Corleone. I expected to find a bloody computer monitor in my bed the next day."[14]

"We're gonna smoke 'em."[15] (Microsoft being the intended smokee.)

"No horse head in the bed yet."[16]

"Those idiots up in Redmond."[17]

"The beast from Redmond."[18]

---

[14] Ibid, p. 52.

[15] Rivlin, op. cit., p. 195.

[16] Rivlin, loc. cit.

[17] Rivlin, loc. cit.

[18] Rivlin, loc. cit.

"They can't keep up."[19] (Referring to Microsoft's inability to out-code the tyros from Netscape.)

"The Evil Empire."[20]

"Godzilla."[21]

Andreessen also discovered that, like Bill Gates, he had an affinity for the camera. In a 2-year period he appeared in or was profiled by every major news and business magazine. He appeared on the cover of *Time* magazine seated on a golden throne. George Gilder, prophet of everything high tech, pronounced Andreessen Earth's most supercalifragilisticexpealidotious person. A *Forbes* article proclaimed Andreessen was the "next Bill Gates."

Merry Pranksters

Inspired in part by Netscape's irrepressible vice president of technology, AOL, another fierce Microsoft competitor, embarked on a path of merry pranksterism. The company flew a blimp over the rollout of Windows 95 with the word "Welcome" emblazoned on its side. (This stunt had a shining precedent: Steve Jobs's condescending 1981 newspaper ads "welcoming" IBM to the microcomputer industry. Today, Apple and Netscape [now owned by AOL] each hold about 4 percent shares in their respective markets. As Marx noted, history **does** repeat itself.) All the while Netscape was indulging itself in displays of high spirits, the company was developing a reputation of being just as arrogant and hard to deal with as Microsoft.

Meanwhile, back in Redmond, Washington, the real Bill Gates, not the simulacrum from Netscape, paid Andreessen the very highest compliment of all. He took him seriously and dedicated all his time and energy to destroying Andreessen's company. The Netscape cofounder personally earned celebrity dartboard status at Microsoft, an honor that had previously been reserved for such luminaries as Philippe Kahn of

---

[19] Rivlin, loc. cit.

[20] Transcript from *Nightly Business Report*, WPBT, September 21, 2000.

[21] Ibid.

Borland. By 1998 it was all over, as shrinking revenues and market share forced Netscape to trade high-tech heaven and independence for the low-tech haven of AOL and subordination.

It's impossible to overestimate the rank stupidity Andreessen demonstrated in his choice of public words and attitude vis-à-vis Microsoft. He'd committed the strategic equivalent of walking into the cage of a hungry tiger, turning around, taping a sirloin steak to his butt, and executing a slow bump and grind. It should have come as no surprise that when he left the cage he had no ass.

The harsh truth is that Netscape wasn't in a position to go head-to-head with Microsoft on anything in 1995. After its IPO, Netscape had $203 million in the bank; Microsoft had $10 billion. Netscape's core products, browsers, weren't hard to build, and Microsoft had the resources to build them. Nor, despite Andreessen's boasts, was Netscape a stronger development organization than Microsoft; in fact, the reverse was true. As already noted, by version 3.0 of IE, Microsoft was winning the product review battles in the press.

The release in 1997 of Netscape Communicator, designed to be an IE killer, drove the point home. Communicator quickly developed a widespread reputation for being slow, flaky, and overloaded with features such as an e-mail manager that never really worked. Netscape's server-based programs were also regarded as second-rate efforts, and many of the products the company claimed to have under development were vaporware. Java as a replacement for Windows proved to be a fantasy. Nor was Netscape smart enough to develop or acquire a robust web design tool à la FrontPage, one of the few places in the Internet bubble where real and sustainable profits could have been made.

Netscape, of course, faced an incredibly difficult challenge. Its initial strong success with Navigator and highly visible IPO guaranteed the company would attract Microsoft's attention. The intelligent thing for Netscape to have done during the period when Microsoft was considering what to do about the Internet would have been to immediately sew Marc Andreessen's lips shut and be as meek and unassuming as possible. Company executives should have publicly fainted when anyone suggested that Netscape technology would ever replace Windows as an applications platform. Netscape should have pledged eternal fealty to Windows, offered to partner with Microsoft (with the full understanding that Microsoft would eventually turn on them), and bought enough time for the company to cement its third-party relationships, make money, and build a more unassailable market position. In point of fact, Netscape **did** try to do this as the full weight of Microsoft's marketing panzers bore down on it, but after Andreessen's series of trenchant observations, Microsoft wasn't buying. What Netscape needed to survive the inevitable Microsoft onslaught was to buy as much time as possible, but the moments allotted by circumstances of its own making turned out to be not enough.

After the sellout to AOL, Marc Andreessen found his role in the industry had changed from young Internet über-man to personal geek assistant to Steve Case. After realizing his career at AOL was going to consist mainly of teaching members of the executive staff how to program their VCRs, he left to form a new Internet services and infrastructure company called Loudcloud. In view of Andreessen's previous performance at Netscape, it was perhaps an unfortunate choice of name. The company finally changed it to Opsware.

eleven

PURPLE HAZE
ALL THROUGH MY BRAIN:
The Internet and ASP Busts

WHEN THE INTERNET EXPLODED on the public consciousness in 1994, one of the reasons for the early excitement was that it seemed so fresh and new. This freshness was, as much else about the Internet proved to be, illusory. The Internet was a child of the 1960s finally all grown up, and it was about as new as LSD. And, like the notorious psychedelic elixir of the era of free love, flower power, and peace, those who partook of the Internet's dot-com drug in the late 1990s experienced an amazing and mind-bending experience that often detoured into a bad trip of bankruptcy, unemployment, and day-after flashbacks of disbelief.

~

Child of the '60s: The Internet

The Internet received its conceptual send-off in the early 1960s from the research and work of Paul Baran and Bob Taylor. Baran, a Rand company employee and computer scientist, wrote a series of papers for the Pentagon dealing with the problem of the U.S. military control and command structure during a major war. During this period, the nation's communications networks were highly centralized. A first strike on the system by either conventional or nuclear forces could have decapitated the military's communications command and control structures, rendering it unable to coordinate an effective retaliation.

To deal with this problem, Baran proposed building a distributed network based on digital technology at a time when all U.S. communications were based on analog systems. This system would pass messages from node to node via "message blocks." No one node would be responsible for end-to-end communications; instead, each would have a store and forward capability, allowing the message blocks to travel via the best or only path available. Using Baran's work as a foundation, in 1965 Rand proposed to the U.S. Air Force that it build a prototype of Baran's network, test it, and then go operational. The Air Force's different radio and TV experts took a dim view of all this talk of "digital transmission" and shot the idea down.

While Baran was working on preparing for nuclear apocalypse, Bob Taylor, head of NASA's Advanced Research Projects Agency (ARPA) unit, was wondering why the three computer terminals in his office couldn't talk to one another. ARPA had been started in 1958 as an Air Force project designed to help the United States pick up the technical gauntlet thrown by the Soviet Union with its successful launch of Sputnik I. The agency was moved over to NASA later that year, and though most of its attention was focused on the space race, there was still plenty of money floating around to fund some interesting research into communications.

Taking advantage of the opportunity, Taylor scooped up millions of taxpayer dollars to fund the development of a system that would allow his terminals to chat and hired MIT graduate Larry Roberts to lead the effort. Roberts began the design and implementation of what was soon to be known as ARPANET, the Internet's direct ancestor. In October 1969, the system went live when a message from the second node on the system to the first caused a system crash. The Internet had been born.

From this inauspicious beginning, the Internet grew from its original two nodes to over 100,000 hosts by 1989. In 1983, MILNET, reserved for military use, was spun off from ARPANET. In 1990, ARPANET was transferred over to the National Science Foundation (NSF) and renamed NFSNET. ARPANET was officially shut down and replaced by the Internet.

The Internet received its first taste of front-page publicity in 1988 courtesy of wiseacre Robert Morris, Jr., a Cornell graduate student in computer science who released a worm onto the Internet. A *worm* is a form of digital virus that infects a system, replicates, and then transmits itself to other systems where it attempts to repeat the cycle.

Morris may have gotten good grades at school, but the world soon found out he wasn't much of a programmer. His worm had a big bug in it, one that allowed the virus to replicate and spread much faster than he'd anticipated. Site after site on the Internet crashed as the worm overloaded hard drives and jammed transmission lines at facilities that included universities, military sites, hospitals, and government offices. The estimated cost of clearing out the virus from infected systems reached into the millions. Morris was convicted of violating the newly hatched Computer Fraud and Abuse Act and promptly became an iconic figure to subsequent generations of socially inadequate, smarter-than-you geeks who today follow in his inglorious footsteps by making everyone's life miserable via the regular creation and release of new Internet-transmitted viruses.

Despite the hullabaloo surrounding Morris's exploit, many people who read about him weren't sure what it was he'd actually done. Despite its rapid growth, the Internet had failed to catch the public's fancy. The various software programs used to browse the system employed primitive interfaces, and though standards had been developed for transmitting data across the Internet, none existed for locating files and documents. As a result, the Internet remained a semiprivate reserve used mainly by academics, the military, and IT workers in a variety of different industries.

The British Invasion

The Internet took a giant step forward in usability with the development of the World Wide Web by British software engineer Tim Berners-Lee. Berners-Lee was a regular Internet user but found the organization of information on the system fragmented and cumbersome. To overcome the problem, he developed a series of protocols and technologies that provide a foundation for what is now called the Web.

Berners-Lee designed the Web to sit on top of the Internet and to use its existing protocols and infrastructure. The Web added three new facets to the system:

- Hypertext Transfer Protocol (HTTP), a methodology for jumping directly from one file to another on the Internet

- The concept of the uniform resource locator (URL), a virtual "address" that can be assigned to any file on the Web

- Hypertext Markup Language (HTML), which controls text formatting for viewing an Internet site

Berners-Lee also created a primitive web browser to help test his initial work, but interestingly enough, browsing technology wasn't a part of his original specification.

The world's first website, http://www.info.cern.ch, went live in 1990, and Paul Kunz of the Stanford Linear Accelerator Center (SLAC) posted the first American website in August 1991. That same year, the U.S. government made the decision to turn over NFSNET to commercial companies and open the system up to commerce. In 1993, CERN, which owned the rights to Berners-Lee's work, announced anyone could use the Web's protocols and underlying technology royalty-free.

By the end of 1992, the Internet had more than a million users, but only 1 percent of that traffic represented web usage. A final element was needed before the Internet's formula for mass-market acceptance was complete: an easy-to-use graphical interface that would make the system attractive and accessible to the millions of PC users still using bulletin-board systems and proprietary services. The earliest web browsers were clunky, character-based systems; the Berners-Lee browser, for example, could display only one line of text at a time. More sophisticated UNIX-based programs were available, but they were difficult to install and UNIX was regarded by many PC and Mac users as a tool of Satan. Marc Andreessen's aforementioned (see Chapter 10) release of the Mosaic browser provided the final piece to the puzzle, and the modern Internet was born.

Up to this point in time, the Internet story made sense. A complex communications network first conceived of in the 1960s is slowly built and extended over the decades. Piece by piece, new capabilities and features are added to improve the system's performance, reliability, and usability. Public participation steadily grows until the technology reaches a critical mass. When it does, businesses jump into the new market to take advantage of new commercial opportunities. Some make a great deal of money, and others fall short and fail.

The Netscape IPO in August 1995 changed all that and sparked a speculative bubble focused on dot-com companies and their stocks the likes of which hadn't been seen since the late 1960s, when investors had lost their heads and portfolios over "technology" companies such as National Video[1] (they were going to build video players for the masses more than a decade before this was actually feasible) and conglomerates such as Ling-Temco-Vought (they were going to build everything). Within a year of the Netscape IPO, thousands of companies were being formed to create the "new economy," a world of web-based e-commerce ventures that seers and visionaries proclaimed would uproot and replace every existing business model and distribution system. The resulting mania drove the Dow Jones Industrial Average (it tracks the average value of 30 large, industrial stocks) from 5,000 to almost 12,000 and the technology-focused NASDAQ (it tracks many of those "dot-bomb" stocks that ruined your portfolio) from the 1,000 range to more than 5,000.

---

[1] My father worked as a stockbroker during the 1960s and 1970s, and I can remember him discussing National Video in the same terms people discussed the dot-com companies of the late 1990s. National Video was an early "high-tech" high flier that sucked up great wads of investor cash before disappearing from the scene.

Magic Carpet Ride

The book that best describes the late 20th century's dot-com bubble was written in the 19th century by Charles MacKay, thought by many to be the Nostradamus of marketing. MacKay's opus is entitled *Extraordinary Popular Delusions and the Madness of Crowds*[2] and it chronicles a long series of manias and speculative booms that have afflicted Western society since the Crusades. Reading through this classic treatise, you can find descriptions of events and circumstances that both presage and prophesy the dot-com boom. For instance, consider alchemy, the centuries-old belief that different substances could be transmuted to gold. Many think that MacKay was trying to warn future generations of the folly of buying stock from TheGlobe.com. When the company went public in November 1998, the stock opened at an incredible $87.00 and reached a high of $97.00. The company's assets? A not-very-quick nor comprehensive search engine, web pages filled with warmed-over links, and a revenue model that lost $4.00 for every $1.00 it earned. Fool's gold, and TheGlobe.com turned back into lead with its shutdown in August 2001.

In a similar vein, others believe *Extraordinary Popular Delusions and the Madness of Crowds'* description of the craze for exotic tulips that spread throughout 17th-century Holland was a warning of another sort. The chapter on "Tulipomania" describes how in the space of a few months the cost of a rare bulb skyrocketed from the merely expensive to the incredible. For a brief period, the sale of a single pretty flower was enough to enable a person to retire wealthy for life. Scholars believe this tale was intended to warn us about Amazon.com stock, which at the height of the bubble reached a high of $113.00 per share, while at the same time the company was bleeding copious amounts of red ink and company CEO Jeff Bezos was telling everyone he had no idea when Amazon would ever turn a profit. By August 2001, the stock was trading at around $9.00 per share, less than the single bulb price of many collectible tulips.

MacKay also cast a jaundiced gaze on witchcraft and the persistent human belief in spirits and the supernatural. When he wrote that chapter,

---

[2] As a young man my father had worked for Farrar, Straus, and Giroux, the American publisher of *Extraordinary Popular Delusions and the Madness of Crowds*, and he brought home a copy. I first read through the book as a young boy and still have it in my family library.

he may have been inspired by a future vision of Kozmo.com, the best known of several dot-com delivery services that sprang up during the boom. Kozmo's original business model consisted of sending people on bicycles to deliver videos, condoms, gum, and Twinkies to lazy New York City yuppies and hungry potheads. This particular venture sucked up more than $250 million in investment capital and almost made it to an IPO. Because it cost the company an average of $10.00 in labor and overhead to fulfill the $12.00 average Kozmo order, a sum that didn't account for the company's cost of goods and marketing expenditures, it truly would have required supernatural intervention for Kozmo to have ever turned a profit.

One thing that *Extraordinary Popular Delusions and the Madness of Crowds* doesn't do is explain the root causes of these speculative bubbles. No one ever has. They usually share factors such as good economic times, easy access to credit, and sometimes the development of new technology, but the combination of all these circumstances usually **does not** generate a bubble. Many reasons for the dot-com boom have been offered, but all are somewhat unsatisfactory. The most common explanations postulate the following:

Major technological breakthroughs often spark speculative fever. Perhaps, but the introduction of the airplane, TV, CB radios, and, most recently, the personal computer did not. And it could be argued that the Internet, although a significant advance in communications, was hardly a technology breakthrough even on the scale of refrigeration, which transformed the American South from a backwater into the country's most vibrant economic region. On the other hand, railroads, the high-tech darlings of the 19th century, triggered a speculative mania that helped contribute to a depression, as Charles Kindleberger points out in *Manias, Panics, and Crashes: A History of Financial Crises* (the second-best book ever written about the dot-com boom). But why trains and not TVs?

The number of people investing in the stock market had increased tremendously over the past 30 years, making the market more volatile. This contradicts mathematics and experience. The larger markets become, the more overall stability they tend to achieve. In the post–Civil War era, "robber barons" such as Jay Gould and Jim Fisk were able to attempt to corner the U.S. gold market (and were only prevented from doing so by President Grant's direct intervention).

The Hunt brothers would attempt to reprise this feat with silver in the 1980s. But by the early 1990s, public participation in the stock market put such an enterprise beyond the power of any individual or even any group of speculators.

The stock market had undergone continuous expansion since the Reagan recovery of 1982. Unfortunately for this theory, few stock market expansions spark speculative bubbles.

Everyone who had lived through the stock market crash of 1929 was now dead, and the U.S. school systems do a rotten job of teaching children about important events in American history and why they occur. This theory makes a lot of sense.

The Internet, a technology child of the 1960s, functioned not only as a communications medium but also as a virtual magic mushroom that clouded the brains of people worldwide. Though somewhat metaphysical, this theory also makes a lot of sense.

Wall Street is full of idiots. This theory is both popular and has a lot going for it.

The people who bought stock from the idiots on Wall Street were also idiots. What?! Are you implying that the American people's failure to, when confronted with IPOs that reeked of red ink and gobbled on about idiotic schemes to sell 30-pound bags of pet food directly to consumers at a guaranteed loss (Pets.com), not fall laughing hysterically to the floor before kicking these IPO turkeys out the door somehow makes them responsible for their own losses? This sort of speculation isn't even worthy of a reply!

Whatever the precise reasons for a particular speculative bubble, its life cycle follows a set course, though it's difficult to predict the exact timing of the sequence of events. First, there's an initial boom period during which insiders get rich and the public "discovers" what's going on. The bubble then grows larger as early skeptics enter the maelstrom and make money while sensible people stand on the sidelines scoffing at their foolishness. The speculators then turn around and make fun of the naysayers, who, embarrassed at their failure to "get it," rush in to scoop up their fair share of the plunder before the opportunity vanishes. At this point, the bubble reaches it maximum expansion and seems to pinch off from normal reality to become a universe of its own. The normal rules of profit and loss no longer apply in this alternate realm; all that matters is supply and demand.

At this point, the smart money tries to bail out before the inevitable crash. A few do succeed in escaping with their riches, and their exit begins to deflate the bubble. The rest of the occupants become uneasy and begin to edge toward the exit as well. For a while, the bubble seems to reach a state of equilibrium as the last group of idiots on the outside rush in to search for now nonexistent profits within the doomed alternate universe. Then contraction occurs, suddenly, and the bubble bursts. Seemingly overnight, profit, wealth, and happiness are replaced by loss, poverty, and misery.

Reflecting the morality of another age, *Extraordinary Popular Delusions and the Madness of Crowds* doesn't waste much pity on bubble participants. In his examination of the South Sea mania, a weird 18th-century scheme that involved buying shares in companies that were going to do business of some sort on the coasts of South America, Mackay writes

> *Nobody seemed to imagine that the nation itself was as culpable as the South-Sea company. Nobody blamed the credulity and the avarice of the people—the degrading lust of gain, which had swallowed up every nobler quality in the national character, or the infatuation which had made the multitude run their heads with such frantic eagerness into the net held out for them by scheming projectors. These things were never mentioned. The people were a simple, honest, hard-working people, ruined by a gang of robbers, who were to be hanged, drawn, and quartered without mercy.*[3]

Although such observations are not politically correct in an era of universal victimhood, they're fair. As the dot-com bubble grew and swallowed increasing volumes of innocent cash, the fact that many of the original business assumptions associated with Internet and web commerce were proving invalid was no secret. At least one prediction about the Internet and e-business was proving true: When things happened,

---

[3] Charles MacKay, *Memoirs of Extraordinary Popular Delusions and the Madness of Crowds* (New York: Farrar, Strauss and Giroux, 1932), p.72.

they happened quickly. The Web's hyperlinked architecture made measuring response and results fairly straightforward and ensured you could learn the depressing news quickly.

The Pusher Man

Banner advertising was e-commerce's first bad trip. Most sources credit the Coors Brewing Company with placing the first web banner. The ad, a bit larger than the 468×60 pixel form factor that would become a Web standard, was one element in a national campaign on behalf of Zima, a new clear malt "beverage" (otherwise known as "beer") Coors hoped would attract barhopping urban professionals everywhere. The banner was placed in October 1994 on the HotWired site, at the time one of the Web's most active, and was a hit. Response rates (measured by how many times people clicked the banner) averaged between 5 percent and 10 percent over the life of the campaign.

Unfortunately for Coors, its ad campaign was so successful that many people actually ran out and tried Zima,[4] only to find the stuff had about as much taste and charm as a glass of warm bathwater. Worse, the initial response to the banner encouraged e-commerce fans to predict that the Zima campaign would be representative of future Web banner performance. It wasn't. Once the novelty of banners had worn off, response rates plunged. By 1998, average banner hit rates had dropped from figures of 3 percent to 5 percent to numbers that ranged between one-tenth to one-quarter of a percent on average.

This drop was entirely predictable. A standard 480×60 pixel Web banner consists of about 5 square inches and takes up less than 5 percent of the real estate on a 17-inch computer monitor. Colors, animation, and interactivity are limited by the bandwidth of the ad server system and the need to ensure that Web pages load quickly. Complicating things further is the easy availability of technology capable of blocking most ads, though they're so easy to ignore most people don't bother. By contrast, an ad on a 25-inch TV consists of about 400 inches of uninterrupted pulsating pixels that talk, sing, and dance while imploring you to buy something. Channel surfing to avoid ads doesn't help, because most stations run their commercials at the same time. Another option is to learn

---

[4] I drank a glass of the stuff once. Ugh.

how to program your VCR, DVD, or similar recording device, but most people prefer the ads.

The Internet's next psychedelic nightmare was *frictionless* e-commerce. On the face of it, this was the most intriguing argument made to justify the existence of many dot-com ventures. Web-based companies, the theory went, would "disintermediate" the middlemen (i.e., distributors and resellers) because people could simply buy products directly via their browsers. One writer for *NewMedia* magazine breathlessly predicted that the Internet would soon obsolete the country's malls and retail stores. Replacing them would be a vast sprawl of distribution centers and warehouses serviced by fleets of vans designed to deliver purchases to your door within 4 to 6 hours.

This was truly stupid stuff. If we've learned anything from history, it's that new methods of distribution and payment rarely supplant existing systems; either they're integrated into the existing system or they become an additional enhancement. If you doubt this, take a coin out of your pocket and inspect this product of Bronze Age technology carefully. Coins are heavy, hard to store, and difficult to transport. Are they obsolete? Ask a vending-machine operator or a Las Vegas casino. Scattering vast new warehouse complexes around the country sounded nice to some, but where were they going to be located? There are areas of the country where building a new gas station or restaurant is reason enough for environmental angst.

And direct marketing with overnight delivery was nothing new. Not surprisingly, people who enjoyed direct shopping via the mail also enjoyed direct shopping on the Web, and there are few complaints about the current efficiency of the delivery system for goods.

Another obvious problem with the concept of disintermediation was that people like to go out and shop. We've enjoyed the experience for several millennia, and we're not going to drop the habit just because the Internet showed up. In 1998, total retail sales on the Internet were $15 billion and projected to reach $1.3 trillion by 2003. A healthy figure, but contrast this number with the 2.3 trillion in-store shopping dollars targeted by Sears and Wal-Mart **alone**. In the United States, and increasingly in the rest of the world, shopping is a necessity and entertainment all rolled into one. Rather than replace retail channels, the Internet is being integrated into the existing system. Web-based kiosks, for example, allow shoppers to browse through a store's inventory and special-order items not found on the floor. New advertising "billboard" displays make use of Web technology to dynamically change their content based on the time of day, promotions, and even estimates of current store demographics.[5]

The rise and fall of ValueAmerica.com, one of the Internet's most storied e-tailers, best exemplifies why the pursuit of frictionless e-commerce was a chimera. If you traveled regularly on business trips in the late 1990s, you probably stayed at one of those hotels that likes to shove a copy of *USA Today* under your door at 5:00a.m. As you staggered down to breakfast with McPaper under your arm and waited for that first cup of coffee to kick start your day, you may remember seeing full-page ads on the back pages of the paper for portable computers, desktop PCs, consumer electronics, barbecue grills, and so forth. If you do, that was your introduction to Value America (which, by the way, generated most of its sales from those newspaper ads).

Value America was the brainchild of sell-your-mother sales wunderkind Craig Winn. Earlier in his career, Winn had built a successful home-lighting business, Dynasty Classics Corp., and then promptly turned around and drove it into the ground. Dynasty's collapse revolved around Winn's managerial incompetence combined with his continued insistence on butting heads with major distributors and resellers such as Wal-Mart. Like many other entrepreneurs before him, Winn resented the distribution system's power to dictate prices, margins, and even packaging to vendors and suppliers.[6] Value America, in addition to making Winn very rich, was also intended to be his revenge on the U.S. distribution system.[7] It would be the system, however, that would have the last laugh.

Value America's business model was both simple and unworkable. The company presented itself as a giant online store. In truth, it was simply a

---

[5] To get a sense of what awaits you in the future, I strongly suggest you see *Minority Report*, the 2002 sci-fi thriller starring Tom Cruise. The film depicts personalized digital advertising displays that greet you by name via scans of your retinal patterns. To depress you further, you should also see *Gattaca*, a scary and prophetic look into a biometric future. Much of *Gattaca* was shot at the Marin County Civic Center, a leaky edifice that was designed by Frank Lloyd Wright and known only semiaffectionately by the natives as "Frank Lloyd Wright's last erection." To many people, the building resembles a giant . . . well . . . you get the idea. I passed this building every day on my way to my job as a product manager at MicroPro corporate headquarters on North San Pedro Road.

[6] Winn blamed Wal-Mart for the bankruptcy of his first company, Dynasty Classics, in an interview in 2000 with *Business Week* magazine.

[7] J. David Kuo, *Dot.Bomb: My Days and Nights at an Internet Goliath* (New York: Little, Brown and Company, 2001).

middleman between buyers and manufacturers. Value America's plan was for the company to never to have shelves or warehouses and the costs that accompany them. When a customer placed an order, Value America passed the request on to a manufacturer, which shipped the item directly to the consumer. Buyers were instructed to ship returned items directly back to the manufacturer. Value America was ostensibly supposed to make money by "reselling products" at a 1 percent markup over cost. For a bricks-and-mortar retailer this is a suicidal price structure, but Value America's inventory-free model supposedly made it possible to achieve profitability with this microscopically thin margin.

Despite the patina of high tech the Internet cast on Winn's creation, nothing he was attempting was new. The manufacturer-direct-to-customer approach has been tried before, and it has failed before. Many, many times. The reason for this is simple: Distribution systems congeal out of businesses and industries not because of desire or opportunism but out of sheer necessity. Unfortunately for the poor souls who loaded e-tail stocks into their portfolios, few people advocating inventory-free retailing had much understanding of how and why distribution systems exist.

The usual function of a distributor or reseller is, in the vernacular, to "break bulk" and reduce the many to the one. These entities are experts in receiving orders from multiple sources and fulfilling them via complex and highly automated systems that provide warehousing, credit checking, tracking, fulfillment, returns management, etc., etc. Creating and efficiently managing such systems requires years of acquired expertise and is expensive. Just how expensive is something Amazon.com discovered as it attempted to create in a few years warehousing and fulfillment systems it had taken companies such as Wal-Mart decades to implement and perfect.

Vendors and manufacturers are naturally drawn to the idea of cutting out the middlemen and selling their products and services directly to customers, but few ultimately succeed. In high tech, business-to-business companies such as IBM and Microsoft have in the past attempted to bypass major hardware and software distributors such as Ingram and Tech Data. Eventually, all have been forced to abandon the attempt. Companies discovered that as they added increasing numbers of resellers, the cost of attempting to replicate the specialized expertise of a distributor became prohibitive. It was more cost-effective to simply ship large quantities of product X (the bulk) to distributor Y (the one) and let them worry about the logistics of shipping the stuff out to various resellers (the many). In consumer retailing the same logic constantly repeats itself, with the sheer volume of companies and customers making the need for a distribution channel even more critical.

There are companies that are able to buck the system, computer manufacturer Dell being one of high tech's most notable. Dell's direct-to-consumer model has flourished because computers are comparatively high-dollar purchases, possess a highly standardized form factor, and are easy to ship via mail. The majority of Dell customers are more interested in price and availability than brand equity and service, and because Dell assembles its own inventory, the company can closely manage demand and fulfillment. With all these contingencies in its favor, Dell's direct business approach can succeed.

None of these aforementioned factors applied to Value America, however. Because it stocked and built nothing, once an order was received and transmitted to a manufacturer, tracking and delivery was out of Value America's control. And, as a business-to-consumer enterprise, it carried the additional burden of coordinating the sales of hundreds of thousands of orders from customers with thousands of manufacturers. Value America never developed inventory management systems that came close to the power and sophistication needed to manage such a complex task.

This wasn't the only drawback to the company's inventory-free model. Manufacturers that sold only a few items via recommendations from Value America gave those orders low priority. In some cases, once they realized that Value America wouldn't be selling significant amounts of product, they didn't bother to fulfill them at all. (In point of fact, many manufacturers required Value America to buy their products from distributors, because they had little interest in attempting to become distributors themselves. This in turn helped undermine the company's "1 percent over manufacturer cost" revenue model.) And though vendors receiving higher volumes of orders from the company were quicker to respond to customer issues, Value America's primitive order tracking and fulfillment systems often made finding and fixing problems difficult, if not impossible.

The company also didn't understand that when you sell something to a customer, you "own" that customer and all the customer's associated problems, including the problem of customer dissatisfaction with a purchase. Despite its claims to have no shelves and no warehouses, Value America soon acquired both in order to manage product returns.

J. David Kuo, in *Dot.Bomb: My Days and Nights at an Internet Goliath*, his I-was-there description of the rise and fall of Value America, described how the situation developed:

> When Winn created Value America, an important part of the model was not holding any inventory, anywhere, at any time. But a strange thing began to happen as the company sold more and more merchandise. When people didn't like a product or changed their mind, or when the product didn't work, they returned the product to Value America. Despite the fact they were **told** to send it back to the manufacturer, they did what shoppers everywhere do. They returned it to the place they purchased it. [8]

At one point Value America found itself managing hundreds of pallets of returned goods sitting in a rented warehouse. And as products aged, many manufacturers refused to take them back, requiring the inventory to be dumped at a loss.

The result of all these problems was that before its inevitable demise, Value America was perhaps the Internet's most reviled e-store. Credit-card returns could take as long as 45 days to process. Items listed as in-stock on the Web site often weren't. Holds on customer service phone lines averaged 45 minutes. Chat rooms and discussion sites that rated online shopping experiences reviled Value America, and the company's online popularity rankings were bottom of the barrel.

Value America, which went public in April 1999 and saw its stock shoot to $73.00 per share on its first day of trading, was in bankruptcy by August 2000. Type in Value America's domain name on the Internet today, and you'll be redirected to an obscure direct marketing firm.

The strength of America's shopping habit was illustrated by the rapid rise and just as rapid demise of Webvan and eToys. Webvan was the brainchild of Louis Borders, founder of the Borders bookstore chain, who conceived it as a national grocery delivery service that would ship food to the domiciles of hungry, time-starved yuppies. The company's debut in Oakland, California, showcased Webvan's commercial heart: a state-of-the-art warehouse festooned with refrigerators, conveyer belts, and lots of plastic baggies (each green pepper sold, for instance, was assigned its very own plastic pouch). The warehouse in turn serviced a

---

[8] Ibid., p. 59.

fleet of vans that delivered your vittles supposedly within 30 minutes of receiving an order. The whole system took $1.2 billion to build.

For a number of people, Webvan was a godsend, and they were happy to pay a premium for their food in return for the convenience of not having to go out and shop. (Not coincidentally, a high percentage of Webvan customers were themselves dot-com types, a nice example of drinking your own triple espresso chocolate latte mocha.) Unfortunately for Webvan, this number of people was small. A warehouse designed to service 8,000 orders per day was fulfilling a few hundred. It turned out most people still preferred to go out and pick out their own peppers for consumption, even if they didn't come wrapped in plastic. Before the company went public in 1999, its prospectus revealed Webvan had lost $35 million on sales of just $395,000.00. This grim financial fact didn't prevent the market from bidding the stock up from $15.00 to $26.00 per share on Webvan's first day of trading.

Another problem with Webvan was the fact that anyone who'd ever gone to a supermarket knew that a reliable infrastructure for the delivery of home groceries already existed. Depending on where you grew up, it might be a kid on a bike with a basket hanging off the front of the handlebars or someone driving a beat-up jalopy with a large trunk, but this system worked and still does. But it didn't seem to occur to anyone that spending $1.2 billion to reinvent a highly functional wheel didn't make a lot of sense.

Webvan stopped wrapping veggies in plastic and closed its doors for good in July 2001. Before the end, its stock was trading for around $.50 per share. About the cost of a single ripe green pepper, sans plastic baggie.

This isn't to say that online shopping for groceries on the Web is extinct. Today in New York City, you can order food on the Internet from upscale stores such as D'Agostinos and Gristede's via your browser. In some cases, you drive to a local store to pick up your order; in others, the supermarket drops your food off at your house. If you're a mensch,[9] you give the delivery kid a nice tip.

In contrast to Webvan, eToys, the now defunct online toy store, had far more success in selling mass quantities of Barbies and LEGOs to America's youth; sales at its peak reached about $200 million. Unfortunately, to ensure the on-time delivery of all that brightly colored plastic to kids the world over, particularly during Christmastime, the toy

---

[9] A Yiddish term for "nice guy."

industry's make-or-break season, the company had to invest in building a $900 million warehouse and fulfillment system. Shipping individual toys presents a particular challenge because they come in a maddening variety of shapes and sizes and vary widely in durability, ranging from incredibly fragile to simply very easy to break.

And though the eToys Web site was widely praised for its interface and usability, it proved unable to replace the experience of bringing your 6-year-old into a store and having him sit down in an aisle, become hysterical, and refuse to move until you gave in and bought him the latest object of his desire. After burning through more than $200 million in real—not Monopoly—money, the company went bankrupt in early 2001 and sold off its $40 million toy inventory to the KB Toys chain for $5.4 million. KB Toys shipped the inventory out to its stores, and if you were a smart shopper you saved a few bucks on your Christmas shopping for the kids if you hit the malls at the right time.

The next group of theories focused on the Internet's direct marketing capabilities. Here the pundits appeared to be a bit more on target. By 1999, it was apparent that e-mail would slowly chew up the U.S. Post Office and replace conventional mail, direct marketing's primary vehicle. Online list brokers such as PostMasterDirect appeared and began doing a lively business creating and renting a wide variety of e-mail databases targeting an increasingly large variety of industries. One writer at *The Industry Standard*, a magazine that lived and died by the dot-com boom, predicted that Web-based infomercials would revolutionize e-tailing.

The pundits, however, had again missed the point. Direct marketing in the United States has traditionally supported conventional retail operations. On average, for every one product sold directly via mail or e-mail, two or more will be sold at a store as a result of a direct offer. Infomercials operate on the same model; most break even on their direct sales of various types of successful infomercials. Profits are made by driving customers to retail stores to buy the latest Ronco breakthrough in better living.

Finally, as all else failed, the theory of *momentum* was introduced to justify the billions being poured down various Internet financial rat holes. The momentum theory boiled down to the belief that if you were losing money at low sales volumes, ramping sales up would demonstrate your business was capable of "scalability" and that this would eventually lead to profitability. It apparently never crossed the minds of many people that the reason dot-com losses grew as sales increased is that many of these businesses were inherently unprofitable. Accelerating sales volumes thus meant you were scaling up to reach insolvency at a greatly increased velocity.

Up, Up and Away

From 1996 to 2000, the dot-com bubble grew with amazing speed as venture capitalists (VCs) and investors poured seemingly endless streams of cash into hundreds of various Internet ventures. The valuation models advanced by Wall Street and the VC community were particularly interesting. Most were based on the concept of *multiples of forward revenues,* an accounting practice that in other times and places might get you sent to jail for fraud.

In this valuation model, if dot-com company A received $100 million in investment capital in year 1, used that cash to generate $200 million in revenues in year 2, and then borrowed another $100 million to generate an additional $200 million in revenue in year 3, the company would be evaluated at $800 million (2 × $400 million) come IPO time. Except no one was actually waiting for year 3 to come around before going public: 8 to 9 months was the usual target. And none of the models seemed to take into account the obscure notion of "profits." All that seemed to matter was "building brands" and generating "momentum" (i.e., serving up millions of profitless page views and selling lots of stuff to lots of people regardless of whether sales of the stuff made any money).

The mania reached its height in 1999 and early 2000, with more than $160 billion being pumped into more and more dot-coms of increasingly dubious bona fides. The bubble burst in April 2000 and was followed by 3 years of a declining stock market and hemorrhaging portfolios. The fallout from the crash dragged into 2002 and helped drive the Dow Jones Industrial Average below 8,000 and the NASDAQ to 1,200. When it was all over, the dot-com winners included the following:

> *eBay.* A solid success, eBay was a Web translation of all those local *Bargain News* and *Buy Lines* newspapers we'd all grown up with. Unlike many other Web businesses that tried to make this claim, eBay's model was truly and inherently "inventory-free."

E*TRADE. Hmmm. There's a problem here. E*TRADE was only sort of a dot-com. The company had actually been offering online stock trading since 1983, and CompuServe and AOL had carried the service since the early 1990s.

America Online (AOL). Well, sort of. AOL had preceded the Internet boom by many years and made a lot of money as the leading proprietary network before the Internet meltdown. But after the merger with Time Warner, creating a new company, AOL Time Warner, the online giant's advertising model promptly tanked, leaving everyone marveling at AOL founder Steve Case's impeccable timing in buying a larger, more profitable company than his own with inflated stock that begin to deflate almost minutes after the acquisition. The new company managed to lose $50 billion in a single quarter in 2002, leaving everyone longing for the good old pre-Internet days when the company sold you online access by the minute. Case and most of the AOL side of the company were summarily kicked out or "resigned" from the merged mess, while the survivors got to work figuring out how to remove the "AOL" from the company logo. Maybe not such a good example after all.

Yahoo. OK, maybe profits were pretty scarce the last several years and revenue growth was flat, but the company made some money during the dot-com boom. But income went south as Web-based advertising income collapsed. And having a stock that plummeted from a high of $348.00 per share to $8.00 per share made everyone cranky.

eBay. Sorry, I already mentioned them, didn't I?

Amazon.com. You must be joking. The company, founded in 1995, finally turned a net profit of a giant, huge, unbelievable $5 million after losing over $500 million the year before. It then turned around and lost another $23 million in the first quarter of 2002. But, good news—this was down from $234 million in the year-earlier quarter. And sales jumped 21 percent to $847 million! Money managers swooned at genius CEO Jeff Bezos's newly found ability to simply lose money, not lose it hand over fist. As the year 2003 hove into view, the hope of sustained profitability by Amazon warmed the hearts of Internet advocates everywhere. It would have been nice if the company had waited until then to tout the stock.

Priceline.com. OK, it had lost a lot more money than it had ever made, and in 2001 its profits were a paltry few million, but it did seem as if there were some money to be made selling unfilled airline seats and hotel rooms at a discount on the Internet. And one advantage to the collapse was that we didn't have to listen to William Shatner sing anymore. Then he came back. But at least he didn't sing.

The Wall Street Journal (WSJ) Online. Another problem. Most of the people who subscribed to the WSJ online also bought the paper edition. Is this really an example of dot-com success? Oh, what the heck! Let's say yes!

Monster.com, HotJobs.com, etc. Yep, like eBay, a solid success. There's a pattern here. If a dot-com is selling an information commodity that by its nature requires no inventory to be managed, it can sometimes make money.

eBay. Did I mention eBay?

Of course, if you dig hard enough, it's possible to find some small success stories here and there, companies that serve small niche markets and make modest profits. For instance, a new Web site, F*****Company.com, sprang up in 2000 with the mission of documenting the ongoing collapse of the dot-coms. The site offered visitors the opportunity to bet on when the next e-venture would fail, advice on the best time to loot your cubicle before you were thrown out of the building, tips on how to keep hold of your company-issued laptop, and the chance to slander upper management with no fear of reprisal. The brainchild of Philip J. Kaplan, known informally as "Pud," the site soon started to do a nice business in sales of T-shirts, a book bearing the Web site's euphonious name, and subscriptions to the site's inner sanctum of information and tips. In the same vein, several firms found there was money to be made in liquidating the assets of failed dot-coms.

There were also a few dot-coms that crawled out from beneath the rubble of the dot-com collapse, dusted themselves off, and put together sensible business plans that offered some hope of success. Like, for instance, eHobbies. Dedicated to serving the needs of those obsessive-compulsive types driven to re-create the world in miniature, the company had burned through $20 million in venture funds while building up a payroll of more than 150 people and had quickly gone insolvent. Two former employees bought what was left from the meltdown and relaunched the site with no venture capital and no payroll (the founders couldn't afford one until they were making some money). A few months after its resurrection, the founders of the new slimmed-down eHobbies were profiled on National Public Radio extolling the virtues of minimal overhead, low payrolls, and real profits.

And that was about . . . it. Depending on your scoring generosity, you could count the number of major dot-com successes on the fingers of one hand. All in all, not much of a return on investment to show for all those billions of dollars spent. (Yes, I hear you. What about Google? Sorry, Google showed in 2004, three years after the meltdown. Doesn't count.) Not to mention the trillions of dollars of paper wealth pulled from the portfolios of hapless investors worldwide as the dot-com bubble burst. As the new economy disappeared behind stacks of unsold inventory and piles of bankruptcy applications, the old economy reappeared and promptly fired hundreds of thousands of people from their jobs.

~

The Last Days of Disco: The ASP Craze

By 1998, a gimlet-eyed observer would have noticed that there was something rather . . . well . . . odd about the "high technology" boom sweeping the nation. The problem was that if you looked closely, there was precious little that was high tech about it. What, exactly, was so new millennium about selling books, furniture, food, wine, toys, stamps, and pornography directly to consumers while building warehouses to store the books, furniture, food, wine, toys, and pornography? (No one bought the stamps—people went to the post office instead. Or used e-mail.) Yes, you needed a Web browser to surf the Internet, and this had been very leading-edge stuff in 1994, but by 1998 your kid knew more about how to surf the Internet than you did, just like he was the only person in the house who knew how to program the VCR. And what was so high tech about a VCR?

As the Internet bubble reached the outer limits of its expansion, there was no question that real high tech was feeling left out of all the fun, particularly the software firms. The hardware companies were actually doing OK. Before the dot-coms shut down their warehouses and left piles of pet food and peppers wrapped in plastic baggies rotting on the loading docks, they were buying expensive Sun Microsystems servers by the thousands and truckloads of Cisco routers. The result was that the stock prices of the hardware companies looked pretty good—not inflated-past-the-limits-of-all-human-intelligence-Amazon.com good, mind you, but very respectable nonetheless.

By contrast, the software guys were wondering where **their** Internet riches and glory were. After all, it was software that had made the dot-com phenomenon possible. The whole thing ran on Web browsers, application servers, Internet protocols, and HTML, but look how it had all turned out. Netscape had burned brightly for a while but then was smothered into submission by Microsoft and Internet Explorer. There had been a couple of mildly hot start-ups such as Vermeer Technologies and FrontPage (Microsoft had promptly snapped them up), and Allaire with its ColdFusion products. E.piphany, a publisher of customer relationship management (CRM) software, had enjoyed watching its stock, driven by Internet mania and interest in this new product category, reach heights unjustified by its sales and profitability.

And for a few weeks in 1999, the Linux guys had done OK in the market. Companies such as Red Hat and VA Linux Systems had taken advantage of the dot-com boom to go public and had seen their stock prices driven to very temporary but giddy highs by the Internet mania. But almost as quickly as their stocks rose, they fell as people realized that there were few profits to be made in a market dedicated to selling a free version of UNIX for PCs that anyone could download from a Web site if so inclined.

But these minor successes aside, most of the software firms had been relegated to the role of selling the virtual equivalent of pans, picks, and shovels to others mining Internet gold. It was a profitable endeavor, but not a very glamorous one for an industry that since the early 1980s had become accustomed to being fawned over as American business's precious new young thing.

But software was ready with a riposte. If the 1960s could make a comeback in the form of the Internet, was there any reason why the 1970s couldn't do it as well? It was time for the rebirth of . . . time sharing! (Computers, not condos.)

Disco Inferno

Time sharing was the mainframe-based centralized model of computing that dominated the industry to the end of the 1970s.[10] It worked by permitting an individual to access mainframes via terminals and work in virtual sessions that created the illusion that each user had control over the whole machine. Time share software was paid for on a rental basis, and the applications available were limited, expensive, and proprietary to particular companies and/or machines. By the mid-1980s, time sharing was moribund, driven out of most markets by networked PCs running comparatively inexpensive desktop applications, though the technology did hold on in areas such as the airline industry's SABRE flight reservation system.

Software vendors quickly realized this old wine in a new bottle deserved a new appellation, and one was promptly coined: application service providers (ASPs). Advocates explained that the ASP schema would replace PCs, or *fat clients,* running desktop applications such as Microsoft Office or Macromedia Dreamweaver with *thin clients* called *network computers* (NCs) running software programs being dished up by banks of remote servers. As with time sharing, applications would be rented or used on an as-needed basis, and boxed/licensed software would soon be a thing of the past.

The NC was the brainchild of Larry Ellison, founder of database powerhouse Oracle who, like many high-tech CEOs, has a deep and abiding fear of Bill Gates. An NC was basically a PC with its floppy and hard disk stripped out and was, as conceived of by Ellison, designed to make Windows and Windows-based desktop applications obsolete. Instead of relying on a desktop OS, users would employ Web browsers as their interface to an array of applications stored on the aforementioned banks of servers and fed to users via the Internet. Files and projects would likewise be stored remotely but could be accessed 24/7 via any computer or NC that had Web access.

---

[10] My first experience with time sharing was with a financial modeling package called "Finar" used by my father to perform simulations of intermediate stock market swings. The cost to rent usage of the package was in the thousands of dollars. Finar was later purchased by MicroPro and in 1983 became a PC-based product called "PlanStar," which was available for a few hundred dollars. A better known exemplar of this type of software was introduced a few years later under the name of Javelin. These data modeling packages take a "top-down" approach to spreadsheet creation. Though powerful, these products have never been widely accepted by the market.

The benefits that were supposed to accrue to both companies and their IT departments from this new/old approach were many. NCs were going to be much cheaper than PCs, and corporate accountants could look forward to saving lots of money on a key capital expense. IT loved the idea that it was going be able to "lock down" applications and desktops and return to those halcyon days when MIS gods strode through the corridors of power and told employees that what was good for them was good for the company (digitally speaking).

Users were also going to benefit from being liberated from the necessity to learn how to turn their computers on and off and understand such esoteric concepts as "floppies" and "hard disks." Productivity would also rise as clandestine sessions of Solitaire and stolen moments with Minesweeper came to an end. Everyone could finally forget about all this "knowledge worker" nonsense as employees resumed their proper roles as corporate drones working maniacally on single tasks administered from a central source.

And for the software companies the ASP model promised a revenue nirvana. In ASP World there would be no more expensive upgrade programs with their direct marketing overhead and wads of CDs being tossed around the landscape. Instead, software use and updates would be managed and policed via electronic distribution over the Internet. Even better, in much the same way that renting a home is ultimately more expensive than buying one, software publishers would be able to develop consistent revenue streams from renting their applications and charging more to use them. After all, the ASP model was relieving a corporation's IT department of the burden of having to test and deploy new programs and upgrades, and that was certainly worth a premium!

There was also the delightful prospect of breaking into lucrative markets the "old-line" software firms seemed to have locked up. Microsoft Office has 90+ percent market share in business applications? No problem. Just load that ASP-based office suite into a browser and start making money. And no need to worry about recouping hosting and development costs—you would be able to offer free applications via the Web and have the cost of deploying and maintaining them borne by advertisers! Just look at the response to that Zima banner on the HotWired Web site! Heck, if an ASP generated half that response rate, it was still found money. And once customers were hooked, you'd upgrade them to a premium service that charged real money on a subscription basis. You just couldn't miss with this ASP model.

In a hurry not to let the moment pass it by, the industry leaped enthusiastically into the golden ether. From the late 1990s to 2001, more than 500 companies received more than $10 billion in venture capital. The industry went furiously to work building the infrastructure and software required to retrieve time sharing from the Lost World of Polyester and transport it forward into the Age of the Internet.

The efforts quickly bore fruit. Soon there was an ASP solution for every market and taste. For those who wanted Web-based business applications, there was HotOffice.com. The basic service was free and paid for by banner advertising. Those in need of enterprise resource planning (ERP) and e-commerce for their Web sites could turn to Pandesic, a joint venture between software giant SAP and hardware colossus Intel. If you were intrigued by Web-based time tracking and invoicing, there was RedGorilla.com. And for those concerned about storage costs, sites such as iDrive.com, which allowed you to save your files on Web servers, were built to help. Providing the hardware infrastructure needed to support this new world of time shar– . . . er . . . Web-based software were firms such as Exodus and USI, both of which were spending billions to cover the American landscape with buildings stuffed with servers and bristling with wires.

Nor was that all. Several trade shows dedicated to the ASP market promptly sprung into being. A new ASP industry consortium was formed. New publications with names like *ASP World* were in the planning stages. ASP stock prices promptly headed into overvalued dot-com territory and thousands of paper millionaires began planning their early retirements. The ASP market was ready for launch!

And then the rocket blew up on the pad.

The Last Dance

There were many reasons for the ASP implosion. One was that people who actually used Web-based applications discovered that in terms of usability and power, the applications, well, sucked. The Web in the late 1990s and early 2000s wasn't designed to act as an application interface, but to allow you to jump around from file to file quickly. It did this well enough if you had a reasonably fast connection to the Internet, but it didn't do much else very well. People accustomed to responsive application interfaces, spreadsheets that raced through huge wads of numbers, and word processors that cut and pasted big blocks of text with alacrity rebelled as they fumbled with slow, clunky, Web-based products that felt as if they were being run on a TRS-80 circa 1978. Only slower.

Another problem for ASP World was that the NC was dying, strangled in its cradle by Moore's law as it wound its coils of relentless price erosion around Ellison's fair-haired silicon progeny. Initially designed to be sold at the "bargain" price of about $1,000.00 per unit, the NC soon found itself competing against nicely loaded desktops for around the same price. (And unlike the PC, NCs offered computer resellers no good opportunities for upselling accessories and extra goodies, making them extremely unappealing to the distribution channel.)

Also, as the Internet grew, the desirability of the thin-client model underwent a reexamination. A thin-client computing environment meant fat servers, huge storage centers, and big thick digital "pipes" to provide, store, and transmit applications and data. Such an environment may have been an IT manager's dream, but corporate CFOs blanched when presented with the bills. Maybe it made sense to offload some of these computing expenses onto increasingly dirt-cheap PCs, after all. And heck, even CFOs like to play a quick game of Minesweeper every once in a while.

The Napster tune-swapping service's mass popularization of peer-to-peer computing also led to a reconsideration of the thin client versus fat client debate. Although Napster's approach of using the Internet to allow people to transfer music directly from one PC to another was a smash success (at least in terms of usage; Napster had a hard time demonstrating how you make money from the concept), the system suffered from a fatal flaw. Unfortunately for fans of 24/7 mass violation of copyrights on a global scale, Napster's system used servers to create centralized directories of all those purloined files residing on everyone's hard disk. This weakness allowed the recording industry to convince the U.S. legal system to shut the network down until it mended its ways. (Napster could never figure out how to profit from its "mass theft" business model and was driven out of business by the recording industry. The company's assets were put up for sale at fire sale prices, and the Napster name was bought by Roxio, who went on to create "Napster 2.0," a "pay-for-play" download service most people never use.)

But new peer-to-peer technology didn't suffer from this weakness. Networks such as Gnutella and FastTrack required no centralized servers but relied on individual PCs to store information about file requests, manage transfers, and create virtual directories to speed up performance. The more fat powerful clients out there, the better, as far as these networks were concerned.

Then there was the issue of information control. Many companies, after taking a look at the hosted model, decided there was no way they were going to entrust mission-critical data to unknown third parties. In fact, they weren't going to entrust it to known third parties either. Ditto for anything that involved critical real-time transactions, such as credit card processing. Many companies insisted that ASPs offer their products for sale the old-fashioned way, via the purchase of a license that enabled them to maintain control over both the software and their data.

And on closer examination, although automatic software upgrades sounded great in theory, in reality they introduced a whole new set of headaches. The possibility of incompatible file formats corrupting data and the chance that an automatic upgrade could break macros, scripts, and applications that currently worked fine made many IT professionals nervous. As a result, many companies decided they preferred to continue to manage their upgrades internally, a choice that gave them more control over the process of testing the impact of new software on existing systems.

It also became clear that charging more for rented applications wouldn't be as easy as once thought. When a company was presented with a prospective tab for a software rental, nothing prevented anyone from doing some simple math that totaled up the yearly cost of renting software and comparing it to the cost of licensing the same product. At this point, software companies relearned the lesson that once markets have become used to existing price points and schedules, they're very resistant to attempts to change them. Arguments about IT savings were countered by rejoinders that the software company was saving money by not having to run an upgrade program.

Exacerbating the problem was the fact that many of the proponents of hosted applications were companies in the CRM and ERP markets. Ostensibly designed to offer business executives top-down views and management of every aspect of their company's operations, purchasers of these software products soon began to derisively refer to them as "shelfware." This unflattering designation arose from the fact that once a company bought one of these mega-sized, multimodule pieces of code and attempted to implement part of it, the expense, difficulty, and cost of doing so often led to the rest of the product being shoved on a shelf and buried.

ASPs also discovered that many segments of corporate America were reluctant to give up the "piracy" discount inherent in conventional software purchases.[11] Software companies are fond of bemoaning the fact that in many markets as much as 50 percent of the software used by companies is illegally copied. And the companies are upset by it too! Very, very upset, and they're going to get on top of the problem and take care of it. Someday. Maybe next year. Or decade. Or whenever.

The upshot of it all is that by 2001, the ASP market bore a grim resemblance to the rest of the dot-com morass. HotOffice found out that banner advertising hardly paid for a single server and cooled into Chapter 11. Intel and SAP pulled the plug on Pandesic. RedGorilla.com turned out to be one sick chimp and died. Exodus and USI went bankrupt. People discovered that hard disk storage cost about $1.00 per gigabyte, so what was the point of renting Internet storage space? The trade shows folded. The ASP consortium closed up shop when most of its membership went out of business or decided that old-fashioned software licensing was still the way to go. In a desperate attempt to distance itself from the unrelenting stream of failures, the industry frog marched the ASP label up against a wall and summarily executed the unfortunate acronym. Taking its place were a plethora of new alphabetical appellations—MRPs, HSPs, HRPs, XSPs, etc.—intended to take everyone's mind off the current depressing state of affairs. Most were immediately hunted down and dispatched. The ASP designation crawled back from the grave and resumed its official role as the standard designation for hosted applications, but it was now in official disgrace and no one

---

[11] In early 1999, I was invited to give a presentation at a Software & Information Industry Association (SIIA) seminar on the ASP market and its prospects for success. The SIIA is the latest incarnation of the old Software Publishers Association. One of the reasons consultants and analysts attend these events is to present themselves as experts on a topic and attract future consulting gigs. The hope is that after a stirring presentation, members of the audience will rush up with their business cards outstretched to hire you to put their myriad sales and marketing problems straight. Unfortunately for my plans, I decided to give a straightforward analysis of the ASP market that concluded that most of the current business models and approaches were horsesh– . . . not feasible. I was later informed by the SIIA that many in the audience had found my negative attitude discouraging, and I collected very few business cards (well, none, actually). This experience drove home to me the realization that a herd of lemmings in the act of flinging themselves over a cliff are primed to discuss the importance of teamwork, the need to stay focused on the task at hand, and the necessity of maintaining a positive attitude.

talked to it. It finally expired from all the sheer contempt directed at it in 2005, to be replaced by the fairly unpronounceable "SaaS" (Software as a Service).

To be fair, the news wasn't all bad. There were a few modest successes in certain markets, such as human resources. Although a company's resume database is important, the inability to access it for a few hours or even a day or so isn't critical. In markets with similar characteristics, such as scheduling, project management, and sales force and marketing automation, ASP firms made some headway, especially if their goals were modest and their prices low. By the end of 2001, the ASP market was determined to have generated about $600 million in revenue and very little in the way of profits. And even these figures were somewhat deceptive as many of the surviving ASPs were now also selling their software the old-fashioned way, via licensing. As with the dot-coms, not much of an ROI on a $10 billion investment.

But, good news! By 2002, industry gurus were proclaiming that, yes, there was **indeed** a fortune to be made by hosting applications. It was going to be done via a brand-new technology: Web services, new Internet-based protocols, products, and services that would allow all those desktop applications to communicate and collaborate in new and wonderful ways. And who was going to make all this money? Well, as the June 25, 2002, issue of *Interactive Week* (a publication that soon after folded, itself a victim of the Internet implosion) told us:

> *The key to the paradox is that growth will be driven not by start up ASPs—which have gained mind share but not market share— but by the folks that already sell software by the ton.*[12]

And how were the folks already selling tons of software going to create ASP World? Well, later in the same article, Microsoft theorized that

> *It's a misconception that people will get Office off a Web site. What is Office in a software-as-a-service world? A client, a way for people to access some services.*[13]

---

[12] "Changing the economics of software business," *Interactive Week*, June 25, 2002.
[13] Ibid.

Oh. In other words, get ready to pay for access to an updated spelling corrector for your word processor. Well, it was good to know what the future held. At least we weren't all going to end up having to wear love beads, acetate shirts with floral designs, and ultrawide ties. That was something.

twelve

THE STRANGE CASE OF DR. OPEN
AND MR. PROPRIETARY

As noted in Chapter 2 of this book, the release of the Altair micro-computer in 1975 heralded the beginning of the modern high-tech industry. But observers of the period also believe there was more to the Altair than just chips; the unit seemed to emit a mysterious elixir that entered the body of computer aficionados worldwide and sparked a strange war of the soul that has raged in the body of the computer geekdom for more than three decades. The war is between those who advocate for free software and open, patentless technology available to all and those who believe in making substantial sums of money from selling proprietary software and the vigorous protection of intellectual property. It's the Kumbayahs vs. the Capitalists.

Other influences may be responsible for the ongoing struggle. Perhaps *Star Trek* bears some of the blame. Few in microcomputing hadn't watched the series, and as Captain Kirk, Mr. Spock, Bones, Scottie, and their innumerable successors went gallivanting through the galaxy, they seemed to have no visible means of financial support. No one in the *Star Trek* universe wearing green eye shades ever appeared to worry about the propensity of the various casts to blow up what you'd think were undoubtedly very expensive spaceships, given their capabilities of violating the laws of physics, transporting the crew to numerous planets inhabited by women who spent most of their time wearing lingerie, and dodging ray-gun fire from angry races of aliens who kept screaming "kaplok!" (and who also seemed to have no monetary worries). Perhaps the reason for Captain Kirk's insouciance lay in the fact that everyone in *Star Trek* had access to what were called "transporters," magical devices that could be used to whisk you from the spaceship Enterprise to a planet without having to pay a toll. Later in the series' development, transporters could be used to create chocolate milk shakes, drinks, and even the occasional boyfriend or girlfriend via simple voice commands. And all for free!

Of course, no computer has a *Star Trek*–like transporter system built into it, but from the standpoint of people interested in obtaining software without forking over monetary compensation, software has something almost as good. That good thing is the "copy" command. And since software, unlike milk shakes, drinks, and boyfriends, is already digitized, just about anyone can execute this wondrous command and enjoy a cornucopia of software in an environment free of the distasteful economic friction of "paying."

Technology's interest in the concept of free software was demonstrated almost conterminously with the release of the Altair in the events surrounding the "liberation" of the first BASIC for this pioneering machine. When first available, the Altair had no useful software, and the market was eagerly awaiting the release of Altair BASIC (waiting was something Altairians were very good at doing because Altair maker MITS was legendary for announcing new products it couldn't deliver, a habit the rest of the industry soon learned to emulate). The product had been developed by a small software firm, Micro-Soft, run by two people no one had ever heard of, Paul Allen and Bill Gates. Micro-Soft had cut a deal with MITS to receive a royalty on every sale of Altair BASIC and was eagerly waiting for a stream of revenue to flow into the tiny firm's coffers upon the official release of the new product to a marketer eager to buy it.

Unfortunately for Gates's and Allen's short-term plans, someone had appropriated an early version of Micro-Soft's BASIC, stored on paper tape, at a small MITS trade show held in Palo Alto in 1975. The tape was promptly reproduced and then handed out at such venues as the Homebrew Computer Club, a semilegendary group of computer hackers and enthusiasts who met regularly in Silicon Valley to share information, gossip, advice, and other things, such as "liberated" chips and especially liberated Altair software. Soon, paper tapes containing an early, buggy version of Altair BASIC were in wide use, and oddly enough, no one offered to pay Micro-Soft a dime for the product.

In 1975 there was very little that was kumbayah about Bill Gates, and he responded to the purloining of Microsoft BASIC by writing an open letter to the software liberators, published in the Homebrew Computer Club's newsletter (and in similar publications), chiding them for their thieving ways and asking them to voluntarily pay for the privilege of using his BASIC. His letter made the logical point that if people weren't recompensed for all their time and hard work spent creating new and better software products, they would have no incentive to do so, and the software industry would wither and die.

Gates's pleas for financial remuneration went widely unheeded. The very act of releasing the letter generated generous amounts of sneers and opprobrium from software's kumbayahs, three hundred or four hundred letters addressed to Gates chastising him for his greed, and about three or four voluntary payments for Altair BASIC. Ruined by the premature widespread release of Altair BASIC and the financial loss this entailed, Micro-Soft went out of business, and Gates and Allen were never heard from…aga…errr…no. That's not what happened.

What actually happened was the widespread release of Altair BASIC established the product as the de facto standard for microcomputers. Despite some idiosyncrasies, Micro-Soft's BASIC was regarded as an engineering triumph—lean, loaded with features, and, in comparison with the mainframe and mini-computer BASICs most programmers worked with, incredibly fast. Although everyone didn't want to pay for Altair, which later became Microsoft (with no hyphen) BASIC, everyone wanted to use it. Since Microsoft's deal allowed the company to license the product to other firms, Microsoft was soon enjoying a tidy business licensing its BASIC to a plethora of other computer companies. In point of fact, it was the industry's high regard for Microsoft's BASIC that led IBM to Bill Gates's door and enabled him to take advantage of the biggest business opportunity of the 20th century.

Nonetheless, as the industry began its rapid development, resentment on the part of software entrepreneurs grew as software piracy spread. And make no mistake, spread it did. Copying a software program worth hundreds, or even thousands, of dollars was as easy as inserting a blank floppy disk into a disk drive and typing in your system's version of the "copy" command. Games in particular were the target of frequent liberation efforts, with user groups for systems such as the Amiga and Atari ST sponsoring "swap nights" where members were encouraged to bring in their software collections for communal sharing. Many businesses entered into the kumbayah spirit of things, with it being a common occurrence for a company to buy one copy of a business software package such as WordStar and distributing it to every member of the company.

To counter the practice of software liberation, now usually called "piracy," a whole host of what were eventually called "copy protection" systems and techniques were developed. Most of these focused on protecting Apple software because this computer system attracted the bulk of new software development until the release of the IBM PC. Some of the techniques employed included things such as forcing a disk drive to write to locations on a floppy nominally off limits to the hardware; "Spiradisk," a system that wrote data to the disk surface in a big spiral; hardware "dongles," plastic keys that contained a chip with a software key embedded into it; and so on.

In response to the efforts of one part of the software industry to prevent pirating software, another part promptly launched an effort to thwart the protectors (this had the happy effect of employing more programmers). Anticopy protection systems included software products such as Locksmith, copy-cracking boards that sucked an entire software product into memory and spit it out to disk, products that were capable of reading dongle keys, and so on, and so on, and so on. As soon as one copy protection scheme was introduced, it was immediately under attack by resourceful folks following in the glorious tradition of Altair BASIC and the Homebrew Computer Club.

By the early 1980s, IBM entered the market with its own microcomputer, and the focus of the endless cat-and-mouse game between the Capitalists and Kumbayahs shifted to the PC. The software industry's reaction to rampant software piracy was the general introduction of copy protection for many of the major software packages. WordStar 2000, Lotus 1-2-3, dBase, and other packages incorporated elaborate schemes meant to halt, or at least slow, the piracy tide. For a brief period in the 1980s, almost a dozen software companies were pitching other software companies on the effectiveness of their respective protection systems.

I initially had a great deal of sympathy for the effort. As a field software engineer for MicroPro, I had become quite accustomed to walking into a customer's location and seeing multiple copies of WordStar (which was not copy protected) installed on every computer in the place but being able to spot only one set of manuals available to the "user" base. Some simple math seemed to indicate a lot of bread was being snatched from my mouth, or at least from the mouth of the company paying my salary.

It was also annoying to find myself spending time providing technical support to people who were clearly flying the software Jolly Roger. One of my responsibilities was to take local technical support calls while in the office from people who were having difficulty with our word processor. A disturbingly high number of my calls went something like this:

Me: Hi! This is MicroPro technical support. How can I help you?

The "customer": I need help installing my NEC 3550 printer.

Me: No problem! Please pull out your installation manual, and turn to page 256. (This was an age when users were a manly bunch, with thumbs thickly muscled from paging through software documentation similar in size and comprehensiveness to small encyclopedias. Not the like the effete perusers of PDFs and HTML you find today.) I'll be glad to walk you through the process.

The "customer": Uh, I don't have a manual in front of me.

Me: No problem. I'll hold on the phone until you can get it.

The "customer": Uh, I don't have a manual.

Me: Can I ask what happened to it?

The "customer": Uh, the dog ate it. (Other popular claims focused on thieving kids, roaring fires, and torrential flooding.)

The computing press (the members of which were used to obtaining all the free software they wanted) was, as you might imagine, generally unsympathetic to the plight of the software firms. Despite giving perfunctory lip service to the idea that software companies had a right to protect their property from theft, the companies were (and are) constantly being lectured on "not treating their customers" like thieves, despite the indisputable fact that large numbers of them were (and are). In 1984, MicroPro estimated that eight pirated copies of WordStar were in use for every one sold. In 2005, estimates put software piracy rates in China at more than 90 percent.

And yet, by the end of the 1980s, practically every software that had implemented copy protection dropped it. Several factors were driving this trend. One was that many companies resisted buying copy-protected software because it added complexity and instability to desktop computing systems and strained the resources of IT departments. Another was that copy protection added considerably to the software industry's support burden because users called up to complain about systems that wouldn't install because of hardware peculiarities, lost or damaged "key" disks, arguments about the number of "valid" installs, and so on. And, although our feelings undoubtedly weren't the strongest factor driving corporate decisions, most software firms were hearing whines and groans from their field sales and support personnel about the difficulty of dealing with protected products. WordStar 2000, for example, at one time used a copy protection system that limited users to three installations of the software on different systems. This meant that whenever I or another person had to install WordStar 2000 on a demo system at a remote location, we had to go through a wearying install/deinstall routine while listening to outraged disk drives go AAAHHHHKKKK SKRRRIIIKKK WAAKA WAAKA WAAKA in order to keep our quiver full of demo installs for future use. (Field personnel weren't initially given non-copy-protected products. When we were, the practical facts we created "on the ground" provided another reason to drop copy protection.)

And finally, despite the theoretical losses software companies were suffering from piracy, it was hard to see in reality how piracy was hurting the companies. As the decade progressed, many software companies did indeed stumble and fall, but in no case was it possible to pin the blame on piracy. Also, it started to become apparent to software firms that piracy had a definite upside, as Microsoft had discovered years ago with the Altair. When the number of people using your software increased, your perception as the market leader increased as well. And pirated software functioned as a sort of marketing kudzu, tending to choke out the competition as use of your product spread throughout the computing populace. Once you had displaced the competition, it was possible to convert X percent of the pirates to paid users via various inducements and offers. Corporations, worried about legal liabilities, were also usually not reluctant to buy purloined software if the price was right.

Becoming the market leader also opened up opportunities for bundling and original equipment manufacturing (OEM) deals. At MicroPro, WordStar's early ubiquity made it the favored word processing product to include with such systems as the Osborne, Kaypro, and many others. While OEM products were sold at a considerable discount from the software's retail price, in most case all the software publisher had to do was provide licenses and serial numbers to its customers; the OEM customer usually was responsible for manufacturing and supporting the product. One MicroPro OEM salesman referred to the firm's OEM business as a "money-printing operation." This model worked in the case of such products as WordStar, dBase, WordPerfect, and most notably, Microsoft Windows. Today, Microsoft's Windows OEM business is the most profitable component in the company's bottom line.

In the meantime, while the proprietary software companies were garnering all the attention (and making all the money) from the market, the kumbayah forces, led by an interesting fellow by the name of Richard M. Stallman, were keeping the dream of free software alive. Stallman had entered computing by way of MIT in 1971, where he worked as a systems programmer in the university's AI lab, at that time a hotbed of innovation in such areas as LISP and related languages. Stallman developed a reputation as an ace programmer and while at MIT developed the legendary program Emacs, a text editor backed up by a powerful and extensible macro system. Stallman was a militant believer in what was then called the "Hacker Ethic," a belief system that preached that software and the information it represented should be open and available to all users to change and modify as they saw fit. Stallman was fervent in his belief about the evils of charging for software, at one time proclaiming that "the prospect of charging money for software was a crime against humanity."[1]

Unfortunately for RMS, as his friends called him, by the 1980s the MIT lab was becoming corrupted by the sirens of commerce, who asked why geeks couldn't also have fancy cars, big homes, and gorgeous girlfriends. Two AI companies (both ultimately unsuccessful) dedicated to building LISP interpreters and dedicated LISP machines spun out of the MIT lab, taking with them many of the lab's best programmers and all, in the opinion of RMS, of the lab's kumbayah mojo.

After a period of mourning, Stallman left the lab with a vision fixed firmly in his imagination. He would create a powerful, free, and open software environment that would allow programmers to create new and wondrous products. This environment would be based on the popular (but proprietary) UNIX operating system and, in a display of geek wit, would be called GNU (GNUs not UNIX; I'm sure you appreciate the recursion). And to ensure that what had happened at MIT could never happen again, he'd protect this environment with a new and innovative concept, a "copyleft" agreement that required programmers who used his software to build new software to make the original GNU software, and any changes or improvements made to the software they had created, available for free to anyone who wanted it under the GNU General Public License (GPL). When the GPL was introduced, Stallman became software's Dr. Open, the civilized, reasonable, humanitarian advocate of

---

[1] *Free as in Freedom: Richard Stallman's Crusade for Free Software* by Sam Williams (O'Reilly Media, 2002)

all that was good and pure in the world. (Bill Gates has traditionally played the role of Mr. Proprietary, but since he's supposed to be leaving Microsoft to cure diseases worldwide, Steve Ballmer will be appearing in the part moving forward.)

This was a sharp and revolutionary contrast with the typical end-user license agreement (EULA) that accompanied most proprietary software. Most EULAs allowed "licensees" of software only the right to copy "their" software onto a limited number of computers. In fact, by 2006 the Microsoft retail EULA for Windows allowed you to copy your $100+ copy of Windows XP onto only one computer, regardless of how many computers you owned. And boy, oh boy, better make sure you never, ever, buy a four-core processor in your computer, because that seemed to violate the Microsoft EULA. And if you read the rest of the EULA, it warned of all kinds of other things you couldn't do, and all the warnings were written in the Scary Lawyer dialect of the English language. In fact, most EULAs are full of scary language and all kinds of implied legal threats. Interestingly enough, despite the fact software companies have been using EULAs for decades, it is unclear whether they have any legal validity.[2] Fortunately for the industry, no one actually ever reads an EULA; if they did, everyone would probably use only free software.

Given the current excitement over open source software and technology, it would be easy to think that Stallman's GPL took the industry by storm, but this was not the case. The first GPL was released in 1989, and the second version, the one in current use in high technology, was released in 1991. At the time of their issuance, few people paid them the least bit of attention. One reason for this may be that although Stallman may have thought charging for software was wrong, almost no one else thought so, especially the many programmers who were making good money selling software and didn't want to give up their new cars, houses, and girlfriends. Another was that Stallman's rantings about the evils of for-sale software and rationale for giving it away sounded a bit too close to Karl Marx's formulation of "from each according to his abilities; to each according to his needs." In an era when the Soviet dinosaur was noisily clanking and shaking its way to extinction, Stallman's zeitgeist seemed off to many.

---

[2] http://en.wikipedia.org/wiki/EULA

~

It's Finally GNU for You

But perhaps the biggest obstacle to the widespread acceptance of Stallman's credo was that although he was preaching about the glories of free software created with GNU, he hadn't actually sat down and finished the project. Stallman **had** built a series of software utilities that could be used to create software (an activity beloved by many coders) but had neglected, years after the proclamation of GNU, to provide the system with its key component, an operating system. Instead, it was left to a 21-year-old Finnish student at the University of Helsinki by the name of Linus Torvalds to create a working implementation of Stallman's dream. UNIX, Linux's distinguished father, had slowly been withdrawn from the programming community and had become increasingly proprietary and fragmented. Dozens of companies took their version of UNIX and built custom extensions and walls around the software. This had the effect of raising UNIX prices (and allowing these companies to do a nice business selling their specialized UNIX versions). Dissatisfied with the UNIX clone he was currently using and unable to afford a proprietary version, Torvalds decided to take a stab at writing his own operating system using the GNU tools.

Linux .001 was released in September 1991. Shortly after its introduction, Torvalds invited anyone interested in the OS to contribute to the development of the next release. Many people did, and the most significant open source project in the industry's history was born.

Driven by the enthusiasm of what would become known as "the open source community," Linux made great strides over the next few years, its progress assisted by Torvalds's decision to release Linux under the GPL. Its growth driven by open source aficionados, by the late 1990s Linux began to do serious financial damage to companies such as SGI, Sun, SCO, and others, all of whom soon saw their business models being ravaged by the new upstart.

But while Linux was steadily eating away at the profits of the UNIX firms, the Windows world safely ignored Torvalds and his OS, for the most part. A few hobbyists played with the system,[3] and Microsoft's behavior toward Netscape and the government's antitrust case raised the blood pressure of free software advocates worldwide; however, that was about it. After all, Windows was very, very cheap. Most people received the product for "free" with their hardware and ignored the issue that their purchase price reflected the cost of Windows, something that was easy to do when computers cost $2,000 to $3,000. And even if you bought it, once you factored in the cost of inflation and the ability to install it on every machine you owned (and a few you didn't), the cost per computer seemed very reasonable for an operating system that ran a huge amount of software and seemed to support just about every peripheral you owned.

Also, what many have called "the open source paradox" began to rear its ugly economic head (and still does). The paradox was that although GNU, Linux, and other open source software had been written ostensibly to liberate programmers from a world of evil capitalists, ultimately it seemed the evil capitalists were most likely to benefit the most from the whole movement. After all, although it was nice that car companies, oil companies, lawyers, grocery stores, Burlington Coat Factory, and lots of businesses of all types were saving money on purchases of software, there was no proof that programmers were sharing in the bounty from all these expenditure reductions. And if you looked at some of the companies that expounded the use of Linux the loudest, such as IBM, you couldn't help but wonder. After all, IBM had become America's most prominent business colossus by building the most proprietary of proprietary software and hardware. IBM had been driven from its perch of preeminence by tiny start-up Microsoft, which had then gone on to enrich more geeks than any other company in history. Microsoft had created thousands of millionaire programmers; how many millionaire programmers had IBM ever created? For that matter, if Linux was so great, where were all the **Linux** millionaires?

---

[3] I purchased a retail copy of Red Hat Linux in the 1990s and attempted to install it on my PC. The install promptly failed when Linux failed to know what to do with my then-state-of-the-art Adaptec SCSI interface card. A plaintive inquiry sent to the famed Linux community was answered by a condescending message that since Adaptec wasn't releasing its drivers under the GPL, I shouldn't expect Linux to work. I promptly gave up on Red Hat and Linux and continued using and buying Windows.

~

Some Hot Tunes

In the meantime, while everyone was focusing on software, no one was paying any attention to the music business. There didn't seem to be any reason to do so. After all, we all knew how the music business basically worked. Every few years the youth of the world generated yet another raft of disaffected grungesters, cute girls, cute boys, some performers of indeterminate sex, ghetto rappers, hip-hop blasters, soul throbbers, chanteuses, lounge acts, and so on, and so on, all of whom were signed to contracts by large, institutionally corrupt music companies. These in turn distributed cash, girls (or boys), and cocaine (or the drug of choice) to the band while paying off music stations to play the songs of the performers under contract to the company. When the current crop of crooners aged and lost their appeal or overdosed, they were promptly replaced by a new generation of cute girls, cute boys, and so on, and the cycle continued.

The distribution model was also well understood. Music was sold to the public via albums, stored on cassette tapes, and later almost exclusively CDs. Most of the music on the album was filler, designed to surround the one or two good songs with enough extra musical noise to justify charging $20 per CD, a price that annoyed people who remembered that before the switch to the new technology in the early 1990s, a record had cost about eight bucks. The companies raised prices because they could but justified the new price tags to the public by talking about the expense of producing CDs (despite that it cost less to mass produce them as opposed to vinyl) and to industry insiders by noting that the price of drugs had skyrocketed over the years.[4]

The music industry had known for years that public dissatisfaction with the current state of affairs was high and that people were highly

---

[4] This sounds like a facetious statement. It's not. The field sales office I worked in was located in Secaucus, New Jersey. The MicroPro offices were down the hall from the studios of one of the region's most popular Top 40 radio stations at the time, Z-100, and I became used to seeing a limo periodically drive up to our forsaken location and drop off such music stars as Cyndi Lauper, Bob Geldof, Madonna, and so on, for on-the-air PR appearances. I struck up an acquaintance with one of the DJs who worked there, and he explained in loving detail how the industry worked.

interested in mixing and matching songs to create custom listening sets that matched their interests and moods (I cover this point in greater detail in Chapter 14), but no one in the business cared. The music companies had the entire distribution system, the artists, and the technology under control. In fact, in the early 1990s, the industry was able to strangle a potential threat to its domination, consumer digital audio tape players, by loading them with enough integrated copy restrictions to the point that no one was interested in buying the units. Although some music executives were dimly aware of the problems software companies had with piracy, none thought they had any lessons to learn from high tech's digital travails.

While the music industry was ignoring both the desires of its customers and the advance of technology, software geeks worldwide were busily working on making the life of the jingle moguls miserable. First came the development of MP3 compression, a technology that allowed software to take any music recording and compress it to about a 12th of its original size with very little loss in sound quality. Work on the MP3 format began in 1987, and final specifications for the technology were released to the public in 1994. Once a song had been "MP3'd," it was small enough to be easily and quickly transmitted electronically. The next step was taken with the spread of cheap read/write optical disk systems in the mid-1990s. This in turn drove the development of software that could "rip" (copy) music from CDs to the new MP3 format. The fourth and final piece of the puzzle dropped into place with the adoption of the Internet by the public. A complete solution to bypassing the music industry's lock on the distribution system had come into existence.

The first major company to explore the possibilities the Internet opened up for music distribution was MP3.com. The service was founded in 1998 and offered downloadable musical for free (the artists were compensated via a system that gave them a small royalty payment based on the number of times their songs were downloaded). MP3.com was **not** a music piracy site; a trained staff winnowed through the uploads and stripped out copyrighted material. Everyone thought the site was wonderful, it grew rapidly, and in 1999 MP3.com launched an IPO that netted the company $370 million.

The good times ceased to roll at MP3.com when in January 2000 it launched the My.MP3.com service. This enabled customers to securely register their personal CDs (you had to actually stick the CD in your PC so that MP3.com could scan it) and then stream a digital copy from your system to an online music "locker room" hosted by the My.MP3.com service. At this point, the intelligent thing for the music industry to have done was to study MP3.com, partner with it, and "train" the public to interact with the site and ones similar to it for the benefit of all concerned. Instead, the music moguls, in an act of classic and far-reaching stupidity worthy of such famous moments in rock-star history as Alice Cooper tossing a hapless chicken to its death to a crowd in Toronto or Ozzy Osborne masticating an innocent bat,[5] sued poor MP3.com for copyright infringement and found a judge dimwitted enough to agree with them. Rather than appeal the case, MP3.com handed over the bulk of its IPO money to the recording industry. Fatally weakened, the service gave up the ghost during the dot-com meltdown, to the music industry's immense satisfaction.

The smirking and high-fiving came to an abrupt end with the appearance of a new service, Napster. Based on a peer-to-peer network system that allowed computers to directly transfer MP3 files across the Internet, Napster made little effort to prevent software piracy, and the site soon became one of the most popular on the planet. The music industry, having learned absolutely nothing from the MP3.com incident, sued Napster as well and eventually was able to shut it down. As already noted in Chapter 11, Napster's great vulnerability lay in its use of centralized servers to store the names of the files being offered to other Napster users. Now, with Napster out of business, smart programmers quickly developed new software that didn't require the use of centralized servers but instead relied on individual computer systems located worldwide to manage the task of file coordination. The recording industry's intelligent response to this development was to sue 19,000 parents, children, dead Vietnam vets,[6] and others for copyright infringement, an act that had absolutely no impact on the widespread practice of downloading free MP3-compressed music. The industry also began suing the individual peer-to-peer networks such as LimeWire and Kazaa, but as soon as one network disappeared, another one promptly appeared. The music industry now existed in a Greek hell of its own creating, doomed,

---

[5] *Rock Stars do the Dumbest Things* by Margaret Moser (Renaissance Press, 1998). A long-buried classic worth your time!

[6] "The Shameful Destination of your Music Purchase Dollars" by David Berlind (http://blogs.zdnet.com/BTL/?p=3486), August 14, 2006

like Sisyphus, to push the rock of copyright litigation up and down a terrain that consisted of endless hills of peer-to-peer networks.

~

Getting to the Root of the Problem

The industry's stupidity reached a dizzying crescendo with Sony BMG Music Entertainment's 2004 release to its customers of something that proved to be far more exciting than any music video ever produced—a "rootkit." A rootkit is perhaps the most dangerous of all malware, a vicious piece of Borgware[7] that absorbs your computer's operating system into a vast, evil collective over which you have no control. Rootkits integrate themselves so deeply into a computer's innards that even high-quality antivirus and antispyware products often cannot detect them. The Sony rootkit, targeted primarily at Windows (though it also infected Macs, but to a lesser extent), was loaded onto 52 of its music CDs, and when someone put a rootkit-infected CD into their computer, Sony's malware was surreptitiously installed onto the system. Once there, if detected, an attempt to remove the rootkit resulted in severe damage to Windows and a nonworking computer. Once hidden on your PC, the rootkit prevented you from copying songs from the CD to another CD or to the MP3 format (though this protection was almost instantly circumvented).

The Sony rootkit spread to more than half a million machines and networks, including those in the Department of Defense and other government agencies, before writer and Windows expert Mark Russinovich discovered its existence in October 2005. He posted his discovery online, and news of the rootkit spread worldwide in a matter of hours. (Companies such as Symantec and McAfee were heavily criticized for failing to develop software that detected Sony's malware until Russinovich's disclosure of its existence.)

---

[7] The Borg are *Star Trek*'s baddest bad guys, a race of cyborgs ruled by queens who run around the galaxy in large cube-style ships assimilating other races while announcing "resistance is futile." In high tech, Bill Gates is usually assumed to be the chief Borg queen. However, given Steve Job's recent penchant for suing everyone, Apple's increasing monopoly in the music world, and the suspicious design of the Apple Cube and the Next computer, many people think Apple's CEO may be auditioning for the role.

Sony's handling of its self-inflicted PR nightmare showed the company's collective intelligence was even with that of the wretched headless bat publicly decapitated by Ozzy Osborne. As outrage about the rootkit grew, Sony embarked on a damage control effort that included the following:

- Claiming the rootkit didn't surreptitiously "phone home," that is, use your Internet connection to contact Sony, when it did just that **every time you played a song.**

- Not realizing that the installation of the rootkit left every computer on which it had been installed with a giant security hole any hacker with knowledge of the rootkit's behavior could exploit.

- Releasing an update that supposedly fixed the security hole created by the rootkit that required you to provide your name, e-mail address, and other personal information to Sony. After installation, it continued to send information about your choice of music to Sony, but now it had a name to match up with your playlist.

- Allowing Sony's president of global digital business, Thomas Hesse, to go on National Public Radio and conduct an interview in which he told the listening audience that "Most people don't even know what a rootkit is, so why should they care about it?" The hapless Hesse was apparently too stupid to realize that Sony was in the process of educating most of humanity on the dangers of rootkits.

- Not knowing that the company supplying its rootkits, software firm First4Internet, was using an **open source encoder in the rootkit.**[8]

Class-action lawsuits against Sony were launched in California, New York, Texas, Italy, and lots of other places. Twelve days after the discovery of the rootkit, Sony announced it would no longer sell its self-infected CDs. Then it announced it was recalling all of the infected CDs and replacing them with non-copy-protected disks. Estimates of the eventual financial damages to Sony ran from $50 million to $500 million. (One of the reasons for the uncertainty was that thousands of Sony-infected PCs remain in use and vulnerable. As late as June of 2006,

---

[8] LAME, licensed under the lesser GPL

three virus creators were arrested for exploiting the security vulnerability created by the rootkit.[9])

More to the point, the entire fiasco helped convince millions of potential buyers of online music that the easiest, cheapest, and safest thing you could do was log on to one of those nice peer-to-peer networks where the music selection was wide, the price was zero, and the number of rootkits you could expect to encounter was low.

~

Back to the Future with WGA

The year 2000, a date that saw most of the world looking forward, saw Microsoft looking back to the 1980s and copy protection. That year Microsoft announced its new "product activation" program. The new copy protection system worked by tethering, in theory, your copy of Microsoft Office 2000 to the Internet via a key found on Microsoft servers. The process worked by your first installing Office and then allowing the product activator to snoop through your computer, send a profile of your hardware to the Microsoft server, and receive a downloaded product key from Microsoft that would allow you to actually use the software you had bought. After initial trials, the scheme was extended to Windows XP when it was released in 2001. Soon, the entire copy protection system became known as Windows Product Activation (WPA).

There were, as you can imagine, some delightful aspects to WPA. If, for instance, you decided to change the motherboard, processor, graphics card, or similar hardware on your system, you ran the risk of waking up WPA and having it nag you to reinstall Windows and your other WPA-protected programs, even though the copy you were using was perfectly legal. Reinstalling Windows sometimes meant calling up a special 800 number and sitting through a long and wearying session that

---

[9] "Virus Suspects arrested in UK and Finland" by Quentin Reade. (Webuser, http://www.webuser.co.uk/news/87558.html?aff=rss), June 27th, 2006

required you speak every last number of the CD key that came with your copy of Windows in the hope that the phone god with whom you were communing would deign to give you a new key. If that didn't work, you could look forward to spending some time with someone named "Ramesh" or "Gupta" who was normally sitting in a call center in India or similar exotic location and explaining why you needed a new key that allowed you to actually use the software you'd bought...errr... "licensed."

~

Freedom From Choice Is What You Want

Most people looked at WPA with the same affection shown a turd dropped in a punch bowl at a wedding, but in the main, Microsoft was able to finesse its introduction. There were several reasons for this. One was that many people received Windows bundled with their computer and, as already noted, didn't really think about what they had paid for the product. Another was that, as had happened before, the WPA copy scheme was quickly cracked, and many people simply bypassed WPA. A third was that Microsoft had given "universal keys" to many of its corporate customers; these allowed them to do mass installs of Windows at their business locations without having to waste time going through hundreds or thousands of activations. These keys had quickly leaked into the general public and were employed by many people to use Windows in pretty much the same way they had for more than a decade. All in all, it all turned out that most people could ignore WPA, for most of the time. Which seemed, to most people, fair.

Microsoft now had legally sanctioned monopolies in desktop operating systems and office suites (but no mauling of the competition allowed)! The company seemed on its way to establishing a similar monopoly in network operating systems, had strong positions in the enterprise database market with its SQL product, was selling a great deal of Microsoft Exchange, had a nice business in mice, and by 2002 enjoyed the luxury of having approximately $49 billion in cash sitting in the company's piggy bank. Why would any company in its right mind disturb such a wonderful status quo?

Of course, the open source and free software folks took a great deal of enjoyment in pointing out that Linux, which had steadily increased in functionality and ease of use, was free and never required you talk to Ramesh when changing a motherboard. And in the meantime, an interesting product called first StarOffice, then OpenOffice, had appeared on the scene. StarOffice began its life as an OS/2 office suite developed by a German company in the early 1990s. After the collapse of OS/2, the software morphed into a Windows product that was bought by Sun, ostensibly because it was cheaper for the company to buy its own office software than buy Microsoft's. The real reason was the desire of Sun CEO Scott McNealy to give Bill Gates and his company a case of heartburn, which he attempted to do by open sourcing most of StarOffice's code, which was then transformed into OpenOffice by a series of programmers dedicated to open source ideals (they didn't become millionaires, though). Sun still sells a version of StarOffice, though there's little compelling reason to buy it considering the price, free, of OpenOffice.

On the other hand, although Linux was free, installing it was a royal pain that the vast majority of people had no desire to experience. The price of freedom included the privilege of choosing **which** Linux you would pick from dozens of different packages, called "distros," and then attempting to install your choice on your hardware. This was made more interesting by the fact that although the core Linux operating system was usually (though not always) the same from distro to distro, the various Linux bundles often used different install procedures, had different user interfaces, looked for key files in different places, included different utilities, and so on, and so on. And, although it was nice that OpenOffice was free and that StarOffice was cheap, once one had copied Microsoft Office to all the computers it needed to be on, the price wasn't really that bad after all.

All this changed in 2004 when Microsoft introduced, with an Orwellian fanfare of misleading language, its new Windows Genuine Advantage (WGA) program. Windows users were prompted (under threat of losing access to updates other than ones deemed critical to security) to download a program that checked their product key for authenticity. If Microsoft determined you were indeed "Genuine," you could continue to receive all Windows XP updates. If you weren't, well, no updates for you, at least until WGA was cracked by hackers (it took about a week). Everything seemed to continue on much as it had before, though the I-told-you-so cackling from the free software crowd grew louder, and people started becoming a little annoyed with Microsoft. It bordered on terminal chutzpah to threaten people with the inability to obtain via Microsoft's update system access to such things as the latest version of Internet Explorer, a product that had been allowed to rot for five years after Microsoft dispatched Netscape. It was nice that Internet Explorer 7 would have tabbed browsing and all, but Firefox and Opera had been offering those features for years.

The rootkit hit the fan in July 2006 when Microsoft unleashed part deux of WGA, called "WGA notifications." WGA notifications was a nifty bit of code that reminded everyone very much of a recent music company's malware. Making utterly sure that WGA notifications would be instantly loathed by humanity, Microsoft misled the world by tucking the program onto its servers and transmitting it across the wires in the company of **security** patches with the appellation of a "critical update." (WGA had nothing to do with security.) Once installed, the WGA program revealed the following charming characteristics:

- It phoned Microsoft every time you logged into Windows to tattle on you if it thought your install of Windows wasn't valid (proving that Microsoft had learned absolutely, positively nothing from the Sony rootkit disaster of 2004).

- WGA now forced Windows to display an unending series of nagware messages urging you to get "Genuine," that is, fork over more money into Microsoft's giant cash hoard.

- The EULA that came with WGA notifications was misleading and didn't properly request the user's consent to install the software.

- If you wanted to "Get Genuine," WGA didn't make it easy for you to see other options other than give $149 to Microsoft. And there **were** other options. For example, if a repair shop had loaded an invalid copy of Windows onto your system during an overhaul of your system but you had bought a legal copy that was sitting on your bookshelf somewhere, you could restore your legitimate key to your system in a process that appeased WGA. But it was a genuine pain to find information about this process via all the "Genuine" nag screens.

- WGA was misidentifying hundreds of thousands, maybe millions, of legitimate installs as "nongenuine." Exactly how many was somewhat mysterious, since Microsoft was not very forthcoming on the issue. The company did say that of the 60 million checks it had run, 80 percent of the machines tattled on by WGA were using invalid keys. That left about 12 million "others." High levels of complaints were coming from a wide spectrum of users, particularly people who'd had Windows preinstalled on their laptops. As one blogger asked, "Is Dell a pirate?"

- If you read the EULA that came with WGA notifications, you realized you were being asked to download a **beta** product that had the potential to cripple your copy of Windows.

- WGA provided no advantages at all to the user (but plenty to Microsoft). The program was simply a copy protection/antipiracy scheme, and people weren't stupid.

Reaction to the whole WGA mess was exactly what you would expect. Several class-action lawsuits were launched against Microsoft claiming the company had violated laws against spyware in several states. Microsoft promptly replaced the big tattler in WGA with a littler tattler, one that would only "periodically" call home to tell on you. Microsoft also changed the EULA to inform you more clearly about its informant. A French company quickly released a program called RemoveWGA that kicked the Jewish mother (WGA notifications) out of your computer, though the basic WGA system remained intact. Several Windows pundits such as Brian Livingston began to recommend that people not use Windows Update but to instead rely on third-party services.[10]

Fresh from its initial success, Microsoft announced that the joys of WGA would soon be extended to all the products in its line. And to ensure that there were no embarrassing ambiguities in the future, WGA in all its glory would be directly integrated into Vista, the designated heir to XP whose father may have been Bill Gates but whose mother was clearly Steve Jobs. In the meantime, the chortles and snickers from the open sourcers turned to guffaws and screams of laughter as they fell to the floor holding their ribs from an excess of merriment.

---

[10] Windows Secret Newsletter, issue 78 (http://windowssecrets.com/comp/060629/)

Rumors then began to quickly spread that part three of Microsoft's spyware system would introduce a new friend to WGA's tattler and Jewish mother: an executioner. This would come in the form of a "kill switch" that would allow Microsoft to remotely disable your nongenuine Windows at the behest and whim of Redmond. (Industry wits noted that given the number of security attacks and virus infections afflicting Windows, most people might not notice any difference in operations.) In response to a query from Ziff-Davis columnist Ed Bott, a Microsoft PR representative, speaking in Modern Flack, provided the following chunk of verbiage:

> No, Microsoft anti-piracy technologies cannot and will not turn off your computer. In our ongoing fight against piracy, we are constantly finding and closing loopholes pirates use to circumvent established policies. The game is changing for counterfeiters. In Windows Vista we are making it notably harder and less appealing to use counterfeit software, and we will work to make that a consistent experience with older versions of Windows as well. In alignment with our anti-piracy policies we have been continually improving the experience for our genuine customers, while restricting more and more access to ongoing Windows capabilities for those who choose not to pay for their software. Our genuine customers deserve the best experience, and so over time we have made the following services and benefits available only to them: Windows Update service, Download Center, Internet Explorer 7, Windows Defender, and Windows Media Player 11, as well as access to a full range of updates including non-security related benefits. We expect this list to expand considerably as we continue to add value for our genuine customers and deny value to pirates. Microsoft is fully committed to helping any genuine customers who have been victims of counterfeit software, and offer free replacement copies of Windows to those who've been duped by high quality counterfeiters. There is more information at our website http://www.microsoft.com/resources/howtotell.

A careful reading of this statement revealed plenty of ambiguities (we didn't ask whether WGA was going to shut down the **computer**, but **Windows**), but Microsoft's PR people clammed up and refused to talk further. Not making people feel any better was an online article by respected security analyst Robert Schneier in which he reported that a Microsoft representative had told him that

> *In the fall, having the latest WGA will become mandatory and if it's not installed, Windows will give a 30 day warning and when the 30 days is up and WGA isn't installed, Windows will stop working, so you might as well install WGA now.*[11]

At this point, the open source people were snorting liquids through their noses as they rolled around the floor laughing hysterically, but Windows people were depressed. Forums and blogs exploded with comments from users that now was the time to finally take a look at Linux, OpenOffice, and other open source alternatives to Windows.[12] It made sense. While Microsoft was spending time and energy figuring out ways to torture many of its customers, new versions of Linux had just about caught up to Windows in terms of ease of install, functionality, and peripheral support. There were still problems, but at least you could be sure that if anyone in the open source community attempted to put something like WGA into Linux, Richard Stallman would personally throttle them. No one was enthusiastic about the prospect of allowing Bill Gates and Steve Ballmer to hold a loaded pistol at their PCs on a 24/7 basis. Given the past experiences with WGA, just how could you be sure that some idiot at Microsoft wouldn't inadvertently do something that crippled your system at just the wrong time? Certainly some people thought the possibility existed. Before finishing this book, I spoke to an acquaintance at Microsoft who told me that

---

[11] http://www.schneier.com/blog/archives/2006/06/microsoft_windo_1.html

[12] I have. I'm tired of talking to Ramesh every time I swap a motherboard, something I do fairly frequently.

I recommend to my friends that they always keep a copy of OpenOffice on their systems in the event that MS Office's activation system locks up the software when they're not expecting it and they can't reach a phone or the Internet to reactivate it. Interoperability is excellent and you can usually get something done. It's good protection against our copy protection.

It appeared that open source has a friend in Redmond after all!

thirteen

ON AVOIDING STUPIDITY

I PERIODICALLY GIVE LECTURES at such venues as technology trade shows, product managers' groups, and high-tech councils, and before beginning my talk, I always ask this question: "How many people have read the following books?" I then list some of the seminal publications on the history of high tech. These include such books as *Apple* by Jim Carlton, *Gates* by Steve Manes, and *Hackers* by Steven Levy. Invariably, only one or two hands go up; often, none do.

Then, I ask how many people have read the newest, hottest, the-promised-land-is-within-your-reach-if-you-just-follow-the-diktats-of-this-newest-business-guru wonderbook. The latest wonderbook differs from year to year and from decade to decade. In the 1980s it was, of course, *In Search of Excellence* by Thomas J. Peters and Robert H. Waterman and its myriad of profitable spin-offs (all based on an original foundation of bogus data). In the early-to-mid 1990s it was often *Crossing the Chasm* by Geoffrey Moore and its myriad of spin-offs (all based on product life cycle models that were first introduced in the 1950s). By the late 1990s and early 2000s it was often *The Innovator's Dilemma* by Clay Christensen, which discusses how established companies have a hard time dealing with new ideas and the very successful follow-on, *The Innovator's Solution*, which proposes a solution to the problem the author of the book admits no one has ever actually used (which is a rather innovative way to end a business book series, when you come to think about it).

Now, in all fairness, many of these business books offer practical, if often generic, advice about how to run a business and the best things to do while you're doing it. Like most exercise machines, many of these books "work" if you rigorously follow their commonsense advice. In most cases, thinking up new or improved products or services to sell to people (this process is currently being lionized as "innovation," and businesses have been doing it since the pyramids, but apparently the new label makes everyone feel even better about the process), being open to new ideas, treating customers well, organizing your data, hiring good employees, not committing accounting fraud, and so on, and so on, will certainly improve your chances of success. But this is rather like saying that breathing increases your chance of competing in the 100-yard dash. It will, but mere respiration is not what separates winners from losers in a race.

The danger comes when you dig into the specifics and try to apply the generic to your specific business and its challenges. Most writers of "theory" books can't overcome the tendency to fit the facts into their grand frameworks, leading to a lot of misleading and contradictory advice. You already know the problem with *Excellence*. The *Chasm* books sometimes work well when talking about enterprise markets with fairly well-defined buying processes, but if you had relied on their advice during the microcomputer market's early growth spurt in the 1980s, you would have been caught utterly flat footed by the rapid pace of events (Moore tries to deal with this problem with a later book that acts as a retrofit to the original theory, but it's unconvincing). The *Innovator* books, written by an academic who has never worked in business, proffers a solution that has never been demonstrated to solve anything.

It's not just high-tech firms that get themselves into hot water in this regard. Super-duper consulting firm McKinsey first wrote about and then introduced the concept of "eagles flying high" at Enron, a theory based on the belief that by hiring lots of smart people and letting the wind beneath their super-intelligent wings push them into the stratosphere, Enron profits would soar to ever loftier heights, clutched safely in the talons of all these Einstein flyers. Unfortunately, the theory didn't take into account that really, really smart people might, in the interests of self-enrichment, create myriads of business deals and projects that objectively evaluated had little or no chance of turning a profit and then create a dizzying array of interlocking shell companies where accumulating debt could be buried, all at the expense of stockholders and company employees' retirement funds.

Another problem with all business books that focus on grand theories of business success is that, in a very real sense, no such theory can ever exist. To help understand this concept further, take a quick look at a popular Hollywood fantasy, that of the young go-getter who develops a surefire way to "beat" the stock market. Now, suppose this fantasy could be translated into reality. Imagine that through the use of supercomputers and sheer genius programming, you create a stock-picking system that infallibly predicts which stocks will go up and down and then write a book releasing this information to the world.

What would happen?

What would happen would be that the stock market would immediately congeal into immobility and would have to be rejiggered to work in such a way that all your good advice and smart programming would be rendered useless. This goes back to the fundamental reality underlying all market-driven systems: there must be a winner and a loser in every transaction for the system to work. (It's a grim fact, but before you run shrieking into the comforting arms of Marx and Lenin, the empirical evidence suggests that communism simply creates losers all around.)

This carries over to the competitive environment all companies must endure in market-driven economies. Competition must winnow the myriad of firms over time to ensure the market can function. Failure must happen. But failure must also always have a cause.

~

The Main Causes of Failure

The main reasons for company failure can be broken down into four basic types:

- Your company is based on fraud and/or the sale of illegal products and services.
- Your company is built around an unrealistic or ridiculous business assumption.
- Your company does not have a strategic vision and plan for success.
- Your company has failed to execute business basics in the course of selling its products and services.

In regards to the first two types of failure, I don't have much advice to give. If, like Enron, ZZZBest, and thousands of other companies over the course of the 20th century and continuing into the 21st, your underlying business model is a Ponzi scheme, your business will fail, and maybe you will go to jail. If your company plans to market heroin or cocaine in the United States, you will fail and probably go to jail if someone doesn't shoot or decide to dismember you with a chainsaw first during a dispute about optimal distribution strategies and reseller margins. If, like a very bright gentleman I spoke to during the course of writing the second edition of *Stupidity*, you intend to bring to market a new word processor for Windows, you will fail, and no one will even pay attention to you. If you're the new SoftRam, please send me a shrink-wrapped version of your product for my collection.

The third class of failure, lack of strategic vision and planning, is, as you've seen, the one most business writers like to write about primarily because books about this topic tend to make the most money. Of course, all successful companies have to develop and sell products and/or services people will pay for; this is the essence of modern commerce, and it is here that a "strategic" plan is both useful and necessary. But few companies and theorists are content to leave it at just that. For the past several decades, American business has been obsessed with the idea that somewhere out there exists a grand unified theory of business that explains once and for all how success can be guaranteed if only the theory can be uncovered and explained. For a time "excellence" seemed to provide the Great Answer. Then the path to proven success appeared to encompass leaping like gazelles over chasms. Now, many believe institutionalizing innovation (something of an oxymoron) into the corporate genome is the first step on the path to enlightenment.

American companies are obsessed with this concept of strategy and are always recasting and reorganizing themselves so as to realign with the latest, greatest strategic vision as brought to them by a newly minted business guru or a shiny new CEO. Caught in a tautological loop, farreaching business plans are developed that are excellent or that leap far enough or that are innovative because excellent or leaping or innovating is what we do. Things usually go well at first. Americans, despite romantic self-images of rebel cowboys and sturdy nonconformists, are actually pretty good at organizing themselves and taking orders. We're not as antlike as the Japanese, of course, but we do stand patiently in lines, stop at red lights, wait our turn, and take orders from authority with a fair degree of alacrity. So when plans and dictates come down from on high, companies can usually be whipped into fighting trim in fairly short order. A laser-like focus is brought to the creation of new marketing and sales campaigns. The competitive terrain is analyzed thoroughly via market research and focus groups. The distribution channel is primed with promotional money, advertising, and collateral. New products and services are manufactured in record time with maximum efficiency. The company maneuvers with stereotaxic directness toward its launch point and pauses in readiness, waiting for the command to move out. When the clarion call comes, the entire firm surges forward in lockstep unison, eyes set straight ahead on the prize, moving in a determined sweep to clear from the field of battle any obstacle that stands in the way of the ultimate victory and triumph.

But then things start to go badly wrong. You unleash a new word processor, and your entire company falls into the mud of massive confusion and market resistance because you've made a fundamental positioning mistake (MicroPro). You launch a hot new microprocessor, and because you've failed to realize that now that you're a consumer brand, the PR rules have changed, and the charge forward has been halted by incoming fire from the press (Intel). You become the Internet's most strategic site by dint of a marketing campaign that secures every corner of the globe with platoons of floppies and CDs, and then find yourself in full retreat as everyone stops using phones to connect to the Internet and starts using high-speed connections (AOL). You attack the market for digital content in 1998 with a can't-miss device, an MP3 player the size of today's iPod...and hardly anyone pays attention (Saehan/Eiger Labs).

And then an awful realization bursts upon you. Business is not...war, at least not conventional war. Innovation doesn't always lead to success; failure to innovate sometimes leads to disaster. Markets are not terrains that can be swept clear of enemies in all conquering waves. What is excellence in the context of one industry is a waste of money in another. If business is war, then it's an odd sort of ongoing guerilla conflict in which the enemy can be an opposing company one day and a division or business unit at your own firm the next. Markets are swampy, Escheresque lumps of chaos studded with redoubts and obstacles that disappear and reappear from any direction, studded with over and under ramparts onto which confused invaders stumble and then stagger off from view. And even when you succeed in your objectives and take the field, sometimes the field disappears beneath you, and you find yourself slogging about in a pale foam that obscures your vision and leaves you wandering directionless in a vast wilderness.

And sometimes you get amazingly lucky.

For instance, let's take the success of Microsoft Windows, to date high tech's most dizzying product triumph. Overcoming its humble roots as a clumsy imitation of the far more sophisticated Macintosh operating system, Windows's success from 1990 onward drove Microsoft by 2005 to more than $40 billion in revenue and 60,000 employees, with 2005 profits exceeding $3 billion. Windows was first announced in 1983 when the GUI wars were first taking shape in the wake of Xerox's pioneering work in the field and the first version was released in 1985. Over the years Windows bested GEM, VisiOn, GeoWorks, the Mac OS, and, most notably, OS/2 in the war for supremacy. What clearer example could exist of a company having a strategic vision for a product and then pursuing that vision to ultimate success?

But for Windows to achieve its current monopoly position, the following events had to occur:

- Xerox, the original inventor of what we now call the *graphic user interface*, had to never develop a clue about how to commercialize most of the groundbreaking developments that came out of its PARC labs.

- Digital Research had to blow off IBM when it came calling for an operating system for the original IBM PC.

- IBM, which during the early years of its relationship with Microsoft could have crushed the company like a bug, had to behave as if prefrontally lobotomized from 1985 to 1995 as the gruesome OS/2 saga ground on.

- Apple had to decide to not license the Macintosh operating system, a decision that led to the company going from approximately 30 percent market share in the early 1980s to 4 percent market share by 2006.

Other events that contributed to the eventual success of Windows also encompassed the following:

- The failure of industry pioneer VisiCorp to release a successful version of VisiOn, an early graphical OS for the PC that scared Bill Gates into almost shampooing his hair.

- Apple suing Digital Research over the release of its DOS shell, GEM, shortly after the product's release. GEM was a direct Windows competitor and far more sophisticated than early releases of Windows in its look and feel (it looked and felt like a Mac). Before the Apple suit crippled the product, GEM was on the verge of achieving widespread adoption in the PC market.

- An unexpected run-up in the cost of memory chips (and temporary violation of Moore's law), which helped cripple the release of OS/2 1.0.

Now, how does one fashion a credible strategic plan that assumes your competition will agree to collectively shoot itself in the forebrain while unpredictable market forces break in such a way as to help ensure your eventual success?

The answer is that you can't. Microsoft's success with Windows, which, depending on how you count these things, ranges from $60 to $100 billion (and still counting!) is as much a result of good luck and stupidity on the part of its competition as much as any vision on the part of Microsoft. No strategic plan that anyone would take seriously could include the actual events as they unfolded over the decades. And whatever strategic plans Microsoft had for Windows in 1983 were obsolete by the product's release in 1985. And whatever plans Microsoft had in 1985 were obsolete by 1987, the year of OS/2's release. And certainly by 1990 everyone's plans for Windows were obsolete as a technically inferior but useful DOS shell swept to market supremacy over far more sophisticated and feature-rich rivals that couldn't do much.

But in the meantime, as I've already pointed out, while Microsoft's competition was engaged in various sorts of self-immolation, the company was continually executing business basics effectively. From the early 1980s through the 1990s the company entered the word processing, spreadsheet, and business presentation markets with good products that sold well and received generally favorable reviews. During this same period, Microsoft was creating a PR campaign that effectively developed a pleasing persona around Bill Gates that supported Microsoft's marketing and sales efforts. The company also continuously improved and refined their development products, releasing new IDEs, languages, and tools that were well received by developers. In 1993 the company fortuitously stumbled onto the Office concept and rode its success to even larger profits. It also figured out how to make profits during the Internet bubble by selling products such as FrontPage. In the aggregate, all these events have contributed to Microsoft's success, and little strategic planning was involved. Microsoft simply gravitated to good opportunities, executed well (or at least better than its competitors), and reaped the rewards.

You're not convinced? OK, let's look at another seminal company in the industry, one undergoing a seemingly miraculous rebirth in high tech. Let's look at Apple, a company I had quite a bit of fun with in the first edition of *Stupidity*.

Now, before we go further, I'm going to give you a test. Let's imagine, for a few minutes, that you have gone down to the mall to visit your local Apple store in order to peruse its wares and decide whether you're going to buy a sleek, dazzling new Apple Intel-based Powerbook or save a few hundred bucks and buy a boring but decent Dell laptop. As you fight your way into the place past hordes of crazed shoppers battling to scarf up the latest iPod, a dazzling light suddenly appears from nowhere in the middle of the store's ceiling. The light grows brighter and more intense, and everyone in the place, except you, falls into a deep sleep and slumps gently to the store's floor, still clutching their iPod boxes. As you watch in amazement, the light contracts into a glowing orb that descends to the floor and coalesces into a beautiful girl. (I feel these Disney trappings most appropriate in light of Steve Job's ascension to the Disney board of directors as a result of the Pixar buyout.) This dazzling apparition is dressed in a gown of diaphanous gold filigree and wafts a wand so white it almost hurts to look at it. As you gape in amazement, the wand glows and shimmers while emitting magical sparks that seem to distort reality itself! You reach out in delight to touch this marvelous instrument, but the vision in front of you quickly yanks it away with a warning that the thing scratches like heck. Tucking the wand safely away in a silicon rubber holster, the magical lady explains that she is your Apple Fairy Godmother and that she has come to ask you to develop an enchanted strategic business plan.

You are, she explains as you listen with rapt attention, to help Good King Steve Jobs come up with a wondrous way to help Apple return to the Glory Days of the late 1970s and early 1980s, when Apple was the predominant player in the nascent microcomputer industry. It shouldn't be too difficult, she says, for someone as brave and handsome as you. And, after all, she says with a lustrous smile on her face, Apple has exquisitely designed and colored computers on which reside the industry's slickest and most intuitive GUI, Mac OS X, version Panther, or Tiger, or KittyKat, or something. This is all running on top of a rock-solid, open source foundation called Darwin, a derivative of the widely praised FreeBSD. OS X Server, OS X's bigger, brawnier brother, is a snap to set up and maintain. And the incredible success of the iPod has put Apple's name on every consumer's tongue and in just about every music lover's pocket.

Now, what's your plan? How do you plan to succor Good King Jobs? We'll stop the book for a bit and give you some time to think through what you're going to do.

OK, time is up.

What you do, of course, is smile regretfully and explain to the hallucination in front of you that you intend to quickly recover from the slight concussion you suffered when a shopping-hardened yuppie sprinting up the aisle in pursuit of the last white 6 gig Nano accidentally hit you upside your head with a purse loaded with a PDA, cell phone, and her current fourth-generation 60 gig iPod. Shaking your head vigorously, the fairy disappears with a *POOF* and the shoppers resume their mad scrambles. Then, after browsing quickly through the software displayed on the shelves and spending some time on the store's web kiosk, you bail out of the place. You see, you're a finance guy with an accounting degree working on your CPA, and one day you plan to be a CFO somewhere. You're looking for a specialized package that can roll up budgets across different company divisions and business units and create a unified financial model of the entire company, something you really can't do with plain old Microsoft Excel. No one offers such a program for the Mac, so it will have to be the Dell.

Now, why didn't you let the magic linger a little longer? Why not take a stab at planning to put Apple back on the throne from which it once reigned microcomputing 25 years ago? After all, everyone is bored with Windows and hates its copy protection. Linux, the only possible other competitor, has all the computing charm of a diesel truck and requires a degree in computer science to install. And everything the Apple Fairy Godmother said is true, and she left out some hard revenue facts besides. In 2003, Apple's annual revenue hovered around $6 billion. In 2005, Apple sold more than 32 million iPods, and more than one billion songs were downloaded from its iTunes service by the winter of

2006. Yearly revenues from 2005 were almost $14 billion with more than a billion of that being profit.

Because such a plan is as impossible to write as was a 1983 strategic plan for Windows that possessed any credibility. In 2003, when writing the first edition of *In Search of Stupidity*, I noted that Apple had about 3 percent to 4 percent market share of new computers sold worldwide (an observation that carries over to the Mac OS, which still runs only— officially—on Apple boxes). Actually, I was generous; by the time the book went to print, Apple's share had slipped to less than 3 percent in some analyses. And today, after the iPod's stunning success, Apple's worldwide market share of PCs/operating systems worldwide is now about...3 percent to 4 percent.

It isn't as if Apple hasn't tried to change this. Since Steve Jobs returned to Apple, the company has launched several "switch to the Mac" campaigns, all of which have had little impact on the market. (Apple doesn't even pretend to try hard in the server market, despite its product's excellent performance). Apple has been able to hold onto its installed base, but little more. People seem quite content to connect their Apple iPods to their Wintel machines. Teenagers, always harbingers of new trends and fads, seem happy to rely primarily on Windows-based peer-to-peer networks to "liberate" music via the Internet and break the RIAA's heart. And many I speak to seem quite put out by iTunes's digital rights management (DRM) schemes. Apple's growth is coming from consumer electronics, not computers, and no one on this planet has ever figured out how to take a company from 4 percent market share to industry dominance in the face of an entrenched competitor determined to defend its turf. Apple came close to industry dominance in the early 1970s and 1980s, but this was before IBM woke up. And despite Microsoft's creeping development of the senescence that inevitably afflicts all megasized corporations, unless a big meteor hits Redmond and Bellevue, Apple cannot hope Steve Ballmer and Bill Gates are going to stand idly by while Apple lops off significant amounts of market share and money from Microsoft.

Does this mean Apple will eventually leave the PC business? Maybe. One possible scenario is that the company focuses on building more consumer devices, using the Mac OS as an embedded operating system to run ever more sleek and scratch-prone proprietary gadgets. Perhaps Apple eventually merges with Sony or another major consumer electronics giant and merges their technology with the new company. Apple has already provided their Intel-based computers with an easy way to run Windows, and the company gracefully exits the market with a solution that doesn't leave its customers with the option of running only soon-to-be obsolete software. Given the pace of hardware advancement and evolution, the entire affair would take only two to three years.

Or maybe the market is changing under Microsoft, and Apple is in position to take advantage of the chaos that will ensue. The iPod's success is ushering in a new era of content where music, film, and, eventually, literature is casting off its ties to the physical. Say a permanent good-bye to liner notes and beautiful album covers (two institutions already wounded by the move to CDs). Today's new music consumer expects to take their music with them, be it on an airplane, in a car, or even from their hotel room. iPods are just way stations, disposable transmitters that facilitate the job of providing personalized content 24/7/365 to consumers. And if you want cover art with that music, well, that's what websites and screen savers are for. And isn't it nice those pretty images are also available anytime from anywhere?

In this milieu, what's needed is a beautifully designed and easy-to-use system that seamlessly manages the task of providing, creating, and managing content for both professionals and the masses, a plan that calls for a hardware platform with plenty of oomph. It's called *convergence*, and high tech has been waiting years for it to occur. For Microsoft, the problem is Windows doesn't seem suited to the task; the system is feature laden but hard to use, loaded with extrusions and encrustations that make the heads of people already defeated by the remote control ache. But anyone who has used an iPod knows Apple can build lean, elegant, easy-to-learn interfaces people like. And its computers are certainly powerful enough to handle content management and transmission. So perhaps it's Apple that dominates this new world, leaving Windows to its fate as a backroom grease monkey that does the grimy, dirty work of chugging through spreadsheets and grinding out yet more business memos. The consumer market is now where it's at, after all, with COMDEX replaced by CES as high tech's major show. And now that Steve Jobs is on the board of Disney, where obviously he plans to sit quietly in the background and provide some helpful advice to the new CEO, we can hope the video iPod and its successors will at least provide us with a steady diet of nice cartoons and the latest Pixar/Disney movies.

There are many other possible scenarios. Perhaps Microsoft buys into several key markets and stitches together a convergence solution that, although not as elegant as Apple's, has enough functionality, price advantage, and nonproprietary advantages to succeed in extending Windows into the living room. After all, who wants to bet against Microsoft and all those billions? And Microsoft has already executed such a strategy, with considerable success.

Of course, if you write enough business plans, I suppose one of them will be the right one. But this smacks of hiring a room full of chimps to sit in front of a group of terminals and hack randomly at a business plan software package in the hopes they'll crank out the next Netscape IPO. The last time this worked was during the Internet bubble, and I think you'll have to wait a few more years before you can get away with this.

Another paradox that awaits strategic plans and planners is that, paradoxically, as a company grows larger, its ability to plan strategically withers away. IBM and Microsoft are both excellent exemplars of this principal. In the early 1980s IBM ruled the mainframe world, it was equal with rivals DEC and Data General in midsized systems, and the story of the PC's success doesn't need repeating. IBM was also the largest software company in the world, with its business products in use in practically every industry on the globe. The company even introduced several desktop software titles, such as an editor, that were initially well received. IBM was in a position to buy any company it needed to help ensure its continued supremacy and indeed was at one time or another rumored or actively interested in buying Intel (in which it held a significant minority stake), MicroPro, Microsoft, Novell, Apple, and many others. Yet today IBM is out of the PC business. Microsoft dominates software. The mainframe market is still profitable, but static. Minicomputers are gone. IBM's most successful business is now in consulting, telling other businesses how to use technology that in many cases IBM no longer produces.

The reason for this is that by the late 1980s, as I point out in Chapter 6 of *Stupidity* was that IBM had become too large for anyone to coordinate its various components into a strategic "whole"; the company was simply too big to coordinate the differing agendas of its myriad numbers of divisions, business units, initiatives, alliances, channel, and so on, and so on, into anything resembling a coherent plan. At the end, IBM's strategic plan had devolved to "grow by 10 percent per year." Or 5 percent.

Or **something**. But to achieve even minimal growth, IBM was forced to turn to selling its consulting services and begin shedding different businesses and products (PCs, disk drives, printers, and so on) it could no longer manage effectively and profitably, even though other firms have been able to do just that. Although then-CEO John Akers's 1992 plan for breaking the company into smaller pieces ended when he lost his job, the effective result over time has been exactly that.

The same conundrum now faces Microsoft. As of 2006, Microsoft was launching or continuing initiatives in the following areas:

- A renewed push into the small business and personal finance market, an effort that was thwarted by the feds putting the kibosh on an earlier attempt by Microsoft to merge with Intuit

- Launch of a renewed assault on Sony and Nintendo with its Xbox system

- Announcement of an attempt to create a Microsoft MP3 player to compete with the iPod

- Further attempts by Microsoft to make Larry Ellison's life miserable with a renewed push into the enterprise database with its SQL product line

- New initiatives to displace Lotus Notes and Novell's GroupWise with Exchange

- The creation of a new document format that competes with Adobe's ubiquitous PDF

- The development of a new image package aimed at PhotoShop as well as Sparkle, a Flash competitor

- The launch of a new antivirus and spyware product that takes direct aim at market leaders Symantec and McAfee

- Initiatives into the mobile e-mail market now dominated by RIM, as well as an early stab at VOIP

The "strategic" goal behind all these initiatives? Grow by 10 percent per year. The strategic plan? Act like a giant maw and attempt to slurp up every $1 billion dollar market in reach in order to continue to fuel growth. The final result of this strategy?

See IBM.

So, if thinking "strategically" is a) often impractical and b) impossible, what's left?

Yes, the boring stuff. Executing business basics in the context of your industry's technological, financial, and competitive factors. Checklists. Spreadsheets. God help you, sometimes even meetings. There's no getting away from it.

Of course, companies and far-sighted CEOs will continue to read the latest business wonderbook and develop strategic plans based on them. Just be aware that your plan will almost certainly be obsolete immediately upon completion; that if you're spending more than 5 percent of your time on thinking deep strategic thoughts, you are almost certainly neglecting the important business of running your company; and that payroll is Thursday.

So, in the end, it's all about coming up with a good idea and then figuring out how to go out and do the basic marketing and selling blocking and tackling that leads to success. Now, I fully realize that's a truism, and it's easy for me to say. To make things worse, I'm not even prepared to tell you exactly what blocking and tackling you need to carry out to successfully market and sell your products and services. Why? For two reasons. One is that I'd have to write at least one book within a book, a detailed field manual that breaks down by categories the various components of an effective sales and marketing effort within a specific industry. I have written one such book, *The Product Marketing Handbook for Software*. At almost 700 pages with more than 2,600 to-do items listed in a suggested order of execution, it's a wonderful book for software types but not as useful for builders of PDAs.

The second reason is that over the years I've noted that the ability of companies to execute successful business programs rises and falls in correlation with the certain key characteristics:

- A corporate management structure that intently studies the history of its industry
- Company managers who have a contextual understanding of their industry's business requirements based on their analyses of the preceding
- An understanding of the company's basic "type" (in other words, sales driven, market driven, technology driven, and so on)

- A lack of age discrimination within the firm
- A temperamentally balanced management group
- An interest in providing cross-functional training to company managers

Let's analyze the value of these characteristics one by one.

~

You Shall Study the Past, and the Past Will Make You Less Stupid

The first and most valuable thing most companies can do to avoid acting stupidly is to encourage all employees to learn about the history of the industry in which they compete. The great thing about history (hindsight) is it is full of facts from which you can learn things, such as how to avoid positioning disasters and what to do if a PR roof falls in on you, while many strategic business books are often full of suppositions and untested conjectures. Now please, don't waste everyone's time with an attempt to wiggle out of your required reading by telling us about the "subjectivity" of history; we're all aware that people can differ about the significance of different events. If different writers and historians have different opinions about the facts, read them all, and make up your own mind from an informed viewpoint.

In the spirit of the advice just given, the following sections include my particular lists of "must" and "recommended" reading. Most of these books focus on high tech, but I've thrown in a couple of tomes from other industries to stretch your brain and provide you with some cross-cultural diversity. Feel free to criticize this lineup and add and subtract to it as you see fit. These lists are not that long, and when you are done reading these or similar books, you will have a well-rounded understanding of the forces that shape the high-tech industry, a truly invaluable asset. Both lists are in alphabetical order.

Must-Reads

These are the must-reads:

- *Apple: The Inside Story of Intrigue, Egomania, and Business Blunders* by Jim Carlton. This is a seminal history of how, where, and why Apple lost its bid for market dominance in desktop computing.

- *Big Blues: The Unmaking Of IBM* by Paul Carroll. This book is a well-written account of the critical period in the late 1980s and early 1990s when IBM lost its luster and market leadership.

- *The Dream Machine: J.C.R. Licklidder and the Revolutions that Made Computing Personal* by M. Mitchell Waldrop. This is a fascinating look at developments in the 1950s, 1960s, and 1970s that led to the rise of personal computing. Read the section on the events at Xerox's legendary PARC laboratories carefully.

- *Gates: How Microsoft's Mogul Reinvented an Industry and Made Himself the Richest Man in America* by Steve Manes and Paul Andrews. To date, this is the most comprehensive history of the early and middle years of Microsoft and Bill Gates you can read.

- *Hackers, Heroes of the Computer Revolution* by Steven Levy. This interesting book spans the world of MIT hackers to the founders of some of the first PC games companies. Of particular note is its profile of Richard Stallman, father of the Free Software and open source movements.

- *Joel on Software* by Joel Spolsky. This is a compendium of fascinating ruminations and rants on running a software business and development trends by Joel Spolsky.

- *Marketing High Technology: An Insider's View* by William H. Davidow. A bit rambling and general at times, this is nonetheless a high-tech marketing classic. Davidow was one of the authors of the Intel "Crush" campaign, a marketing program that cemented Intel's lead in the microprocessor market and relegated arch rival Motorola to also-ran status.

- *The Reckoning* by David Halberstam. This big, long book describes how the Japanese kicked the stuffing out of the American auto industry. For a classic example of how companies learn lessons only to forget them, turn to page 558 to read about how Lee Iacocca revived a Chrysler promotional program that offered purchasers of Chryslers a five-year and 50,000-mile warranty to help turn the company around. Decades later, Hyundai would relearn a lesson Chrysler forgot.

- *Selling Air* by Dan Herchenroether. This is the only book ever written that describes accurately the process of selling software in the enterprise. Both highly educational and a fun read.

Recommended Reading

These are recommended reading:

- *Beer Blast: The Inside Story of the Brewing Industry's Bizarre Battles for Your Money* by Philip Van Munching. This is an excellent look at product marketing in an industry dominated by distribution and image advertising. If you're working in a market segment dominated by many products, or which has undergone commodization, this is an invaluable guide to tactical infighting.

- *On the Firing Line: My 500 Days at Apple* by Gil Amelio. This is a very odd book by a very interesting man. Amelio's tenure at Apple was notable for the lack of progress made in halting Apple's sales and marketing slide, and reading his book it is not hard to figure out why. By his own admission, he failed to hire the right people, failed to enforce edicts against channel stuffing and stupid discounting, and eschewed any serious look at the product marketing dilemma facing the then struggling computer company. In fact, one of the striking things about this book is the lack of focus given to Apple's products and marketing. We do read a great deal about Amelio's salary negotiations, which helps explain his failure at Apple and is an instructive point to ponder in an era of silly CEO salaries.

- *Open Source: The Unauthorized White Papers* by Donald K. Rosenberg, Ph.D. This book is an excellent look at the issues and challenges surrounding the development of open source software. The book covers the history of the current general public license (GPL) under which Linux and related products are released, and it covers the different variants that have sprung up over the years. Rosenberg also discusses Microsoft's reaction to the development of Linux and the efforts the company has made to strangle this annoying infant in its crib.

- *Odyssey* by John Sculley. Long out of print, this book should be read after *Apple*. Apple's most significant CEO with the exception of Steve Jobs, John Sculley made some of the worst marketing, technical, and sales decisions ever seen in the industry. This book provides insights (many unintentional) into how he did it.

- *The Product Marketing Handbook for Software* by Merrill R. (Rick) Chapman. One of my other books, this is an extensive field manual for software marketing and sales. At almost 700 pages with more than 2,600 checklist items, it's the most comprehensive book of its kind.

- *The Second Coming of Steve Jobs* by Alan Deutschman and *iCon Steve Jobs: The Greatest Second Act in the History of Business* by Jeffrey S. Young and William L. Simon. Read together, both of these books will help you understand why in the not too distant future, many people at Disney are going to be living interesting times.

- *Once upon a Time in Computerland: The Amazing, Billion-Dollar Tale of Bill Millard* by Jonathan Littman. California, est, and ethics meet in the high-tech distribution channel. Ethics lost, but sometimes there is justice in this world. This buried classic explains how the first and greatest computer chain went to its eventual demise and the rise of the California approach to high-tech business.

~

Now That You Know, Do You Know When to Know It?

Now that you're done reading and your brains are stuffed with knowledge and insight, you're ready to tackle the problem of context, something you can't do until you're well read. In Chapter 4 of *Stupidity*, I describe the fundamental positioning error MicroPro made in the release of WordStar 2000 and its ultimate impact on the company. Over the years, other software companies, including Microsoft, Borland, Novell, Sun, and many, many others in the software business, have repeated the same mistake, with very much the same consequences. But what is a mistake in one milieu does not necessarily carry over to another industry. Context can change everything, which is why you need to study and learn before you are fit to make important decisions.

Shortly after *Stupidity*'s release, an interesting question was raised on the Joel on Software forum (www.joelonsoftware.com). A reader of ISOS asked if the iPod mini, on the verge of its release, ran the risk of running the same positioning conflict as MicroPro did with its WordStars. The astute reader pointed out that the two devices were named the same thing (iPod), did much the same thing, had disturbingly close pricing, and the new iPod mini offered considerably less storage functionality than a full-blown iPod.

The answer was...no. Why? Because in the world of high-tech hardware, small and sleek has huge appeal. Smaller items frequently sell better because they're easier to carry around, and good design reflects directly on the persona of the person buying a gizmo. The fact that the iPod mini offered the functionality it did in the size it came in was enough to separate it from its older brother in the mind of the buying public.

Failure to study and thus understand the context of the market has led software companies to frequently take the experience of hardware and misapply it to software, almost always to bad effect. Over the years, the "lite" word processors, spreadsheets, databases, suites, and graphics packages have not taken the market by storm. Why? Well, software is not carried around (at least not where it can be seen) and applications are used in a wide variety of situations. And a product that's 20 megs in size as opposed to 60 doesn't make you look cooler or help you get dates. And finally, the cost of computer hardware continually drops relentlessly, making the gains realized by tight code irrelevant from the buyer's standpoint.

But for literally over a quarter of a century, the press has bemoaned product bloat in software. For more than a quarter of a century, different software companies have attempted to build "smaller" software products. And for more than a quarter of a century, customers have voted with their dollars almost every time for more powerful software products stuffed with every extra strip of "chrome" and every last power option available. And since software is very cheap (if you doubt this, compare the cost of buying a word processor, spreadsheet, presentation package, and database in 1986 and compare it with the cost today, and then factor in inflation), why not buy the extra dagmars[1] for your PC? Who knows when you might not need to create a slide or two? Or maybe crunch some numbers? The current market for application suite software such as Microsoft Office bears this out; although it is possible to buy just Microsoft Word or Excel, today almost no one does.

It's a factor to keep in mind as "component" computing, now being referred to as "mashups," begins to reappear on the horizon. In the mid-1990s, as object-oriented programming began to sweep through the industry, the concept of "components" appeared in software. Under this new paradigm, users would pick and choose from bundled packages of components and assemble their own spreadsheets, word processors, databases, and so on, thus building their very own personalized applications that had just the right amount of features and avoided the dreaded "bloat." As mashups (mixes of components that are accessed via the Internet) have become more popular, the press (which, because of layoffs and turnover, has as short an institutional memory as the companies they cover) has begun to beat the "bloatware" drum again. And, inevitably, some poor schnook of a software company is going to create a web-based "lite" word processor or spreadsheet or application suite that will do just as well as its floppy and CD-based predecessors.

---

[1] Dagmars were large, black, rubber protuberances found on the bumpers of 1950s cars, most notably Cadillacs. The name was created in honor of a well-endowed actress of the same era.

~

Are We...Are We Ourselves?

O ne of the most valuable exercises a company's managers can undertake is to arrive at a candid assessment of your company type. Doing this helps you understand many of the underlying reasons and motivations for what happens inside your company and others. This in turn will help you successfully maneuver through the shoals of corporate politics and safely pass the rocks of competitive pressure.

The problem with this exercise is 95 percent+ companies that undertake it lie to themselves. When asked, just about every CEO or member of upper management will blurt out they are a "market-driven" organization. Sometimes they are, and sometimes they're lying (usually to themselves).

There are four basic classes of firms:

The technology-driven company: The technology-driven company is controlled by the desires and direction of its development staff and is (naturally) the most common type of high-tech firm. MicroPro, of whom we've read, was a classic example of this company type, and its inherent tendencies explain why the company engaged in the final act of technical immolation I discuss in Chapter 4. The most common problem with the technology-driven company is that it builds products that satisfy its development staff, rather than providing the features and benefits the market wants. A classic example occurred early in WordStar's evolution. Over time, many users requested the ability to format text in side-by-side columns, useful for many types of writing, particularly resumes and newsletters. The development group refused to add this feature to the product and noted that over time requests by users for side-by-side columns diminished. This was absolutely true! Users wanting this feature purchased WordPerfect or Microsoft Word. (To the day the product died, it never had this feature). Novell was another example of this syndrome in action. Its key programmers successfully fought the incorporation of a GUI into NetWare long after it was clear that this was what the market wanted.

The sales-driven company: Ashton-Tate, publisher of dBase, was a classic example of a sales-driven company, myopically focused on fulfilling quarterly sales quotas. When demand for certain products weakened, it would offer product at special prices, bundle slow sellers with quick movers, offer special returns, offer stock swaps— anything in an effort to meet unrealistic quotas. At one point, the distribution system had backlogs of more than 24 months for certain products, but Ashton-Tate had satisfied its quotas, for the time being. Of course, much of this product eventually came back, and the revenue piper had to be paid, with much wailing, gnashing of teeth, and layoffs. Siebel was a more modern example of a sales-driven company; its desire to close business, making it oblivious to the desire of some of its key customers to give the CRM publisher some business back.

The market-driven company: This company is motivated by the needs and desires of its customer base. This is often the most successful of company classes because all functional groups sublimate their egos to their customers' needs. Although this is an easy philosophy to preach, it is a hard one to put into practice. But market-driven companies have their own problems. Often, they lose the will to lead. The company becomes too reactive and fearful of change, waiting for the safe road to appear while missing opportunities stemming from an aggressive but intelligent, proactive development strategy. An excellent example of this phenomenon occurred with WordPerfect. For years, WordPerfect offered toll-free phone support to buyers of its products, a practice that made customers love the company and the company love them back. WordPerfect's legion of loyal DOS users lured the company into thinking that its Windows development effort did not have to be a top company priority. As history has demonstrated, all those DOS fans were wrong.

The finance-driven company: Not many pure finance-driven companies exist in high tech, though some will argue that Dell comes close. Probably the best examples can be found outside of high tech. For instance, during the 1980s, auto-industry observers noted that General Motors was a finance-driven company. The road to upper management usually led through GM's accounting department. Over time, this led to GM implementing many cost-saving programs that made it more economical to create cars that nobody wanted to drive, a practice that helps account for the company's continued shrinkage over the years.

Few companies are perfect examples of any one type. Most are a mix, with one element predominating, but it is important to understand which type(s) best describes your firm. This in turn will provide you with insights into the potential problems your company will likely face and its strengths and weaknesses when dealing with different sets of problems.

~

Never Trust (or Hire) Anyone Over 30

High tech is awash with barely disguised age discrimination. High-tech companies vigorously deny this because U.S. law forbids age discrimination; the companies, of course, are lying. In most cases, if you decide to make a career in high technology, you will be fawned over whilst in your 20s and respected until your late 30s. At age 40+, if you have not escaped into upper management, it is assumed you will be either a) rich from the money you made working for a hot start-up or b) preparing for a second career, perhaps as a fries preparation specialist at the food court of your local mall. At 50+ a perk of your job will include a shiny new shovel, with which you are expected to dig your own grave, jump in, and then drag the dirt over on top of you. If you are 60+ and are spotted in the halls of a high-technology company, it is assumed you are either a) the grandparent of an employee or b) a ghost.

The impact of foolish youth on your company's operations can range from damaging to catastrophic, depending on how unlucky you are. This was brought home to me shortly before the first release of *Stupidity* in 2003. I was contacted to possibly consult with a software company that had recently made a series of missteps in dealing with the press upon receiving less than stellar reviews. Reviews can be very important in a firm's marketing efforts, and bad notices can put a serious crimp in your product's sales. When a reviewer has slammed your product, you can go down two paths. The first path consists of the following:

1. Gritting your teeth and carefully reading the review.

2. Analyzing any mistakes the reviewer has made about your product's capabilities or misapprehensions.

3. Writing a letter of corrections to the editor of the publication and hoping it will be printed in an upcoming issue (your leverage in this regard will be greatly enhanced if you're an advertiser).

4. Contacting your customers to inform them of your efforts. Contact vehicles can consist of letters, white papers, PR releases, blogs, podcasts, TV appearances, and so on.

5. Putting in place a review management program that, you hope, educates the market and future reviewers on your product or service's abilities.

6. And, finally, fixing legitimate complaints and shortcomings in your product.

If executed properly, this type of program can have a positive impact on your future reviews and marketing, though none of this will make your current suffering go away.

The other path usually incorporates the following:

1. Screaming loudly at your employees whilst simultaneously tearing at your hair in agony and disbelief that the cretin putting this bilge to paper has achieved the miracle of somehow succeeding in putting pen to paper when it is clearly evident they don't possess the required gray matter to sustain basic autonomic functions, such as breathing.

2. Calling the editor of the offending rag and hurling threats of defenestration, physical violence, and never, ever advertising in their Codex of Evil ever again (this final threat will be taken seriously by some publications but never works when accompanied by shrieks of fury at the unfairness of it all; rather, this approach is sometimes effective when delivered by a soft velvet touch and will only have an effect on subsequent reviews).

3. Calling the reviewer at his or her home and yelling at them.

The second path, which is the one this prospective consulting customer had chosen, is never effective and usually leads to a company developing a toxic reputation amongst press, an outcome that can have a long-term and devastating impact on your sales and marketing efforts, as I describe Ashton-Tate discovering in Chapter 5.

As part of the "getting to know you" evaluation I conduct before taking on a new client, I first reviewed the company's PR program with the firm's director of marketing, a bright, personable woman with an MBA and two years of post-college experience under her belt. As I had suspected, neither she nor anyone at the company had any experience with the software review process. In the course of the discussion, I was taken on a tour of the company's website. As she showed me one of the site's promotional pages, I noticed an image of a professional golfer—not a first-tier player but a well-known second-tier star with something of a "bad boy" reputation (at least as bad boy as a guy playing golf can get). "That's an interesting choice of an endorser," I told her. "Can you tell me how much he cost?"

"Oh, we're not paying him anything," she said in a sunny tone. "One of our web designers saw the image, liked the way it fit with our campaign, and put it up."

"Uh, you do realize you're running a liability here?" I told her. "You can't just slap up an image of a personality and not pay them or at least get their permission to use their likeness."

"I'm not worried. We're covered under fair use law."

"No, you're not," I said. "You're not a news organization. You're not reporting on anything. You're not conducting scholarly research. You're not writing books on bad golf swings. These are the criteria for using content for fair-use purposes. Sticking this fellow's picture up here doesn't fall under any of these."

She seemed unconvinced, and I let the matter drop. Later I mentioned to the company's CEO that he ought to check with his lawyer about the potential lawsuit issues. (The web page vanished a few days later.) I also mentioned that his marketing department seemed to consist entirely of 20-somethings with very little industry experience.

"I like the energy they bring to the company," he said. "And they work cheap."

"How much do you think those bad reviews you've been getting are costing you in sales and reputation?" I asked.

After this encounter (I wasn't hired by the way; the company founder thought my fees were too expensive), I decided to conduct an impromptu poll of ten small- to medium-sized high-tech companies and asked them to estimate over the last six months how many new hires were 20+, 40+, and 50+ years old, respectively. (This was something of a guerilla poll, since the HR departments at these companies would never have cooperated with me.) The smallest company had $1 million in revenue, the largest more than $70 million. The numbers broke down as shown in Table 12-1.

Table 12-1. *Ages of New Hires*

Age Range	Sales	Marketing	Development
20+	80%	95%	80%
40+	20%	5%	10%
50+	10%	0%	0%

These numbers were striking. Based on them, if you're older than 50, the chances of being hired by a high-tech firm are almost nil (there's some hope in sales, perhaps a reflection of the value of a salesperson's track record and contact list). And even if you're just in your 40s, the numbers are almost as grim, especially in marketing. The reason for amateur behavior on the part of many software companies may be quite simple: Amateurs are running the show.

Shortly after my visit with the software company, the impact of amateurism in regards to fair-use laws came into sharp focus, courtesy of Salesforce.com. Salesforce.com was an early leader in the SaaS (formerly ASP) market, providing customer relationship management (CRM) software you accessed via your web browser. Salesforce.com was a happy green island of profitability in the sea of red ink that subsumed the early ASP market and bluff and very quotable founder and president Marc Benioff became a much-reported-on celebrity in the technology press. As Salesforce.com went public and continued its profitable ways, Benioff and the company marched off to do battle with the likes of Siebel and Oracle under the banner of "The End of Software," a direct challenge to the licensing model that has dominated the industry since its development.

Along the road to sales and IPO success, Salesforce.com also became known as a contributor to Tibetan human rights organizations and causes. Tibet and its exiled leader, the Dalai Lama, are currently the darling of Hollywood, Richard Gere, and the left coast of the United States in general. Tibet is the type of oppressed nation Silicon Valley can get behind; the Dalai Lama is Disney cute, and Tibetan Buddhism's belief in reincarnation is magical and mystical in a way that generates a delicious shiver in the souls of California chardonnay drinkers and Shirley MacLaine acolytes everywhere. Even better, the country's remoteness, mainland China's possession of nukes, and the geological fact that Tibet suffers from a complete lack of oil, means there's virtually no chance the United States will actually **do** anything useful to relieve the sufferings of the oppressed Tibetan people (such as send in the Marines to shoot the oppressors à la Iraq).

Flush from success and a belief in the ultimate holiness of its cause, in 2003 the company was one of several major donors to a September 5th event in San Francisco hosted by the American Himalayan Foundation at which no less an august presence than his holiness, the Dalai Lama, was scheduled to speak. Plugging its role of event donor, in August the company created 500 posters that it sent to local companies and members of the press. The poster featured a photograph of a meditative Dalai Lama (the Pope and the Archbishop of Canterbury presumably being busy that day) beneath a caption that read "There is no software on the path to enlightenment." Beneath the photograph was emblazoned Salesforce.com's "No Software" logo and the subhead, "Salesforce.com celebrates 100,000 enlightened Salesforce.com subscribers."

The Dalai Lama, who to the best of everyone's knowledge, does not currently use hosted sales automation software, was reportedly not amused by a campaign that used his likeness to give an implied commercial endorsement and made his displeasure known. At first, Salesforce.com attempted to blow off the criticism by pointing out its support for all things Tibetan; however, the outcry against the company's commercial crassness refused to die down. Then rumors reached Salesforce.com that the Dalai Lama had retired to a mountain retreat and was praying that the company's marketing and PR group be reincarnated as earthworms. Upon this, Salesforce.com promptly capitulated, the posters were recalled and destroyed (the few that survive are now prized collector items), company president Marc Benioff publicly apologized, and presumably Salesforce.com's marketing personnel will enter the next cycle of existence in the form of creatures whose principal diet does not consist of forest refuse.

~

The Best Generals Hire the Best Generals

In the foreword to *Stupidity*, Joel Spolsky states his belief that high-tech companies can't succeed unless there's a programmer (and we'll assume he's also partial to hardware engineers) at the head of a company. It's a natural assumption; after all, Joel is a programmer, and coders and engineers do tend to be the loci of new ideas and products for high tech. But it's a supposition that's easy to argue with. Ray Noorda was the man most directly responsible for the early success of Novell, and he wasn't a programmer. Steve Jobs was the man most responsible for the rise of Apple and the creation of the Macintosh OS. Jobs was never a programmer and only nominally an engineer. It was Steve Wozniak who did all the significant work in this respect during Apple's early days. Charles Wang, founder of Computer Associates (now CA), may have done some nominal coding, but his main interest was always business. Charles Tate of Ashton-Tate never programmed for a living nor did Scott Cook, founder of Intuit.

Of course, Joel advocates can point to some significant examples that prove his case. Bill Gates was certainly a programmer. Mitch Kapor, founder of Lotus, was a developer as well. John Warnock of Adobe was an engineer and onetime chief scientist at the legendary PARC lab.

But then you look at the history of developers in relation to the companies they either founded or worked for, and the picture again becomes decidedly mixed. The SuperSet helped damage Novell. The WordStar programming team drove the final stake through MicroPro's heart. Dan Bricklin and Bob Frankston, developers of the first blockbuster desktop application, VisiCalc, engaged in a foolish and ruinous fight with the publisher of the product, VisiCorp, that destroyed the spreadsheet cash cow for both companies. Apple's developers made a 20-year career of running amok from time to time. It's probably fair to state that programmers and developers help kill and hurt as many companies as they start.

Many historians believe the principal reason that Napoleon was beaten at Waterloo had little to do with the specific tactics used on the field of battle but by the absence of three men from the campaign: Marshalls Berthier, Lannes, and Davout. Berthier was Napoleon's chief of staff, a master of interpreting Napoleon's wishes and transmitting complex orders in clear, simple terms. After Napoleon's first exile, he switched sides and never switched back. During the battle, his replacement, Marshall Soult, proved unable to provide the same clarity of communications achieved by Berthier, and the French suffered mightily because of it. Lannes, a brilliant fighter who was willing to talk back to the Corsican when he felt he was wrong, couldn't make the big event; he was dead, killed at the battle of Aspern-Essling. Davout, Napoleon's strategic equal and a man who would have crushed the Prussians at Wavre where Marshall Grouchy failed and thus made it likely Napoleon would win at Waterloo, declined to show up for the battle, tired of Napoleon and his endless wars. The marshals who did show up to support the emperor were for the most part brave men and competent, but they were also his managerial second tier.

A well-run company follows the example of Napoleon at his best (I'll pause a moment for all you current and nascent CEOs and future members of upper management to enjoy the frisson this analogy is generating, but please remember we're simply resorting to an analogy here; business is not war) and develops a well-rounded, high-quality management team. An interesting aspect of many of the most successful high-tech companies is that they seem, at least for a time, to follow a "binary star" system, with two people in essence sharing the CEO's job—one person focusing on the technical side of the company and the other on key business issues. Notable examples of this approach include Gates/Ballmer, Warnock/Geschke, Jobs/Wozniak, and Cook/Proulx.

Regardless of how or whether the top job is split up, you're also going to need to establish and manage a management group with a diverse psychological profile. Please note I'm not discussing specific skill sets, such as the ability to write Java code or do basic bookkeeping; it's a given that if you are to build and sell products and services, that you have at least some initial competence in doing so.

What I mean by "diverse" is the mental landscape of your team and the way they choose to use their abilities and ambition. In many companies, the founder and CEO tend to create an upper management team that is a clone of themselves. Each member of the team, when they look around, tends to see a somewhat distorted image of themselves that smiles back in approval and affirmation. In such an environment, a company's upper management functions in almost cult-like fashion—self-referential, self-absorbed, and increasingly cut off from both the rest of the company and the market.

Another extreme is the management theory that the executive suite functions as an analog to the Roman Colosseum in its heyday. Periodically, members of the management team are expected to check in for fights to the death with each other held under the watchful eye of the company founder or CEO. The rationale normally offered for this practice is Darwinian in origin; by encouraging this type of ongoing fratricide, you are supposedly building a tougher, better business executive. Apparently, no one has ever considered the possibility that what you are evolving toward is a manager better adapted toward killing his peers than the competition.

The best management systems I've worked with or observed avoid both of the extremes described. Instead, they seek to blend a psychologically diverse group into an effective group. The best teams at minimum always seem to possess the following:

- Someone with the ability to successfully communicate the CEO's idea and business goals to the rest of the company and its managers. The "Berthier."

- Someone equal in business skills and abilities to the CEO, an individual who can step in and run the company in the event something renders the company's leader hors de combat; this person is also willing to step back into their assigned role and take orders. The "Davout."

- Someone unafraid to challenge upper management's assumptions and beliefs when warranted. The "Lannes."

- Someone with a strong understanding of the company's logistical needs and capabilities (this can include the firm's finances). The "Wellington." (Napoleon and his managerial group never fully mastered the importance of logistics, as the 1812 debacle in Russia demonstrated.)

~

Now That You Know, What Do the Rest of You Know As Well?

My last piece of good advice focuses around the issue of "siloiza-tion," the tendency of key functional groups in high-tech companies (development, marketing, sales, Q&A, and so on) to be ignorant of the value and contribution of other groups. Of course, a great deal of lip service is always being served in this regard. For example, I've actually never had a technologically driven company tell me they think their sales group is worthless; they simply act like it.

Of course, if you've done your reading and learned your history lessons, your managers and employees should be intellectually inoculated against this type of foolishness, but it's one thing to know something and another to feel it. My solution? Encourage members of your company to compete in business simulation games. Simulators from companies such as Forio and the famous Marketplace simulator that is sold by several companies allow your managers to game price wars, brand management, sales and marketing campaigns, distribution strategies, and more. Simulators are a marvelous opportunity to provide your employees with a chance opportunity to test ideas and concepts in cyberspace before they approach your bottom line.

Simulators are also excellent tools for encouraging teaching teamwork and collaboration if members of different groups from your company play in teams. Just about every person who plays in a simulator ends up learning the true value of cash flow and finances in a company's operations. I've played Marketplace; the game has a loan shark if you run out of cash, and you really don't want to meet him.

fourteen

STUPID ANALYSES

~

Chapter 2, "First Movers, First Mistakes: IBM, Digital Research, Apple, and Microsoft"

Perhaps the most telling lesson one can take from Chapter 2 is that both large and small companies can be arrogant and stupid to the point of unreason. In the case of Digital Research, it is hard, even after all these years, to understand how Gary Kildall could have been so cavalier in his dealings with IBM. As the years passed, despite Kildall becoming very rich (though not Bill Gates mega-rich) as a result of his business endeavors in the early desktop computer market, he became increasingly depressed over the unfairness of it all. Before his premature death at the age of 52 in 1994 in mysterious circumstances, Kildall believed he had slipped into obscurity, permanently eclipsed by the shadow of Bill Gates. This is not true; Kildall will live forever in the annals of American business as the man who blew what was perhaps the biggest business opportunity of all time.

On the other hand, IBM, the company that partnered with Microsoft in breaking Kildall's heart, would over the years demonstrate stupidity on a scale that the father of CPM could not have imagined. Over the course of two decades, Big Blue would allow its lead in PCs, software, and other key markets to slip from its grasp one by one. In the end, it would be Bill Gates and Microsoft who would benefit from both companies' foolishness, and neither Kildall nor IBM had anyone to blame but themselves.

Stupidity bites.

~

Chapter 3, "A Rather Nutty Tale: IBM and the PC Junior"

Not much analysis should be necessary at this point since this chapter describes succinctly what was wrong with the PC Junior and includes bullet points in specific detail about what IBM could have done to avoid what happened. The key lesson to keep in mind is that people never want to buy something that is clearly a second-rate version of a prime product. If you want to differentiate your product, instead add features and abilities that appeal to a different audience. Sometimes the feature you add can be as simple as a color choice; women will purchase pink iPod minis and Motorola Razr phones, and men won't. A classic example of the "build towards" strategy in software occurred years ago when WordPerfect Corporation added several features to its word processors of great appeal to lawyers. The legal industry made WordPerfect an industry standard, and even today, despite the Microsoft onslaught, the product has held onto significant market share in law offices worldwide.

~

Chapter 4, "Positioning Puzzlers: MicroPro and Microsoft"

Since Chapter 4 focuses on software companies, I'll discuss positioning issues as they pertain to this industry. Software by its nature is an abstraction; no one can "touch" a software product, though you do interact with it. This makes it often important, if not critical, that you assign your product a physical identity so as to allow the market and potential buyers to "see" the product and easily conceptualize its value.

Assigning software a physical identity is not usually very difficult (though it can be tricky, as the Lotus Notes example demonstrates), but despite all the ink spilled on the topic, many companies and marketing "experts" continue to get software positioning wrong. For instance, in

2004 I attended an industry conference and sat through a presentation given by a consultant who specializes in high-tech "messaging." At one point, his presentation focused on Microsoft's rollout of Windows 3.*x* in the early 1990s. During his presentation, he showed two slides. The first was filled with a fair amount of jargon and wordy gobbledygook. This, the presenter claimed, was Microsoft's original positioning statement. The second slide, he claimed, represented Microsoft's new, successful positioning strategy. It stated the following:

*Windows 3.*x *Will Transform the Way You Use Your Computer*

This is wrong. This is not a "positioning" statement—this is a tag line. You can tell by the generic nature of the phrase, because it can be used to describe *any* product. For instance:

"Binky 3.*x* will transform the way you use mapping software."

"Binky 3.*x* will transform the way you manage shipping schedules."

"Binky 3.*x* will transform the way you live your life."

And so forth.

Now, how exactly did Microsoft position Windows 3.*x*? It was very simple:

Microsoft Windows (finally) makes your PC work like a Mac (for a lot less money than a Mac).

Now, if you want, you could use the tag line:

And thus transforms the way you will use your PC.

In the context of the events surrounding the early 1990s, this was a powerful statement. The Macintosh had been on the market since 1984, everyone who was interested in a desktop computer knew what a Mac could do (and what a PC running DOS couldn't), and IBM had just spent the last several years bungling the release of OS/2. All that Microsoft had to do was produce a product that was good enough to stand up to the market's scrutiny of its claim about Windows working just about as well as a Mac. Despite the beliefs of Microsoft haters and Macophiles, Windows passed that scrutiny, and the rest is history.

Later that evening I had a chance to put my product positioning techniques to work. In addition to writing books on high-tech history and software marketing and sales, I'm also the managing editor of Soft*letter, a bimonthly newsletter dedicated to examining all aspects of the software business. As I was handing out a free sample of the publication at the conference reception, I was approached by a gentleman with some questions on how his company could position their software product.

"OK," I said, "can you first tell me what your software product does?"

"Sure," he said. "It Bzzzzz application Zaaaappppiinn integration MOM Bzzzz diagnostics errrrburrr help desk Xxxxx network architecture."

I blinked at him. "Uh, again, what does your software do? How would I use it?"

"Bzzzzz application Zaaaappppiinn integration...."

"No, wait, stop. What does your software product work with?"

"Applications."

"And how does it work with applications?"

"It monitors them."

"And where does it monitor them?"

"It monitors them on a network."

"And what precisely does it monitor about the applications?"

"It monitors them for their functionality. If an application crashes, it informs a help desk that the application has crashed."

"What else does it tell the help desk? "

"It provides diagnostics that describe the network and user environment when the application crashed."

"OK, that's better. So, how about this? Your application functions as a sort of virtual fireman on call. He monitors your network for application problems. When a program crashes and burns, the fireman tells you that there's a fire and provides helpful information that will assist you in putting the fire out."

He looked at me thoughtfully for a moment. "You know, we paid some consultant thousands of dollars to come out and talk to us about our software. We talked about the fire, but never got to the fireman."

If you need assistance in positioning your product, work your way step by step through the following process. (For your information, this is a streamlined version of the methodology I describe in *The Product Marketing Handbook for Software*.)

Successful positioning consists of working through these steps:

1. *Visualize*: The visualization process begins with writing a description of a product and what it does in 25 words or less. Why 25 words? Because if you exceed this, the person listening to you begins to tune you out because they're overwhelmed by verbiage. The goal of this visualization is to develop a picture of a visceral, physical item or process that you can link to your intangible software product. Once you're done with this exercise (and you'll have to repeat it several times before you zero in on likely candidates), try it out either through formal market research or via some impromptu testing with likely prospects for your products.

2. *Perform image creation and attachment*: The next step in the process is to combine the basic visual identity you've created with favorable images and ideas. Let's step outside the computer industry for a minute to get a different perspective. Let's look at dough. Yes, dough. Now, in and of itself, just about everyone knows what dough is, what it looks like, and what you do with it. And visually, dough is not much to look at.

   Now, just how does one make dough desirable? Fun? Enticing? You build a man made out of dough. He's rather sexless and childlike in appearance, with a round little tummy, a high squeaky voice, and a high-pitched giggle (a series of characteristics common to babies, creatures with strong appeal to women, the principal purchasers of dough). We're talking about the Pillsbury Doughboy, and he imparts to dough about as attractive an image as you could expect it to possess.

In *In Search of Stupidity*, I discuss Microsoft's disastrous "Two Nags" ad, which attached an inappropriate image to its two Windows products. But in 2003, Microsoft demonstrated how effective this technique can be in high-tech marketing with its "Butterfly" campaign. The company spent massive amounts of advertising dollars in this period to promote its MSN service, a direct competitor to AOL. Its ads focused heavily on MSN's "spam-fighting" abilities and the features in the MSN service that protect you and your family from offensive and unwanted e-mail. A natural image to represent this type of activity might be a policeman or burly bouncer, but acting against type, Microsoft chose to use its MSN butterfly logo instead.

The butterfly was reincarnated as a rather nerdy-looking series of gentlemen dressed in ridiculous butterfly costumes who ran around protecting children from sexually explicit posters, dropped spam (represented as long lines of dubious-looking people) through trap doors, and so on. The result of the campaign was to not present MSN's spam filtering as a militaristic strongman or grim censor (an image that Microsoft, given its problems with the government and the public during its antitrust case, probably wanted to avoid), but rather as a friendly and harmless virtual family companion.

3. *Layer*: Finally, after combining visual identity and basic images, the layering process can begin—extending the visual identity and its image to appropriate circumstances For instance, our Doughboy becomes ubiquitous on morning breakfast shows and around major holidays, both times when people are more likely to be thinking about buying baked products. The concept Pillsbury wishes to build in your mind is that dough is the Pillsbury Doughboy who appears at Christmas, which makes you think of delicious things and makes you want to buy dough. Pillsbury dough, to be precise. In high tech, ads for Intuit's widely used TurboTax software appear in the three months before April 15th. Before Christmas, all the main video game systems are heavily advertised.

4. *Build a marketing vocabulary*: The next step after developing a strong visual identity for your product is to build a supporting "marketing vocabulary" around it. In high-tech marketing, the foundations of this vocabulary are jargon and buzzwords. Jargon consists of industry-specific slang and acronyms. Buzzwords are words and phrases that describe desirable features and characteristics. There is a natural tendency for jargon to evolve into buzzwords. A classic example is the term WYSIWYG (what you see is what you get), which was coined by MicroPro founder Seymour Rubinstein, publisher of the one-time market-leading word processor WordStar, to describe the product's text-formatting abilities. When first coined, WYSIWYG had a specific technical meaning; it described a text editor that formatted words in a fashion similar to that of a typewriter. Now, WYSIWYG functions as a buzzword. A product that has WYSIWYG is good, and one that lacks WYSIWYG is not as good.

5. *Create descriptors*: Once the appropriate jargon and buzzwords have been identified or created, we turn our attention to "descriptors," short, pithy, catchphrases and sentences built from your marketing vocabulary that perform several functions simultaneously in the mind of the buyer. For one thing, they reassure the buyer about the nature of the purchase. For example, you don't care if a toothpaste is "easy to use," but you'd like your spreadsheet to be. For another, they serve as category cues, often letting the buyer know more about the nature of the product being discussed. "Powerful and full featured" means "high end." Descriptors can also incorporate "validators," that is, words and phrases that "prove" the truth of the assertions being made. "Market leading," "endorsed by," and "*PC Magazine* Editor's Choice" are all good examples of common validators.

6. *Describe the product*: Visual identity, basic vocabulary, and descriptors are combined to create a product description. Ideally, the description is internally logical and consistent and cues the mind of the buyer almost immediately, describing precisely what the product is, its key characteristics, and the compelling reason(s) to buy it.

7. *Repeat and integrate*: The final keys to successful encapsulation are repetition and integration. Repetition is always critical, but it's even more so when dealing with a product that is difficult to conceptualize. In this case, the marketing campaign must relentlessly and continuously repeat, almost to the point of physical pain, the company's visual concept of the product, and its encapsulated description. The ultimate goal is to establish a mental link between product and concept that is as clear as the link between a word processor and a typewriter. A classic example of this technique in action was Microsoft's relentless use of the phrase "rich text" (later "rich content," "rich capability," "rich *whatever*") to describe its products' abilities to create elaborately formatted text. The press and the competition sneered, but over time Microsoft succeeded in creating an effective buzzword for its products that other competitors began to copy.

The ultimate goal of the positioning process is encapsulation. A properly encapsulated product consists of a series of carefully structured ideas and concepts that are self-supporting, internally logical, and capable of being communicated to potential buyers with a minimum of confusion. The ultimate goal of the encapsulation process is to create a marketing identity for the product that automatically triggers these concepts, ideas, and associations in the buyers' minds without having them to "think" about it.

Another advantage of this process is that it should, if properly executed, help you identify potential positioning conflicts. If during this process you realize you have already created a product with identical positioning characteristics, you have a potential positioning conflict on your hands. Recovering from positioning disasters such as MicroPro's is expensive, ugly, and not always possible. Avoid them in the first place.

~

Chapter 5, "We Hate You, We Really Hate You: Ed Esber, Ashton-Tate, and Siebel Systems"

Many people have pointed to Ed Esber's PR ineptitude as the main reason for Ashton-Tate's demise, but this is wrong. It is rare for PR disasters to destroy a company, though they can certainly hurt it and be very expensive. Ed Esber's primary mistake was in failing to understand that Ashton-Tate wasn't just selling a product; it was creating an ecosystem. dBase was a "platform," a basic set of tools and functions that could be adapted to create applications in a myriad of businesses. As such, its developer community was not simply important to the company's success: it was critical. Once this support was lost, dBase's fate was inevitable.

It is not simply software companies that build ecosystems; hardware companies do it as well. The classic industry example of this is Intel's microprocessor product line. When Intel rolled out its famous 8080, 8086, and 8088 chips, the chips were technically inferior to competing microprocessors from Motorola. (This, by the way, is why Apple was able to release a sophisticated GUI front end for the Lisa and then the Mac systems in the early 1980s while similar attempts for the PC stalled as developers struggled to overcome the anemic performance of the 16-bit Intel chips.) But Intel provided a wealth of development tools and marketing assistance for its silicon and persuaded so many designers to build new systems on top of their microprocessors that they became the market standard. (You will learn more about this strategy after you finish reading William Davidow's *Marketing High Technology: An Insider's View*.)

If you are selling a platform-class product, you will need to do the following:

Make it easy and cheap to build or develop products around your platform: The larger and more successful your ecosystem, the better. Accept that over time, you may have to give your development tools away. That's OK; if you can't figure out how to make money selling classes on developing things with your stuff, training materials, add-ons, publications, conferences, and so on, and so on, you shouldn't be in the business.

Leverage your ecosystem: Had Ed Esber been smarter than he turned out to be, he could have used his platform to supply him with a sellable dBase upgrade in a timely fashion. Of course, he would have had to have been aware that the dBase development process was as deeply flawed as it was to have executed this strategy.

Compete with your ecosystem: It's expected that you will compete with your ecosystem; it's good for you and keeps you on your toes; just make sure you do it fairly. No preannouncements of products you will never ship. No sniping in the press. And if a developer keeps doing things better with your product than you can, buy them.

Support your ecosystem: Support your ecosystem with sales, marketing, and development programs. For an example of how to do this well, spend some time researching Microsoft's various developer support programs. IBM's Eclipse project is also well worth examining. Your ecosystem is a minimarket, and its health and development is an accurate predictor of your future financial fate.

Never go to war with your ecosystem. You will lose.

Siebel was a reprise of Ashton-Tate's sorry story and continued proof of this book's thesis that technology companies continue to repeat the same fundamental mistakes again and again. In Siebel we see a company that, like Ashton-Tate, actually decided to argue with its customers (and remember, dBase developers **were** Ashton-Tate's primary customers) when they took the opportunity to express their unhappiness with the firm's high-handed and unresponsive ways. The stupidity of this should have been immediately apparent to Siebel, but I don't think anyone at upper management had read this book.

A critical point to keep in mind is that Siebel, like Ashton-Tate, was a sales-driven company, and firms with this underlying character tend to make these types of fundamental mistakes. Driven by the need to generate revenue on a quarterly basis and make their numbers, sales-driven companies tend to do and say whatever it takes to get the money. While founder Tom Siebel expressed puzzlement over which of his marquis customers were unhappy with Siebel CRM, the reality is that the Siebel sales force knew exactly which customers were mad at them and why. Siebel just didn't care. It had already sold the software.

~

Chapter 6, "The Idiot Piper: OS/2 and IBM"

Doing an analysis on this chapter is difficult because of the scope of the mistakes IBM made; as I point out, it's difficult to find areas in which it **didn't** botch up the basics. Perhaps the most important lesson that can be drawn from the IBM OS/2 fiasco was that the company had simply grown too large to effectively coordinate the myriad of competing agendas that plagued the doomed OS. The best thing IBM could have done for OS/2 was spin the product off in the mid-1980s and free it from the crushing weight of Big Blue's very big bureaucracy.

Taken point by point, IBM committed the following critical mistakes and blunders:

IBM initially mispriced OS/2: Once circumstances and time had set the price of a desktop OS at $40, even IBM had to live in this pricing environment. It should be noted that adjusted for inflation, the retail price of Windows XP Home Edition, the upgrade version (which most people buy), is currently $100, approximately $40 in 1981 dollars.

IBM stunted the development of its OS/2 ecosystem: IBM priced its development tools too high, failed to create the right mix of marketing and development support to nurture its ecosystem, and confused everyone with its inclusion of Windows into some Warp versions of OS/2.

IBM had a very weak product management system: In a well-run company, product managers (PMs) frequently function as product advocates and coordinators for new and existing products. In some companies they are even given P&L responsibility for their products. At IBM, such product management as the company had did not work well and had little ability to influence the development of a proper ecosystem for OS/2.

IBM made a surprising name mistake with the "Warp" naming fiasco: One thing IBM had no shortage of was lawyers; you would have thought the company would have been aware of the issues surrounding its habit of assigning names taken from the *Star Trek* series to beta versions of OS/2. Although it is beyond the scope of this book to discuss trademark and copyright issues in depth, the following checklist will help you avoid IBM's mistake when naming a product:

- Does the name support or undermine the product's positioning? For example, referring to your product as Tiny ERP (enterprise resource planning) is probably a bad idea; no one expects that planning their business's entire operations is a task that can be handled by a "tiny" anything. (Note: I once looked at a prototype of a product that was named just that.)

- Can the name be confused with another of your products or a competitive product?

- Can the name be trademarked? And even if it is, is the trademark defensible if challenged? If a word is already in use as a generic term, no amount of money spent takes it out of the generic category (at least not in the United States).

- Will the name infringe on a protected trademark? And even if you don't think it does, are you ready to go to court and spend lots of money to prove it?

- Is the domain name available for your Internet website? And if the .com domain is not available, have you considered the alternates, such as .net?

- If it's a software product, have you referred to the product as 1.0? If so, don't. Call the product 1.1 or 1.5. First versions scare people.

- Can the name be shrunk down to an inappropriate acronym? Does it lend itself to an undesirable pun? (For instance, one company selling accounting software once introduced a reseller program whose name shrank to "CPR," a most unfortunate name when selling to a market consisting of middle-aged sedentary males who are wondering if a major chest burster is in their future.)

- Does the name translate into an inappropriate or scatological term in a foreign language? The classic example is the Chevy Nova, which translates into "doesn't go" in Spanish.

- Do you want the name to support a "family" or a brand or company identity? For example, Microsoft Word? Microsoft Office? Microsoft Project?

Finally, remember that when naming a new product, your primary goal is to stay out of trouble! It is difficult to think of a situation where a great name alone led to product success; it's far easier to come across situations where a naming faux pas led to much corporate grief and financial agony.

~

Chapter 7, "Frenchman Eats Frog, Chokes to Death: Borland and Philippe Kahn"

Borland in the 1990s was an example of a technically driven company, one whose primary goals was to fulfill the dreams and desires of its development group (I cover this topic in greater detail in Chapter 13). This led to the plethora of different database projects and releases that in their totality confused the marketplace and robbed Borland of focus and direction at a critical time. (An interesting fact that buttresses this point is that in the first edition of *In Search of Stupidity* I made no mention of ICE, yet another database project under the control of Paradox developer Rob Shostak.)

One can argue whether the Ashton-Tate purchase was a mistake. Certainly Borland purchased very little in the way of technology resources; on the other hand, it could, briefly, claim to be the market share leader in desktop DBMSs after the acquisition, a talking point of some value. And Borland did use mainly its own stock to make the purchase, though shareholders suffered from dilution as Borland began to experience hard times.

However, there is no dispute that after the purchase Borland mishandled the takeover in several ways:

Creating a positioning conflict between Paradox and dBase: Both dBase products were development "platforms" and should have been treated as different worlds with little interaction between them. This strategy can be successful; for example, Computer Associates (now CA) over the years has bought several major mainframe databases with an eye to buying revenue streams that enrich the company's coffers. Borland's initial attempt to position Paradox as an "end user" problem was ridiculous; the product was every bit as powerful as dBase, and if it had been repriced to match a "lite" database's cost, Borland would have been leaving money on the table.

Not enhancing dBase in a timely fashion: This is probably the single biggest mistake Borland made in the dBase acquisition. Since what Borland was buying was market share and an installed base, to squander these assets was senseless. It was vital that Borland immediately throw resources into transforming dBase into a competitive product ASAP. This could have been either through an internal development effort or via an acquisition. After the publication of the first edition of *In Search of Stupidity*, I learned from an impeccable source that Borland's initial strategic plan for dBase after the Ashton-Tate buyout consisted of **not releasing an upgrade for the product for 18 months.** Madness.

Alienating key personnel at a critical time: Since Borland was buying not technology but a relationship with an installed base, it was important for the company to retain and assuage anxious employees who were in a position to soothe and reassure an anxious ecosystem on the verge of collapse. Borland's failure in this regard exacerbated an already bad situation.

Building a consumer campaign around an arcane technical capability: Borland's attempt to sell object technology to spreadsheet users and people who wanted to use their databases as simple filing systems was clearly misguided and a waste of money. Worse, the effort distracted the company from releasing their products with timely upgrades and new features their users wanted.

Now, it **is** possible to sell technical abilities to nontechnical users via top down "branding campaigns," discussed in greater detail in Chapter 8. Branding campaigns are tautological crusades that basically say, "Good this is so it is good." Such a branding campaign might have resorted to jingles like this:

> "Objects Are Great" (to be sung all together, upbeat tempo)
> *Objects are great and really so cool*
> *The girls all want them but not Bill Gates*
> *With Objects you'll always have a really hot tool*
> *So program in Paradox and get more dates!*
> (Repeat 100 million times.)

The problem with these types of branding campaigns is that they are incredibly expensive and don't sell things directly. Borland couldn't afford to run them.

In all fairness, many of Borland's developers **were** intrigued by object technology, but Borland's object campaigns addressed their market as a whole.

Many Borland promotional programs were stupid: I think the chapter does a good job of analyzing why, so let's move on.

~

Chapter 8, "Brands for the Burning: Intel, Motorola, and Google"

As Chapter 8 points out, branding campaigns are expensive and should be attempted only by very large companies with big marketing budgets. How big should you be? I recommend at least $1 billion+

in yearly revenue and the bigger the better. Intel's budget for its "Intel Inside" campaign is estimated to be $1 billion+ alone (Intel's 2005 revenues were nearly $40 billion). But much of the money spent on Intel's program is in the form of rebates given to chip buyers; these rebates in turn drive further purchases of Intel chips (and help keep AMD locked out of the market). Nonetheless, all major branding campaigns consume much corporate coin.

If successfully executed, a branding campaign can indeed contribute to a company's bottom line (as does Intel Inside), but the campaign must be of long-standing duration, repeat a key point relentlessly, of necessity spend much money, and be targeted at the right audiences. (Also, most successful branding campaigns avoid being tied to a specific technology like the plague.) As we've seen, the Motorola campaign failed on all of these counts. It should be noted that Digital DNA was not a corporate campaign but one conceived of and launched by a division within the company, a major contributing factor to its failure.

Motorola's recent "Hello Moto" branding campaign is a more successful effort on the company's part, though how successful it will be over time remains to be seen. "Hello Moto" sells the concept that its phones are cool toys for cool EuroTrash; therefore, cool EuroTrash you are if you own a Motorola phone. Unlike Digital DNA, the concept is aimed at phone buyers, not phone makers. Also, it's useful that Motorola can project its tautology into the market's mind via its control over the sign-on screens of the phones it manufactures in much the same way that Intel has pounded its jingle into the heads of consumers worldwide.

But having made the commitment to create a brand, a company must vigorously defend it when the brand promise is compromised by misfortune and adversity. The most effective way to do this is face up to the problem, fix it, and put together a PR program that takes control of the story by giving the press a new tale to follow, one of an evil knight menacing a beautiful princess, the appearance of a white knight who will save the fair maiden, a battle, and the triumph of virtue. Yes, this is the fairytale format, an archetypal story. When Intel's chips stopped counting and Google started snooping, both companies should have done the following:

- Fully acknowledged the problem (the black knight appears).
- Proclaimed itself the protector of its customers (the fair maiden).

- Announced that the company will make its customers whole or protect them from harm. (The white knight appears, and please note he's your company.)
- List the steps the company will take to solve the problem. (The white knight challenges the black knight to mortal combat for the hand of the fair maiden.)
- List a timetable for when these events will take place (the gauntlet is thrown).
- Report to the press and your customers on your progress (the battle is joined).
- Report to the press and your customers on the final resolution of the problem (the black knight is slain).
- Obtain quotes from affected customers on their satisfaction with your solution (happy ever after).

Two wonderful things happen when a company follows this course (as opposed to the ones these companies actually took). The first is that your company immediately undergoes a glorious transformation from black knight to white. The second is that this approach changes the arc of the story from a focus on how the fair maiden has been besmirched by the black knight to a rousing yarn of the white knight riding to the rescue and saving our menaced heroine. And the press, like everyone else, always enjoys a happy ending with a nice touch of humbleness and corporate redemption thrown it.

With this methodology in mind, how should Google have reacted to the CNET/Eric Schmidt contretemps? Well, Google was being positioned by the press as the black knight in pursuit of the fair maiden, privacy. This is a legitimate concern, one that Google would have been intelligent to acknowledge. After doing this, Google might perhaps have announced a program or series of actions it would undertake to help save the fair maiden. These actions could consist of a host of things, including setting up an advisory board within the company to monitor privacy concerns, working with outside bodies to establish privacy "standards," and creating a privacy conference and related activities. The result would have been to transform Google's (and Schmidt's) snarling visage into something far more charming.

A last word about Google: The company has executed a daring branding gambit by attaching a moral promise to its business operations. This gambit has been accepted by the market, and now Google is on the hook to keep its brand promise of "Do No Evil." Cooperating in a massive censorship operation with a repressive and dictatorial government that from time to time invades other companies for the purpose of territorial expansion and murders its own citizens is a fairly evil thing to do regardless of the various rationalizations offered. Google must keep its brand promise or drop its "Do No Evil" proclamation. To continue down the path it has chosen will lead to erosion of its brand image and an endless stream of sniggers and derision over the company's perceived hypocrisy.

~

Chapter 9, "From Godzilla to Gecko: The Long, Slow Decline of Novell"

In examining what happened at Novell, we again see how the intrinsic weaknesses of a technology-driven company can damage a company if not controlled and compensated for by an alert upper management team.

Novell's key mistakes included the following:

Not allowing an ecosystem to flourish and grow around NetWare: That Novell blithely went ahead and shut down a key component of its third-party support system with barely a second thought was the act of a company completely cut off from reality. By the time it had become irrelevant, Novell's failure to provide a powerful development environment for building NetWare applications had become an industry joke.

Developing a weak product management system within the company: A strong product management system would have perhaps forced the Superset to end its defiance of market trends and wishes.

Developing an unbalanced management system: The Superset had too much power at Novell. This was not the fault of the Superset but rather of CEO Ray Noorda, who was responsible for putting together a balanced managerial team at Novell.

Creating a positioning conflict within the company via the acquisition of UNIX from AT&T: As has happened at so many companies, Novell was never able to reconcile the internal contradictions a positioning mistake of this type generates, and the company suffered mightily as a result.

~

Chapter 10, "Ripping PR Yarns: Microsoft and Netscape"

The decades-long Microsoft PR campaign that focused on building Bill Gates into Microsoft's primary branding element shows both the power and the danger inherent in such an approach. Using a company founder or CEO to directly represent a company has been successful for many companies, including Chrysler (Lee Iacocca), Perdue (Frank Perdue), Wendy's (Dave Thomas), and even Martha Stewart, despite her felony conviction for lying under oath and obstructing justice.

However, if the founder or CEO's image is seriously dented or scratched, the company's brand value will suffer in direct proportion to the damage being meted out to the hapless executive. Bill Gates' behavior during the DOJ's antitrust trial led to his leaving his CEO position at Microsoft in order to avoid doing more collateral damage to Microsoft. But since his departure, the image-mending process I described in the first edition of *In Search of Stupidity* has continued apace. Over the past several years, most media coverage of Gates has focused on his charitable work, with the Bill and Melinda Gates Foundation contributing almost $5 billion to efforts to control AIDS and malaria in Africa and India. While I'm sure Gates's concern for poverty-induced suffering is genuine, it certainly doesn't hurt Microsoft to have the company's bruised branding symbol reborn as a beneficent spreader of balm and hope to the world's poor, sick, and hungry; and it certainly beats the robber-baron image Gates acquired as a result of his meltdown during the DOJ depositions.

The damage the loss of the case caused Microsoft has continued, however. Periodically the European Commission drags the hapless software maker into court and fines it for failing to build versions of Windows nobody wants and being mean to open source companies and for being a very successful American company. The Koreans have joined in the fun as well. To just make them all go away, Microsoft handed out large bundles of cash to Novell, Sun, Real (even Be got into the action for $23 million, for god sakes), and a whole wad of state governments. And every time an attorney from Microsoft opens his mouth, he or she gets to listen to a succinct recitation of "the guilty of abusing your monopoly power" verdict as brought to the world by no less a body than the U.S. government. As a result, Microsoft can expect to be reaching for its checkbook on a regular basis well into the future.

Another consequence of the legal debacle is that Microsoft increasingly resembles the IBM of the 1980s in several interesting ways. Plenty of lawyers are now running around the halls of Redmond making sure the company stays out of further legal trouble. A wealth of committees and oversight groups are dedicated to making sure Microsoft plays nice with the market, at least nice enough to keep the feds at bay. Microsoft is now a middle-aged place to work and has a hard time recruiting the hottest talent, though the company remains solidly profitable and can expect to make money over the next few years at a measured pace. That's what the middle-aged do.

Of course, that's not what Microsoft wants. Microsoft wants to remain eternally young, eternally exciting, and eternally on the cusp of what's new and relevant. But those are characteristics reserved for smaller, leaner, more driven firms with both more to gain and more to lose. The only way for Microsoft (or any giant company) to regain its lost youth is to break itself up into smaller firms that will need to scramble and innovate to survive.

But they never do.

~

Chapter 11, "Purple Haze All Through My Brain: The Internet and ASP Busts"

There's not much proactive analysis I can give on the topic of economic bubbles. I don't know why they form, I don't know how long they will last when they do form, and I can't accurately predict how long the bubble will live; therefore, I can't give advice on how to time your market entry and exit so as to avoid being crushed by the Greater Fools rushing for the entrance when the bubble collapses. My best advice is to avoid them.

That said, you can draw several powerful and practical lessons from the Internet and ASP meltdowns. One of the most important is the realization that the concept of disruptive change and paradigm shifts, as described by most pundits and analysts, is dangerously misguided and has convinced many people to throw their money into ventures that are doomed because true disruption is very, very rare indeed. A true disruption is a rapid change in a market that destroys or overthrows an existing business or industry. For instance, the development of CD-based encyclopedias in the mid-1990s destroyed the concept of selling home encyclopedias within a few years of their introduction. But most disruptions are really simply adaptations—alterations made by companies in response to a constantly evolving market. The Internet was widely described as a "disruptive" technology that would change everything, but in the end it disrupted only some things, changed others, and had minimal impact on yet others. And even apparent cases of disruption are almost always less dramatic than they appear. For a market to undergo significant change, fundamental building blocks that support change must be in place. If they are not, disruption cannot take place. If more people had been doing their homework during the Internet bubble, less money would have been lost.

To illustrate what I mean, let's discuss the music industry, a business that is facing disruption of its current business model (caused in part by its own stupidity). When I was a boy I was introduced to the joy of buying 45 records by a boyhood chum who took me in tow to purchase copies of "Let's Hang On" by the Four Seasons and "Hang On Sloopy" by the McCoys. This type of vinyl was popular through the 1950s to the late 1960s, and if you had a record changer, you became used to piling a stack of 45s onto a spindle in any order you liked and enjoying your own private mix (think of the system as an analog iPod).

A hit 45 cost approximately a dollar or so in the 1960s, making them highly accessible to kids, but the quality of the records and the record players was low and the durability of your average 45 was poor. Any collection soon became badly damaged. Then the late 1960s and 1970s saw the release of classic rock albums such as *Sergeant Pepper's*, *Tommy*, and *Dark Side of the Moon*, and the prevailing teen/young adult zeitgeist shifted from dance parties to getting stoned and sitting around listening to 33s while attempting to decode the secret messages everyone was sure were embedded in those spinning grooves. Interest in 45s vanished.

By the late 1980s the album craze was over, and most people had woken up to the fact that most of the records they bought usually had only one or two good songs they wanted to hear. The rest were often filler material churned out by the band to create an album that the record companies then turned around and sold to you for the price of about ten 45s. People didn't appreciate this, and the desire to create custom mixes of just the songs you wanted to hear grew steadily. Unfortunately, the only way most people could create a mix was with a combination of a receiver, tape recorder, and record player. This was expensive if you bought top-of-the-line equipment, the process was laborious and slow, and the mixes created were often sonically inferior to the original content you had purchased on an album.

In 1989 while working for a small software start-up in New York, I was approached by the company's CEO and told about a ground-floor investment opportunity in which I might be interested. A business acquaintance of my boss had developed a kiosk-based system that allowed you to step into a booth, look at a menu of contemporary songs, and then have them burned from a hard drive onto a tape cassette while you waited. The process took only a few minutes, you could buy as many songs as would fit on the cassette, and you were charged on a per-song basis. Your mix tape ended up costing about as much as an album. The record companies, agreeing to license their music, received the lion's share of the revenue, but the kiosks, if people liked them, were still almost money-printing machines for the new company.

I thought it was a great idea. Several trial kiosks had been set up in the city, and I tried the system. It worked as advertised. I loved it, and the people I watched stepping up to the system loved it too. "This can't miss," I thought, and I prepared to open up my piggybank and do some serious investing. "I'm in," I told the CEO. I thought I might get rich.

After several weeks passed and I didn't heard any more about the mix system, I asked my boss what was the story with the company and the kiosks. "It's not going to happen," he told me with a long face. "The record companies decided not to license their music; they're making too much money from album sales."

A few years later, the industry switched over to CDs and took the opportunity to jack up the price of an album by 40 to 50 percent for hot sellers, ostensibly because of the cost of the changeover. However, prices stayed high even after everyone had thrown out their turntables and bought CD players despite CDs being cheaper to manufacture in bulk than vinyl records. And the CDs still had one or two really good songs and a lot of filler.

Then MP3, Napster, and the Internet appeared, and we all can see how that's turning out.

Now, it's easy to criticize the greedy record companies, and their behavior since the digital wave swept over the industry in regards to fighting the decades-long desire of people to assemble their own custom assortments of tunes is immensely stupid. But it's impossible to see how a record company executive in 1989 can be faulted for refusing to look 10 years ahead and predict the Internet, high-speed bandwidth, a highly effective compression format for digital music that preserves 95+ percent of the original's sonic quality, Napster, peer-to-peer networking, the iPod, and so on. And I don't think you can do it, because if you could, you'd be a multibillionaire; and there's only a few of them out there, and the odds that one of them is reading this book at any particular minute is low.

But what we can do is analyze what factors have to be in place before a technology becomes truly disruptive, track it against a highly touted current technology, and see whether the needed factors are in place to support a disruptive change.

For a disruptive idea or technology to take hold, the conditions in Table 14-1 must occur.

Table 14-1. *Custom Music Mix Change Model*

Condition	Status
There must be an idea for change.	In the case of music, the idea of allowing people to quickly create their own music mixes existed for decades.
There must be a market desire for change.	As my 1989 experience demonstrated, there was.
There must be an advantage to change.	The advantage was a customized music-listening experience.
There must be an infrastructure that supports change.	In 1989, there was. It's not as sophisticated as an Internet download to an iPod, but it got the job done well enough for people who had only a painful alternative.
There must be a distribution mechanism for change.	In 1989, there wasn't. The record companies were in a position to block distribution of music via their control of the means of distribution, that is, stores, and this meant disruptive change could not occur.
Change must come at the right price.	In 1989, the price was right for the customer (though not for the record companies).
There must be an acceptable quality of experience when change occurs.	Although cassette tape systems in 1989 were not as good as today's portable MP3 systems, they were good enough.

As we can see, lack of a distribution mechanism in 1989 was enough to prevent the development of a potentially disruptive technology from emerging. It's also interesting to realize that while the record companies had no interest in using the Internet as a distribution vehicle, being quite happy with the existing system as it was, the very existence of this mechanism was enough to allow the market shift to occur.

Now, let's use this model to track the ASP market of 1999–2001 to understand why it failed to ignite as predicted and why it is in the process of recovering under the rubric of SaaS (see Table 14-2).

Table 14-2. *ASP/SaaS Change Model*

Condition	Status
There must be an idea for change.	There is. Providing computer applications online has been done since the 1960s.
There must be a market desire for change.	There was. Many companies had become disillusioned with the difficulty of maintaining applications internally via large IT staffs.
There must be an advantage to change.	1999–2001: The early ASP companies had difficulty in clearly articulating the advantage of change to many companies. They were unable, particularly in the "office" application markets, to provide a clear reason to change. 2004–Present: SaaS application developers are now focused on opening new markets by providing many companies with access to capabilities they can't obtain any other way. For example, online marketing and sales promotions software for gas stations and auto repair shops.
There must be an infrastructure that supports change.	The infrastructure of 1999–2001 was immature and had difficulty supporting certain classes of applications, but this was probably not a determining factor. Most companies had access to high-speed Internet connections in this time period, a critical infrastructure issue.
There must be a distribution mechanism for change.	The Internet provided such a distribution mechanism.
Change must come at the right price.	1999–2001: ASP companies not only didn't offer attractive pricing for their services; in many cases they attempted to charge **more** for online applications. Companies that did comparison pricing analyses were frequently unimpressed. 2004–Present: Most successful SaaS companies have brought their cost structures in line to either compete with or beat the costs of traditional software purchases.

Condition	Status
There must be an acceptable quality of experience when change occurs.	1999–2001: In most cases, there wasn't. Early ASP applications were clumsy and slow. Online applications that attempted to compete with desktop applications suffered greatly by comparison in terms of power, interface, and overall usability. 2004–Present: As Ajax technology takes hold, web-based applications are starting to match their desktop counterparts in interface quality and power, though it will take time for them to match many desktop products.

The case for SaaS should not be overstated. Although the future does lie in online applications, the change will be slow in many market segments, many companies will retain their current software systems for many years, and there will be situations where using applications on a local computer will remain the best way to get something done.

Now, let's use this model one last time to track the progress of a technology that received a great deal of attention in the early 2000s but has failed to catch fire: e-books. Companies such as Adobe have spent much time and energy pushing the technology with little to show for it to date. Paper books are bulky, they age and decay, and they are difficult to store. E-books offer readers potential access to an infinite number of publications that can be manipulated and accessed in ways we haven't yet even explored. For example, business books could be automatically updated on a periodic basis to ensure they are current (I've tested the technology that can do this). Books could contain live pictures and interactive content (you can imagine just what the comic books of the future will look like). Finding information in e-books is a snap compared to their paper equivalents.

So why haven't e-books taken off to date? Let's look at the model (see Table 14-3).

Table 14-3. *E-Book Change Model*

Condition	Status
There must be an idea for change.	There is. E-books exist and are being sold, though not in large numbers.
There must be a market desire for change.	There is. Many companies and people are interested in saving trees, time, and money by reducing the amount of printed material they must manage. In corporate America, despite their powerful drawbacks, e-books are becoming more and more popular.
There must be an advantage to change.	There are many advantages to e-books.
There must be an infrastructure that supports change.	The infrastructure does not exist. Current e-book readers and displays are very inferior to paper.
There must be a distribution mechanism for change.	The Internet provides such a distribution mechanism.
Change must come at the right price.	E-book pricing is comparable to printed books.
There must be an acceptable quality of experience when change occurs.	E-books are not close to providing an acceptable quality of experience to most people. The books are too heavy, the displays are too limited in contrast and quality, and storage is too limited.

So when do e-books begin to disrupt the print business? At the point when an e-book reader weighs about 6 ounces, has a form factor of a mid-sized paperback (though the unit will be less than an inch thick), the screen can be read in full sunlight while you're at the beach, screen resolution is comparable to the 1,500 to 3,000 dots per inch typical on a printed page, the book has between 500 gigs to 1 terabyte of integrated storage, and wireless Internet access is integrated into the system. The price should range from $250 to $500. When will it be possible to build such a system? My estimation of the current pace of hardware development says between 6 to 10 years.

I'll be investing in a good e-book company around that time.

~

Chapter 12, "The Strange Case of Dr. Open and Mr. Proprietary"

The Sony Rootkit Fiasco

The Sony rootkit disaster is a perfect example of what happens when an industry stubbornly refuses to listen to its market and instead tries to sue it. The desire of people to mix and match music to meet their particular tastes tracks back to the 1950s and the development of the first record changers. By the late 1980s, as this book documents, technology had developed to the point where this customer need could be met (and very profitably). By the late 1990s, only a true pack of idiots would have missed the handwriting on the wall and not moved proactively, in concert with an MP3.com or Napster, to meet the clearly inevitable future. By the millennium's end, you didn't need a crystal ball to see what was coming; all you had to do was take some time out from sucking up to rock gods and snorting cocaine and go out and buy an MP3 player and download some jingles. Instead of suing Shawn Fanning, creator of Napster, one of the music companies should have had enough sense to buy out Napster and make Fanning its VP of business development. Sony's idiocy has only helped establish free MP3s downloaded from peer-to-peer systems as the preferred way to obtain music. When one discusses making **money** from online music sales, Apple and its iPod hardware platform have a chokehold on the music companies. To understand how anomalous this is, imagine one of the turntable companies of the 1970s or 1980s, perhaps Dual, Thorens, or Garrard, having the power to dictate the price of record albums. The mind boggles.

The facts are these: Music is rapidly decoupling itself from physical mediums such as CDs, DVDs, or whatever their successors may be. And the iPod and competing systems function merely as way stations that allow a person to manage, transmit, and play their musical/video environment as they see fit. The consumer of the future will demand that this environment be portable, of the highest quality, and protected against loss, with buying opportunities (at reasonable prices) integrated directly into the experience. MP3s, MPEGs, higher-quality formats, and satellite radio will increasingly be expected to be flexible, integrated, and available 24/7. As Apple has demonstrated, people will buy music online. What Apple has failed to realize (or least not solved technically) is that people will not endure being locked into an environment where an accident (your MP3 player is lost, breaks, or is stolen), copy protection, or a technology change destroys or damages their personal entertainment environment.

This presents an opportunity for the music industry. Instead of fruitless attempts to put the online genie back in the bottle, consider some fresh thinking. Here are few ideas the industry could consider:

- Selling higher-quality audio files to audiophiles with "golden ears." (These are the people who claim to have the ability to hear upper frequencies commensurate with bats.)

- More aggressively integrating sales opportunities into the online presentations of your musicians. For example, with the demise of vinyl came the loss of an art form, the album cover. Websites can function as online album covers and sell posters. I've visited a half dozen websites plugging different artists and albums; I have yet to see a site where I can buy an album cover/poster for these forthcoming releases.

- Consider encouraging artists to step outside the album and three-minute-tune format and experiment with new approaches. And then be prepared to be the first to sell the new tracks.

- Take a hard look at MP3.com's music locker concept. Didn't it ever occur to anyone in the business that serving as the trusted storage repository for your customer's music might be a **good** thing?

- Stop suing people. It's fruitless, it angers your market, and it diverts the industry from figuring a way out of the pickle it has put itself in. Recently, the music industry has begun suing websites posting **tablatures** online. A "tablature" is a form of musical notation that tells players where to place their fingers on a particular instrument rather than follow standard musical notation. Of course, the industry offers no intelligent online alternative for consumers, with the result that the best tablature websites can now be found in places like Russia.

A final suggestion is that decreased drug use by industry executives might lead to clearer thinking.

WPA, WGA, and All That Jazz

Let me be direct. Microsoft should immediately stake WPA, WGA notifications, and all the rest of them through the heart, cut off their heads, stuff their mouths with garlic, and bury them in unhallowed ground. The minor reasons for this are as follows:

- Microsoft is attempting to reprice its software out of historic bounds. In 1981, the introduction of PC DOS reset the price for desktop operating systems to $40.00. Today, that same $40.00 is worth $89.50. The base version of Windows XP, XP Home, currently costs $100.00 (and Microsoft's power in the distribution system makes sure it stays sct close to those levels). That doesn't seem like much of a difference, but when you bought the original DOS, you were able to install it on any machine you owned. Up until the introduction of WPA and WGA, you could do this with Windows. Now, if you have more than one PC in your home without an operating system, the cost of Windows is $200.00,[1] a 100 percent increase. Add a third system, and you suffer another 100 percent increase.

- Microsoft is attempting to convince new markets in countries such as China and India to adopt Windows instead of Linux. To do so, the company will have to provide Windows at prices greatly reduced from U.S. retail levels. It's already doing this in Thailand (cost of a basic copy of Windows is $36.00) and Malaysia, and you can expect the Chinese and Indians are going to want prices that are at least as good. If not, they're in a position to mandate the use of Linux in their markets. Offering the people who brought you Tiananmen Square sweetheart prices on the world's favorite OS will be very, very unpopular in the U.S. market. And having a little tattler, Jewish mother, and executioner in your computer isn't going to make people feel better about the situation. Worse for Microsoft,

---

[1] Actually, if you own one retail copy of Windows, you can buy an additional "license" and get a whopping $15 off the retail price. However, almost no one knows about this program because Microsoft does little to publicize it.

I don't think those governments are going to allow Windows to stick kill switches in the software sold in their countries. This will make Americans feel even worse and Linux and open source increasingly attractive.

- Microsoft's behavior with its copy protection systems is starting to make people remember the DOJ trial and "guilty of monopoly abuse" verdicts. It's also likely to attract the attention of European commissions, groups that like to hand out big fines to the Redmond giant. Windows is becoming the most expensive component in the purchase of a computer. As noted in this chapter, when computers cost $2000.00 to $4000.00, as they did in the period during which Microsoft was establishing its desktop OS monopoly, the cost of the operating system was easily overlooked. But this has changed. Highly functional systems for home and regular office use can now be purchased for less than $499.00, and prices continue to slide. In the 1980s, companies such as WordPerfect found it impossible to sell $499.00 word processors to people buying $499.00 Amigas and Ataris. Microsoft increasingly finds itself in a similar dilemma. If you're buying a computer without an operating system, paying from $100.00 to $150.00 for a copy of Windows Professional for a computer that costs less than $500.00 has many people scratching their heads. For system builders such as Dell, Lenovo, and HP, OEM prices for Windows range from $30.00 to $80.00, depending on the number of licenses ordered and your ability to negotiate a good deal with Microsoft. For many of the systems built by manufacturers, this makes Windows the single most expensive item in the bill of materials. As a result, more and more PC builders are looking at Linux with deep longing.

- WPA, WGA, and all the rest of it make Microsoft look old and out of touch. With the Indian and Chinese markets exploding, SaaS opening new markets, open source pushing along the process of commoditization of operating systems and desktop applications, and the digital revolution in entertainment and personal information spreading daily, are copy protection schemes the best things Microsoft can focus on? The company grew to its current status of software colossus without help from copy protection. Perhaps Microsoft is feeling arthritic and wants to turn Windows into a sinecure? WPA will keep Granny Microsoft safe and secure while she sips her cup of warm milk, allows inspissation to clog her arteries and tamp down the fires of innovation, and reflexively smacks her toothless gums while endlessly reminiscing about the good old days of ATs, floppy disks, and how she once spanked those whippersnappers VisiOn and OS/2.

The major reason to drop copy protection is that Microsoft is placing itself athwart the rails of new trends as the engine of change bears down on it. Since the introduction of the original IBM PC, I have never bought a fully configured Intel-derived computer. I've always bought either stripped units or component parts and configured or built my own systems. I do this because a) I enjoy it (sort of), b) to save money (not really anymore), c) to learn about how new hardware interacts with new software, and d) to give myself the best chance to move my files and programs over to the new system with a minimum of agony and loss.

I have recently built a new system and spent weeks being stymied in my attempts to preserve my current computing environment. The image management system I've been using allows me to create backups of my partitions and move these to my new computer, but attempting to boot the computer with these partitions immediately crashed the system. Not even Windows XP's Safe Mode can handle the transferred environment.

I did have an alternative to what I attempted, one that has been suggested by several computing experts. I could take "advantage" of the situation to simply do a clean "reinstall" of my Windows system, on the theory that after several years of use, all Windows' installations become "gunked up" and sluggish because of performance and safety degradation (an odd concept when you consider that software can't rust or decay). This is finally what I was forced to do, but the new computer has been sitting idle for months after its purchase and assembly. That's because the path of a clean install means I'm throwing away the most valuable computer asset I own, my working "environment." The idea of throwing away four years of accumulated tweaking and alteration of my virtual workbench throws me into the same kind of cold sweat felt by those who lost their Day-Timers on innumerable trains, taxis, cars, and airplanes during the 1980s and early 1990s. My computing environment is more than a workspace; in an increasingly real sense, it's my "life."

It's also extremely valuable. In 1981, the cost of a fully loaded IBM PC, with all the associated accessories and software you needed to be productive, ranged from $4,000.00 to $8,000.00 (and could easily go higher). That amount of money bought you a car back then. Today, a highly functional PC with equivalent accessories and software costs you about $500.00 to $800.00 (adjusted for inflation, that's about $300.00 to $600.00 in 1981 dollars). That buys you a set of tires for your car. Laptops prices are also plummeting rapidly, with mid-level units now costing from $400.00 to $700.00, on average.

But what is the time cost of replacing your computing environment? First, let's define what your computing environment comprises. It can include the following:

- Your applications
- Your files (documents, music, data, and so on)
- Your hardware settings
- Your PC's BIOS settings
- All DRM (digital rights management) protection that has been applied to copy-protected products such as Windows and Office
- Fixes to Windows, Office, and all other applications you have installed
- Your Internet bookmarks, cookies, saved passwords, and so on
- The organization of your desktop
- Custom configurations you may have applied to your system, including color choices, taskbar arrangement, registry tweaks, integrated services, and so on, and so on
- All data that drives applications; for instance, lists of keywords and phrases that drive a macro program, Skype addresses, AIM custom-configured buddy lists, and so on
- Images and backups of your data
- And anything else I've neglected to remember

What do you estimate the cost of replicating all this would be, assuming you do a ground-up rebuild of your system? And just how do you propose to manage the process? I'm not aware of any tool that allows you to inventory and track all the myriad adjustments and changes you can and do make to a workspace you've developed over the years. Furthermore, how many of you have kept track of all the serial numbers, passwords, and configuration data you'll need to reinstall and reconfigure your various programs and access the various websites important to your business and work requirements?

There are programs that purport to make this process easier; I've used several, and they all have severe restrictions. Some of these products barely, or don't, work (as I'm finding). Most, of course, don't deal with files; that's the responsibility of backup. None, so far as I can tell, quite know what to do about DRM. Some standards groups are looking at the problem, most notably U3 (http://www.u3.com), a portable computing environment standard being pushed by companies such as SanDisk. I think they're heading in the right direction for the Windows world, but it's too early to know how effective their standard will be and even U3 doesn't have an answer for WPA and WGA.

I sat down and estimated that a complete reinstall and reconstruction of my current computing system would take approximately 100 hours (this counts the time required to locate all applications, locate all documents associated with the applications, request lost documents and configuration information, physically reinstall them, and then test and "debug" the new environment to try to discover what I've missed and which products no longer work). Since I've had to create "from scratch environments" more than 25 times over the years, this number is not based simply on supposition but on hard-won personal experience.

Let's assume you're a working professional who bills out their time at $50 per hour, with 50 hours needed for a complete rebuild (generous estimates) of your computing workspace. That means the replacement cost of your environment is $2,500.00; that's not counting lost opportunity expenses you may incur as you attempt to reconstruct a lost or corrupted environment. I've spoken to professionals who peg the value of their environment at far higher levels; one attorney I spoke to estimated the cost of rebuilding her environment from scratch to be $20,000.00. And the costs of your environment are steadily rising; after all, most of us are not relying less on computing power and Internet access to do business, but more. Increasingly, more people are going to expect that their personalized computing environments are permanent and valuable investments that will "die" only when they do (and maybe not even then).

Despite this, many practices in the software industry, such as the reintroduction of copy protection, make computing environments more fragile and easily damaged or lost. This places customers and companies at cross-purposes to each other and presents major problems for the next release of Windows, Office, and other platforms. For the most part, these products are very insensitive to the value of an environment; worse, their greater complexity, combined with such delights as WPA and WGA, makes them increasingly unable to be "fixed" in case of a problem. Conversely, major opportunities exist for products and services that can harden, protect, and guarantee the survival of a user's most valuable computing asset. Open source products help meet this need. So does SaaS, at some levels.

But Windows, with its tattler, nag, and executioner, doesn't. For an example of how this can be expected to play out, all Bill Gates and Steve Ballmer have to do is buy an iPod, download some MP3s, and let Steve Jobs and Napster's heirs rock their world.

AFTERWORD:
Stupid Development Tricks

THE COMPLETE TITLE of *In Search of Stupidity* includes the phrase "High-Tech Marketing Disasters," and from these words you might conclude that it's a firm's marketers who usually bear the chief responsibility for major corporate catastrophes. This isn't true. To be worthy of mention in this book, it took the combined efforts of personnel in upper management, development, sales, and marketing, all fiercely dedicated to ignoring common sense, the blatantly obvious, and the lessons of the past. Major failure doesn't just happen: To achieve it, everyone must pull together as a team.

Chapter 4 of *In Search of Stupidity* helps drive this point home. For MicroPro to plummet from the software industry's pinnacle to permanent oblivion took a) upper management's mishandling of development and market timing, b) the marketing department's idiotic decision to create a fatal product-positioning conflict, and c) the development team's dimwitted decision to rewrite perfectly good code at a critical time because it wanted to write even better code that no one really needed. A magnificent example of different groups within a company all cooperating to ensure disaster.

In this spirit, I've decided to include selected portions of an interview with Joel Spolsky that ran on SoftwareMarketSolution (http://www.softwaremarketsolution.com), a website sponsored by the author of this book that provides resources and information on products and services of interest to high-tech marketers. (By the way, this interview was "picked up" by Slashdot [http://www.slashdot.org], a website dedicated to technology, coding, open source, and all things nerd. It generated a considerable amount of comment and controversy. You can search the Slashdot archives to read what other people thought and gain further insight into Joel's opinions.)

I regard Joel Spolsky, president and one of the founders of Fog Creek Software (http://www.fogcreek.com), as one of the industry's most fascinating personalities. He worked at Microsoft from 1991 to 1994 and has more than 10 years of experience managing the software development process. As a program manager on the Microsoft Excel team, Joel designed Excel Basic and drove Microsoft's Visual Basic for Applications (VBA) strategy. His website, Joel on Software (http://www.JoelonSoftware.com), is visited by thousands of developers worldwide every day. His first book, *User Interface Design for Programmers* (Apress, 2001), was reviewed on SoftwareMarketSolution, and I regard it as a must-have for anyone involved in developing and marketing software.

Why this interview? If you've ever worked on the software side of high technology, you've probably experienced the following: After a careful analysis of your product's capabilities, the competition, and the current state of the market, a development and marketing plan is created. Release time frames are discussed and agreed upon. Elaborate project management templates are built, and milestones are set. You post the ship date up on a wall where everyone in your group can see it, and your team begins to work like crazed beavers to meet your target.

Then, as the magic day looms nearer, ominous sounds emit from development. Whispers of "crufty code" and "bad architecture" are overheard. Talk of "hard decisions" that "need to be made" starts to wend its way through the company grapevine. People, especially the programmers, walk by the wall on which you've mounted the ship date, pause, shake their heads, and keep walking.

Finally, the grim truth is disgorged. At a solemn meeting, development tells everyone the bad news. The code base of the current product is a mess. Despite the best and heroic efforts of the programmers, they've been unable to fix the ancient, bug-ridden, fly-bespeckled piece of trash foisted on them by an unfeeling management. No other option remains. The bullet must be bitten. The gut must be sucked up. The Rubicon must be crossed. And as that sinking feeling gathers in your stomach and gains momentum as it plunges toward your bowels, you realize that you already know what you're about to hear. And you already know that, after hearing it, you'll be groping blindly back to your cubicle, your vision impeded by the flow of tears coursing down your face, your eyes reddened by the sharp sting of saline. And you've already accepted it's time to get your resume out and polished, because the next few financial quarters are going to be very, very ugly.

And then they say it. The product requires a ground-up rewrite. No other option exists.

Oh, you **haven't** been through this yet? Well, just wait. You will. However, as you'll learn, what you're going to be told may very well not be true. After reading this interview, you'll be in a better position to protect your vision and your career in the wonderful world of high tech.

And now . . .

~

An Interview with Joel Spolsky

SoftwareMarketSolution: Joel, what, in your opinion, is the single greatest development sin a software company can commit?

Joel Spolsky: Deciding to completely rewrite your product from scratch, on the theory that all your code is messy and bug-prone and is bloated and needs to be completely rethought and rebuilt from ground zero.

SMS: Uh, what's wrong with that?

JS: Because it's almost never true. It's not like code rusts if it's not used. The idea that new code is better than old is patently absurd. Old code has been used. It has been tested. Lots of bugs have been found, and they've been fixed. There's nothing wrong with it.

SMS: Well, why do programmers constantly go charging into management's offices claiming the existing code base is junk and has to be replaced?

JS: My theory is that this happens because it's harder to read code than to write it. A programmer will whine about a function that he thinks is messy. It's supposed to be a simple function to display a window or something, but for some reason it takes up two pages and has all these ugly little hairs and stuff on it and nobody knows why. OK. I'll tell you why. Those are bug fixes. One of them fixes that bug that Jill had when she tried to install the thing on a computer that didn't have Internet Explorer. Another one fixes a bug that occurs in low-memory conditions. Another one fixes some bug that occurred when the file is on a floppy disk and the user yanks out the diskette in the middle. That LoadLibrary call is sure ugly, but it makes the code work on old versions of Windows 95.

When you throw that function away and start from scratch, you are throwing away all that knowledge. All those collected bug fixes. Years of programming work.

SMS: Well, let's assume some of your top programmers walked in the door and said, "We absolutely have to rewrite this thing from scratch, top to bottom." What's the right response?

JS: What I learned from Charles Ferguson's great book (*High St@kes, No Prisoners* [Crown, 1999]) is that you need to hire programmers who can understand the business goals. People who can answer questions like "What does it really cost the company if we rewrite?" "How many months will it delay shipping the product?" "Will we sell enough marginal copies to justify the lost time and market share?" If your programmers insist on a rewrite, they probably don't understand the financials of the company, or the competitive situation. Explain this to them. Then get an honest estimate for the rewrite effort and insist on a financial spreadsheet showing a detailed cost/benefit analysis for the rewrite.

SMS: Yeah, great, but, believe it or not, programmers have been known to, uh, "shave the truth" when it comes to such matters.

JS: What you're seeing is the famous programmer tactic: All features that I want take 1 hour, all features that I don't want take 99 years. If you suspect you are being lied to, just drill down. Get a schedule with granularity measured in hours, not months. Insist that each task have an estimate that is 2 days or less. If it's longer than that, you need to break it down into subtasks or the schedule can't be realistic.

SMS: Are there any circumstances where a complete code rewrite is justified?

JS: Probably not. The most extreme circumstance I can think of would be if you are simultaneously moving to a new platform and changing the architecture of the code dramatically. Even in this case you are probably better off looking at the old code as you develop the new code.

SMS: Hmm. Let's take a look at your theory and compare it to some real-world software meltdowns. For instance, what happened at Netscape?

JS: Way back in April 2000, I wrote on my website that Netscape made the single worst strategic mistake that any software company can make by deciding to rewrite their code from scratch. Lou Montulli, one of the five programming superstars who did the original version of Navigator, e-mailed me to say, "I agree completely; it's one of the major reasons I resigned from Netscape." This one decision cost Netscape 4 years. That's 3 years they spent with their prize aircraft carrier in 200,000 pieces in dry dock. They couldn't add new features, couldn't respond to the competitive threats from IE, and had to sit on their hands while Microsoft completely ate their lunch.

SMS: OK, how about Borland? Another famous meltdown. Any ideas?

JS: Borland also got into the habit of throwing away perfectly good code and starting from scratch. Even after the purchase of Ashton-Tate, Borland bought Arago and tried to make that into dBASE for Windows, a doomed project that took so long that Microsoft Access ate their lunch. With Paradox, they jumped into a huge rewrite effort with C++ and took forever to release the Windows version of the product. And it was buggy and slow where Paradox for DOS was solid and fast. Then they did it all over again with Quattro Pro, rewriting it from scratch and astonishing the world with how little new functionality it had.

SMS: Yeah, and their pricing strategy didn't help.

JS: While I was on the Excel team, Borland cut the MSRP on Quattro Pro from around $500.00 to around $100.00. Clueless newbie that I was, I thought this was the beginning of a bloody price war. Lewis Levin,[1] Excel BUM (business unit manager) was ecstatic. "Don't you see, Joel, once they have to cut prices, they've lost." He had no plan to respond to the lower price. And he didn't need to.

SMS: Having worked at Ashton-Tate, I have to tell you the dBASE IV code base was no thing of beauty. But, I take your point. Actually, I saw this syndrome at work in Ashton-Tate's word-processing division. After they bought MultiMate, they spent about 2 years planning a complete rewrite of the product and wasted months evaluating new "engines" for the next version. Nothing ever happened. When a

---

[1] Lewis Levin got his start in the industry as the product manager for MicroPro's PlanStar.

new version of the product **was** released, it was based on the same "clunky" engine everyone had been moaning about. Of course, in those 2 years WordPerfect and Microsoft ate Ashton-Tate's word-processing lunch.

JS: Ashton-Tate had a word processor?

SMS: Yes, but nothing as good as WordStar, mind you!

JS: Hmm. That reminds me that Microsoft learned the "no rewrite" lesson the hard way. They tried to rewrite Word for Windows from scratch in a doomed project called "Pyramid," which was shut down, thrown away, and swept under the rug. Fortunately for Microsoft, they did this with parallel teams and had never stopped working on the old code base, so they had something to ship, making it merely a financial disaster, not a strategic one.

SMS: OK, Lotus?

JS: Too many MBAs at all levels and not enough people with a technical understanding of what could and needed to be built.

SMS: And I suppose building a brand-new product called "Jazz"[2] instead of getting 1-2-3 over to the Mac as quickly as possible, thus staking Microsoft to a 2-year lead with Excel, is an example of the same thing?

JS: Actually, they made a worse mistake: They spent something like 18 months trying to squeeze 1-2-3/3.0 into 640KB. By the time the 18 months were up, they hadn't succeeded, and in the meantime, everybody bought 386s with 4 megs of ram. Microsoft always figured that it's better to let the hardware catch up with the software rather than spending time writing code for old computers owned by people who aren't buying much software any more.

SMS: WordPerfect?

JS: That's an interesting case and leads to another development sin software companies often make: using the wrong-level tools for the job. At WordPerfect, everything, including everything, had to be written in assembler. Company policy. If a programmer needed a little one-off utility, it had to be hand-coded and hand-optimized in assembler. They were the only people on Earth writing all-assembler

---

[2] Jazz was intended to be the Macintosh equivalent of Symphony for the PC. Like most of the integrated products, it managed to do too much while not doing anything particularly well.

apps for Windows. Insane. It's like making your ballerinas wear balls and chains and taping their arms to their sides.

SMS: What should they have been coding in?

JS: In those days? C. Or maybe Pascal. Programmers should only use lower-level tools for those parts of the product where they are adding the most value. For example, if you're writing a game where the 3D effects are your major selling point, you can't use an off-the-shelf 3D engine; you have to roll your own. But if the major selling point of your game is the story, don't waste time getting great 3D graphics—just use a library. But WordPerfect was writing UI code that operates in "user time" and doesn't need to be particularly fast. Hand-coded assembler is insane and adds no value.

SMS: Yes, but isn't such code tight and small? Don't products built this way avoid the dreaded "bloatware" label?

JS: Don't get me started! If you're a software company, there are lots of great business reasons to love bloatware. For one, if programmers don't have to worry about how large their code is, they can ship it sooner. And that means you get more features, and features make users' lives better (if they use them) and don't usually hurt (if they don't). As a user, if your software vendor stops, before shipping, and spends 2 months squeezing the code down to make it 50 percent smaller, the net benefit to you is going to be imperceptible, but you went for 2 months without new features that you needed, and **that** hurt.

SMS: Could this possibly account for the fact that no one uses WordStar version 3.3 anymore despite the fact it can fit on one 1.4 meg floppy?

JS: That and Control-K. But seriously, Moore's law makes much of the whining about bloatware ridiculous. In 1993, Microsoft Excel 5.0 took up about $36.00 worth of hard drive space. In 2000, Microsoft Excel 2000 takes up about $1.03 in hard drive space. All adjusted for inflation. So stop whining about how bloated it is.

SMS: Well, we've had much personal experience with the press slamming a product we were managing. For example, for years reviewers gave MicroPro hell over the fact it didn't support columns and tables. Somehow the fact that the product would fit on a 360KB floppy just didn't seem to mean as much as the idea that the reviewer couldn't use our product to write his or her resume.

JS: There's a famous fallacy that people learn in business school called the 80/20 rule. It's false, but it seduces a lot of dumb software start-ups. It seems to make sense. Eighty percent of the people use 20 percent of the features. So you convince yourself that you only need to implement 20 percent of the features, and you can still sell 80 percent as many copies. The trouble here, of course, is that it's never the same 20 percent. Everybody uses a different set of features. When you start marketing your "lite" product and you tell people, "Hey, it's lite, only 1MB," they tend to be very happy, then they ask you if it has word counts, or spell checking, or little rubber feet, or whatever obscure thing they can't live without, and it doesn't, so they don't buy your product.

SMS: Let's talk about product marketing and development at Microsoft. How did these two groups work together?

JS: Well, in theory, the marketing group (called "product management") was supposed to give the development team feedback on what customers wanted. Features requests from the field. That kind of stuff. In reality, they never did.

SMS: Really?

JS: Really. Yes, we listened to customers, but not through product management—they were never very good at channeling this information. So the program management (design) teams just went out and talked to customers ourselves. One thing I noticed pretty quickly is that you don't actually learn all that much from asking customers what features they want. Sure, they'll tell you, but it's all stuff you knew anyway.

SMS: You paint a picture of the programmer almost as a semideity. But in my experience, I've seen powerful technical personalities take down major companies. For instance, in *The Product Marketing Handbook for Software* (Aegis Resources, 2006), I describe how the MicroPro development staff's refusal to add the aforementioned columns and table features to WordStar badly hurt the product's sales.[3] How do you manage situations like these?

---

[3] Over time, the programming staff noted that requests for this feature from users were dropping. This was absolutely true, because people who wanted this capability in a word processor bought other products.

JS: This is a hard problem. I've seen plenty of companies with prima donna programmers who literally drive their companies into the ground. If the management of the company is technical (think Bill Gates), management isn't afraid to argue with them and win—or fire the programmer and get someone new in. If the management of the company is not technical enough (think John Sculley), they act like scared rabbits, strangely believing that this **one** person is the only person on the planet who can write code, and it's not a long way from there to the failure of the company.

If you're a nontechnical CEO with programmers who aren't getting with the program, you have to bite the bullet and fire them. This is your only hope. And it means you're going to have to find new technical talent, so your chances aren't great. That's why I don't think technology companies that don't have engineers at the very top have much of a chance.

SMS: Joel, thank you very much.

GLOSSARY OF TERMS

ARPANET

The immediate precursor to the Internet created by the Advanced Research Projects Agency (ARPA). No one lost any money on the ARPANET, a fact that leads many people to remember it fondly.

ASP

Acronym for *application service provider*. Software usage and distribution systems in which programs are hosted on servers, not installed on separate desktops. In the late 1990s, the perceived advantages of this approach included providing a steady revenue stream for software companies, less software piracy, and easier management of upgrades. The disadvantage to these systems was that nobody bought them.

banner ad

A type of web-based advertisement. The standard banner size is 468×60 pixels (about 5 square inches). Nobody watches them.

beta

A prerelease software product sent to end users for testing and evaluation. Right.

branding

A marketing process that attempts to attach desirable intangible qualities to products and services. The process reached its apotheosis during the dot-com boom, a time when sock puppets and incredibly expensive Super Bowl ads featuring things like computer-generated herds of cats wasted amazing amounts of money with no discernible ROI.

channel

An industry term for the high-tech distribution system. The term is used somewhat loosely and often refers to a channel segment, as in "the reseller channel." The channel is sometimes also referred to by hardware and software vendors as "bloodsuckers," "vampires," "weasels," and "those thieves." The channel has its own special vocabulary for the vendors.

channel stuffing

A sales tactic where product is sold into a distributor's or reseller's inventory despite a lack of end-user demand for the product. Channel stuffing can take many inventive forms, such as selling product to a distributor just before the end of a fiscal quarter and then taking the product back immediately after the quarter ends, shipping bricks to a distributor instead of actual products (a hard drive manufacturer once pulled this stunt), etc.

chiclet keyboard

Used on the PC Junior. A membrane-based keyboard technology that companies insist on periodically trying to sell to people even though past experience has taught them no one wants it.

click-through

An Internet ad model that measures response by the number of users who click an ad that links to the advertiser's site. Most response figures use numbers that hover close to the value "zero."

collateral

All material created to support a product, including brochures, posters, sample product, demonstration disks, mobiles, and T-shirts. Frequently referred to as "junk" by members of the press, who often seem to prize obtaining the stuff nonetheless.

competitive upgrade

A software promotion designed to drain sales away from a competitor's installed base. Usually the product is sold at a price close to or below the upgrade price of a competing product. At Borland, these programs are sometimes referred to as "hoist by your own petard."

CRM

Acronym for *customer relationship management*. This category of software is descended from the various sales contact management software packages that became popular with businesses beginning in the late 1980s through the early 1990s. Many of the CRM systems installed in the late 1990s and early 2000s were derisively referred to as "shelfware" because many of the packages didn't work, hurt relations with customers, and were eventually "installed" on shelves across corporate America.

Dali Lama, The
The exiled political and religious leader of Tibet. If it would get the Chinese out of his country, he'd use a hosted online CRM system.

demo dolly
An individual assigned to demonstrate a product, often to a member of the press or an industry analyst. Demo dollies can be of either sex. The most important personal characteristic of a successful demo dolly is the ability to nod wisely even when a member of senior management says something inane.

DOJ
Acronym for *Department of Justice*. This part of the U.S. government occasionally sues large companies who violate U.S. antitrust laws. It's believed by some in the high-tech industry that the DOJ only does this after inspecting the entrails of a chicken and deciding that the omens are right.

ERP
Acronym for *enterprise resource planning*. A class of software designed to integrate every aspect of a company's operations, from customer service to warehouse management. Frequently, use of these products requires a business to "reengineer" its business processes, which in turn often leads to the need to placate angry customers who are receiving multiple bills for items they didn't order. This helps drive purchases of CRM software.

evil
See Google, Yahoo, and MSN.

est
A system of self-awareness, self-actualization, and self-fulfillment developed in California. est graduates and practitioners are sometimes referred to as "sociopaths."

Google
Currently the leading web search firm in the world. When Google is not assisting the Chinese government in censoring the Web so as to prevent the Chinese people from learning about their government's violations of human, civil, and religious rights, the company operates under the motto of "Do No Evil."

gray market
A system designed to sell products outside of normal "authorized" reseller channels. Gray markets usually spring up when large companies buy more products than they can sell in order to achieve bigger discounts, and then turn around and sell their excess inventory "out the back door" to smaller resellers. These resellers in turn sell the product to customers (sometimes without warranties or service agreements). Everyone in high tech is constantly bemoaning the existence of gray markets, but they never seem to go away. Participants in these markets can be distinguished by their nervous tics, an unfortunate byproduct of their constant winking.

GPL
Acronym for Gnu Public License. A license agreement for software that requires the software developer to provide the source code of their product free of charge to all users (you can charge a fee for warranties and the costs of physical transport), who must in turn offer the same source code with all changes they have made to it to their users under the same terms. The GPL was created by Richard Stallman, a programmer who lives with no visible means of support.

GUI
Acronym for *graphical user interface*. A software operating environment that provides users with a visual desktop metaphor. The modern GUI avoids the trash-can icon because its use usually leads to a lawsuit by Apple.

hindsight
Also called "history." A process whereby you study others' mistakes so as not make them yourself. The concept is despised by masochists.

HTML
Acronym for *Hypertext Markup Language*. A formatting language designed for viewing documents posted on the World Wide Web. Also known as "Greek" to people not familiar with the 1970s concept of editor/formatter text processing.

IDE
Acronym for *integrated development environment*. A software development tool used by programmers to write programs. A good-quality IDE is often named as a respondent in the divorce proceedings between a programmer and his or her spouse.

iPod

An expensive, easily-scratched MP3 player sold by Apple with an almost impossible-to-replace battery. Everybody wants one.

infomercial

A form of television advertising designed to elicit a direct response to an offer via a phone call or visit to a website. Cher can often be seen on these programs, if you're a fan.

Internet

A worldwide system of interconnected computer networks. Because it's supposed to make information free, everyone wants to control it.

IPO

Initial public offering (of stock). During the dot-com boom, IPOs were often used to legally defraud millions of people who should have known better.

ISP

Acronym for *Internet service provider*. A company that provides access to the Internet.

ISV

Acronym for *independent software vendor*. A developer or publisher of software products.

Java

A programming language designed to compile and run under a virtual microprocessor or "machine."

LAN

Acronym for *local area network*. A group of PCs linked to run in a cooperative fashion.

Linux

An open source UNIX derivative for Intel systems developed under the GPL. At Microsoft, this operating system is sometimes called "Apocalypse Now."

malware

A class of software that includes viruses, spyware, and rootkits. Sony's favorite form of malware is the rootkit.

marcom

Short for *marketing communications*. The department in a business responsible for creating and administering collateral development, PR, and advertising, along with the scheduling of trade show participation.

MDF

Acronym for *marketing development funds*. Refers to a type of promotional program widely used in high-tech marketing. MDF programs usually involve a vendor paying funds to a distribution partner in return for access to a sales channel or to a manufacturer to obtain discounts on purchases. In some industries this process is called "bribery," "extortion," or "payola."

MP3

A digital compression format that makes it easy for your kids to steal music worldwide.

MSN

See *evil*.

Moore's law

Not actually a law, but an observation. Moore's "law" states that the number of transistors contained in a microdevice doubles every 18 months. Moore's law accounts for the fact that the new computer you just bought will be worth the price of a boat anchor 6 months after purchase. Actually, the boat anchor will be worth more.

NIC

Acronym for *network interface computer*. A PC without a disk drive designed by Larry Ellison that no one buys.

NOS

Acronym for *network operating system*. An operating system designed to run a network of desktop computers.

OOP

Acronym for *object-oriented programming*. A programming methodology that combines code and data in "packages." The technology is incomprehensible to most users of software.

open source
Both a movement and a process of creating software that believes that the underlying source code of products should be freely accessible to users. Many open source programmers believe Bill Gates is Satan. Bill Gates believes many open source programmers are communists.

OS
Acronym for *operating system*. A program that allows a computer system to operate its internal hardware, manage its memory, communicate with application programs, and make Bill Gates richer than God.

peer-to-peer
A networking technology that allows computers to communicate and exchange information directly instead of through a server. Peer-to-peer networks are most frequently used to defraud record companies, whom no one likes anyway.

positioning
A marketing process that attempts to "place" a product in a desirable "location" in a prospective buyer's mind. The most successful positioning strategies in high-tech consist of first telling people what the heck it is you want them to buy.

p-System
A 1980s "write once, run anywhere" precursor to Java. The performance of p-System programs tended to be poor, and figuring out how to properly capitalize the name of the OS drove everyone crazy.

RDBMS
Acronym for *relational database management system*. A methodology for storing and retrieving data from computer systems that relies heavily on tables. Periodically, database programming specialists engage in abstruse arguments about which database system is more or less relational than another. These arguments can sometimes reach levels of ferocity equivalent to those seen during the Thirty Years War, but because programmers are poor fighters, no one is usually hurt.

ROI
Acronym for *return on investment*. The amount of money earned on investing in a particular program or business. The concept wasn't in use during the dot-com boom.

rootkit
A form of malware popularized by Sony.

SaaS
Acronym for Software as a Service. Software usage and distribution systems in which programs are hosted on servers, not installed on separate desktops. Some people are buying these systems as long as everyone agrees to never, ever say "ASP."

search engine
A program designed to search and index information on the Internet.

server
A computer running a NOS or a web-based application such as e-mail.

shelfware
Unused software. *See also* CRM.

Siebel Systems
At one time the leading CRM company in the world. Before it was taken over by Oracle, Siebel no longer had good relations with some of its key customers.

SIG
Acronym for *special interest group*. A subdivision of a user group, dedicated to examining one particular application category or product. For example, a user group may have a word-processing SIG, which might, in turn, be divided into smaller SIGs dedicated to specific word-processing products.

SOHO
Acronym for *small office/home office*. A class of products aimed at small, independent businesses and entrepreneurs.

SRP
Acronym for *suggested retail price*. The price no one actually pays for a product, except in the case of Microsoft Windows.

Stallman, Richard M.
The inspiration behind the Father of Linux, Linus Torvalds, who created Bill Gates' and Steve Ballmer's worst nightmare.

subtractive marketing

A marketing process that strips desirable features out of a successful product and then attempts to position the pathetic, leftover hulk as a good "value." Marketers who rely on subtractive marketing must hope that their customers are idiots. Usually, this hope is disappointed.

Torvalds, Linus

The Father of Linux, Bill Gates' and Steve Ballmer's worst nightmare.

URL

Acronym for *uniform resource locator*. A "virtual" address for a website. Used by web browsers to locate things to buy, communities to argue in, and pornography to view. Fortunately, no one ever goes to the porn sites.

WGA

Short for Windows Genuine Advantage. The product is considered by many observers to open source's best friend.

WPA

Short for Windows Product Activation. A copy protection scheme introduced by Microsoft in 2000. Considered by many observers to be open source's second best friend.

Yahoo

A leading web portal that has never promised not to be evil and therefore has no compunctions about helping the Chinese government jail journalists.

SELECTED BIBLIOGRAPHY

Auletta, Ken. *World War 3.0: Microsoft and Its Enemies*. New York, NY: Random House, 2001.

Bank, David. *Breaking Windows: How Bill Gates Fumbled the Future of Microsoft*. New York, NY: The Free Press, 2001.

Carlton, Jim. *Apple: The Inside Story of Intrigue, Egomania, and Business Blunders*. New York, NY: HarperBusiness, 1998.

Cassidy, John. *Dot.Con: The Greatest Story Ever Sold*. New York, NY: HarperCollins Publishers, 2002.

Chapman, Merrill R. *The Product Marketing Handbook for Software, Fifth Edition*. Killingworth, CT: Aegis Resources, 2006.

Cringely, Robert X. *Accidental Empires: How the Boys of Silicon Valley Make Their Millions, Battle Foreign Competition, and Still Can't Get a Date*. Reading, MA: Addison-Wesley, 1992.

Davidow, William H. *Marketing High Technology: An Insider's View*. New York, NY: The Free Press, 1986.

Dvorak, John and Adam Osborne. *Hypergrowth: The Rise and Fall of Osborne Computer Corporation*. New York, NY: Avon, 1984.

Ferguson, Charles. *High Stakes, No Prisoners: A Winners Tale of Greed and Glory in the Internet Wars*. New York, NY: Times Books/Random House, 1999.

Halberstam, David. *The Reckoning*. New York, NY: William Morrow, 1986.

Kaplan, Philip J. *F'd Companies: Spectacular Dot-Com Flameouts*. New York, NY: Simon & Schuster, 2002.

Kindleberger, Charles P. *Manias, Panics, and Crashes: A History of Financial Crises, Fourth Edition*. New York, NY: John Wiley & Sons, 2000.

Kuo, J. David. *dot.bomb: My Days and Nights at an Internet Goliath*. New York, NY: Little, Brown and Company, 2001.

Levy, Steven. *Hackers: Heroes of the Computer Revolution*. New York, NY: Dell, 1984.

MacKay, Charles. *Memoirs of Extraordinary Popular Delusions and the Madness of Crowds*. New York, NY: Farrar, Strauss and Giroux, originally published in 1841 with some additions in 1852.

Manes, Stephen and Paul Andrews. *Gates: How Microsoft's Mogul Reinvented an Industry—and Made Himself the Richest Man in America*. New York, NY: Simon & Schuster, 1994.

Peters, Thomas J. and Robert H. Waterman, Jr. *In Search of Excellence: Lessons from America's Best-Run Companies*. New York, NY: Harper & Row, 1982.

Peterson, W. E. Pete. *Almost Perfect*. Roseville, CA: Prima Publishing, 1994.

Rivlin, Gary. *The Plot to Get Bill Gates: An Irreverent Investigation of the World's Richest Man . . . and the People Who Hate Him*. New York, NY: Times Books/Random House, 1999.

Rosenberg, Donald. *Open Source: The Unauthorized White Papers*. Foster City, CA: IDG Books Worldwide, 2000.

Segaller, Stephen. *Nerds 2.0.1: A Brief History of the Internet*. New York, NY: TV Books, 1998.

INDEX

You Need the Companion eBook

Your purchase of this book entitles you to buy the companion PDF-version eBook for only $10. Take the weightless companion with you anywhere.

We believe this Apress title will prove so indispensable that you'll want to carry it with you everywhere, which is why we are offering the companion eBook (in PDF format) for $10 to customers who purchase this book now. Convenient and fully searchable, the PDF version of any content-rich, page-heavy Apress book makes a valuable addition to your programming library. You can easily find and copy code—or perform examples by quickly toggling between instructions and the application. Even simultaneously tackling a donut, diet soda, and complex code becomes simplified with hands-free eBooks!

Once you purchase your book, getting the $10 companion eBook is simple:

1. Visit **www.apress.com/promo/tendollars/**.

2. Complete a basic registration form to receive a randomly generated question about this title.

3. Answer the question correctly in 60 seconds, and you will receive a promotional code to redeem for the $10.00 eBook.

2560 Ninth Street • Suite 219 • Berkeley, CA 94710

eBookshop

THE EXPERT'S VOICE™

Offer valid through 4/9/2007.